MW00575785

Michael Higgins'
EXPLORING WINE REGIONS

The Central Coast of California

Written & Photographed by

Michael C. Higgins, PhD
Author, Photojournalist & Publisher

The Foreword by

Dany Rolland, Oenologist, Partner and Manager of the Dany and Michel Rolland Wine Estates and Rolland Laboratories

Richard Sanford, Vintner, Pioneer of the Sta. Rita Hills Appellation in Santa Barbara County

Ian Brand, Winemaker/Vintner, I. Brand & Family Winery

David Glancy, Sommelier, Certified Wine Educator, Founder & CEO San Francisco Wine School

Published by
International Exploration Society
United States of America

On The Cover: The beautiful landscape of JUSTIN Vineyards & Winery in Paso Robles
Above: The massive slope on which Booker Vineyard grows their vines in Paso Robles
Next Page: Bud break in the Beckmen Vineyards in Santa Barbara

ExploringWineRegions.com

Bud break of Cabernet Sauvignon vines at Beckmen Vineyards in the Los Olivos AVA, Santa Barbara County

WORK SPACE. I sure love my work. Dining room view at the Sunstone Winery's castle

WHY CALIFORNIA'S CENTRAL COAST?

California is my home. I was born and raised here, and I have lived in Southern California my entire life. Although I have traveled to thirty-one countries (just getting started), it has been such a blessing to live in this state filled with extraordinary wine regions. I have been to almost all of them and do not have enough fingers and toes to count the number of times I have enjoyed visiting California wineries. For decades here, I have photographed and written numerous articles published in magazines.

To say the least, I know the California wine regions very well. I have numerous vintner, winemaker and chef friends. I am a California Wine Appellation Specialist with honors from the San Francisco Wine School. It makes sense that I put my knowledge into an *Exploring Wine Regions – California* book. And so, I began. My development of the book, though, led me to focus on the Central Coast wine regions. I realized that the extraordinary quality of wines being produced along California's Central Coast really must be brought to life. The wines here compete strongly with wines from Napa and Sonoma. And the tourism is extraordinary. The people in the Central Coast are very friendly and inviting, and want us to come enjoy their wines and activities. There is nothing stuffy about California's Central Coast wineries. And I want to show you just how excellent it is to spend time there.

This Central Coast book includes Monterey County to the north, San Luis Obispo County in the middle (including Paso Robles) and Santa Barbara County in the south. Every type of wine is made here. The terroir is incredibly diverse, allowing for the optimum growing of just about any wine grape. Central Coast winemakers tend to be less rigid, more creative, and inventive. The tourism is better than you can imagine. Restaurants and accommodations at wineries are becoming common here.

Something very important about this book is how I show you the ways to find your favorite wines based on the grape's optimum terroir. California wines are generally purchased by the grape, so I have organized how you can find your favorite wines based on their perfect terroir. The diversity of wine regions in the Central Coast is extensive. Some places are hot and others cold. Some soils have stones, others clay, and yet others are seabeds or volcanic. This diversity of terroir is what makes the Central Coast capable of delivering super-high-quality wines when properly planting grapes in the right terroir, optimizing viticulture techniques and utilizing winemaking proficiency and expertise.

As a California book, I explored the Valle de Guadalupe wine region in Baja California. Still California, different country. The wines, gourmet foods and luxurious accommodations in Valle de Guadalupe will surprise you. Since this book now focuses specifically on California Central Coast, next year I will release an *Exploring Wine Regions – México* book, focusing on this Valle de Guadalupe wine region as well as some other special wine regions in México important to explore.

While my journeys through the California Central Coast encompasses decades, the focus now to create this book is 2021-2023. It is important to remember that wineries continue to introduce new wines and restaurants change menus. Things will change, but you will get the essence of what each winery, restaurant and lodging will be able to offer. This is a survey, not a census. It is my subjective journey through these wine regions giving you a snapshot of what is amazing here. If you find a mistake in these 436 pages, I will cringe, and would still like to hear from you.

As usual, everything I cover in this book is from my own personal experiences. I was there. The photos are authentic from my camera and my eye. Everything I write is from my journeys.

So now it is time to go explore and go enjoy the journey.

Happy Tasting,

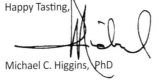

Michael C. Higgins, PhD

Michael C. Higgins, PhD
Author, Photojournalist & Publisher

For more than twenty years, author, photographer and wine expert Michael C. Higgins has been the publisher of *Flying Adventures*, a lifestyle travel magazine for food and wine lovers who own and travel on private airplanes. As a private pilot, travel enthusiast, and food and wine lover himself, Higgins continues to live the story he's been sharing for decades.

Between the magazine and this book series, Higgins has participated in some of the most extraordinary experiences. He has virtually done it all: from pruning vines, picking grapes, working alongside winemakers, to participating in blind tastings, food and wine pairings, judging Cru Bourgeois wines, and sharing many meals with world-renowned winemakers, over countless hours, discussing everything wine. His time in wine regions adds up to thousands of days and counting. And as an accomplished photographer, he has captured even more spectacular images of the wine world.

Higgins has participated in many unique wine experiences, indulged in the most exclusive culinary affairs, been pampered in highly luxurious destinations and jumped into the wildest of adventures. His goal is to inspire his readers to join him in exploring the wine regions of the world and experiencing the unimaginable. Higgins has a BA in Commercial Art, an MBA and a PhD in Business Administration. He is a California native and lives in Pasadena, California.

THE FOREWORD
The Magic of Terroir

It is important that we talk about terroir before we begin exploring this book. Terroir (ter-ˈwär). My definition of terroir is very simple. It is the unique distinction of land, climate and people for vineyards. Webster says: *the combination of factors including soil, climate and sunlight that gives wine grapes their distinctive character.* While most definitions speak primarily of soil, topography and climate, the people who work the land are also a critical component to terroir.

So commonly in California and other New Worlds, wines are chosen by grape variety. May I have a glass of Cabernet Sauvignon? Grapes are identified on the bottle making it easy to choose by grape. And when we want to drink a Cabernet Sauvignon, we ask for Cabernet Sauvignon. When we feel like Pinot Noir, we choose Pinot Noir. This is the New World.

In the Old World (Italy, France, Spain) it is different. Grape names are not on the bottles. This can be very frustrating at times. Wines are identified by place. Identified by the winery and its specific location where the vineyards surround the winery. This is a choice of terroir. It becomes necessary to know the winery and its location (terroir) to know the wine.

In Bordeaux France for example, if you choose a winery from the Margaux appellation, being in the Left Bank Médoc you will know the grape will be primarily Cabernet Sauvignon. Other Bordeaux grapes may also be part of the blend. Choosing Margaux specifically means you like the softer more feminine style to Cabernet Sauvignon this terroir creates. Choosing the exact château is the further definition of the specific soil and people of that château. This requires knowing terroir to find your favorite wines. The more we use terroir choosing techniques in the New World, in California, the better the wines we will drink.

As **oenologist Dany Rolland** (partner and manager of the Dany and Michel Rolland wine estates and Rolland Laboratories) explained to us in our previous Bordeaux France book: "understanding the qualities of a grape based on which appellation they are grown in is not so simple. The notion of terroir adds to the complexity. To achieve excellence, we need soils, subsoils, climate, landscapes, work and know-how. And when this synergism occurs, the result is exceptional." Dany could not be more correct, and she articulates this point very well.

Terroir can be complicated, as I'm sure you are beginning to realize or already knew. The more precise and specific we can be about terroir, and the grapes that are growing in that terroir, the better chance we are going to be drinking more exceptional wines. And isn't that the point?

People love to invite me to dinner at restaurants (oh yes, please ask) because I will find the better wines off of a wine list even when I do not know any of the wines or wineries. This is because of terroir. If I look for the grape they want to drink at the table and match it up with its perfect terroir, the wine will most likely be exceptional.

As you read this book, consider the wines you like and find the optimum terroir where these grapes grow best. This will result in you finding your best wines. I promise you, if you choose your wineries to visit in this terroir method, you are going to have a great time and drink better wines.

I am forever learning. In researching for this book, I found new places with exceptional terroir for certain grapes. This caused me to discover new excellent wines. Grapes that were not my favorites became wines I actually loved. When grapes are in the right terroir, the resulting wines can be amazing.

In the opening of each appellation in this book, I give you the specifics about the terroir and which grapes excel in that appellation. This will help in finding the wineries that make the wines you love most.

Left page:
Cabernet Sauvignon vineyard
in terroir of gravel and stone soil at
Star Lane Vineyards in the Happy Canyon AVA

Dany Rolland, Oenologist
Partner and Manager of the Dany and Michel Rolland
Wine Estates and Rolland Laboratories
RollandCollection.com

THE FOREWORD
The Magic of Terroir

Richard Sanford, Vintner

Pioneer of the Sta. Rita Hills Appellation
in the Santa Ynez AVA, Santa Barbara County
AlmaRosaWinery.com

Ian Brand, Winemaker

Winemaker/Vintner, I. Brand & Family Winery
IBrandWinery.com

I discussed terroir with **winemaker Richard Sanford**, the pioneer of the Sta. Rita Hills appellation in Santa Barbara County known for its remarkable Pinot Noir. Richard planted the very first vineyard here in 1971. As Pinot Noir became immensely successful here, it also created an incorrect association with the climate of the rest of the Santa Ynez Valley appellation.

The problem Richard explains is the cool climate of this westerly valley was not in the Santa Ynez Valley AVA, an appellation that generally produces Rhône varietals (Syrah, Viognier, Grenache, etc.). Rhône varietals need a warm climate different than Richard's cold valley producing the cold Burgundian varietals of Pinot Noir and Chardonnay. It was necessary to establish a distinction. They were not the same terroir. Not even close!

Richard formed a group with other vintners in this cold valley. They all knew their terroir was completely distinct from the rest of the Santa Ynez Valley. They began by defining the perimeters of this special cold place. In the center of the valley is a hill called Santa Rita Hills. This is where they got the name for the new appellation Sta. Rita Hills AVA. They presented the facts to the approving government entity: Alcohol and Tobacco, Tax and Trade Bureau (TTB), and after roughly ten years of process, the TTB (government is so slow) gave approval for their sub-appellation.

You can see the importance in appellations and sub appellations being the definition of terroir. This is what you want to know in seeking the terroir of the grapes for the wines you like most. For example, if you want to taste some of the best Pinot Noir in all of California, you must visit the wineries and taste the wines in the Sta. Rita Hills AVA.

What a pleasure it was discovering **winemaker Ian Brand** and his wines. We are both terroir geeks! Ian is a winemaker sourcing fruit from numerous appellations within the Central Coast. He finds unique vineyards with extraordinary terroir. He chooses very specific blocks, even specified rows, in order to make unique wines that not only represent the perfection of the place (terroir), they are also extraordinarily delicious wines. With his passion, I had to ask Ian to express his insights on the terroir here in the Central Coast...

"California's Central Coast stretches two hundred and fifty miles between Monterey and Santa Barbara. The redwoods fade into chaparral scrub on the rugged ridges of Big Sur, which ease southward into golden hills toward Morro Rock and terminate in the eastward folds of the Transverse Ranges. It is a region, seemingly more than any other, defined by the vast, cold Pacific Ocean. Fingers of fog and cold marine air funnel through every gap and crevice in the coastal ranges and, in contradiction to the latitude, feed some of the most temperate winegrowing regions in the world. The imprint of the ocean is seen on the soils. Largely west of the San Andreas Fault, the Central Coast is the only North American winegrowing region not on the North American plate (see map next spread). Our mountains are formed from the ocean sediments and granitic intrusions, scraped into ridges as the Pacific Plate collides with and is subducted by the continental shift. Every now and again the ground shakes."

"I've been sifting through this dirt for nearly twenty years, refracting the lens of wine in search of the idea of the Central Coast 'terroir' as broadly defined, describing the interaction of a place and a people through wine. It's a living theory, constantly changing, shared with vibrant, curious communities in and around food, wine and agriculture. In these communities I've found a collection of the best souls I've met anywhere. Like the landscape they are expansive, engaging and kind, unimpressed by the trappings of wealth and protective of our collective legacy."

THE FOREWORD
The Magic of Terroir

"From a winegrowing perspective, the Central Coast is newer to the international stage. While the first commercial vineyards in the region coincided with the gold rush, planting did not begin in earnest until the early 1970s. We are still very much in our exploratory phase, allowing our concept of what the terroir can be to evolve with our deepening knowledge of place. The region remains full of possibility, an ingenue with few resources can still find the space to build a successful winery or a landowner can pivot to grapes and turn up incredible potential lying in plain sight. This possibility extends into a passion for place by residents. Visitors will, as likely as not, find proprietors opening bottles or behind the counter, ready to proclaim this the best piece of coastline anywhere in the world. There's a solid chance they're right."

"My favorite Central Coast wines are woven of these threads. The coastal sunshine coaxes a pure, fruited ripeness balanced by an acidity nurtured in cool nights and Pacific tempered days. The wines are built on the lean minerality of the new soils – calcareous, granitic, siliceous – thrust up in slow tectonic fury. Hints of marine salinity lend a savory accent, which can be underscored by the Central Coast variation on garrigue – less rosemary, thyme and sage and more chaparral, manzanita and dried grass. There's a consistent freshness, reminiscent of how the sunshine on the beach refracts through the sea spray and the salt air fills your lungs, and a direct purity, because the verses of this ground can't be spoken in any other voice."

Let me introduce you to **Master Sommelier and Certified Wine Educator David Glancy**, one of only twelve people in the world to have both credentials. David is the founder and CEO of the San Francisco Wine School. I met David as a result of enrolling in one of his courses, the *California Wine Appellation Specialist* (CWAS) credential program. This is one of many wine-education programs he has authored.

Being a terroir geek, I want to know everything about appellations anytime and anywhere, and that is why I chose this course. Certainly, there is a lot to learn from David Glancy's intense knowledge and experience, and this would also be valuable in researching and writing this book. If you really want to understand terroir, I highly suggest you take this course as well. The topics will very much enrich the beginner wine enthusiast; however, the sophisticated content will also provide critical knowledge to a wine professional.

All that being said, I got a lot out of this course (graduated with honors) and thought it would be valuable to have David share his insight here on the magic of terroir. This is what David has to say...

"The climate of California is often simplified as being Mediterranean and ideal for wine-grape growing; however, the reality is more complex with some of the hottest spots in the world such as Death Valley and the Mojave Desert, located here. The much cooler land along the Pacific Coast is cooled by deep, cold ocean currents and the Coriolis Effect bringing their cool temperatures to the surface. This cool-water upwelling contributes to coastal fog and breezes. Gaps in the Coast Ranges allow the cooling to encroach inland in many places."

"The geography and geology are equally complex due to the intersection of the Pacific and North American tectonic plates (map next page). California has many volcanic mountains, uplifted Coast Ranges, rivers, lakes and the former ancient sea beds of the coastal regions. As such, there are over 100 different soil variations in the state with various combinations of sand, silt, loam, clay, limestone, granite, iron-rich volcanics and more. The Central Coast has all of these, creating very diverse soils, terrains and temperatures."

"Combining all of this with numerous grape varieties within the species Vitis Vinifera and wine can seem daunting. Some grape varieties, like Chardonnay and Pinot Noir, prefer cool climates while grapes like Zinfandel and Grenache are very heat tolerant. Grapes have some soil preferences but are fairly flexible.

David Glancy, MS, CWE
Master Sommelier and Certified Wine Educator
Founder & CEO, San Francisco Wine School
SanFranciscoWineSchool.com

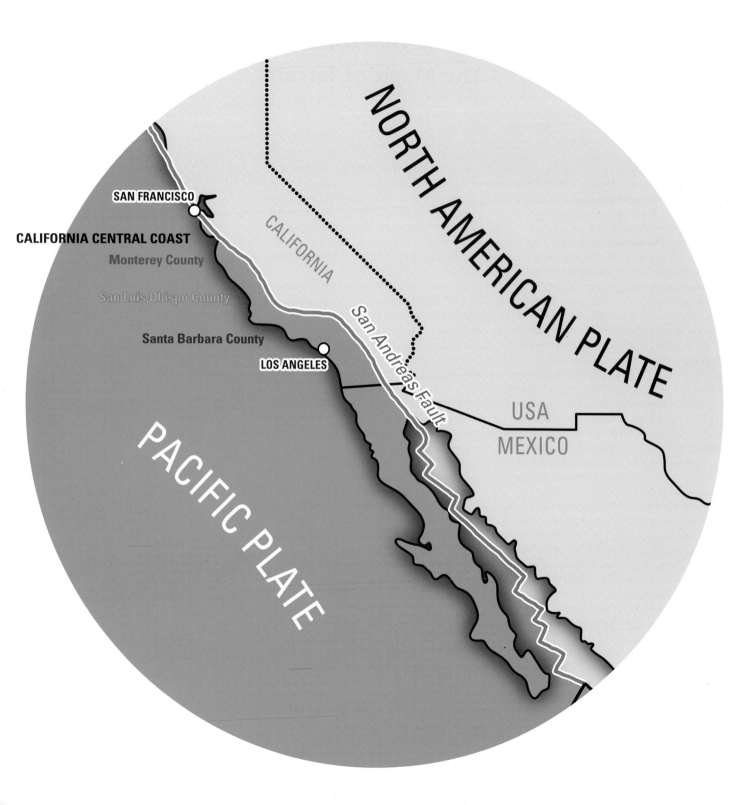

NORTH AMERICAN PLATE

PACIFIC PLATE

CALIFORNIA

San Andreas Fault

USA

MEXICO

SAN FRANCISCO

CALIFORNIA CENTRAL COAST

Monterey County

San Luis Obispo County

Santa Barbara County

LOS ANGELES

THE FOREWORD
The Magic of Terroir

The combination of the climate and the soil is often more important as some soils are cool, water-retaining soils that delay ripening, and others are warm, well-draining soils that might speed up ripening. In much of the world, latitude is what gives us an idea of how cool or warm a region is, but in California longitude – or more precisely, proximity to the coast – is a much more significant determinant of climate. The gaps in the Coast Ranges regularly make areas along east-west running rivers cooler than what would be expected for their distance from the coast."

"American Viticultural Areas (AVAs) are legally defined areas that are specific to wine-grape growing and ideally have some unifying element, potentially based on soil, elevation, bodies of water or climate. The Central Coast AVA is the largest in California and over 90% of the Central Coast's vineyard acreage is in the three counties covered by this book: Monterey, San Luis Obispo and Santa Barbara. These counties are the heart of the Central Coast AVA and are home to roughly 90,000 acres of vineyards, over 650 wineries, and over seventy different grapes. They also have thirty-three AVAs nested within the larger Central Coast AVA. This represents roughly one-fifth of the state's acreage, wineries, and AVAs, and arguably half of the premium-quality wines."

"*Exploring Wine Regions – California Central Coast* will connect the soil, climate and grapes and make exploring wine a pleasure. This book will guide you through the deep, cool Monterey Bay to the cool to moderate AVAs of Arroyo Seco, Santa Lucia Highlands and Chalone. The warmer portions of southeastern Monterey County have very few wineries but thousands of acres of grapes often contributing to bulk wines labeled as Monterey County, Central Coast, or simply as California. The Salinas River Valley, with its howling winds, lies at the center of Monterey, framed by the Santa Lucia Mountains and Gabilan Mountains. Soils range from alluvial gravel to limestone and more. Cool climate-loving grapes, like Chardonnay and Pinot Noir, thrive in the cooler coastal regions, and Cabernet and other thick-skinned red grapes do better in the warmer portions."

"San Luis Obispo County is equally diverse, ranging from the warm Paso Robles AVA and its eleven districts to the cooler coastal regions of Edna Valley AVA and the new-in-2022 San Luis Obispo Coast AVA (SLO Coast AVA). Even Paso Robles has more variety than one might expect, with gaps in the coastal mountains, such as Templeton Gap, cooling portions of the larger AVA. The rainfall and soils change just as rapidly in this area, leading wineries to grow over sixty different grape varieties, depending on their situation. Chardonnay and Pinot Noir thrive in the cool portions, and in SLO, they are joined by Albariño, Grüner Veltliner and more. In the warmest places Cabernet, Zinfandel and GSM blends and varietal wines reign supreme."

"Santa Barbara County sees many of the same patterns but has its unique features with the Transverse Range shifting the Coast Range 90° and creating a channel for cooling fog and breezes inland. With climbing temperatures moving from west to east, Santa Maria Valley AVA and Sta. Rita Hills AVA specializes in Chardonnay and Pinot Noir, while inland, in Ballard Canyon AVA and Los Olivos District AVA, there are more Syrah and other Rhône grapes, and easterly is Happy Canyon AVA, with Cabernet Sauvignon and other thick-skinned grapes are grown."

"In this book, and Michael's prior two, he not only covers the regions, grapes and wineries, he also dives into travel options, hotels, restaurants, and activities. Each chapter includes maps and breathtaking photos. Every detail and bit of insider information is included from his many visits and interviews. It's all you need to maximize your wine-travel experiences throughout the Central Coast."

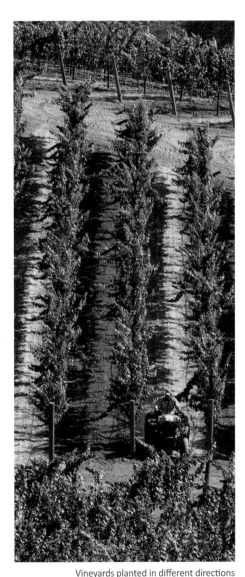

Vineyards planted in different directions
to optimize the terroir in this hilly environment
of Opolo Vineyards in Willow Creek AVA, Paso Robles.

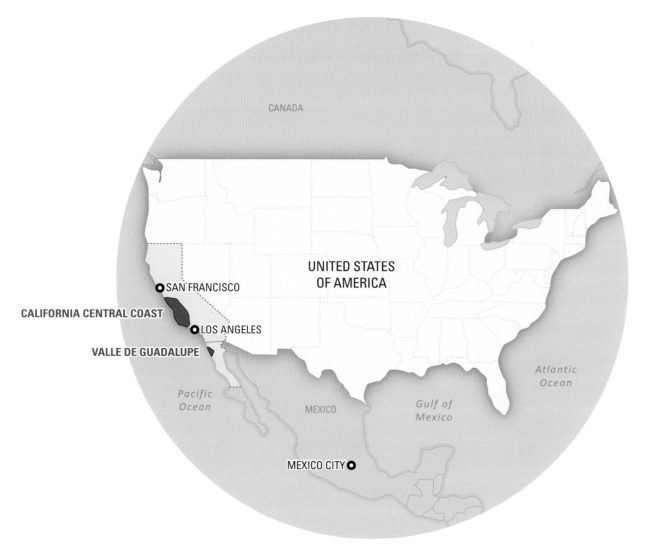

EXPLORING WINE REGIONS™ • 3RD EDITION • CALIFORNIA CENTRAL COAST, USA

ISBN 978-0-9969660-4-7 - Printed Edition   •   ISBN 978-0-9969660-5-4 - eBook Travel Edition

Published by: **International Exploration Society**
Box 93613 • Pasadena, CA 91109-3613 • USA • +1 626 618 4000

CONTENTS

18   OF CALIFORNIA CENTRAL COAST
Why is Central Coast Special 18
The Geography Of California 20
How to Best Read this Book 22

24   MONTEREY COUNTY
Monterey Downtown 24
The Monterey Wine Trail 44
   - Santa Lucia Highlands AVA 44
   - Arroyo Seco AVA 60
   - Chalone AVA 66
Carmel Valley Country Charm 72
   - Carmel Valley AVA 72
   - Carmel Valley Village 82
Coastal Wine Tasting 86
   - Carmel by-the-Sea Village 86

92   SAN LUIS OBISPO COUNTY
York Mountain AVA 98
Paso Robles AVA 102
   - Estrella AVA 108
   - Geneseo AVA 122
   - El Pomar AVA 144
   - Adelaida AVA 150
   - Willow Creek AVA 176
   - Templeton Gap AVA 198
Tin City, Templeton 210
   - Santa Margarita Ranch AVA 214
Paso Robles Downtown 220

230   SAN LUIS OBISPO COUNTY (cont)
SLO Coast AVA 230
   - San Simeon and Cambria 234
   - Avila and Pismo Beach 250
   - Edna Valley AVA 258
   - Arroyo Grande AVA 277
San Luis Obispo Downtown 284

298   SANTA BARBARA COUNTY
Santa Ynez AVA 306
   - Buellton Downtown 326
   - Solvang Downtown 328
   - Sta. Rita Hills AVA 340
   - Ballard Canyon AVA 352
   - Los Olivos AVA 360
   - Happy Canyon AVA 374
Alisos Canyon AVAs 386
   - Los Alamos Downtown 392
Santa Maria Valley AVA 398

410   BAJA CALIFORNIA, MEXICO

417   CONCLUSION
The Index 418
Collect Our Books 420
Travel with Us 425
Get Extra Chapters - Free 427
Glossary 420
eBook Travel Edition 421
Acknowledgements 428
Media Resources 429

WHY IS **CALIFORNIA CENTRAL COAST** SPECIAL

The Geography has Micro-Pockets of Very Special Terroir

Cabernet Sauvignon Vineyards of JUSTIN Winery in Paso Robles

*W*ine is a living legend
It is a craft, enduring and profound

In the vineyard, it is growing
In the winery, it's evolving
In the bottle, it is alive

Tannins group and sink to the bottom
allowing the wine to age
developing complexity in aromas
smoothing flavors and mouthfeel

In the bottle, wine changes in texture
in a way that cannot be mimicked

Every moment you open a bottle
it is its own moment for the wine

The older she gets
the more seductive she becomes

Wine is meant to be shared
in romance and friendship

Wine is the art of living

– Michael C. Higgins

So you love California wines? So do I.

Have you done much exploring in the Central Coast of California? The big names of Napa Valley and Sonoma County get so much attention, attracting many tourists and grabbing lots of wine shelf space. The Central Coast, though, offers so much to the winemaker and tourist as those big names... and more!

Are you a lover of Cabernet Sauvignon and have many bottles in your collection from Napa? So do I. Napa has excellent Cabernet. In the Central Coast; however, the Adelaida District in the Paso Robles AVA, for example, is producing Cabernet Sauvignon with scores hitting 100 points and winning blind competitions against the names of Napa.

A lover of Chardonnay? Have you tried the Chardonnay from the Edna Valley AVA in San Luis Obispo? The wines here more closely represent Burgundy France than anywhere else in California.

Are you a Pinot Noir lover? Do you relish the delicious fruit and delicateness of this grape? I am a huge fan of California Pinot Noir, and the Central Coast has some of the very best terroir to grow this grape. When you look at the wines from the Santa Lucia Highlands in Monterey County and Sta. Rita Hills in Santa Barbara County, you will discover that this terroir is so good, you could almost make a great Pinot Noir with your eyes closed.

Love the Rhône wines of Syrah, Grenache and Viognier? Paso Robles in San Luis Obispo County and the Santa Ynez Valley in Santa Barbara County rock these wines like no other place in California. The terroir here is absolutely perfect for these grapes. And winemakers have made these wines their talent. Even the French from the Rhône Valley are here because they know.

The California Central Coast is not small to winemaking, it is home to thirty of California's 147 Appellations (AVAs: American Viticultural Areas). Of California's 4,700 total wineries, there are more than 600 wineries in the Central Coast. This is a special place worth exploring.

The old winery of Sanford & Benedict Vineyard in Santa Barbara

THE GEOGRAPHY **OF CALIFORNIA**

The Pacific Plate's Ancient Movements Created Unique Growing Conditions Exclusive to the Central Coast

The Central Coast from Templeton Gap (Paso Robles) to Morro Bay (San Luis Obispo)

THE TERROIR OF CENTRAL COAST

The United States is the fourth-largest wine producing country in the world (behind Italy, France and Spain, respectively) with California being the leader as the largest wine-producing region in the USA.

California is fortunate to have such diversity in terroir that every type of wine grape can find its perfect home here. And the Central Coast is just the same, with excellent terroir for growing all types of wine grapes. And there are valid arguments that the soil of the Central Coast is significantly better than the rest of California. Unfortunately, the Central Coast has been hidden behind the well-known names of Napa Valley and Sonoma County.

The Central Coast being hidden has nothing to do with its high-quality grapes and the excellent wines produced here. A great way to know just how good the wines are here in Paso Robles, for example, is to ask a Napa winemaker. For decades, Napa wineries have been purchasing generous portions of Cabernet Sauvignon from Paso to blend into their wines. They know how good the grapes are here.

Let's step back 130 million years, give or take a few decades, when a huge tectonic plate in the Pacific Ocean collided with the North American continent. This began as a series of events over the next 100 million years whereby the Pacific Plate rose from deep in the ocean and eventually hit the North America Plate.

When the Pacific and North American plates met, they moved laterally aside each other. This line of continuing movement is what we know today as the San Andreas Fault. West of the fault line is the Pacific Plate, leaving the rest of California and North America on the North American plate.

The Central Coast of California is a little sliver of land that runs from south of San Francisco all the way down the coast to include all of Baja California (see map on right page). This excludes Napa, Sonoma and Lodi, for example. This makes the Central Coast wine regions geologically distinct from the rest of California with thick layers of ocean sediment, hard granitic rock, quartz diorite, and serpentinite rocks.

MONTEREY COUNTY has seven appellations that flow along the Salinas Valley, all having significant influence from the large Monterey Bay, sporting the cold Pacific Ocean. These AVAs are perfect for Burgundy varietals (**Pinot Noir** and **Chardonnay**). I find the Santa Lucia Highlands AVA particularly exceptional for **Pinot Noir**. The Carmel Valley AVA is a very different appellation here because of its elevation being above the fog line. This gives them warm days, reaching 100° at times, making it ideal for the Bordeaux varietals of **Cabernet Sauvignon** and **Merlot**.

SAN LUIS OBISPO COUNTY has two very distinct wine regions. To the north is Paso Robles, the largest geographic appellation in the state and the fastest-growing wine region as well. Because of its size, in 2014, Paso Robles created eleven sub-appellations to more accurately distinguish this big area. Paso Robles is the warmest wine region in the Central Coast and primarily produces red wines. Paso Robles is known for excelling in three types of wines: Bordeaux (**Cabernet Sauvignon**, **Merlot**, etc.), Rhône (**Syrah**, **Viognier**, **Grenache**, etc.) and **Zinfandel**. To the west and south is the SLO Coast AVA known for cool-weather grapes, significantly representing Burgundy style wines (**Pinot Noir** and **Chardonnay**).

SANTA BARBARA COUNTY has three very distinct wine regions. The primary region is the central Santa Ynez Valley AVA, which excels with Rhône varietals (**Syrah**, **Viognier** and **Grenache**). To the east is the Happy Canyon AVA, a newer appellation known for its excellence in Bordeaux varietals (**Cabernet Sauvignon**). To the west is the Sta. Rita Hills AVA, one of the finest growing regions for Burgundy varietals (**Pinot Noir** and **Chardonnay**). Because of the plate movements we discussed, the mountain range here moves east-west (unlike North American ranges being north-south) which funnels cool morning and evening air from the Pacific Ocean into the vineyards.

BAJA CALIFORNIA, MÉXICO, is still California, but a different country. It is also on the Pacific Plate and has the ocean influence into the valley through Ensenada. All types of grapes are being grown here. I found the grapes doing better to be **Nebbiolo** (Italian), **Tempranillo** (Spanish) and **Syrah**, **Mourvèdre** and **Sauvignon Blanc** (French).

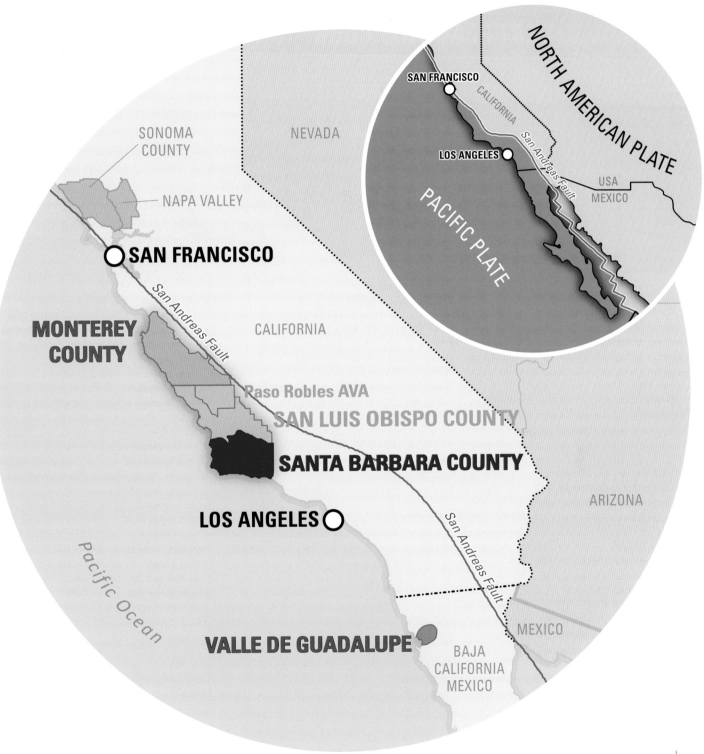

SONOMA COUNTY

NEVADA

NAPA VALLEY

SAN FRANCISCO

MONTEREY COUNTY

San Andreas Fault

CALIFORNIA

Paso Robles AVA

SAN LUIS OBISPO COUNTY

SANTA BARBARA COUNTY

LOS ANGELES

ARIZONA

San Andreas Fault

Pacific Ocean

VALLE DE GUADALUPE

MEXICO

BAJA CALIFORNIA MEXICO

NORTH AMERICAN PLATE

SAN FRANCISCO

CALIFORNIA

LOS ANGELES

San Andreas Fault

USA
MEXICO

PACIFIC PLATE

HOW TO **BEST READ THIS BOOK**

Rodney's Vineyard at Fess Parker Winery in Santa Barbara

NAVIGATING CALIFORNIA

Being methodically organized and geographically oriented, I like to make it simple to navigate and easy to find places. This should help you tremendously as you make your way through this book and the Central Coast of California.

The Central Coast is located south of San Francisco and north of Los Angeles, and along the Pacific Ocean coast. Highway 101 runs from San Francisco directly through the cities of the wine regions to Los Angeles. This makes Los Angeles and San Francisco the two primary airports arriving to the Central Coast of California.

I have organized this book traveling from north to south. There are three Central Coast counties I have covered between San Francisco and Los Angeles.

The first county is Monterey County. Then San Luis Obispo County, which includes Paso Robles. And third is Santa Barbara County. Each of these three counties also have commercial airports. There are regular airline shuttles to each of them from San Francisco and Los Angeles. Plus, several airlines travel to these smaller airports from many locations throughout the USA. All of these smaller airports have rental cars available too.

Continuing even further south, past Los Angeles and San Diego, we enter México in Baja California. An hour and a half south of the US/México border is the Valle de Guadalupe wine region and their port town of Ensenada.

THINKING TERROIR

As you travel the Central Coast, remember to be thinking terroir, terroir being the climate and soil most optimum for each grape variety. We buy our California wines based on grape varieties; however, if you think terroir, you will discover how to find the best quality of the wines you like.

The proper relationship between the soil, grape and climate is the magic inside any wine. This is an important threesome that, if you are looking, thinking and asking, will help you discover the tremendous differences and subtle nuances that make your favorite wines their best.

In addition to your inquiries during your own journeys, I am ahead of you in the expedition so you can know in advance where you want to go to drink the best of what you want to try. I have delineated the terroir as it relates to grape variety throughout this book so you know where to find the very best wines of the grapes you love.

Opolo Vineyards in Paso Robles

HOW THE BOOK IS LAID OUT

I just described the geographic order of the book. Then, within each county, I distinguish the wine regions by appellation and sub-appellation. Wineries are included and presented within their respective appellation.

Maps. I love maps, which is why there are thirty in this book. They separate and lead each wine region, their appellations and sub-appellations, followed by its characteristics and uniqueness.

The light-gray side column provides the basics: wine region and appellation, business type, name, price range, address, phone, e-mail, website, and the days and hours they are open. For wineries, I list all their wines in this right column. I start with the red wines and order them by quality/price. Then I move on to white wines, and end with sweet and sparkling wines. I also include a photo of a bottle for label recognition, and that bottle also represents my favorite wine I tasted.

ARRIVING & TRAVERSING

From north to south, here are the airports for each of the wine regions and the two major airports north and south of them. Highways 101 connects all of them together.

San Francisco International Airport (SFO)
Located thirteen miles south of downtown San Francisco and seventy-five miles south to Monterey, the first Central Coast wine region in the north of the book.

Monterey Regional Airport (MRY)
Located three miles southeast of downtown Monterey and only a few miles to the beginning of the Salinas Valley wine regions.

Paso Robles Municipal Airport (PRB)
Located four miles northeast of downtown Paso Robles and in the middle of the wine regions. No commercial airlines here; however, rental cars are available for private pilots.

San Luis Obispo County Regional Airport (SLO)
Located three miles southeast of downtown San Luis Obispo and is adjacent west of the wine regions. Paso Robles is thirty miles north on Highway 101.

Santa Barbara Regional Airport (SBA)
Located seven miles west of downtown Santa Barbara and forty-five miles north over the mountain range to the wine regions.

Los Angeles International Airport (LAX)
Located twelve miles southwest of downtown Los Angeles and 140 miles north to the Santa Barbara wine regions.

Cabernet Sauvignon

WHO GOT IN?

Not everyone. With over 600 wineries, I had to make deliberate choices on who to include.

My first priority was that every winery must be open to the public for visits. California wineries are generally known for being open; however, some are not. They make wine, leave them alone. So, I left them alone.

Next, they must make excellent wines and go beyond the step-up-to-the-bar to taste wine.

Tourism is key to what I look for to include in the book. They must provide wine experiences for their guests at their property. Some have become quite creative and innovative with experiences that you have never seen before. Read what I have written and find what appeals to you.

Many wineries now have food experiences to go with wine tastings. Some have full-on restaurants at the winery. Others offer food and wine pairing experiences. I look for interesting experiences, like horseback riding through the vineyards, cooking with chefs, wine blending with oenologists, and overnight accommodations in the vineyards. There are a lot more of these that you might imagine, so I find them and bring them to you in this book.

Every place I have written about in this book is from my own personal, hands-on experience. No one has paid me to write any of these reviews.

Networking has been key. I worked extensively with locals, wine lovers, winemakers, publishers, travel and tourism professionals, wine councils, chefs, restaurateurs, sommeliers, government officials, and other organizations at the forefront of food, wine and tourism in California.

Who is out? If all they do is offer a tasting? Boring! If they do not even open the doors? No way! If the wine is not excellent? Why bother? Life is too short to drink bad wine. What you can count on from me is that I was actually there, I know the experiences and I know the wines are excellent. And some will simply blow you away.

PRICING SCALE

Wineries (Price Per Bottle)
$ - < $20
$$ - $20-$50
$$$ - $50-$100
$$$$ - $100-$200
$$$$$ - $200+

Culinary (Price For Entrée)
$ - < $10
$$ - $10-$20
$$$ - $20-$50
$$$$ - $50-$100
$$$$$ - $100+

Lodging (Price Per Room/Night)
$ - < $100
$$ - $100-$200
$$$ - $200-$400
$$$$ - $400-$600
$$$$$ - $600+

Pinot Noir

CALIFORNIA · **MONTEREY COUNTY (MRY)**

The Deep Cold Monterey Bay Produces an Extraordinary Environment for Viticulture

The Monterey Bay as seen from the beautiful beaches of Pacific Grove at the tip of the Monterey Peninsula

Monterey's beautiful sailing marina

The Beautiful Colors of the Monterey Fisherman's Wharf

F rom the Monterey Bay National Marine Sanctuary, to the expansive
wine regions, to cute little villages with many wine-tasting rooms.

MONTEREY COUNTY

Let's begin with the county of Monterey, at the north of our California's Central Coast wine regions. Monterey is the name of the county and of the third largest city with a population of 30,000 people. Salinas is the capital and the largest city with over 150,000 people. Monterey AVA is also the name of the overall appellation here for viticulture.

Further, Monterey is the name of the bay, which is an official **National Marine Sanctuary**. It is considered the "Serengeti of the Sea," with extensive wildlife. It is America's largest and most diverse marine sanctuary. You may be visiting Monterey for the wineries and their wines; however, don't leave without seeing this extraordinary marine sanctuary.

Speaking of why one would visit Monterey. I have been to Monterey many times for so many of its beautiful attributes; however, it never occurred to me that Monterey had wine regions. I am still today a bit dumbfounded that it never really dawned on me. Certainly, I knew the Santa Lucia Highlands, so famous for its Pinot Noir, and I have

numerous bottles in my wine cellar. Just to open your eyes a bit further and to put all this in perspective, Monterey County has the same number of acres of vineyards as Napa County. This is no small wine region; it is significant in the world of wine.

When you don't see something right in front of your eyes, often times you don't think it's there, and I think this is the case with the wine regions of Monterey. The closest vineyards to Monterey are a thirty-minute drive up the Salinas Valley. River Road is the **Monterey Wine Trail**, traversing the appellations and reaching the wineries to explore.

I suggest getting out and seeing the vineyards. Make the drive. See the expansive wine region and visit a few wineries. If you don't want to get out into the farmland, then there are two excellent options.

Carmel-By-The-Sea Village. This is a cute storybook village along Hwy 1, just fifteen minutes west of Monterey, on the ocean. Totally walkable. Filled with art galleries, cafes, restaurants, and inns. Plus, wineries have set up shop with tasting rooms. I counted eighteen tasting rooms in the village.

Carmel Valley Village is a little town along the roadside going through the Carmel Valley AVA. This appellation is at a much higher elevation, away from most of the cool marine fog. It has a much warmer climate than the rest of Monterey County, so they are producing more full-bodied wines (Cabernet Sauvignon, Merlot). When Monterey and Carmel are filled with fog, as they often are, take this beautiful drive into the Santa Lucia Mountains where the Carmel Valley brings you sunshine and magnificent landscapes. The Carmel Village has twenty-three wineries with tasting rooms to visit. Nice restaurants too.

The **Monterey Regional Airport** (MRY) has forty direct flights daily from ten major airports, and is only ten minutes from downtown Monterey.

Don't forget that **Monterey City** is a beautiful area located right on the water of the bay. They have a sailing marina, yacht club, Fisherman's Wharf, Monterey Bay Aquarium, Cannery Row, and numerous excellent restaurants. This is the source for numerous water activities: sailing, boat tours, kayaking, scuba diving, whale watching, etc.

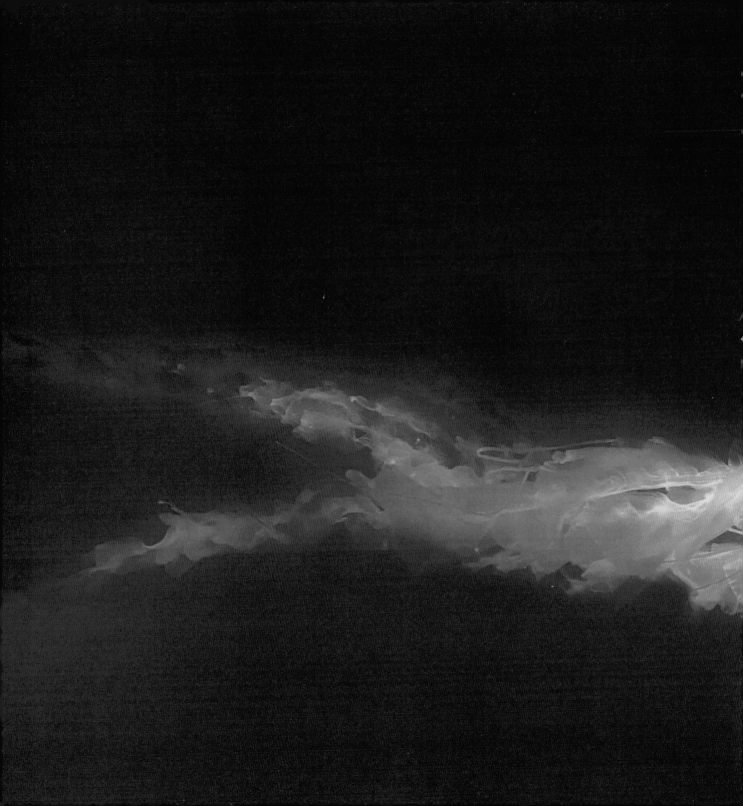

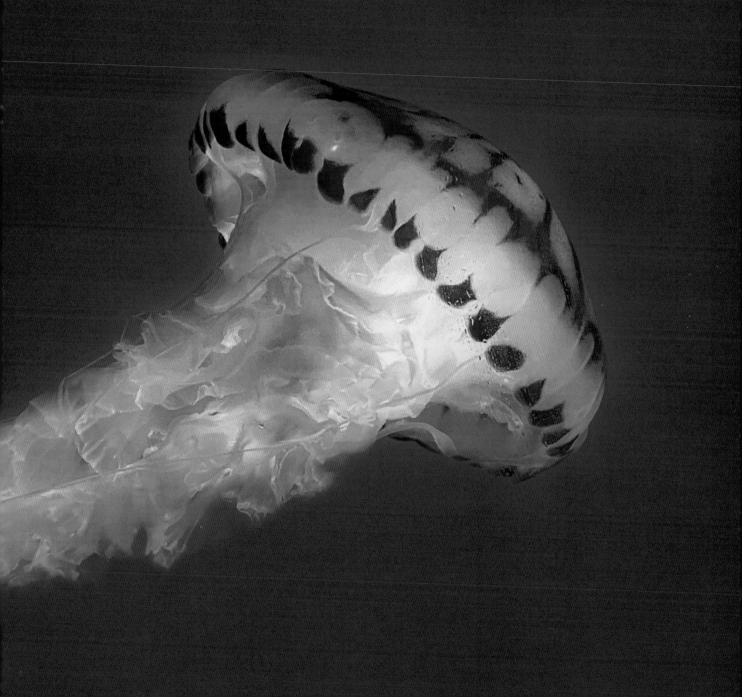

THE UNDERSEA WORLD IS MESMERIZING HERE

The Monterey Bay is most interesting. It is a protected marine sanctuary of breathtaking nature. It has extensive kelp forests, underwater canyons and deep ocean environments very close to shore, all creating a habitat for a huge variety of marine life, including thirty-six species of marine mammals, more than 180 species of birds, more than 500 species of fish, plus thousands of invertebrates and algae. It is the largest, most diverse marine sanctuary in the country.

Put away your scuba diving equipment, the Monterey Bay Aquarium has brought the Monterey Bay indoors in a most spectacular way. Every minute, 2,000 gallons of the ocean is pumped into the aquarium from the bay. First, this fresh seawater arrives into their **Kelp Forest** (photo below right) before circulating throughout the aquarium's 200 exhibits. It is three-stories tall of glass viewing, holding 343,000 gallons of water, and is the very first and largest live kelp forest ever created outside the ocean. I think they are very successful because they bring the ocean directly into this exhibit every day. It's not just the live seawater, it's everything that comes with it out of the ocean (hundreds of species of fish, invertebrates and algae) that makes the environment a real ecosystem. The kelp grows three to five inches every day in this healthy environment.

The exhibits are truly mesmerizing as they captivate you with the wonderment of the ocean. Just look at that **decorator crab** (left page). Isn't he cool looking? He is a seafloor scavenger consuming scraps of dead animals. The **purple-striped jellies** are particularly fascinating to me (see photo on previous spread). Their flowing tentacles, the way they undulate and how they glow ever so beautifully, I can watch them for hours. And there are hundreds of them in a huge wall aquarium.

Check out the colorful **anemones** (photo left page, lower left). These are actually predatory marine organisms, consuming prey that comes within reach of their tentacles and immobilizing it. There are numerous **live corals** at the aquarium. See their unique beautiful colors and shapes (photo left page, lower right). There are several hands-on touching of plants and animals. You can even pet bat rays (photo below left) in their **Bat Ray Touch Pool** as they swim around and come up to you for your affection.

They have a very impressive deep-sea exhibit, **Into The Deep: Exploring Our Undiscovered Ocean**. This is the largest collection of deep-sea animals in North America. The deep-sea is the part of the ocean that is deeper than 660 feet. Species here must adapt to a world of little to no light and no boundaries, water temperatures close to freezing, and enormous water pressure. Yet these animals are so numerous they outnumber animals on land.

They have an **Open Sea** exhibit too. It is a massive: 90' wide and 35' tall glass wall (photo below center). It is 52' front to back, holding 1.2 million gallons of seawater, home to **green sea turtles**, **hammerhead sharks**, a massive school of **pacific sardines**, elusive **ocean sunfish**, and **flashing mahi mahi**, just to name a few. It is a grand sight to see!

886 Cannery Row
Monterey, CA 93940

+1 831 648 4800
Aquarium@MBayAq.org

MontereyBayAquarium.org

All tickets must be purchased online
MontereyBayAquarium.org/visit

Open: Every Day, 10am-5pm

I recommend planning to spend the day here:
200 Unique Exhibits Around The Aquarium
They have numerous programs throughout the day:
15-minute Educational Programs At Exhibits
Live Feeding Programs In Your Presence
Behind-The-Scenes Private Tours

Restaurant
MONTRIO BISTRO

$$$-$$$$

414 Calle Principal
Downtown Monterey, CA 93940

+1 831 648 8880
Montrio.com

Open: Every Day, 5pm-9pm (Fri/Sat 10pm)

Pavlova (top): a totally vegan dessert made of blood orange-grapefruit mousse, marinated citrus, and blood-orange sorbet on an airy, crisp meringue shell, and topped with sprinkles of dark chocolate.

Hiramasa Crudo (below center): thinly sliced raw yellowtail kingfish, blood orange aqua chili, avocado, cured tomato, compressed Thai basil, and California arbequina olive oil. Lots of delicious juices and big flavors, and a bit spicy with the serrano peppers.

Braised Beef Short Ribs (below right): decadent short ribs slowly simmered in their juices, glazed root vegetables, garlic mashed potatoes, in a classic homemade Bordelaise sauce of dry red wine, bone marrow, butter, shallots, in a demi-glace marchand de vin sauce.

V ery healthy fine dining from a celebrity chef, in a historic fire station.

LUXURY DINING IN A CERTIFIED GREEN RESTAURANT

Did you realize there is a green certification for restaurants? This luxury restaurant is honored with that status. Montrio Bistro uses sustainable seafood: local, organic produce; prime meats; homemade sauces, and homemade desserts. The food is creatively gourmet, locally derived, fresh, delicious, and healthy.

They define their cuisine as "cutting edge Californian." I call it European-influenced American food. Seasonally inspired. Small plates and main courses.

This is a glamorous atmosphere in a renovated historical fire house. White tablecloths. Excellent wine list. Exceptional service. This restaurant offers a beautiful evening you will remember.

MONTEREY CANNERY ROW

Cannery Row is the famous waterfront street in Monterey where the once-burgeoning sardine-canning factories thrived. The last cannery closed in 1973 when, well, all the sardines were gone. Where did they go? Simply, they went into cans. Over-fished! It was not until 1999 that the sardines fully recovered. It was officially named Cannery Row in 1958 to honor John Steinbeck and his well-known novel *Cannery Row*.

Today, the abandoned factories have been converted into restaurants, shops, the Monterey Plaza Hotel, Coastal Kitchen, and the Monterey Bay Aquarium.

In his book, *Cannery Row*, John Steinbeck described this street as...

"a poem, a stink, a grating noise, a quality of light,
a tone, a habit, a nostalgia, a dream."

Restaurant at Monterey Plaza Hotel
COASTAL KITCHEN

$$$$$

+1 831 645 4064
CoastalKitchenMonterey.com

Open: Wed-Sat, 5:30pm-8:30pm
RSVP Online or Call

My inspiration is to showcase the bounty of the Monterey Peninsula in an elevated setting where guests can celebrate special occasions and make lasting memories.

— **Michael Rotondo, Executive Chef**

Japanese Wagyu Beef (right): a duet of beef with a horseradish infused beet reduction sauce, grilled ramps, local nasturtium, and a celery seaweed vinaigrette, perfectly paired with an exquisite Nebbiolo from northwest Italy.

Miso Marinated Black Cod (below right): a locally fished black cod, marinated in miso with grated carrot, kishu mandarin, shitake tempura, and a silky yellow curry sauce.

Tortellini En Brodo (below center): is a special pasta course of the evening whereby the tortellini is cooked slowly inside a Moonflower cheese bowl, then served tableside, placed on top of purple broccolini, spigarello kale, prosciutto, mint, and a brassicas' inspired minestrone broth.

Valrhona Ispahan (below left): is inspired by the legendary pastry chef Pierre Herme's Valrhona. Chocolate Isapahan with pink peppercorn, lychee and raspberry sorbet. Decadently beyond delicious.

O ver looking the Monterey Bay, this elegant restaurant is delivering a very special menu.

TABLE D'HÔTE

Enter a kitchen that is on its way to a Michelin star. Chef Michael Rotondo arrived in Monterey in 2021 to create this new restaurant Coastal Kitchen at Monterey Plaza Hotel. He came from the San Francisco Ritz-Carlton, as the executive chef of their award-winning Parallel 37.

This is one of your ultimate food and wine experiences to have in Monterey. Between the chef and his sommelier, they have crafted a very special culinary experience. I could say a lot about how delicious and creative the cuisine is here; however, the pictures really tell you the most delicious story.

This is a *table d'hôte* (prix-fixe) menu, newly crafted each month, and modified daily with fresh opportunities. This is Chef Michael's creativity with flavors, design and local ingredients to expressive eight unique courses of magnificence.

MONTEREY **DOWNTOWN MONTEREY** ■
Hotel, Restaurant & Spa
MONTEREY PLAZA HOTEL

$$$-$$$$-$$$$$

400 Cannery Row
Monterey, CA 93940

+1 831 920 6710
Reservations@MontereyPlazaHotel.com

MontereyPlazaHotel.com

LUXURY HOTEL CANTILEVERED OVER THE MONTEREY BAY

There is so much to love about this hotel. The location is ideal: in Monterey, right on the bay (view from the rooms above), in Cannery Row, down the street from the Monterey Bay Aquarium. This hotel is close to many excellent restaurants, including two of their own: Schooners, a casual ocean front dining restaurant (7am-9pm) and their formal Coastal Kitchen (left page) where you will experience some of the finest food and wine pairings.

Get one of the rooms that are cantilevered over the water (photo below right) where you can open the doors and hear the waves crashing, watch the seals and otters playing, and gaze at the sailboats drifting by, all as you enjoy one of the very best coffees you can make in your hotel room. That was an exceptionally special extra.

Go rooftop for an amazing view of the bay from their sundeck. Enjoy the outdoor fireplace or soak in a whirlpool tub overlooking the bay (photo below).

Inside, they have a beautiful lounge, a living-room-comfy environment, fireplace, live music and full-service of drinks and snacks (photo right).

CALIFORNIA · MONTEREY COUNTY WINE TASTING

The Wine Trail, Coastal Tasting and Country Charm

The mountaintop vineyards of Albatross Ridge

Chardonnay harvest at the Albatross Ridge vineyards

VISITING WINERIES IN MONTEREY COUNTY MADE EASY

If you are like me, you have visited Monterey for its beauty and not yet realized there is a wine region with acreage as big as Napa Valley. This is an exciting discovery. While the cool environment here focuses on Pinot Noir and Chardonnay, all types of grapes can be found grown in the different appellations here.

This is not your typical wine region where you visit appellations to find the wines that you enjoy. Instead, the wineries primarily set up tasting rooms in two of the villages for you to come visit them and taste their wines. The wineries both grow and source their fruit in the different appellations all over Monterey County and beyond. This makes it very easy to park your car once and walk around to the different wineries and enjoy all aspects of the villages. If you want to go out into the agricultural areas, you can still go visit wineries surrounded by vineyards.

Here are the three places to go visit wineries...

THE WINE TRAIL

The Monterey Wine Trail (page 44) is out in the *Salinas Valley,* where you will find wineries among the vineyards to visit. It is about a thirty-minute drive to The Wine Trail where there are several wineries open to the public. Not many, so I point you to the ones to visit. Even though it is a distance from the city, it is definitely worth the trip.

Traverse the River Road. It runs along the base of the foothills of the Santa Lucia Mountains, primarily running at the edge of the Santa Lucia Highlands Appellation. As you continue farther south, you go into the Arroyo Seco Appellation. Most of the wineries are located along River Road with a couple of them off the road and into their appellations. At this time, there are less than ten wineries open to the public here. Hopefully this will continue to grow.

COASTAL WINE TASTING

Coastal Wine Tasting (page 86) happens right in the city, *Carmel-By-The-Sea*, a very charming village located right on the beach in Carmel Bay. No driving out into the valleys to visit wineries. There were eighteen wineries with tasting rooms when I visited.

Carmel-By-The-Sea Village is a charming town where the original Hansel and Gretel fairytale cottages were built (and are still there) and inspired numerous other homes and businesses to carry on this interesting theme.

You can park your car once, and then visit the wineries to taste wines created from many Monterey appellations. There are an abundance of restaurants, shops and galleries that fill this darling little place. And at the edge of the village is the beach for a nice excursion.

COUNTRY CHARM

Carmel Valley Coastal Charm (page 72) is a short distance from Monterey and Carmel into a long beautiful valley in the middle of the Santa Lucia Mountains. The valley is significantly warmer than cool Monterey. The sun burns off the fog quickly here, if the fog even shows up at all.

The *Carmel Valley Appellation* offers terroir unique in Monterey with a warm climate for Bordeaux, Rhône and other varietals. There are a couple of wineries here that you can visit that are on their estate of vineyards. The rest of them are located in the *Carmel Valley Village*.

There is an abundance of wineries here with their excellent tasting rooms, and very comfortable and stylish tasting areas in which to enjoy your experience. There were twenty-three wineries here when I visited.

MONTEREY COUNTY (MRY)
Appellations

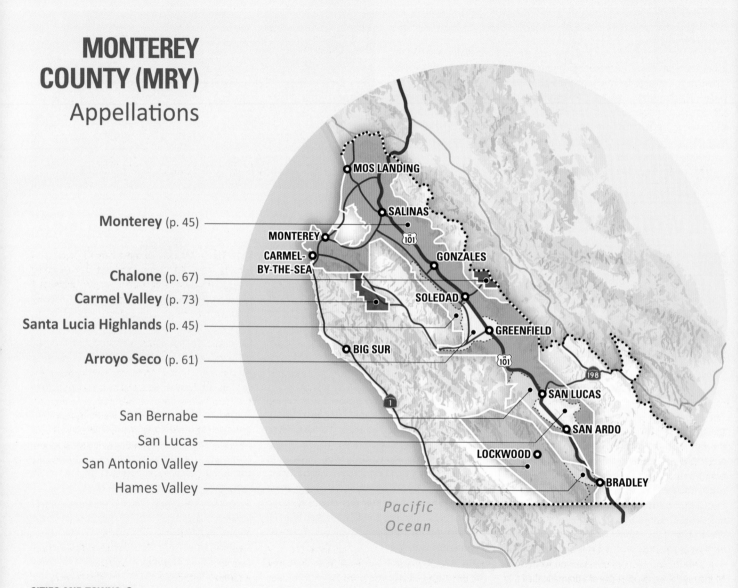

Monterey (p. 45)

Chalone (p. 67)
Carmel Valley (p. 73)
Santa Lucia Highlands (p. 45)

Arroyo Seco (p. 61)

San Bernabe

San Lucas

San Antonio Valley

Hames Valley

MOS LANDING

SALINAS

MONTEREY

CARMEL-
BY-THE-SEA

GONZALES

SOLEDAD

GREENFIELD

BIG SUR

SAN LUCAS

SAN ARDO

LOCKWOOD

BRADLEY

*Pacific
Ocean*

CITIES AND TOWNS ⭘
Appellations ━━━━━•
County limits ···········

M onterey climate is ideal for cool-weather wine grapes; particularly Pinot Noir and Chardonnay are the super-stars here.

MONTEREY APPELLATIONS

Monterey County (MRY) has nine appellations. The primary appellation is the **Monterey AVA**, with six sub-appellations, plus two appellations (outside of Monterey AVA) **Carmel Valley AVA**, and **Chalone AVA**. These two appellations are at higher altitudes above the fog line, providing a significantly warmer climate for heavier red-grape varieties.

The Monterey AVA is dramatically influenced by the cold Pacific Ocean filling its valley with fog. Just 100 yards off shore is a unique feature known as the Blue Grand Canyon, named because of its size similarity to the famous above-ground Grand Canyon. The Blue Grand Canyon is sixty miles long and 16,000' deep (the Grand Canyon is only 6,000' at its deepest). Most large canyons in the ocean are in deep water a distance from the shore. This canyon is right in the bay, creating ideal weather onshore for farming cool-weather-crops, from lettuce and broccoli to the cool-weather wine grapes, particularly Pinot Noir and Chardonnay.

Here is how this submarine canyon works. The Monterey Bay sits on the edge of a dramatic shelf that drops 5,000 meters into this canyon. The floor is thick with decaying matter from the remains of life above that have sunk and decomposed. Strong offshore winds push the surface water away into the ocean,

forcing this deep water to rise with all of its nutrition, also bringing up very cold water to the surface.

This creates an explosion of life, from mammoth to microscopic species, all living in a gigantic kelp forest growing as much as 100 meters a day. There are 300 species of fish, 1,000s of invertebrates, creating the largest, most diverse marine sanctuary in the country.

What I find fascinating is how the balance of nature works here. Preventing the fast-growing forest of kelp from getting out of control is a huge number of sea urchins that vigorously consume the kelp. At the surface lies a single keystone species, guardians of the kelp forest, that maintain the balance of life here, sea otters. Otters are ravenous consumers of urchins as they can easily consume fifty urchins per day per otter.

What further happens with the upwelling of the extremely cold water from the canyon floor, is it also cools the marine air, creating fog that blankets the bay and significantly fills the agricultural valley.

As the southern end of the valley warms up, which happens faster than in areas near the shore, the rising warm air pulls the cold marine air down the valley, creating ocean winds as an air-conditioning system, mitigating temperatures and extending growing season.

The **Monterey Wine Trail** is where you can visit the actual wineries in this valley. The first appellation you reach on this Wine Trail is the **Santa Lucia Highlands**

AVA. This is Monterey's most famous appellation growing world class Pinot Noir. Most of the wineries are just outside the appellation, along the main road. Many of the wineries throughout Monterey County buy fruit from here for their premium Pinot Noir wines.

Next along the Wine Trail is the **Arroyo Seco AVA** with wineries inside and outside the appellation, and many wineries in the county buying their fruit from this excellent terroir. Across the valley and up the mountain is the **Chalone AVA**. Following Arroyo Seco west into the mountains is a beautiful drive that leads you back around to the **Carmel Valley Village** and then **Carmel-By-The-Sea Village**. These two locations are where you will find numerous winery tasting rooms.

Here are some helpful driving distances and times to make it easier to get around.

Driving Distance to Monterey from...
- **San Francisco**   120 mi (2 hrs, 00 min)
- **Paso Robles**   115 mi (1 hrs, 50 min)
- **San Luis Obispo**   142 mi (2 hrs, 15 min)
- **Los Angeles**   320 mi (5 hrs, 00 min)

Driving Distance from Monterey to...
- **Carmel-by-the-Sea**   4 mi (15 min)
- **Carmel Valley Village**   17 mi (30 min)
- **Santa Lucia Highlands AVA**   20 mi (30 min)
- **Arroyo Seco AVA**   40 mi (50 min)
- **Chalone AVA**   52 mi (70 min)

Beautiful lake and vineyards at Chalone Vineyard

MONTEREY COUNTY WINERIES

The Wine Trail (page 45)	Number of Wines	Red Wines	White Wines	Rosé Wines	Sweet Wines	Sparkling Wines	Wine Shop	Boutique	Lodging	Restaurant	Food Options	Food & Wine Pairings	Tours	Educational Workshops	Fun Activities	Pinot Noir	Chardonnay	Syrah	Other
Santa Lucia Highlands Area																			
Odonata Winery	21	√	√		√		√									√		√	√
Rustique Wines	5	√	√	√			√						√	√		√	√		
Pessagno Winery	21	√	√	√	√		√	√	√						√	√	√	√	√
Puma Road Winery	20	√	√	√	√		√		√						√	√	√	√	
Wrath Wines	19	√	√	√			√						√		√	√	√	√	
Hahn Estate	27	√	√	√	√		√	√		√			√			√	√	√	
Arroyo Seco Area																			
Joyce Estate Winery	13	√	√				√						√		√	√	√	√	
Scheid Vineyards	40	√	√	√	√	√	√			√	√		√		√	√	√	√	√
Chalone AVA																			
Chalone Vineyard	9	√	√				√								√	√	√	√	
Country Charm (page 73)																			
Carmel Valley																			
Folktale Winery & Vineyards	25	√	√	√	√	√	√	√		√	√	√		√		√	√	√	√
Holman Ranch	24	√	√	√	√		√	√	√	√			√		√	√	√	√	
Albatross Ridge Vineyards	11	√	√	√	√		√			√	√				√	√			
Carmel Valley Village																			
Albatross Ridge	11	√	√	√	√		√			√	√				√	√			
Bernardus Winery	22	√	√	√			√			√	√				√	√		√	
Boekenoogen Wines	10	√	√				√	√							√	√		√	
Holman Ranch	24	√	√	√	√		√	√	√	√			√		√	√	√	√	
I. Brand Winery	15	√	√	√			√								√	√	√		
Joyce Wine Company	13	√	√	√			√						√	√		√	√	√	
Scratch Wines	7	√	√	√	√		√								√	√	√	√	
Windy Oaks Estate	22	√	√	√			√	√							√	√			
Coastal Wine Tasting (page 87)																			
Carmel-By-The-Sea Village																			
Albatross Ridge	11	√	√	√	√		√			√	√				√	√			
Blair Estate	10	√	√	√			√	√		√					√	√		√	
Caraccioli Cellars	12	√	√	√	√		√								√	√	√	√	
De Tierra Vineyards	19	√	√	√	√	√	√			√				√		√	√		√
KORi Wines	9	√	√	√			√						√	√		√	√		√
Lepe Cellars	6	√	√				√	√								√	√		√
Silvestri Vineyards	20	√	√	√	√		√						√	√		√	√	√	√

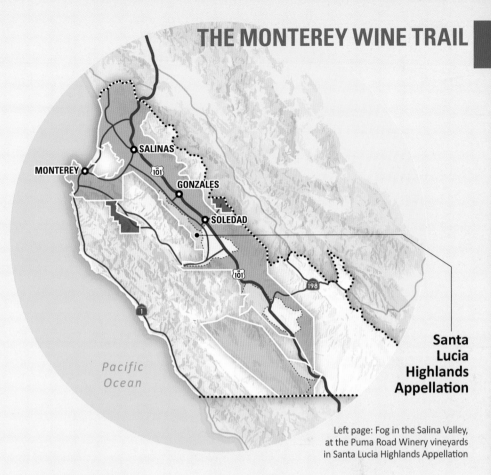

THE MONTEREY WINE TRAIL

SALINAS

MONTEREY

GONZALES

SOLEDAD

Pacific Ocean

Santa Lucia Highlands Appellation

Left page: Fog in the Salina Valley, at the Puma Road Winery vineyards in Santa Lucia Highlands Appellation

MAGICAL TERROIR

The **Monterey Wine Trail** is a small group of wineries in the Salinas Valley that are open to the public. Heading south from Monterey, the first appellation that you reach within the **Monterey AVA** is the **Santa Lucia Highlands AVA** (SLH).

SLH is an eighteen mile stretch of vineyards along the foothills of the Santa Lucia Mountain Range. Being just twenty miles from the bay, SLH has optimum impact from the marine influence. Cool, thick fog every morning and afternoon winds are constant, predictable, daily occurrences.

This wind and fog produces cool air conditioning to make for a very long growing season. And with poor soil, it forces the grapes to work extra hard. The results are vines that produce tiny clusters with little berries of intense flavor.

The primary grapes planted here are Pinot Noir and Chardonnay. The wines are rich, fruit forward, silky vibrant wines (I just love this style). Wineries from all over Monterey County – and all over California, for that matter – purchase the extraordinary fruit produced here in SLH.

Most of the wineries here are not within the appellation. They are located at the base of the Highlands along **River Road**, where the wineries have easy road access for production and tourists. I have organized them by distance from Monterey.

Here are the wineries to check out.

- Odonata Winery, page 47
- Rustique Wines, page 49
- Pessagno Winery, page 51
- Puma Road Winery, page 55
- Wrath Wines, page 57
- Hahn Estate, page 59

$$

645 River Road
Salinas, CA 93908

+1 831 566 5147
Info@OdonataWines.com

OdonataWines.com

Open: Every Day, 11am-5pm

Collection of Wines

Pinot Noir (Santa Lucia Highlands)
Pinot Noir (Santa Cruz Mountains)
Pinot Noir (Silacci Vineyards)
Petite-Sangio (Petite Sirah, Sangiovese)
Black Darter - Rhone Blend (Grenache, Mourvèdre, Syrah)
Carbonic Carignan (Carignan)
Malbec Et (Malbec fermented with Viognier)
Cabernet Sauvignon (Carmel Valley)
Durif (Reserve Petite Sirah)
Syrah (Hook Vineyard)
Syrah (Soberanes Vineyard)
Sangiovese, Grenache, Malbec, Petite Sirah
Dessert Zinfandel (Zinfandel)

Sparkling Blanc De Blanc (Chardonnay)
Sparkling Grenache Rouge
Sparkling Albariño
Sparkling Riesling

S parkling wines that will get your attention in both quality and uniqueness.

CLOSEST WINERY TO MONTEREY

As we start out on **The Wine Trail**, Odonata Winery is the first winery we reach. They are very close to Monterey, eight miles from the water. They are on River Road before you get to the *Santa Lucia Highlands Appellation*.

The winery is adjacent to their small estate vineyard of Viognier (photo left and above). Why Viognier you ask, and I asked? Owner/winemaker Denis Hoey loves to co-ferment with Viognier. He sees it as his salt. And he only needs a little salt. Four to five buckets of Viognier to co-ferment with Syrah, for example. So, who is going to sell him four to five buckets whenever he needs it? Now he has his "salt" growing at the winery as he needs.

Did you know adding a little Viognier (a white grape) to Syrah (a red grape) enhances the red color. Logic would think the opposite. The chemical compounds of Viognier help stabilize and retain the color of the Syrah during the fermentation process. It also enhances the aromas by bringing beautiful floral, spice and peach notes. Also plum, tobacco, black pepper, and even bacon fat, in the mouth.

Chemistry sure is amazing!

This Viognier concept began in Côte-Rôtie, a wine-growing region in Northern Rhône France, where Viognier often grows alongside Syrah. Winemakers simply went with what they had, producing a "field-blend" wine. And it worked, magically! And thus, the Viognier co-fermentation concept was discovered.

Other than his Viognier salt, Denis purchases all of his fruit from sources with extraordinary vineyards. From his neighboring Santa Lucia Highlands (where he makes three excellent Pinot Noirs) to notable vineyards around Monterey County and beyond. He looks for vineyards that have great representation of the terroir so he can make his distinguished wines.

Let's talk bubbles. I really like his traditional Champagne-style *Blanc de Blanc*, Chardonnay from the acclaimed Escolle Vineyard in the Santa Lucia Highlands. But there's more. Have you ever tasted sparkling wines from Albariño or Riesling? Here is the place to discover. And you must try their Grenache sparkling. It is a red sparkling, strawberry in color, with lots of delicious fruit flavors.

$$

1010 River Road
Salinas, CA 93908

+1 831 320 8174
Sara@RustiqueWines.com

RustiqueWines.com

Open: Friday-Sunday, 11am-5pm

From Rancho de Guadalupe, comes an estate vineyard of Pinot Noir and Chardonnay.

YOUTHFUL ENERGY

This is the second-closest winery to Monterey as you head out onto **The Wine Trail**. This is a large ranch located on River Road just before you get to the *Santa Lucia Highlands Appellation* (photo above). There is a big history here, and you will see it with the restored-barn tasting room (photo left page), and other historic buildings on the property.

It was 1873 when the Rancho de Guadalupe was subdivided into seven parcels in the initials of the family. In 1923, the Sargeni family partitioned 1,235 acres of this ranch for their dairy business. Today, Sargeni's great-grandson Chad Silacci is the winemaker endeavoring this viniculture opportunity on the ranch.

In 1999, 22.5 acres of Pinot Noir and Chardonnay were planted for selling the grapes. This family is a huge lover of wine, and many of them are working in the industry (note: family member Michael Silacci is winemaker at Opus One in Napa Valley). In 2006, they started making wine for themselves, family and friends.

Harvesting 2.5 acres of Pinot Noir and 1 acre of Chardonnay, the Silaccis had a lot of wine for everyone they knew. People loved their wines, and the cellar was filling fast with extras. This became the time to get serious and become a commercial winery. It was official in May of 2021. They are just getting started with twelve years of experience.

They hired excellent winemakers to set their course, including Denis Hoey at Odonata Winery down the street (see previous pages), where they still make their wines today. Chad Silacci became good friends with Denis and inspired him to go to college to study viticulture and oenology.

Today, Chad and his sister, Sara, run the business. Both in their early twenties, putting youthful energy into their new business, with drive to make it a success.

Most of their wines are sold direct to consumer, so you might as well show up to the ranch and have a good time with them. It is a super-casual environment with very nice people.

And, they have fifteen years of library wines to share with you. This is the way to do tasting if you would like to get into their aged wines.

Collection of Wines

Rustiqué Pinot Noir (Silacci Vineyard)
Rustiqué Rosé (Pinot Noir)
Rustiqué Chardonnay (Oak Aged)
Rustiqué SS Chardonnay (Stainless Steel)

$-$$-$$$

1645 River Road
Salinas, CA 93908

+1 831 675 9463
Info@PessagnoWines.com

PessagnoWines.com

Open: Every Day, 12pm-5pm (Sat/Sun 11am)

A thirty-year dream of luxurious wines created by two passionate owners.

WINE, MUSIC, LODGING

At this point along **The Wine Trail**, we are now reaching the *Santa Lucia Highlands Appellation*. To the west of River Road is the appellation, and to the east of the road is Pessagno Winery. The winery has a view of the beautiful Santa Lucia Mountains and appellation.

Three miles south on River Road is Pessagno's sister winery, Puma Road Winery. Both of these wineries have accommodations (see next page), homes next to the winery and vineyards. It is not common here for wineries to have lodging, and there are no hotels. More so, this is a great way to stay in the middle of the wine regions in such a beautiful agricultural area against the mountains.

This winery has a thirty year history, and was a passionate dream for its previous owner and winemaker, Stephan Pessagno. His dream was to produce exclusive wines from prestigious vineyards. In 2014, the Franscioni family took over this dream to continue the legacy of the luxurious wines here.

The Franscionis are four generations of farmers here, and the owners of Puma Road Winery (page 55).

They bring their expertise and reputation of growing the finest grapes to some of the industry's best-known winemakers. They have over a thousand acres of vines in the Santa Lucia Highlands, the appellation that focuses on Burgundy varietals. Burgundy is also the focus at Pessagno Winery.

The Franscionis also brought their exceptional winemaker to Pessagno to expand the quality and styles of the wines here. Winemaker Olivier Rousset comes with great knowledge from France. His experience in Burgundy and Bordeaux France, makes him an ideal oenologist to create the best wines for Pessagno and Puma Road wineries. Olivier also worked with Napa and Sonoma wineries to achieve top scores for their wines.

Yes, it certainly is unusual to see a French winemaker in Monterey. With a notable accent, Olivier is making excellent Pinot Noir and Chardonnay in the Santa Lucia Highlands AVA for Pessagno. And also using Santa Lucia Highlands AVA and Paicines AVA grapes for Puma Road.

Don't miss the fun of **Tastings & Tunes**, live music and wine every Saturday (Puma Road Winery) and Sunday (Pessagno Winery) afternoons.

Collection of Wines

Four Boys Pinot Noir (Santa Lucia Highlands Estate)
Pinot Noir (Santa Lucia Highlands Estate)
Pinot Noir (Pedregal de Paicines Vineyard)
Pinot Noir (Central Avenue)
Syrah (Santa Lucia Highlands Estate)
Pinot Noir (Santa Lucia Highlands Estate)
Grenache (Pedregal de Paicines Vineyard)
Zinfandel (Pedregal de Paicines Vineyard)
GSM Blend (Pedregal de Paicines Vineyard)
Mourvèdre (Monterey County)
Sangiovese (Paicines, California)
Quattro Red Wine Blend (Cabernet Franc, Merlot, Cabernet Sauvignon, Malbec)
Tre Red Wine Blend (Cab Sauv, Malbec, Petite Sirah)
Due Red Wine Blend (Cabernet Sauvignon, Petit Verdot)

Viognier (Pedregal de Paicines Vineyard)
Intrinity Chardonnay (Santa Lucia Highlands Estate)
Chardonnay (Pedregal de Paicines Vineyard)
Pinot Gris (Santa Lucia Highlands Estate)

Hames Valley Port

When you are traveling through **The Wine Trail**, you will quickly notice that there are no restaurants or hotels, only wineries, vineyards and row crops. This is truly an agricultural region. The Salinas Valley is often nicknamed the "Salad Bowl of the World," as roughly 70% of the nation's lettuce crop is grown here.

The Salinas Valley does have Highway 101 running through the middle of it with a couple little towns, **Gonzales Village** and **Town of Soledad**, which are ten to fifteen minutes from River Road. In both these two towns, you will find an abundance of local authentic Mexican food, plus some extras that I share with you below.

Luigi's Italian Restaurant
+1 831 675 7800 • 346 Alta Street, Gonzales
Open: Mon-Fri 11am-9pm, Sat 12pm-9pm

LuigisPasta.net

Directly from Italy, authentic recipes and the devotion to freshly made Italian food began three generations of this heartfelt Italian family creating delicious Italian meals here since 1975. Today, Luigi's has taken over a bank building in the center of town.

There is nothing like their homemade lasagna. The noodles were perfect. The sauce unbelievable. The cheeses were glorifying this beautiful dish.

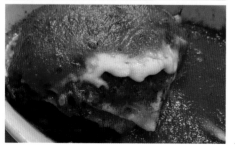

Taste Of The Pinnacles Wine Bar
+1 831 237 5321 • 148 Main Street, Soledad
Open: Wed-Sun, 3pm-10pm

TasteOfThePinnacles.com

As I walked in the door, I was greeted by a very happy welcoming. I found myself sitting at the bar enjoying the best quesadilla (photo) I've ever eaten, discovering that this happy gentleman is the ex-mayor of Soledad and this is his retirement business.

Not just lots of wine, microbrews on tap as well. The food is simple, yet delicious. The tri-tip sandwich you see below was quite yummy.

$$$

Pessagno Winery
1645 River Road
Salinas, CA 93908
+1 831 675 9463
AirBnB Link at: PessagnoWines.com

Their sister winery has accommodations too
Puma Road Winery
32720 River Road
Gonzales, CA 93926
+1 831 675 3548
Airbnb Link at: PumaRoad.com

ENJOYING HOMES IN THE VINEYARDS

Passagno Winery and its sister Puma Road Winery have homes to rent in the vineyards on their winery properties. These photos here are of the home at Pessagno Winery. Other than roadside motels on Hwy 101, there are no nice hotels in the wine regions. These are nice homes available on Airbnb (links on their websites).

The homes are right in the middle of the Santa Lucia Highlands wine region along River Road. To the west, you will see this impressive appellation in the foothills of the Santa Lucia Mountains. To the east, is an abundance of prolific farmlands with a diversity of row crops as far as you can see.

The homes are well maintained, clean and well supplied. The customer service is always available and responsive. Full kitchens have all the essential cooking tools.

$$-$$$

32720 River Road
Gonzales, CA 93926

+1 831 675 3548
Info@PumaRoad.com

PumaRoad.com

Open: Thursday-Monday, 12pm-5pm

Collection of Wines

Pinot Noir (Apex Vineyard - Santa Lucia Highlands Estate)
Pinot Noir (Santa Lucia Highlands Estate)
Pinot Noir (Pedregal de Paicines Vineyard)
Cabernet Sauvignon (Pedregal de Paicines Vineyard)
Merlot (Pedregal de Paicines Vineyard)
Cabernet Franc (Pedregal de Paicines Vineyard)
Malbec (Pedregal de Paicines Vineyard)
Petit Verdot (Pedregal de Paicines Vineyard)
Tannat (Pedregal de Paicines Vineyard)
Cache (Cabernet Sauvignon, Merlot, Cabernet Franc)
The Predator (Cabernet Sauvignon, Merlot, Cabernet Franc,
Petit Verdot, Malbec)
TKO (Cabernet Sauvignon, Petite Sirah, 36 mo. in new oak)

Chardonnay (Pedregal de Paicines Vineyard)
Chardonnay (Vigna Monte Nero - Santa Lucia Highlands)
Silvio's Vineyard Pinot Gris (Santa Lucia Highlands Estate)
Sauvignon Blanc (Monterey County Estate)

Rosé of Grenache (Pedregal de Paicines Vineyard)

Blanc de Noirs (Santa Lucia Highlands Estate)
Blanc de Blancs (Santa Lucia Highlands Estate)
Cuvée (Santa Lucia Highlands Estate)

Four generations of farmers in Monterey and the Santa Lucia Highlands Appellation.

WINE, MUSIC AND LODGING

Three miles south of Pessagno Winery (page 51), also on River Road, is the Puma Road Winery along **The Wine Trail**. The winery is directly east of the road, with thousands of acres of row crops decorating the agricultural landscape behind them. To the west, Puma Road Winery views the beautiful *Santa Lucia Highlands* appellation and mountain range.

Both Puma Road and Pessagno wineries have accommodations (see previous page). These are homes next to the wineries and vineyards. It is not common here for wineries to have lodging. And there are no hotels. This is a great way to stay in the middle of the wine regions in this beautiful agricultural area against the mountains.

Puma Road Wines was created by Ray Franscioni, fourth generation of farmers here since the 1890s. The Franscioni family started with dairy operations and quickly expanded into a row crop farming as they saw the value of the soil and climate here. They now farm a massive 6,000 acres of row crops.

In the 1990s (a hundred years after arriving), Ray Franscioni decided to expand their farming business into vineyard operations. Ray has planted roughly a thousand acres in the Santa Lucia Highlands AVA (Burgundy varietals) and another thousand acres in the Paicines AVA (Bordeaux varietals).

The Franscionis achieved an excellent reputation, as other wineries buying their fruit were making wines that were gaining top scores from the critics. It was time for Ray Franscioni to start his own label from these excellent grapes. This happened ten years later, in 2003.

Ray was very smart to hire an excellent winemaker, Olivier Rousset, who comes with great knowledge from France. His experience is from Burgundy and Bordeaux France, as well as Napa and Sonoma wineries that achieved perfect scores from critics for their wines.

It is unusual to see a French winemaker here in Monterey. Olivier is making excellent Pinot Noir and Chardonnay from the Santa Lucia Highlands AVA (SRH) and Bordeaux wines from the Paicines AVA. And, you must try their line of sparkling wines made from SRH.

Don't miss the fun of **Tastings & Tunes**, live music and wine every Saturday (Puma Road Winery) and Sunday (Pessagno Winery) afternoons.

$$-$$$

35801 Foothill Road (at River Road)
Soledad, CA 93960

+1 831 678 2992
Info@WrathWines.com

WrathWines.com

Open: Friday-Monday, 11am-5pm

A beautiful afternoon of lakeside tasting.

GRAPES OF WRATH

Well, actually, Michael Thomas, the owner and winemaker at Wrath Wines, says it is more about the "Wrath of Gods" from the Led Zeppelin song. Further, wrath is the diurnal wall of maritime fog that regularly rolls into the Salinas Valley followed by persistent afternoon winds that relentlessly scream into the vineyards.

Michael is an archaeologist, a professor at the University of Texas, and leads a team of archaeologists in Italy that is uncovering an ancient Roman wine distribution center under a town that was smothered during a volcano eruption in 79 A.D. Interesting artifacts are being discovered, for example: more than four hundred amphoras, which are large ceramic wine vessels.

As an archaeologist, Michael has to believe in terroir and has brought this forth in his vineyard-specific wines in Monterey. I am particularly impressed with his single-vineyard wines, as they are representing the specific terroir and clones of each site.

They have three levels of wines. *The Ex Anima Series*: which are fresh, cleanly made, unoaked wines at very affordable prices. *The Single Vineyard Series*: focuses on Pinot Noir, Chardonnay, Grenache, and Syrah, primarily from the Santa Lucia Highlands AVA. *The Winemaker Series*: experimental wines, playing with clonal selections and blends, and trying unusual grapes, like Falanghina from Italy. Have you ever heard of this grape? Me neither. It is definitely a unique wine worth trying.

Speaking of experimental, Michael hired Sabrina Roadem, owner of Scratch Wines (page 83), who is a very creative and talented winemaker (Viticulture and Enology degrees from UC Davis). They bring their art and science to making some excellent wines.

I particularly enjoy tasting through their single-vineyard wines, especially the Pinot Noir wines from different vineyards in a Santa Lucia Highlands. It was a difficult choice between so many great wines, yet my favorite was the single vineyard **KW Ranch Pinot Noir** from the Santa Lucia Highlands.

This is a beautiful place to hang out for the afternoon. They have tours around the property. One of the best experiences is the natural lake (photo left page) where you can sit back and enjoy one of their delicious wines, and gaze across the lake, vineyards and the Santa Lucia Mountains in the backdrop (photo above).

Collection of Wines

Single Vineyard Series
Pinot Noir (Boekenoogen Vineyard)
Pinot Noir (Cortada Alta Vineyard)
Pinot Noir (San Saba Vineyard)
Pinot Noir (Tondré Grapefield)
Pinot Noir (KW Ranch)
Grenache (Alta Loma Vineyard)
Syrah (San Saba Vineyard)
Syrah (KW Ranch)
Chardonnay (Boekenoogen Vineyard)
Chardonnay (San Saba Vineyard)

Winemaker Series
Pinot Noir (Clones: 115 and 667)
Pinot Noir (Clones: Swan and 828)
Pinot Noir (Clones: Pommard 4 and 777)
Ex Vite Pinot Noir (Whole Clusters)
Saignée Pinot Noir (Rosé)
Fermenta Chardonnay
Chardonnay (Clone 3)
Falanghina (Falanghina Grape)
Destruction Level Grenache-Syrah

$$-$$$

37700 Foothill Road (inside the AVA hills)
Soledad, CA 93960

+1 831 678 2212
Info@HahnFamilyWines.com

HahnWines.com

Open: Thursday-Monday, 11am-5pm

Collection of Wines

Lucienne Pinot Noir (Smith Vineyard)
Lucienne Pinot Noir (Lone Oak Vineyard)
Lucienne Pinot Noir (Doctor's Vineyard)
Lucienne Pinot Noir (Hook Vineyard)
SLH Reserve Pinot Noir (Santa Lucia Highlands)
SLH Pinot Noir (Santa Lucia Highlands)
SLH Grenache (Santa Lucia Highlands)
SLH Orchestral Pinot Noir (Chardonnay)
Smith & Hook Reserve Cabernet Sauvignon
Smith & Hook Cabernet Sauvignon
Smith & Hook Malbec
Smith & Hook Cabernet Sauvignon (Paso Robles)
Smith & Hook Proprietary Red Blend (Cabernet
Sauvignon, Merlot, Malbec, Petite Sirah)
SLH Rosé (Santa Lucia Highlands)

Lucienne Chardonnay (Smith Vineyard)
Lucienne Chardonnay (Lone Oak Vineyard)
SLH Chardonnay (Santa Lucia Highlands)
SLH Pinot Gris (Santa Lucia Highlands)

Winery Selection Sparkling Blanc de Blancs (Chardonnay)
Winery Selection Sparkling Blanc de Noir (Pinot Noir)

E xperience the one winery located in the middle of the Santa Lucia Highlands Appellations.

BEAUTIFUL PINOT NOIR

Now we are at the southern end of this eighteen-mile appellation *Santa Lucia Highlands*. Still on **The Wine Trail** and just off of Puma Road, Hahn Estate brings you into the appellation, in the middle of the vineyards, up at elevation, with spectacular views. Hahn is the only winery in the appellation that is open to the public. The entrance sets a great stage. It is a long drive up the hill, maybe a mile, an awesome driveway through trees and vineyards.

I am sure you have heard of Hahn Winery, as they are big, producing over five hundred thousand cases of wine annually – and excellent wines. I have been drinking their Pinot Noirs for decades and have bottles in my cellar right now. For me, this visit was an opportunity to try some of their special wines not in distribution, as well as other varietals I was unaware they made.

For example, they make Bordeaux style wines under the label of **Smith & Hook**. This is where it all began for the founders Nicky and Gaby Hahn when they came to the Santa Lucia Highlands in the late 1970s. They loved Cabernet Sauvignon and planted

vineyards. Soon, they realized the cool climate was better suited for Burgundian grapes. Cabernet vines came out, and Pinot Noir and Chardonnay were planted. This was the beginning of the stellar Pinot Noir the Hahn Estate winery produces.

Smith & Hook is back better than ever, with winemaker Megan McCollough seeking excellent fruit from places like Paso Robles where Cabernet Sauvigon excels. Megan, checking her wines in the cellar (left page), has already achieved 95 points from Decanter magazine for this wine.

Back to the essence. I am a Hahn Pinot fan. What I spent my time discovering on my visit was their Lucienne wines. These are their top premium Pinot Noir wines, single-vineyard bottled. The ultimate for me was the **Lucienne Pinot Noir, Smith Vineyard**. These grapes grow at their highest elevation vineyard at 1280' in the Santa Lucia Highlands AVA. The wine was beautifully fragrant with the delicious black cherry flavors I love so much about Pinot Noir. This wine had soft tannins and an elegant finish. And the pricing is extremely fair.

Now don't forget the view. This is one of the best parts of drinking wine here. Look at the photo above. Isn't this the best patio ever?

CALIFORNIA • MONTEREY **ARROYO SECO AVA**

Diversified Terrain, Soils and Climates in this Cool-Climate Appellation

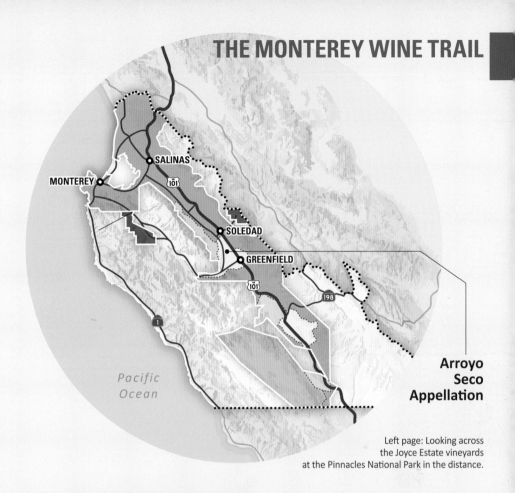

THE MONTEREY WINE TRAIL

Pacific Ocean

Arroyo Seco Appellation

Left page: Looking across the Joyce Estate vineyards at the Pinnacles National Park in the distance.

CLEAN WATER, MARINE INFLUENCE

The Arroyo Seco appellation is central in the Salinas Valley and one of the important sub-appellations of the Monterey AVA. The appellation is thirty-five miles from the Monterey Bay and gets direct marine influence. The nights and mornings fill the appellation with fog, plus the afternoon winds cool the grapes, all tempering the grapes' growth and intensifying their fruit flavors for great Burgundian wines.

The Arroyo Seco appellation begins in a steep narrow gorge at the foothills of the Santa Lucia Mountains. Moving east into the valley, the topography widens and eventually opens up to warm, fertile soil in the Salinas Valley. The canyon and valley have very different microclimates and soil types. Deep in the canyon, vineyards are less fertile and are shielded from afternoon winds

creating warmer temperatures. As the canyon opens to the valley floor, the afternoon winds from the cold ocean cools the grapes.

"Arroyo Seco" is Spanish for "dry riverbed." Underground is the Arroyo Seco River, considered one of the cleanest rivers in California, providing excellent clean irrigation for the vines.

There are numerous vineyards in the Arroyo Seco, over seven thousand acres of vines in the appellation. There are primarily farmers here, with many wineries in Monterey, and elsewhere, desiring these grapes to make their wines.

There is one winery to visit in the appellation, **Joyce Estate Winery**, and another just outside the AVA, **Scheid Vineyards**. Both are easily accessible.
• Joyce Estate Winery, page 63
• Scheid Vineyards, page 65

$$-$$$

38740 Los Coches Road
Soledad, CA 93960

+1 831 659 2885
Info@JoyceWineCo.com

JoyceWineCo.com

Open: Friday-Sunday, 12pm-5:30pm

Carmel Valley Village Tasting Room (page 82)
Open: Every Day, 12pm-6pm

A young entrepreneur, inspired with creative ideas, passionate about making great wine.

ARROYO SECO, SLH & MORE

It all started when Russell Joyce was a little boy working in a little four-acre vineyard on the hillside behind his house. He learned how to tend to those vines, harvest the grapes, make the wine, rack the barrels, and hand-bottle and label the wines. This was an inspiration! Russ knew then he wanted to learn the techniques and traditions of world-class winemaking.

In 2010, Russ started his official brand, began production in an industrial winery and opened a tasting room in the Carmel Valley Village. It was a big success. The tasting room has a fun and lively atmosphere. More than a wine-tasting room, it is a place of refreshing summer drinks and outrageous parties. This is the hip place to hang out.

Joyce has kept his focus on hand-crafted wines from small lots. His specialty is Pinot Noir. And I was totally impressed that each wine was as excellent as the last. His Pinot Noirs are excellent across each of the six different vineyards. Primarily, the Arroyo Seco AVA (where the new estate winery is now located) and the Santa Lucia Highlands, most famous for their excellent Pinot Noirs.

In March of 2021, Joyce had the opportunity to purchase a winery facility in his beloved Arroyo Seco AVA. His vineyards were now directly across the street (photo on previous page) and neighboring the iconic wineries of Kendal-Jackson and J Lohr. They know where to grow excellent wine grapes.

This new acquisition was not what you would expect of a winery facility; this was a worn out, dilapidated barn. Joyce put his hard-work ethics to full momentum, and within several months he had completely restored that barn into a quality working winery, now housing modern winery equipment and ready to receive this year's harvest. I was fortunate to taste his new Chardonnay right out of the tank (photo left page of Russell Joyce).

The new winery has an excellent tasting room inside the barn (photo above). Such a cool authentic atmosphere. And a **spacious outside tasting** area with **outdoor games** and **picnic benches** to bring your lunch to taste with the wines. It is worth the drive to Arroyo Seco appellation to see Joyce.

Collection of Wines

Submarine Canyon Pinot Noir (Arroyo Seco AVA)
Escolle Vineyard Pinot Noir (Santa Lucia Highlands AVA)
Tondré Grapefield Pinot Noir (Santa Lucia Highlands AVA)
River Road Pinot Noir (Santa Lucia Highlands AVA)
Joyce Estate Pinot Noir (Carmel Valley AVA)
Gabilan Mountains Pinot Noir (Gabilan Range)

Tondré Grapefield Syrah (Santa Lucia Highlands AVA)
Rosé (Mourvèdre, Grenache) (Arroyo Seco AVA)

Submarine Canyon Chardonnay (Arroyo Seco AVA)
Escolle Vineyard Chardonnay (Santa Lucia Highlands AVA)

Sauvignon Blanc (Arroyo Seco AVA)
Albariño (Arroyo Seco AVA)
Dry Riesling (Monterey AVA)

$$-$$$

1972 Hobson Avenue
Greenfield, CA 939627

+1 831 386 0316
Contact@ScheidVineyards.com

ScheidVineyards.com

Open: Every Day, 11am-6pm

Carmel-By-The-Sea Tasting Room
Open: Every Day, 12pm-7pm (Fri-Sat 8pm)

Collection of Wines

Reserve Wines
Pinot Noir 115, Pinot Noir 667, Pinot Noir 777,
Pinot Noir SLH, Pinot Noir POM, Pinot Noir Calera,
Kurt's Cabernet Sauvignon, Appassimento Cabernet
Sauvignon (Amarone style), Syrah Reserve,
Cabernet Franc, Claret Reserve,
Riverview Chardonnay, SLH Chardonnay,
Sauvignon Blanc, Isabelle Sparkling (Méthode
Champenoise of Chardonnay, Pinot Noir)

Red Wines
Pinot Noir, Cabernet Sauvignon, Merlot, GSM
Petite Sirah, Tannat, Barbera, Zinfandel, Dolcetto

White Wines
Chardonnay, Viognier, Grenache Blanc, Pinot Blanc,
Sauvignon Blanc, Roussane, Petit Manseng,
Grüner Veltliner, Gewürztraminer, Dry Riesling,

nvesting in vineyards started as a big tax write-off
for wealthy investors, now it's a huge wine success.

SUSTAINABILITY

Nothing romantic about getting into the wine business for investment purposes. In fact, many people say the best way to make a million dollars in the wine business is to start with ten million dollars. Not for Al Scheid.

Al Scheid was a very successful investment banker with clients he helped become wealthy. This success created large tax burdens! Al made use of the tax laws in the 1970s to offset income by purchasing agricultural land for vineyards. It is a large investment on the front end and no income for at least five years. And that is exactly what he did. He formed Vineyard Investors Limited Partnership and starting buying vineyards in Monterey.

Tax monies were saved; however, there was an abundant demand for his grapes. Al was able to get 100% of the grapes sold prior to planting vineyards. So he kept buying land and planting vineyards. By 1997, he had amassed seven thousand acres of vineyards and decided it was time to start making wine. And Scheid Vineyards winery was born.

Scheid has two wine businesses. First, he partners with major retailers to private label wines for them. This has now turned into seventy different labels and a million cases of wine annually. Second, he harvests the top 1% of his best grapes to make his own wines. You can taste and buy these wines in their tasting room (wine list to the right).

Scheid's sustainability goes far beyond the agricultural methods in the vineyards. In 2017, they installed a windmill on the property (left page), which fully operates their massive winery operations (photo above), plus provides power to 125 of their residential neighbors. Such a great environmental benefit, and now a couple more wineries have put up windmills.

Have you ever seen a massive winery operation? When you visit the winery, you can **tour** inside, as well as through their boutique winery, and get the picture of what 10,000 acres of vines produces today!

Every Sunday, they have **food trucks** and **live concerts** on their expansive property. And there are monthly **Paint & Sip** events. In December, they have **Reef Making** from the freshly trimmed vines.

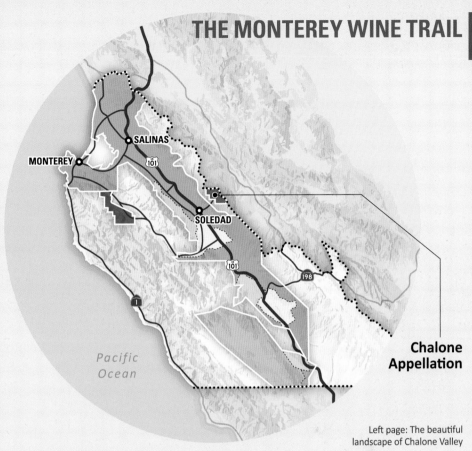

**Chalone
Appellation**

Left page: The beautiful
landscape of Chalone Valley

MOUNTAINOUS TERROIR

The Chalone Valley is where the business of great wines began in Monterey County. The very first winery and the oldest vineyards live here.

A quarter of the way up the Salinas Valley (forty miles from Monterey city) is a small town called Soledad on Hwy 101. Head east on Hwy 146 into the Gavilan Mountains another ten miles and you will arrive at the Chalone AVA and **Chalone Vineyards**. It is a total of about one hour and fifteen minutes from Monterey city to Chalone Valley.

The Chalone Valley is beautiful with its rolling hills of vineyards, trees and volcanic rocks protruding out of the soil. And the soil here is special. It is limestone, very similar to the terroir of Burgundy France. When you taste the Chardonnay and Pinot Noir here, you will understand this Chalone AVA.

At 1,800 feet elevation, Chalone appellation is above the Monterey fog, yet it still gets the light cool breezes from the marine effects of the bay. Add that to the mountain coolness and the amazing volcanic limestone soils, and you have extraordinary terroir for Burgundian wines.

Adjacent to the Chalone Valley, and only three more miles drive up the road (ten minutes), is **Pinnacles National Park**. You can see the Pinnacles from the vineyards at Chalone Vineyards. This is definitely a good side trip if you love hiking, nature and ancient history.

There is only one winery in the Chalone AVA, and it is definitely worth your visit.

• Chalone Vineyards, page 69

$$-$$$

32020 Stonewall Canyon Road
Soledad, CA 93960

+1 707 933 3235
Info@ChaloneVineyard.com

ChaloneVineyard.com

Open: Thursday-Sunday, 11am-5pm

The origins of Monterey wine greatness began here in this special mountain terroir.

HIDDEN TERROIR OF BURGUNDY

Are you aware of Chalone Vineyard, hidden in the Gavilan Mountain Range 1,800 feet above Monterey? Chalone has the oldest vineyards in Monterey County. It is also the first commercial winery in the county. This is a special place in its own unique Chalone Valley, and the only winery today in the Chalone AVA. With 1,000 contiguous acres, they have 250 acres planted to vines focusing on Pinot Noir, Chardonnay, Chenin Blanc and Syrah.

This remote area is below an extinct volcano and has limestone soils similar to Burgundy France. When the wines reached connoisseurs, the word got out, and while there was no telephone service here until 1990, the demand became so abundant that Chalone grew rapidly and became the first winery to become a publicly traded company.

Then, the notable French Rothschilds (Lafite) became partners and eventually purchased the company making it private again. Ultimately, Bill Foley, known for acquiring exceptionally great properties, acquired Chalone into his portfolio.

Now the property is available for visitors. It is an hour and fifteen minutes drive (50 miles) from Monterey, twenty minutes up the mountain from Hwy 101. It is worth the time to get there. The drive in the mountains is stunning. Made me want to arrive on my motorcycle. And the majestic Pinnacles in the backdrop makes this a magical place. Well, the special terroir makes this a place magical!

Over 100 years ago (1919), Chenin Blanc was planted here (photo left page). This is a wine to experience. It brings out the minerality of this terroir showing the sweet richness of mango, pear and honeysuckle like only 100-year-old vines can express.

I am personally a fan of their Pinot Noir. In this cool mountain limestone grows delicious Pinot! I tasted from the barrel what the new winemaker Greg Freeman has been experimenting with perfecting the property and winemaking.

This is a beautiful day trip. Visit the neighboring Pinnacles National Park (next page) in the morning and then enjoying Chalone Vineyard wines afterwards. Bring a lunch; it is a beautiful place to appreciate the afternoon.

There is an indoor and outdoor deck (photo above) to taste their wines. They are planning for various activities and areas of the property to be available for guests. Check with them on what is available.

Collection of Wines
All wines exclusively from their estate in the Chalone AVA

Chalone Vineyard Estate Reserve Pinot Noir
Chalone Vineyard Estate Grenache
Chalone Vineyard Estate Syrah
Chalone Hidden Barrel Estate Cuveé (Grenache, Syrah)

Chalone Vineyard Reserve Estate Chardonnay
Chalone Vineyard Estate Chenin Blanc
Chalone Vineyard Estate Chardonnay Musqué
Chalone Vineyard Estate Pinot Blanc
Chalone Vineyard Estate Chardonnay

23 MILLION YEARS AGO

The Pinnacles are an interesting geological formation that formed 23 million years ago from an ancient volcano. This is a stratovolcano, a formation of many layers of lava and explosive bursts of rocks from eruptions of great violence. Several million years of erosion later, the Pacific Plate collided with the North American Plate at this point lifting up the remnants of this volcano into the beautiful rock formation known today as the Pinnacles. Forces of water and wind also caused large boulders to slide down the steep canyon walls, creating what are now the caves. Not real caves, rather narrow passages created under the piles of boulders. The Pinnacles are a geologist's playground peppered with silica-rich rhyolite, layered lava flow bands and perlite pockets of green volcanic glass. A fascinating exploration experience! And an opportunity to see the uniqueness of the Pacific Plate that made the terroir of the California Central Coast wine regions so special.

HOME TO TWENTY DIFFERENT TYPES OF RAPTORS

Raptors are birds of prey and are commonly seen here, especially during the breeding season of January to August. Raptors are strategic and effective hunters with powerful beaks and talons for tearing apart prey. They have telescopic vision and can see small prey from miles away. The geography here provides raptors with ideal nesting sites on inaccessible cliffs and rock formations. It is a spectacular and beautiful sight to see these falcons, eagles, owls, kestrels, and a variety of hawks (red-tailed hawks, cooper hawks, sharp-shinned hawks, red-shouldered hawks), and the massive California condor.

EXCELLENT DAY TRIP

Imagine a beautiful day here in the mountains. A nice morning hike when the air is fresh to see the spectacular Pinnacles. Bring a lunch to eat out on the trail in the park or to take to Chalone Vineyards to do with some wine tasting in the afternoon. It's the perfect day.

MONTEREY **CHALONE VALLEY**
Ancient Hiking Attraction
PINNACLES NATIONAL PARK

West Entrance
5000 Highway 146
Paicines, CA 95043

+1 831 389 4486

Pinnacles.org
NPS.gov/pinn

Open: All Year, Every Day
West Entrance (Chalone Valley): 7:30am-8pm
East Entrance: 24 hours

(no through the park access
to the east and west entrances)

The One Warm Appellation in Monterey, Growing Bordeaux Varietals

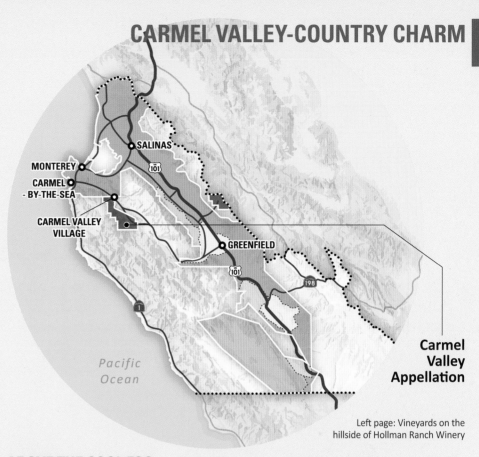

SALINAS

MONTEREY

CARMEL
- BY-THE-SEA

CARMEL VALLEY
VILLAGE

GREENFIELD

*Pacific
Ocean*

**Carmel
Valley
Appellation**

Left page: Vineyards on the
hillside of Hollman Ranch Winery

ABOVE THE COOL FOG

Monterey is known for its cool foggy weather to grow cool-climate grapes for Chardonnay and Pinot Noir. Differently, Carmel Valley is up in the Santa Lucia Mountains at elevations from 846' to 2,762', where they get very little fog, and when they do, it burns off fast. Lots of warm sunny days here. They have mountainous hillside vineyards producing full-bodied wines like Cabernet Sauvignon and Merlot.

This is a dense-growth mountainous region that is engagingly beautiful looking through the valley. The vineyards and wineries are hidden amongst the trees, up in the canyons and along the hillsides. Because of this, there are very few wineries open to the public. For an extra-beautiful adventure, continue down the road past the village and you will wind through some stunning landscapes. It's a great drive that will ultimately lead you into the Salinas Valley to the vineyards of Arroyo Seco AVA.

The Carmel Valley Village is a small country village at the north entrance to the valley closest to Monterey (about thirty minutes). It is filled with wine-tasting rooms, plus restaurants and shops. I counted twenty-three tasting rooms when I was there.

Open Winery Properties
• Holman Ranch, page 75
• Folktale Winery, page 81
Spectacular High-Elevation Vineyards
• Albatross Ridge Vineyards, page 79
Village Tasting Rooms
• Albatross Ridge, page 82
• Holman Ranch, page 82
• Joyce Wine Company, page 82
• Scratch Wines, page 83
• Windy Oaks Estate, page 83
• I. Brand Winery, page 83
• Bernardus Winery, page 85
• Boekenoogen Wines, page 85

$$-$$$

<u>Ranch, Vineyards and Winery</u>
60 Holman Road
Carmel Valley, CA 93924
+1 831 659 2640
Info@HolmanRanch.com
Open: All Year, By Appointment

<u>Village Tasting Room (page 82)</u>
18 W Carmel Valley Road
Carmel Valley Village, CA 93924
+1 831 601 8761
Wines@HolmanRanch.com
Open: Thursday-Monday, 12pm-6pm

HolmanRanch.com

A̶ n exclusive opportunity to do wine tasting on a ranch in a historic hacienda.

A RANCH OF HOSPITALITY

In the hills, just above the Carmel Valley Village, is the 750 acre estate of the Holman Ranch rising from 500' to over 2,000' elevations. The ranch began when the governor of México gave 6,000 acres of this valley to Corporal Manuel Boronda in 1769 as a gesture of gratitude for his service. It wasn't for 159 years later, until Gordon Armsby opened Holman Ranch for hospitality.

So, in 1928, Gordon builds a hacienda here, deep into the property and nestled in an oak tree forest. The hacienda was made from local materials, Carmel Stone, terracotta roofing and oak-beamed ceilings. It quickly became a Hollywood retreat. For example, Clark Gable and Marlon Brando loved to escape to here. One of the homes is now named **The Charlie Chaplin Suite**, after one of their most frequent famous guests. It is located inside the historic hacienda and opens into an inner courtyard.

In 2006, Holman Ranch was purchased by the Lowder family, who restored the hacienda to its original perfection. They also built two new Ranch Houses to expand to fourteen guest accommodations.

They also planted eighteen acres of Pinot Noir, Chardonnay, and Pinot Gris vineyards this year. Then 2009 became their first wine. A wine cave was built, not just for aging barrels, the entire winemaking process occurs inside the cave.

The Holman Ranch Estate Vineyard & Winery is now born and thriving. They are proud that 100% of their wines come from their estate grown vineyards on the ranch. The hillsides make great terror for the vineyards and spectacular views for us visitors.

They have three types of wine tastings. The first is at their **Carmel Valley Village Tasting Room** (page 82). Next is the **Hacienda Tasting** on the ranch in their beautiful historic hacienda (photo above and left page). Wine tasting at Holman Ranch is by appointment only on their website.

The experience you really want to do is the **Full Vineyard Tour and Tasting**. It's an extensive tour throughout their property on an ATV. It includes visiting the wine caves and off-roading to the upper vineyard on their property where you will taste the reserve and library wines, all while enjoying spectacular views of Holman Ranch and the beautiful Carmel Valley (photo previous page).

Collection of Wines

Reserve Jarman Pinot Noir
Hunter's Cuvée Pinot Noir
Three Brothers Pinot Noir
Heather's Hill Pinot Noir
Kelly's Press Pinot Noir

Reserve Jarman Sparkling Brut Rosé (Pinot Noir)
Susan's Saignée Rosé of Pinot Noir
Rosé of Pinot Noir

Estate Syrah

Reserve Jarman Chardonnay
Estate Chardonnay
Pinot Gris

A RANCH OF HOSPITALITY

This is the only experience like this in all of Monterey County. And the only winery in the Carmel Valley Appellation that allows visitors at the winery, has wine tasting on the ranch and provides accommodations. There are two very large suites available inside the original historic hacienda, plus an additional twelve rooms in the guest house buildings.

The Charlie Chaplin Suite is named after one of the most frequent famous guests and is located inside the historic hacienda and opens into an inner courtyard.

The Hacienda Suite is a full-scale luxury residence inside the original historic hacienda. It has a full kitchen, dining room, living room (photo below), an underground wine cellar, and a wrap-around deck outside under the oak trees. The bathroom is spectacular (see photo below bottom). The bedroom is so full of luxury you will never want to leave (photo below right).

The Ranch Rooms were built in 2006 to expand accommodations here. They are two ranch-style buildings, with six private rooms and baths each, built outside the courtyard in the oak grove.

Weddings and Events are common here. When you book the ranch for an event, you get everything. It includes all fourteen rooms for your guests, the beautiful grounds, courtyards and the hacienda living area.

$$$-$$$$-$$$$$

Ranch, Lodge, Winery, Vineyards
60 Holman Road
Carmel Valley, CA 93924

+1 831 659 2640
Info@HolmanRanch.com

HolmanRanch.com

Private Estate Open: By Appointment Only

$$$-$$$$

Carmel Valley Village Tasting Cottage
19 East Carmel Valley Road
Carmel Valley, CA 93924
+1 831 298 7388
Open: Thursday-Sunday, 12pm-6pm

Carmel-By-The-Sea Village Tasting Room
Dolores St, Between Ocean & 6th Ave
Carmel-By-The-Sea, CA 93923
+1 831 293 8896
Open: Every Day, 12pm-7pm (Fri/Sat 8pm)

AlbatrossRidge.com
Info@AlbatrossRidge.com

O n top of the Santa Lucia Mountains, the highest vineyard in the Monterey Appellation.

OCEAN VIEW

You've heard me say: *wine grapes are very smart, as they live in the most beautiful areas of the world.* At the Albatross Ridge Vineyards, these grapes live on top of a stunning ridge, a mountaintop with a direct view of the ocean. We pay big dollars to have our homes with a great view of the sea. These are very happy grapes.

In the Monterey Appellation, these vineyards are at the highest elevation, on top of the Santa Lucia Mountains. The terroir is exceptional. Check out the numerous stones in the vineyard. They get direct ocean breezes in the afternoons. The unique conditions here cause harvest to be earlier and for the crop to be naturally small, with only two tons per acre. All of these great conditions make the fruit here extra-high quality. And the wines are uniquely excellent.

The history is very interesting. In the 1930s, famed engineer and pilot William Hawley Bowlus, whose pioneering sailplanes are in the Smithsonian now, used to fly gliders off the ridges of Monterey's majestic Carmel Coast. Eight decades later, his grandson and great-grandson unknowingly came

to these same mountain slopes and established their most distinctive vineyards. Brad and Garrett Bowlus purchased this mountain ridge in 2008 and planted four clones of Pinot Noir and two clones of Chardonnay. They focus on these two cool-climate varietals exclusively. And the wines are showing it.

After planting the vineyards, Brad and Garrett were searching for a name. They discovered an old book about Monterey history and discovered something remarkable, a photo of Hawley Bowlus launching his Albatross Sailplane off the same high mountain slopes where they planted their vineyards. It affirmed everything they had been working so hard to achieve. And the appropriate name was born.

The Albatross Ridge winery and vineyards are not open to the public. As such, they have tasting rooms in both Carmel Valley Village and Carmel-by-the-Sea Village. All their wines are at both places along with some nice appetizers for pairings.

Above is Garrett Bowles, winemaker/ viticulturist, traversing his special vineyards, keeping an eye on everything to be sure the harvest is optimum. These beautiful vineyards can be seen on the left page, page 36, and page 38.

Collection of Wines

First Flight Pinot Noir
Estate Reserve Pinot Noir
Cuvée Vivienne Pinot Noir
Cuvée Owen Pinot Noir
Santa Lucia Highlands Pinot Noir

Pétillant Natural Rosé (Sparkling Pinot Noir)
Pet Nat Sparkling Rosé (Sparkling Pinot Noir)

First Flight Chardonnay
Cuvée Beaudry Chardonnay
Beton Chardonnay
Estate Chardonnay

MONTEREY **CARMEL VALLEY**
Winery, Restaurant, Giftshop
FOLKTALE WINERY & VINEYARDS

$$-$$$

8940 Carmel Valley Road
Carmel Valley, CA 93923

+1 831 293 7500
Info@FolktaleWinery.com

FolktaleWinery.com

Open: Thurs-Mon, 11:30am-8:30pm (Sunday 10am-4pm)

Collection of Wines

The Hound (Cabernet Sauvignon, Malbec,
Merlot, Petit Verdot, Cabernet Franc)
Eden Rift Vineyard Pinot Noir
The Creator Pinot Noir
The Ruler Pinot Noir
Central Coast Reserve Pinot Noir
Santa Lucia Highlands Reserve Pinot Noir
Le Mistral Joseph's Blend (Grenache, Syrah, Mourvèdre)
Le Mistral Brosseau Vineyard (Syrah)
Le Mistral Syrah
Carbonic Sangiovese
Piquette (Gamay Noir)
Blade and Talon Négrette (Négrette Grape)

Talon Rose Madder (Cabernet Sauvignon Rosé)
Estate Rosé (Pinot Noir Rosé)

Santa Lucia Highlands Reserve Chardonnay
Estate Chardonnay
Albariño (Albariño Grape)
The Lion 4 Real (Chardonnay and Riesling)
We Are A Flower (Sauvignon Blanc, Semillon)
Blade and Talon Falanghina (Falanghina Grape)

Muscat Hamburg (Muscat Desert Wine)

Sparkling Brut (Chardonnay)
Sparkling Rosé (Pinot Noir)
Talking Animals Pétillant Natural (Grenache Blanc)

The only winery in Monterey County with a restaurant. And the largest gift shop too!

AFTERNOON RESTAURANT DELIGHT

As you enter the Carmel Valley, before reaching the appellation and before reaching the village, you will find Folktale Winery & Vineyards along the roadside. This is truly the ambiance of the **Monterey Country Charm in Carmel Valley**.

The property is a sixteen acres estate of Sangiovese vineyards. They also have 300 acres of vineyards in the Arroyo Seco Appellation. In Carmel Valley, the beautiful warm sun graces this countryside creating the perfect setting for this winery, it's attached restaurant and the luxury gift shop, all amongst the vineyards.

The **Folktake Rosé Sparkling Wine** is the perfect refreshment for a beautiful afternoon lunch here outside on their spacious patio of mature trees, rose gardens and wine barrels. Plus, the indoor seating is open to the outdoors (photo left page).

The Rosé Sparkling is the wine that put this winery on the map. It is really delicious. And refreshing. A watermelon and strawberry delight in your mouth. It's creamy and has a light effervescent. It is 80% Pinot Noir and 20% Chardonnay.

The dining is casual. They have some interesting small plates (lamb meatballs and scallop crudo for example), creative flatbreads (pizza), a variety of salads and entrées like the Winery Burger on the left page. Also a mushroom truffle ravioli and a charred Spanish octopus, both of which I need to go back and experience.

The beautiful dining patio is also where you do wine tasting. You don't have to order food to taste wines: they can bring out a flight of five different wines and pair them with foods. Or you can have just the flight. Or you can pair their wines to the food that you order. It's as you wish.

The gift shop experience here is a beautiful endeavor. It was created by Temia Demakopoulos, who moved from San Francisco where she managed the legendary Gump's. This is a treat in stunning homeware, art pieces, decadent candles, beautiful ceramics, handmade textiles, and on and on. The apothecary items are of ultimate quality. Made just for them, in small batches of nutrient dense, active plant ingredients in their natural state. Indulge!

CARMEL VALLEY VILLAGE

So you have come out to Carmel Valley. Maybe visited one of the few wineries here open to the public. You have definitely noticed that Carmel Valley is a lot warmer than the rest of Monterey, and Carmel-by-the-Sea. The elevation is higher here, and the fog rarely rolls in. And when it does, it burns off fast. This is the ***Carmel Valley Country Charm.***

The Carmel Valley is a short distance from Monterey and is a long beautiful valley in the middle of the Santa Lucia Mountains. **Carmel Valley Village** is located right on Carmel Valley Road at the beginning of the *Carmel Valley Appellation,* which offers terroir unique in Monterey with a warm climate for Bordeaux, Rhône and other varietals.

There is an abundance of wine-tasting rooms here in the village. I counted twenty-three wineries when I visited. There are restaurants, specialty markets and stores too. You can park once and enjoy as many wine-tasting experiences as you desire.

### Albatross Ridge Tasting Cottage	### Holman Ranch Tasting Room	### Joyce Wine Company
+1 831 298 7388 • 19 East Carmel Valley Road	+1 831 601 8761 • 18 West Carmel Valley Road	+1 831 659 2885 • 1 East Carmel Valley Road
Open: Thursday-Sunday, 12pm-6pm	*Open: Thursday-Monday, 12pm-6pm*	*Open: Every Day, 12pm-6pm*
AlbatrossRidge.com	HolmanRanch.com	JoyceWineCo.com

See full review of Albatross Ridge Winery at page 79

See full review of Holman Ranch Winery at page 75

See full review of Joyce Wine Company at page 63

The Albatross Ridge vineyards and winery are not open to the public. They have two very nice tasting rooms, here in Carmel Valley Village and also in Carmel-by-the-Sea Village.

Holman Ranch is one of the few wineries open to the public. By appointment only. It is definitely worth going up to the ranch. In the meantime, they have a large tasting room in a historic road house from 1928.

The Joyce Winery is located out on **The Wine Trail** in the *Arroyo Seco Appellation.* Here in the village, they have a beautiful tasting room with lots of fun and lively entertainment.

CARMEL VALLEY VILLAGE

Scratch Wines

+1 831 320 0726 • 1 East Carmel Valley Road
Open: Every Day, 12pm-7pm (Fri/Sat 8pm)

ScratchWines.com

From the beginnings of working in the film and theater industry, to obtaining a Master of Science in Viticulture and Enology from UC Davis, Sabrine Rodems brings us some of the most inspired wines and the most beautifully creative wine-tasting atmosphere to enjoy her wines.

Now twenty years later, Sabrine has a reputation being in demand by other wineries, including winemaker at Wrath Wines on **The Wine Trail**. Her labels (below) speak to her creativity as well.

Spoken from the winemaker herself...

What I love most about Monterey, Arroyo Seco, Santa Lucia Highland and Santa Cruz Mountains is that I have four geologically different sites at my fingertips. Getting to work with bench Pinot Noir, riverbed Riesling and Grenach, and Coastal Cabernet, makes my work exciting and the wine exciting as well. Winemaking is the best of both worlds, the amalgamation of science and art.

Windy Oaks Estate

+1 831 298 7083 • 19 East Carmel Valley Road
Open: Thursday-Monday, 12pm-5:30pm

WindyOaksEstate.com

An American corporate attorney, residing in London, drinking and visiting Burgundy, Jim Schultz knew it was time to retire and pursue his passion.

Burgundian at heart, with very special friendships at the vineyards, Jim obtained the most amazing gift we can all only dream about. Jim received Pinot Noir cuttings from the most sacred site in Burgundy. Yes, the top 2% of the highest quality level in Burgundy, a Grand Cru. And yes, I must keep it a secret.

However, I will not keep Windy Oaks Estate a secret. As you can imagine, the red and white Burgundies here are extraordinary. The vineyards are now over twenty years old. The winemaking style here emulates Burgundy. In fact, Jim personally travels to Burgundy to choose his Burgundian oak barrels from the cooper.

Here is a unique opportunity to taste wines with a pedigree that you cannot find anywhere else in California. Enjoy!

I. Brand & Family

+1 831 298 7227 • 19 East Carmel Valley Road
Open: Thursday-Monday, 11am-6pm

IBrandWinery.com

It is a great pleasure to know Ian Brand, as we are kindred spirits in the love of terroir. To us, terroir is the essential ingredient in happy vines that produce exceptional wine grapes.

It is Ian's passion and endless pursuit of unique vineyards that have extraordinary terroir for the grapes being cultivated. Not just vineyards, certain blocks in vineyards, even specific rows, that he would call idiosyncratic sites. Ian loves dirt roads, discovering remote challenging vineyards that possess special terroir and grapes that magnify excellence.

Ian is a master of knowing terroir, and has built a collection of wines that are all terroir driven wines. Every wine in his collection defines its place. This is a tasting room to discover terroir. Ian has geological maps on the walls, rocks on the counters and the most amazing wines in the bottles.

As each bottle was opened, it became my next favorite. The Cabernet Franc... hmm... wow!

MONTEREY **CARMEL VALLEY**

Restaurant

LUCIA RESTAURANT & BAR

$$$-$$$$

Bernardus Lodge & Spa
415 West Carmel Valley Road
Carmel Valley, CA 93924

+1 831 658 3400
BernardusLodge.com

Open: Every Day, 7am-10pm

King Salmon (top): summer corn succotash, cherry tomatoes, golden potatoes, and patty pan squash, in a scallions, red pepper, and buttermilk emulsion.

Salt Roasted Beet Salad (below center): Swank Farms greens, preserved lemon ricotta, housemade granola, whole-grain mustard vinaigrette.

Chocolate (below right): a luscious surprise to discover inside those chocolate balls.

Beautiful food, farm-to-table, in a white-cloth luxury environment of very attentive service.

LIVE MUSIC AND LUXURY DINING

Lucia is a luxury restaurant in the Bernardus Lodge & Spa, a four-star hotel in the Carmel Valley. It is open for breakfast, lunch and dinner. They also have a beautiful lounge and bar, and live music nightly.

Truly an authentic farm-to-table experiences with the culinary team having access to some of the freshest produce in their own twenty-eight acres of extensive vegetable gardens, organic herbs and fruit trees. Such an inspiration for seasonal ingredients to inspire the menu.

Don't be discouraged by the online dining apps and the restaurant's own website saying that the restaurant is full and has no more reservations. I just showed up, and there were plenty of tables available.

Bernardus Winery

+1 831 298 8021 • 5 West Carmel Valley Road
Open: Tuesday-Saturday, 11am-4pm (Fri/Sat 5pm)

Bernardus.com

Bernardus Pon was a forward thinker, believing that Carmel Valley had different terroir than the rest of Monterey (and it does), making it possible to grow Bordeaux varietals. In 1990, he purchased 210 acres in the higher, more southern part of the valley, specifically a sun-trapped bowl shielded from the coastal fog. The elevation is 1,200' high. The vineyards were planted facing west for maximum afternoon sun.

Bernardus planted all five Bordeaux varietals: Cabernet Sauvignon, Merlot, Cabernet Franc, Malbec, and Petit Verdot. It was perfect for these grapes. The daily temperatures can exceed 100° during the day and drop to 50° at night. The bowl traps the heat of the day, while elevation and ocean proximity produce cool nights. These are awesome diurnal effects that wine grapes love.

Bernardus continued his forward thinking by opened the first tasting room in the Carmel Valley Village. Indoor, outdoor, private rooms, and a bar.

Boekenoogen Vineyards & Winery

+1 831 659 4215 • 24 West Carmel Valley Road
Open: Every Day, 11am-5pm

BoekenoogenWines.com

This is a fifth-generation ranching family that embarked on the vineyard business in 1998. They moved their cattle to another property from the Santa Lucia Highlands after they saw vineyards arising and great wines being made there. It was time for them to plant and cultivate great vineyards in this excellent appellation.

You will notice that the Boekenoogen Vineyards are being proudly displayed on other wineries labels. Excellent grapes come from here and the vineyards are becoming icons.

With the results of such excellent grapes, in 2006 the Boekenoogens decided to produce their own wine. They built a winery in the middle of their vineyards. Boekenoogen Winery is one of very few wineries that grows, produces, and bottles on site. Not open to the public though.

The Boekenoogen tasting room in the village has a very knowledgeable and entertaining team.

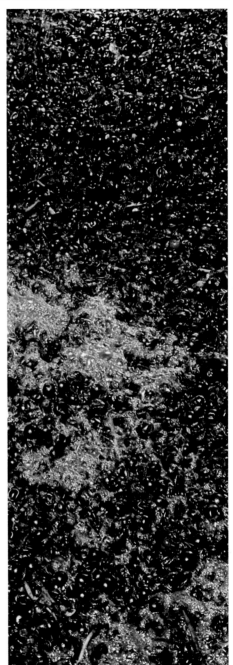

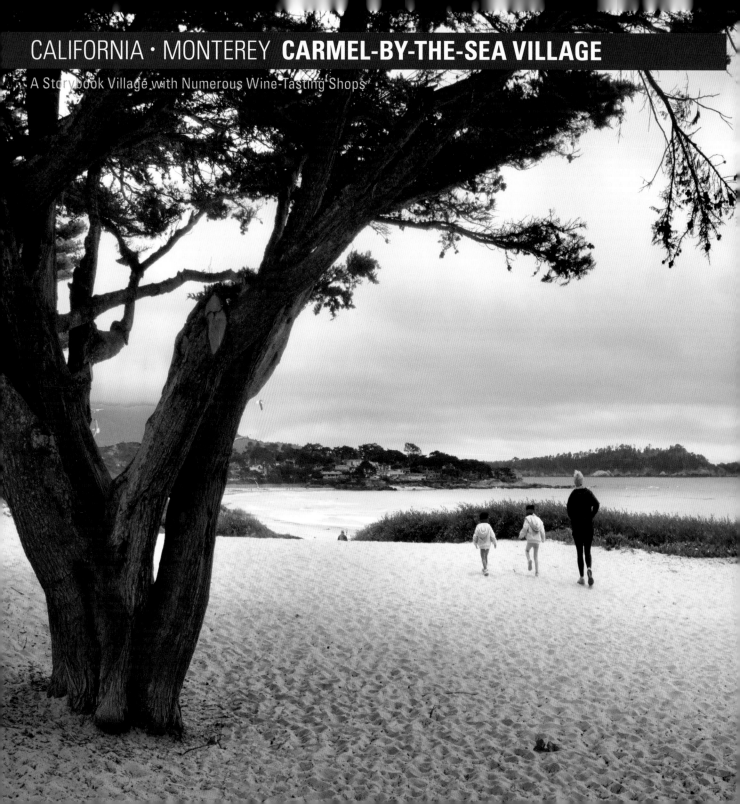

CARMEL-COASTAL WINE TASTING

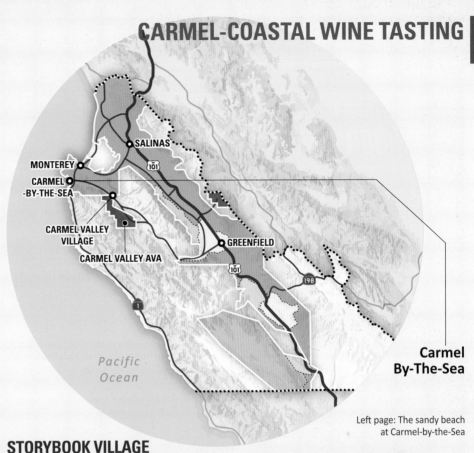

Carmel By-The-Sea

Left page: The sandy beach at Carmel-by-the-Sea

STORYBOOK VILLAGE

This is where the original **Hansel and Gretal Cottages** (c.1924/25) were built, inspiring the building aesthetics of Carmel-by-the-Sea over the next century. This is a very cute storybook town with picturesque structures in a whimsical style, as if straight out of a children's book. From the steep-pitched roofs, rustic stone chimneys, and arched windows and doors, it is like experiencing a fairytale come to life. The village has been a haven for famous artists, poets, musicians, and writers.

The **Carmel-by-the-Sea Village** is such a joy to walk around (about ten blocks square) and take in the fanciful architecture. You will discover numerous shops, cafés, art galleries, inns, restaurants, and adjacent sandy beaches. Plus, wineries have set up tastings here to make it easy to access their wines without having to travel into the appellations. I counted 18 wine tasting venues when I was there.

Being a city of dreamers, artists and story-tellers, there are no addresses or postal delivery. The 3,700 residents rebel being citified; instead they use names for a sense of camaraderie and personality.

This is a small beach city with adjacent white sandy beaches. It is bird-rich, with abundant sea animals, surfing, scuba diving, and scenic paths. Directly north is Americas #1 golf course, **Pebble Beach Golf Links**. Carmel's **Mission San Carlos Borromeo** is the most authentically restored of California missions.

Here are the wineries I visited. They are quite diversity in the types of wines offered.

Village Tasting Rooms
• Albatross Ridge, page 88
• Blair Estate, page 90
• Caraccioli Cellars, page 90
• De Tierra Vineyards, page 90
• Lepe Cellars, page 91
• KORi Wines, page 91
• Silvestri Vineyards, page 91

Albatross Ridge Tasting Room
+1 831 298 7388 • 19 East Carmel Valley Road
Open: Thursday-Sunday, 12pm-6pm

AlbatrossRidge.com

See full review of Albatross Ridge Winery on page 79

The Albatross Ridge vineyards and winery are not open to the public. They have two very nice tasting rooms, here in Carmel-by-the-Sea Village and also in Carmel Valley Village.

Cultura, Comida Y Bebida (Mezcal)
+1 831 250 7005 • Dolores Street, btw 5th & 6th Ave
Open: Tuesday-Sunday, 5pm-9pm

CulturaCarmel.com

The owners come from a renowned restaurant where they bring the knowledge of quality cuisine and their shared passion for the foods and mezcal of Oaxaca.

Cultura is known for their unique cocktails. Below is the *Cultura Craft Margarita* - Bravo Orange Curaçao, citrus simple, lime, mezcal and two tequilas.

Anton & Michel Restaurant (French)
+1 831 624 2406 • Mission Street & 7th Ave
Open: Every Day, 11:30pm-4pm, 5pm-9pm

AntonAndMichel.com

Indoor or outdoor poolside (photo below), this luxurious French restaurant delivers beautifully delicious and unique cuisine.

Imagine the *Seafood Fricassée* (below): grilled shrimp, scallops, smoked salmon ravioli, asparagus-mushroom cream sauce, and chipotle pesto. Yum!

1900s RYAN'S RANCH HOMESTEAD

Tarpy's Roadhouse Restaurant is known for being Monterey's best steakhouse. And they sure do deliver. Not just a wide variety of quality steaks to choose from (prime angus sirloin, prime select filet mignon, prime select ribeye, grilled New York steaks with truffle butter, and on and on and on), they also deliver them with creativity. Look at the interesting ingredients in the meatloaf and short ribs below. They also have a huge selection of fish fillets and shellfish.

Just outside of Carmel-by-the-Sea Village is this historic steakhouse that is a very delicious experience. They have historic patios outdoors, if you would like that experience, plus a beautiful indoor dining room and several small dining rooms for lots of privacy. The inside is uniquely creative, for example the cat and dog sculptures that greet you as you enter the restaurant (photo top right).

This Historic Stone House was built by Charles Ryan. It took him ten years to build his dream home. Charles built the house all by himself, and every stone in the building came from the property. As he finished portions of the home, he would move in his family.

They lived there until 1943, when Ryan sold the property to a restaurateur. It was several restaurants before Tarpy's Roadhouse began in 1992, and they have been there ever since.

Classic Meatloaf (photo below): with garlic mashed potatoes, green beans, and a delicious Madeira mushroom gravy.

Braised Short Ribs (photo right): red-wine demi, roasted garlic mashed potatoes, green peas, caramelized cipollini onions, and fresh thyme.

Chocolate Cake (photo below right): decadence beyond decadence in chocolate, homemade whipped cream and vanilla ice cream.

$$-$$$

2999 Monterey Salinas Highway
Monterey, CA 93940

+1 831 647 1444
Banquet@Tarpys.com

Tarpys.com

Open: Every Day, 11:30am-8pm (Fri/Sat 9pm)

Blair Estate

+1 831 625 9463 • Carmel Plaza, 7th btw Mission & Juniper

Open: Every Day, 11am-6pm (Fri/Sat 7pm)

BlairWines.com

For five generations, the Blair family has lived and farmed the Arroyo Seco Appellation. Their focus is Pinot Noir. They love how the terroir here represents Pinot Noir excellently. And professionals agree. *Wine Enthusiast* has scored them 91-points. They are winning Double Gold medals in important wine competitions. I tasted their 2017 *The Reserve, Pinot Noir, Delfina's Vineyard* when I was there. It was a beautiful presentation of dark fruits and soft tannins.

This was a hand sampling of the very best Pinot Noir from their vineyards. Only four barrels' worth, yet with the complexity of seven different clones and two different coopers for their barrels. In the end, this equates to only 100 cases of wine for us to enjoy. It's a limited quantity of the very best of what they do.

They have other Pinot Noirs as well as Chardonnays. The tasting room is in a nice plaza with a central outdoor dining area to enjoy a lunch at the restaurant with their wine.

Caraccioli Cellars

+1 831 622 7722 • Dolores St. btw Ocean & 7th

Open: Every Day, 12pm-6pm (Fri-Sun 11am)

CaraccioliCellars.com

This is as close to a Champagne house as you can get outside of France. The Caraccioli family hired international winemaking consultant and Champagne guru Michael Salgues to create their sparkling winemaking program. They modeled the traditional French winemaking standards and Champagne law requirements and modernized the process to enhance and improve the sparkling wine.

Champagne houses in France are bound by strict laws. For example, by law, they must use the first 150 of the 180 gallons of juice extracted from each ton. Caraccioli Cellars raises the bar on this regulation, as they only use the first 120 gallons per ton. This provides what they call *the best heart juice* from each grape and allows their wines to shine in their purity. The secondary fermentation goes four years, with an additional year of aging under cork.

Their sparkling wines are sophisticated, and very refined and elegant within every sip.

De Tierra Vineyards

+1 831 622 9704 • Mission St. btw 5th & 6th

Open: Sunday-Thursday, 2pm-7pm (Fri/Sat, 8pm)

DeTierra.com

Back in 1998, Salinas row crop farmer Tom Russell, passionate about wine, teamed up with Italian winemaker Lucio Gomiero, and they started planting an organic vineyard in the Corral de Tierra Valley. This valley is in a very unusual place, southeast of Monterey in the Santa Lucia Mountains.

They started as farmers selling their grapes and ultimately decided to start making their own wines. With winemaking, they expanded out of the valley and started purchasing grapes from all over Monterey County and beyond to nine varietals: Pinot Noir, Chardonnay, Riesling, Sangiovese, Syrah, Cabernet Sauvignon, Merlot, Cabernet Franc, and Petit Verdot.

The wines here are excellent. It is nice to have the variety all in one place, and they were all very good. My favorite though is their Russell Estate Cabernet Franc. This is from the vineyard of their original property in Corral de Tierra Valley. The nose is amazing, with super-rich cherries on the mouth.

Lepe Cellars
+1 831 597 2029 • Dolores St. btw Ocean & 7th
Open: Friday-Monday, 1pm-7pm

LepeCellars.com

Here is a unique winery tasting experience with the tasting being connected to a fine art gallery. As you enter the building you walk through the wine-tasting bar on your way into the art gallery (photo below). You can taste wine while you browse the art gallery. And the gallery is very nice.

Miguel Lepi is a young guy who found a very clever way to start his wine business. He did a Kickstarter campaign. How cool is that? Miguel studied enology and viticulture at Cal Poly San Luis Obispo and has been working for some well-respected winemakers. And still does.

Now he is taking an adventure with his own wines. He buys all his fruit from vineyards that meet his viticulture standards. He makes his wines at one of the wineries he works. Miguel now has a tasting room and his wines are really good. My favorite is his Pinot Noir from the Santa Lucia Highlands. This is a great opportunity to support a talented new winemaker.

KORi Wines
+1 831 877 0888 • Mission St. btw Ocean & 7th
Open: Every Day, 1pm-6pm (Fri-Sat, 7pm)

KORiWines.com

KORi Wines started as a partnership between Santa Lucia Highlands grape grower Kirk Williams and his step-daughter Kori Violini. KW Ranch Vineyards is for Kirk's initials and KORi Wines is for, well, hmm...

The original vines were planted in 1998, with the first release of wines in 2007 from ten-year-old vines. The focus is Pinot Noir, and they have been getting high scores and winning competitions.

KORi Wines are strictly single-varietal wines. As they added wines, they chose other great vineyards in Santa Lucia Highlands and Arroyo Seco appellations with best-suited terroir for each varietal. I particularly loved their Sauvignon Blanc from the Griva Vineyard, a special terroir in Arroyo Seco appellation.

While their only tasting location is in Carmel-by-the-Sea, they have special invitations to go to their KW Ranch, where you can see the Pinot Noir vineyards. This is a tasting experience in the vineyards, and you are welcome to bring a lunch.

Silvestri Vineyards
+1 831 625 0111 • 7th btw San Carlos & Dolores
Open: Every Day, 12pm-6pm

SilvestriVineyards.com

Movie posters in a wine shop, I questioned? *Back to the Future, Castaway, Romancing the Stone,* and more than a hundred more. Alan Silvestri is the music composer for some of the greatest films made.

Alan's grandparents left Italy in 1908 on an adventure to America and landed in New York City in the restaurant business. Five decades later, Alan took his adventure westbound to Hollywood in pursuit of his love of music. Later, to adventure again, to Carmel for his passion of food and wine.

The Silvestri Vineyards were planted in a special spot in Carmel Valley with different altitudes and slopes, allowing them to grow diverse varietals. First, it was the Pinot Noir, Chardonnay and cool-weather Syrah. Later, Cabernet Sauvignon was planted high on the slopes above the fog line, where it could thrive.

All wines are estate grown and express the beautiful characteristics of this unique terroir.

CALIFORNIA · **SAN LUIS OBISPO COUNTY (SLO)**

The Central Coast Comes Alive with Beauty and Winemaking Excellence

The fog rolling in over the vineyards of Edna Valley

Exploring Delicious Canapés
at JUSTIN Restaurant in Paso Robles

Front: Garden tart, sumac Greek yogurt,
estate strawberries, pickled onion,
bachelor button and onion flowers
Back left: Beef tartar, pecorino, and tuille
Back right: Kushi oyster, rose and raspberry mignonette espuma

Downtown San Luis Obispo

I magine the happiest city in America, surrounded by numerous wine regions, sporting a multitude of outdoor activities, and attracting amazing chefs, winemakers and other artists... Then you have discovered the magnificent San Luis Obispo.

SAN LUIS OBISPO COUNTY

Now let's journey through the San Luis Obispo County wine regions. San Luis Obispo is the name of the county and also its largest city, with a population of nearly 50,000 people. Both the city and county have adopted the nickname SLO by both locals and regular visitors.

SLO is central within the Central Coast wine regions, with Monterey County to the north and Santa Barbara County to the south. Its wine regions span almost the full length of the county along the ocean and the inland valleys: of approximately fifty miles north-south, and forty miles east-west.

While the soil can be diverse in each of the appellations around SLO, the Pacific Ocean is a key element in the terroir for all of the appellations. In fact, this maritime influence is absolutely essential for both the cool appellations and the warm and hot appellations.

The city of San Luis Obispo started with the **Mission San Luis Obispo de Tolosa**, established in the 1700s, and the city grew around it. Today, the mission and museum is open for visitors. This downtown area is filled with cute little shops, bookstores, delicious restaurants and other interesting eateries, museums and art galleries, plus wine and craft beer tasting rooms. It is a great little walking town. Also, SLO has been ranked as one of the top **happiest cities in America** by a Gallup Index. Now this is a place to getaway.

The **San Luis Obispo County Regional Airport** (SBP) has direct flights from eight major airports, and is only a five-minute drive from downtown SLO.

The wine regions are close by with hundreds of tasting rooms to explore. The Edna Valley AVA is just ten minutes southeast of downtown SLO, with Arroyo Grande Valley AVA adjacent to the east. The newest AVA, SLO Coast AVA, expands in several directions around the city and up the coast.

To the north is the Paso Robles AVA, the largest wine region in SLO County with over 250 wineries. Paso Robles has prospered with much acclaim for outstanding wines and culinary attractions. Wines are receiving high scores from major critics, and winning awards against well-known Napa Valley wineries. Paso Robles AVA starts just ten minutes north of downtown SLO, and the city of Paso Robles is about a thirty minute drive on Highway 101.

The SLO coast has beautiful beaches on which to relax, play and explore an abundance of sea-life, plus several cute little beach towns to hang out in, like **Cambria** in the north and **Avila Beach** in the south. This is also where you will find the famous **Hearst Castle**.

The well-known **Cal Poly San Luis Obispo** is located just north of downtown SLO. Significantly important to this university are their viticulture, oenology and wine marketing departments providing knowledgeable people to the wine industry here.

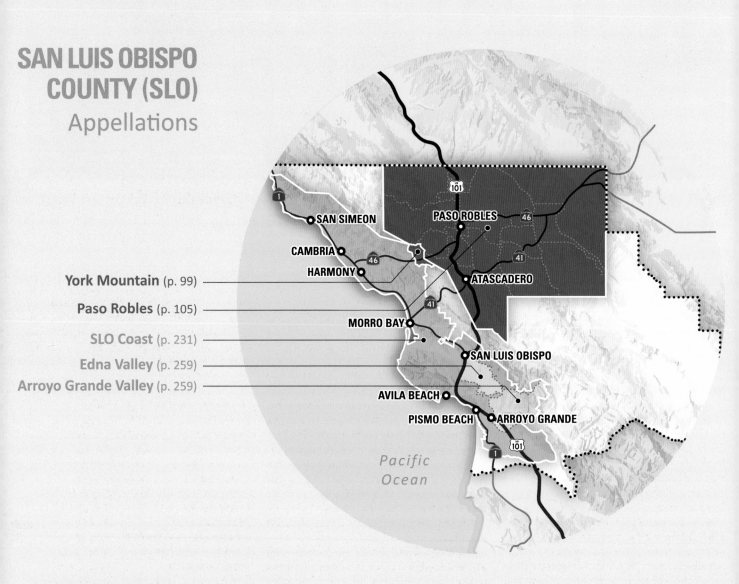

SAN LUIS OBISPO COUNTY (SLO)
Appellations

York Mountain (p. 99)

Paso Robles (p. 105)

SLO Coast (p. 231)

Edna Valley (p. 259)

Arroyo Grande Valley (p. 259)

SAN SIMEON

PASO ROBLES

CAMBRIA

HARMONY

ATASCADERO

MORRO BAY

SAN LUIS OBISPO

AVILA BEACH

PISMO BEACH

ARROYO GRANDE

Pacific Ocean

CITIES AND TOWNS ⦿
Appellations ————•
County limits ··········

S an Luis Obispo has France written all over it, from cool Burgundian weather to warm Bordeaux and Rhône Valley climates.

APPELLATIONS OF SLO COUNTY

San Luis Obispo County (SLO) has five appellations, well, technically sixteen AVAs when you consider Paso Robles has eleven sub-appellations. Paso Robles AVA is the largest and most well-known appellation in the county, with ten times the number of wineries than the rest of the county.

Most of us have heard of Paso Robles as they have become quite well-known for their wines lately. The wines have been winning top awards and the well-known critics are scoring them very high points, including 100-point wines! It has taken a while; Napa Valley vintners have known for a very long time as they have been purchasing Paso Robles fruit here for decades.

While the Paso Robles AVA was established in 1983, it took another three decades to further define the terroir here and create the eleven sub-appellations in 2014. You can read more about Paso Robles and its sub-appellations on page 105.

The **Paso Robles AVA** is in the north half of the county. The **York Mountain AVA** is adjacent to the west of Paso Robles AVA in the Santa Lucia Mountain Range.

York Mountain AVA is where the very first winery began in SLO County in 1895. Andrew York first purchased property here in 1892, and started planting Zinfandel grapes. York Mountain became an official AVA in 1982. York Mountain is at 1,500 feet elevation and only seven miles from the Pacific Ocean. York Mountain is cooler and wetter than Paso Robles. There is only one winery here. More on page 99.

In the southern part of the county, south of the city of San Luis Obispo, the terroir is much cooler; this is where the other AVAs are located. **The Edna Valley AVA** is immediately to the southeast of the city and is where most of the wineries are located in south SLO county. Edna Valley AVA is one of the oldest grape-growing regions in SLO county because of the Mission San Luis Obispo and the Spanish missionaries making wine there. You can read more on page 259.

The **Arroyo Grande Valley AVA** is immediately adjacent southeast of the Edna Valley and has a similar climate for Burgundian varietals. Along the entire coast of the county, also encompassing Edna and Arroyo Grande AVAs, is the newest AVA in SLO county, **SLO Coast AVA** established in 2022. Again, cool Burgundian climate for these varietals.

Think of French wines in SLO County. Both York Mountain and Paso Robles AVAs are focused on Bordeaux and Rhône Valley varietals, while the Edna Valley, Arroyo Grande Valley and SLO Coast AVAs focus on Burgundy varietals. SLO County definitely speaks France!

Here are some helpful driving distances and times to make it easier to get around.

Driving Distance to San Luis Obispo from...
- **Los Angeles**   190mi (3 hrs, 30 min)
- **Santa Barbara**   94mi (1 hr, 30 min)
- **San Francisco**   230mi (3 hrs, 45 min)
- **Monterey**   140mi (2 hrs, 15 min)

Driving Distance from San Luis Obispo to...
- **SLO Coast AVA**   5 mi (10 min)
- **Edna Valley AVA**   5 mi (10 min)
- **Arroyo Grande Valley AVA**   13 mi (20 min)
- **York Mountain AVA**   30 mi (35 min)
- **Paso Robles AVA**   10 mi (13 min)
- **Paso Robles Downtown**   30 mi (30 min)
- **Cambria**   34 mi (40 min)
- **Morrow Bay**   13 mi (16 min)
- **Avila Beach**   10 mi (13 min)

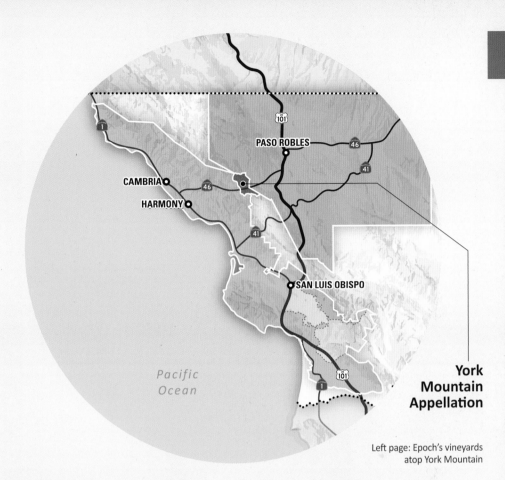

**York
Mountain
Appellation**

Left page: Epoch's vineyards
atop York Mountain

HIGH-ELEVATION TERROIR

York Mountain is said to be where the first bonded winery began in San Luis Obispo County (SLO). While York Mountain did not become an official AVA until 1982, the trailblazing Andrew York purchased property here and started planting Zinfandel grapes in 1882. His winery, Ascension Winery, which later became York Mountain Winery, was built in 1895.

The York Mountain AVA is adjacent to the west edge of the Paso Robles AVA, in the Santa Lucia Mountains, just seven miles from the Pacific Ocean. Most vineyards are planted around 1,500 feet elevation. York Mountain is cooler and wetter than Paso Robles. While a few smart winemakers have vineyards in this special mountain terroir, only one winery exists in the AVA, **Epoch Estate Wines** (descendants of York Mountain Winery).

In the 1913, fame arrived in SLO as the great Polish pianist and prime minister, Ignacy Paderewski visited Paso Robles seeking the healing effects of its hot sulfur-rich mineral baths for his rheumatism. Paderewski fell in love with the area and purchased 2,000+ acres, established Rancho San Ignacio, and planted Zinfandel and Petite Syrah. Paderewski went on to create award-winning wines, all at the York Mountain Winery.

Today, Andrew York's winery has been restored into a beautiful tasting room by the current owner of **Epoch Estate Wines**, who continues to harvest the prized grapes from the Paderewski vineyard.

Here is the one winery of York Mountain.
• Epoch Estate Wines, page 101

SAN LUIS OBISPO **YORK MOUNTAIN** ■
Winery and Restaurant
EPOCH ESTATE WINES

$$-$$$

7505 York Mountain Road
Templeton, CA 93465

+1 805 237 7575
TastingRoom@EpochWines.com

EpochWines.com

Open: Every Day, 10am-4pm

IN THE MOUNTAINS

Let's start with a very interesting talent of the winemaker here. Jordan Fiorentini does not write the typical winemaker notes. For her, wine is a sensation. She sees wine in abstract shapes and intersecting lines that she calls *Vinpressions*. They are visual tasting notes communicated in drawings of how her wines smell, taste and feel as you sip them (Jordan and her drawings, left page).

The drawings express her palate left to right as the wine enters and evolves in her mouth as a time lapse. The drawings develop how and where the wine expresses sensation. In the cheeks, across the tongue, back along the roof of the mouth, and so forth... Each sensation is recorded as its unique expression in the mouth. Remarkable!

Jordan brings unique creativity to winemaking, along with an analytical methodology that comes from her undergraduate degree in engineering. She also has a master's degree in viticulture from UC Davis. She makes single varietals as well as blends; the ultimate creativity of her expressions.

This is a beautiful property to visit. Hey, it's in the mountains, how can it not be beautiful? And it's unique as the only winery in this appellation.

In 2010, geologists Bill and Liz Armstrong purchased this property, changed its name, and constructed a brand-new winery. A mixture of rustic and modern, the winery is mostly underground into the hill, blending into the landscape and providing a natural temperature for the wine, while providing the winemaking team the ultimate facility for making great wines.

While the original winery was built in 1882, it fell apart over a century of use and weathering. Then the San Simeon earthquake of 2003 finished it off, making it condemned by the county. Reconstruction by the new owners took four years (2013-2016). Honoring the structures historic integrity meant literally brick-by-brick and stone-by-stone reinstalling each of them in their original exact locations, including the original redwood beams. This space is really cool (photo above), with great ambiance to relax and enjoy their wines... as it is now Epoch's new tasting room.

Collection of Wines

Block B (Syrah)
Sensibility (Grenache)
Tempranillo (Tempranillo)
Zinfandel (Zinfandel)

Authenticity (Syrah, Mourvèdre)
Mourvèdre (Mourvèdre, Grenache)
Creativity (Viognier, Roussanne)

Estate Blend (Syrah, Mourvèdre,
18% Grenache, Tempranillo, Graciano)
Ingenuity (Petite Sirah, Syrah,
Mourvèdre, Grenache)
Possibility (Syrah, Petite Sirah,
Grenache Blanc)

Veracity (Mourvèdre, Grenache, Syrah)
Rosé (Mourvèdre, Grenache, Syrah)
White (Grenache Blanc, Viognier, Roussanne)

Tasting Kits (Five Different Mini-Bottles)

The rolling hills and vineyards of Pomar-Junction Vineyard & Winery in Paso Robles

PASO ROBLES
Appellations

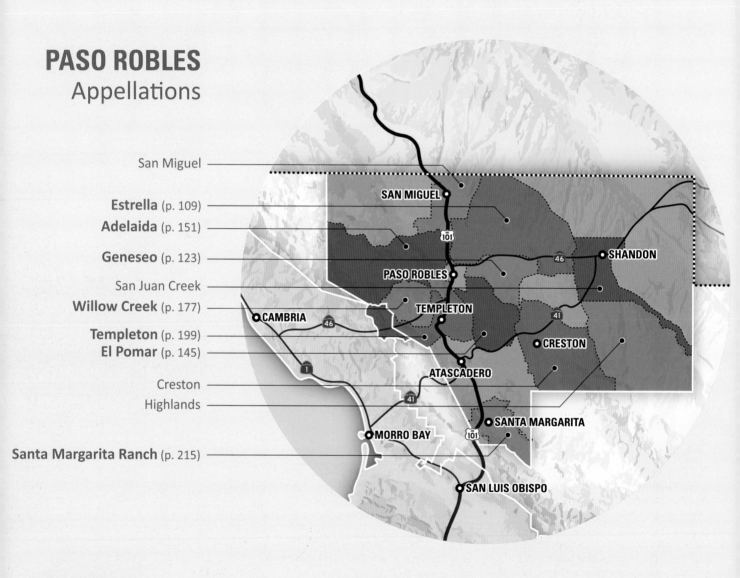

San Miguel

Estrella (p. 109)

Adelaida (p. 151)

Geneseo (p. 123)

San Juan Creek

Willow Creek (p. 177)

Templeton (p. 199)

El Pomar (p. 145)

Creston

Highlands

Santa Margarita Ranch (p. 215)

SAN MIGUEL

SHANDON

PASO ROBLES

TEMPLETON

CAMBRIA

CRESTON

ATASCADERO

SANTA MARGARITA

MORRO BAY

SAN LUIS OBISPO

CITIES AND TOWNS ⊙
Appellations ————•
County limits ···········

Pomar Junction Vineyard & Winery in Paso Robles

California's Wild-West wine region, where trailblazing winemakers innovate extraordinary wines. This terroir has proven to be special for Zinfandel, Bordeaux blends and Rhône style wines.

APPELLATIONS OF PASO ROBLES

Formally, the town is **El Paso de Robles**, which means "the pass of the oaks" in Spanish. In short, Paso Robles, and locally known as just Paso. Paso Robles is located exactly halfway between Los Angeles and San Francisco, and is in the northernmost part of San Luis Obispo County. And you guessed it, there are many oak trees.

This is a place of rugged ranchlands and cowboy ambiance. A place where winemakers showed up to do what they wanted, like cowboys, doing whatever they damn please. There were no rules. And most of the time, the rules were deliberately broken. Paso Robles is truly one of the world's most dynamic winegrowing regions as a result.

Originally, Paso Robles was known for its thermal waters flowing from the ground. People came for the therapeutic health benefits of soaking in mineral waters. Today, these baths have all disappeared. Paso Robles also had the world's largest concentration of almond orchards. Almond orchards slowly moved to the central valley for the abundance of water and flat land more conducive for harvest. The almond groves were replanted into vineyards and the wine industry was begun.

Without the Santa Lucia Mountains and the Templeton Gap, Paso Robles would not be the excellent wine region it has become. The Santa Lucia Mountains lines the coast insulating Paso Robles from the cold Pacific Ocean, trapping the daytime heat needed for growing grapes. In the evening, the Templeton Gap (a notch in the mountain range) allows the cold marine weather to flow into the vineyards. This creates temperature swings of as much as 50° during the summer and fall harvest months. Such conditions are called the diurnal effect, optimal for the Bordeaux and Rhône varietals, in which Paso excels.

Paso Robles used to be just one appellation (AVA) established in 1983. It was the largest un-subdivided AVA in California. Then, in 2013, Paso Robles established eleven sub-appellations to distinguish the differing terroir throughout the region. To understand this in perspective, the Napa Valley AVA has sixteen sub-appellations within 225,000 acres. Paso Robles now has eleven sub-appellations within three times the area of 614,000 acres.

Paso Robles has now grown to over 250 wineries, most have tasting rooms, many have restaurants or food service and some have accommodations.

This is cowboy country meets world-class wine. If you have not been here in a while, you will not recognize Paso. With the same small-town feel where you can still meet the farmers and winemakers in the tasting rooms, the wine quality is through the roof.

The sophistication has expanded. Restaurants have become gourmet. This is an agricultural community, so farm-to-table takes on the best of this meaning. Even Michelin has discovered Paso, handing out a star here. And wineries now have accommodations in the vineyards, both luxury and creative.

Beyond wineries, Paso now has a host of microbreweries, craft distilleries and olive oil artisans. The coast and Cambria is close by if you would like to visit the beach. All of this and more, you will find in the following pages. Enjoy!

Below are distances and times (without traffic) to reach Paso Robles.

Driving Distance to Central Paso Robles from...
- **Los Angeles**   205mi (3 hrs 15 min)
- **San Francisco**   205mi (3 hrs 15 min)
- **Monterey**   115mi (2 hrs)
- **San Luis Obispo**   31mi (32 min)
- **Cambria**   31mi (39 min)

Ziplining through a barn and across vineyards at Ancient Peaks Winery in Paso Robles

PASO ROBLES WINERIES	Number of Wines	Red Wines	White Wines	Rosé Wines	Sweet Wines	Sparkling Wines	Wine Shop	Boutique	Lodging	Restaurant	Food Options	Food & Wine Pairing	Tours	Educational	Fun Activities	Bordeaux Varietals	Rhône Varietals	Zinfandel	Other
York Mountain AVA																			
Epoch Estate Wines	16	√	√	√			√										√	√	√
Estrella AVA																			
J. Lohr Vineyards & Wines	38	√	√	√	√		√									√	√		√
Villa San-Juliette	13	√	√	√			√			√	√					√	√	√	
Allegretto Vineyard Resort	13	√	√	√			√	√	√	√	√	√	√	√	√	√	√	√	
Geneseo AVA																			
Eberle Winery	17	√	√	√	√		√	√		√	√		√		√	√	√	√	√
Robert Hall Winery	23	√	√	√	√		√			√	√	√	√	√	√	√	√	√	
Paris Valley Road Winery	20	√	√	√		√	√			√	√		√	√	√	√	√	√	
Cass Winery	16	√	√	√		√	√		√	√	√		√	√	√	√	√		
El Pomar AVA																			
Pomar Junction Vineyard	32	√	√	√	√		√									√	√	√	
Bovino Vineyards	15	√	√	√			√		√	√			√			√	√	√	
Adelaida AVA																			
Adelaida Vineyards & Winery	13	√	√	√	√	√	√			√	√		√		√	√	√	√	√
JUSTIN Vineyards & Winery	18	√	√	√			√	√	√	√	√	√	√	√	√	√	√	√	
Tablas Creek Vineyard	34	√	√	√	√		√						√	√	√		√		√
Daou Vineyards	18	√	√				√	√				√	√			√	√		√
La Cuvier Winery	11	√	√				√			√	√					√	√	√	
Alta Colina	15	√	√	√			√		√				√		√	√	√		
McPrice Myers Winery	19	√	√	√			√						√			√	√	√	
Six Mile Bridge	7	√	√	√			√									√			
LAW Estate Wines	11	√	√	√			√												
Willow Creek AVA																			
Opolo Vineyards	14	√	√	√	√	√	√		√	√	√	√				√	√	√	√
Denner Vineyards	11	√	√	√			√									√	√	√	
Booker Vineyard	8	√	√	√			√						√		√	√	√	√	
Niner Wine Estate	14	√	√		√	√	√	√		√	√	√	√		√	√	√	√	
Barton Family Wines	29	√	√	√	√	√	√	√		√	√						√		
Hunt Cellars	20	√					√									√	√	√	
Turley Wine Cellars	6	√					√			√									
Templeton Gap AVA																			
Castoro Cellars	17	√	√	√	√	√	√	√							√	√	√	√	
Hope Family Wines	12	√	√				√						√	√		√	√	√	
SummerWood Winery & Inn	15	√	√		√	√	√	√	√		√					√	√		
Peachy Canyon	18	√	√	√			√	√							√	√	√	√	
Santa Margarita Ranch AVA																			
Ancient Peaks Winery	15	√	√	√	√		√			√	√		√		√	√	√	√	√

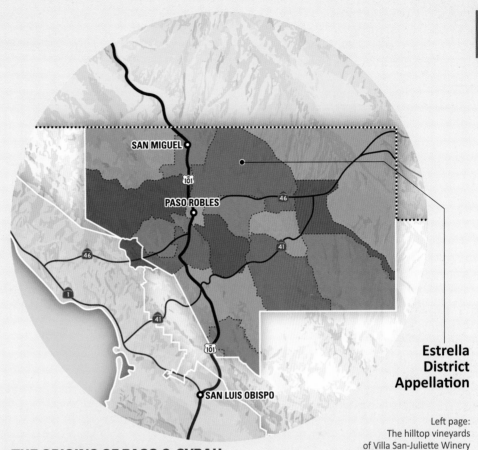

Estrella District Appellation

Left page:
The hilltop vineyards of Villa San-Juliette Winery

THE ORIGINS OF PASO & SYRAH

The Estrella District was officially established as an AVA in 2014 as one of the eleven Paso Robles Districts, located on the north and east side, up against the foothills. While the Greater Paso Robles AVA was established thirty-one years previously in 1983, the Estrella District was becoming known more than a century earlier, right after California became the 31st state in 1850.

Ranchers began to move to this area, raising cattle and sheep, while farmers set roots here to grow grains and feed. Dry-farming, if you can imagine that! It was 1888 that marked a significant growth as the railroad was built connecting this area with San Francisco and Los Angeles. The ranchers and farmers now had the transportation needed to sell their goods, also inviting more people to move here.

Earlier in San Miguel, adjacent west of Estrella, wine grapes started in 1797 at the **San Miguel Mission**, a national historical landmark worth visiting.

Pioneer Gary Eberle (page 125) propagated French Syrah cuttings in the Estrella District in 1975, thinking Rhône varietals would excel here (he was right), creating the first Syrah wine in the USA at the Estrella River Winery.

Estrella ("star" in Spanish) was named from the star-like pattern made by the ridge lines of the topography. The important river that flows through and feeds agricultures here, was named Estrella River.

This AVA has excellent wineries, unique vineyard accommodations, delicious restaurants, and lots of activities to make your trip special.

Here are some excellent properties to visit here.
- J.Lohr Vineyards & Wines, page 113
- Villa San-Juliette Vineyard & Winery, page 115
- Allegretto Vineyard Resort, page 117

JERRY LOHR
VISIONARY OF THE CENTRAL COAST

Even though the terroir was unrecognized for its quality, Jerry believed and invested in planting vineyards along California's Central Coast.

"Getting to know all that I can about dirt is my thing."
— Jerry Lohr

A FARM BOY FROM SOUTH DAKOTA

You never know how life will evolve. Jerry Lohr grew up in a farming family in a very tiny South Dakota town. He was one of only nine graduates from the local school. Jerry found himself at South Dakota State University where he graduated with honors in civil engineering. Then on to Stanford University for master's and doctorate degrees in civil engineering. Being in California, Jerry pursued designing and building new custom homes, 962 homes to be exact. When the housing boom began to change, Jerry starting looking to diversify and add another business to his portfolio. And his roots in farming arose.

Jerry saw the demand for wine on the increase. He studied everything wine he could get his hands on, especially viticulture. With soil maps, weather and heat pattern data, Jerry roamed California in search of perfect terroir. Of course there was Napa Valley, but Jerry felt this area was already developed. Jerry was looking for his niche, just like he did in the housing business. Then he found Monterey California. While there was an abundance of agriculture here, there was not viticulture.

Jerry loves dirt, and this dirt caught his attention. It was well-drained alluvial soil washed down from the mountains with proper amounts of magnesium and calcium, all in a maritime climate. And the Monterey Bay has a huge effect on the climate here. Jerry thought this was perfect for Chardonnay and he purchased and planted his first 280 acres. He was right about the terroir here, and the proof was in the extraordinary qualities of wines he produced.

Not all was a success though. He tried Cabernet Sauvignon and Merlot to great dismay. He quickly figured out he needed a much warmer environment for Bordeaux varietals, and so he headed one hundred miles south and discovered Paso Robles, also an area not yet realized for its potential. This is where Jerry found the perfect terroir, particularly the diurnal day/night temperature differences of as much as 50°F in which Cabernet Sauvignon thrives at its best.

In the beginning, there were lots of skeptics thinking this was a huge gamble for Jerry to believe in the Central Coast for viticulture. Now, five decades later, Jerry is producing over 20 million bottles of wine from more than 4,000 acres along the Central Coast. My math puts J. Lohr as the 21st largest winery in America, and the largest winery in the California Central Coast. Jerry's vision has had a remarkable success that has me in awe every time I think about it.

Jerry is properly recognized for his pioneering spirit here in discovering the potential and creating acclaim for this region that greatly benefits us wine lovers (as well as those in the wine and tourism businesses). The honors and awards are too numerous to list. Highlighting... **Oenological Award of Excellence** by *The Quarterly Review of Wines,* **Professional Excellence in Oenology** by the New York Institute of Technology, **American Winery of the Year** by *Wine Enthusiast* magazine, and **Winery of the Year** by *The Tasting Panel*. And most special was Jerry Lohr becoming the third person in history to be honored by *Wine Enthusiast* magazine as an **American Wine Legend**.

While Jerry still works long farmer hours, he always finds time to give back. His impact on industry organizations and educational institutions is tremendous. He has personally contributed thousands of hours and raised tens of millions of dollars to important causes. Jerry is very appreciative and generous with his second family, his 250 employees that he feels made his success possible. Jerry has shared the wealth and success of the winery by instituting an employee stock ownership plan so his employees can share in the profits of J. Lohr Vineyards & Wines.

In his eighties, Jerry remains passionate about wine and can be found at the winery, where I met him, sharing with visitors his wines out of the barrel (photo below left) as well as contemplating their next wines and strategizing perfection with Director of Winemaking Steve Peck (photo below right).

$-$$-$$$-$$$$

6169 Airport Road
Paso Robles, CA 93446

+1 805 239 8900
PRWineCenter@JLohr.com

JLohr.com

Open: Every Day, 10am-5pm

Collection of Paso Robles Wines

Signature Cabernet Sauvignon
Cuvée POM (Merlot, Malbec)
Cuvée St. E (Cabernet Franc, Cabernet Sauvignon)
Cuvée PAU (Cab Sauv, Cab Franc, Merlot, Petit Verdot)

Hilltop - Cabernet Sauvignon
Beck Vineyard - Cabernet Sauvignon
Shotwell Vineyard - Cabernet Sauvignon
Home Ranch - Cabernet Sauvignon
Shotwell Vineyard - Malbec
Home Ranch - Petit Verdot
Beck Vineyard - Syrah

Gesture Syrah
Gesture Zinfandel
Gesture Mourvèdre
Gesture GSM (Grenache, Syrah, Mourvèdre)

Pure Paso, Proprietary Red Wine
(Cabernet Sauvignon, Petite Sirah, Syrah, Malbec)

Seven Oaks (Cabernet Sauvignon)
Los Osos (Merlot)
South Ridge (Syrah)

Gesture Viognier
Gesture Grenache Blanc
Gesture RGV (Roussanne, Grenache Blanc, Viognier)
Gean Vineyard - Grenache Rosé

The largest winery along the Central Coast, producing both affordability and excellence.

TRY THESE 36 WINES

Certainly you know the *J. Lohr Seven Oaks* as they produce a whopping twelve million bottles annually of this Cabernet Sauvignon wine. And it's a good wine. Surprisingly, at $17 a bottle, this wine is aged in real oak barrels. Great quality for the excellent price.

For the other eight million bottles of wine they produce, this is what lots of cash, expertise, terroir, and passion creates. I am a real fan of their *Signature Cabernet Sauvignon*; released on Jerry Lohr's eightieth birthday, with his signature, it culminates his five decades of history and experience into a single bottle. In contrast, only 9,600 bottles are made of this stellar wine.

J. Lohr produces twenty-three different wines in Paso, all from Bordeaux and Rhône grapes (wines listed in right column). An additional twelve cool-weather wines from Monterey, and one special Cabernet Sauvignon from St. Helena, Napa Valley, named after Jerry's late wife, Carol, with $3 from every bottle donated to the National Breast Cancer Foundation. All wines are available by visiting or calling their J. Lohr Wine Centers in Paso Robles or San Jose, California.

J. Lohr wines are accessible to everyone with prices and perfection ranging from $10 to $100. Their website has a very cool "Wine Locator" to find their wines local to you.

But visit them! They have remodeled their Wine Center with new reimagined tasting experiences. They have a new indoor tasting room inspired by Jerry's South Dakota farmhouse roots. Outdoor tasting is on the veranda overlooking their vineyards.

• **Seasonal Experience**. This is a seated tasting of their current seasonal releases focused on J. Lohr's winery-exclusive wines. A charcuterie and cheese board can be added to this experience.

• **Legacy Experience**. A curated seated tasting by a J. Lohr Wine Educator, in their special Tasting Salon, of their winery-exclusive, club-only, and library wines, and thoughtfully paired with included charcuterie and cheeses included.

• **Signature Experience**. An ultimate experience in a private VIP room, led by an advanced-level J. Lohr Wine Educator, tasting their iconic gems, including *J. Lohr Carol's Cabernet Sauvignon*, the *J. Lohr Cuvée Series*, library selections, and the *J. Lohr Signature Cabernet Sauvignon*.

$-$$-$$$

6385 Cross Canyons Road
San Miguel, CA 93451

+1 805 467 0014
TastingRoom@VillaSanJuliette.com

VillaSanJuliette.com

Open: Thursday-Monday, 11am-5pm
Tuesdays and Wednesdays by appointment

F rom the hills of northern Paso Robles comes a picturesque destination with delicious terroir.

DREAMS COME TRUE

Nigel Lythgoe and Ken Warwick, childhood friends from Liverpool and creators of the Emmy award-winning *So You Think You Can Dance* and *American Idol*, respectively, had an exciting dream of owning their own vineyard. Most of us wine lovers have considered this romantic ideal at some time or another. Nigel and Ken made it happen with the purchase of this property in 2005.

Over the next ten years they completely redeveloped this property. They built an ever-so-charming Italian villa, naming it after Romeo & Juliet, replanted 50% of their a 120 acres of vineyards, and hired a very talented winemaking team to produce high-scoring wines you will love.

Today, this Tuscan estate is worth your visit. It makes for the perfect afternoon, relaxing outdoors on their patio listening to the beautiful fountain, or under the shade of their massive oak tree, or under their large pergola overlooking the vineyards and the Paso Robles valley below. Grab a glass or bottle of your favorite wine (they have thirteen different wines to choose from) and find your perfect spot.

This is a wonderful place to spend the afternoon, with its light fresh breeze and picturesque view across the rolling hills of vineyards. Their on-site Italian chef provides a gourmet bistro-style menu every day for a delicious lunch on the patio.

My romantic nature comes alive here. Tuscan grounds, picturesque views, delicious cuisine, comfortable furniture (love seats), and nice places to stroll around holding hands. My favorite wine here is none other than *Romantique*, a special blend of all five Bordeaux varietals from the very best of their property.

There are many tasting opportunities, including a flight of nine different wines. Imagine a seven-wine flight with lunch at a very affordable price.

The menu is ever changing and creative. Above are their crab cakes, scrumptiously delicious, and the rémoulade is homemade. Below is the most delicious avocado toast you will ever encounter. Heirloom tomatoes, savory mascarpone cheese and drizzled with a rich balsamic reduction. Yum!

Collection of Wines

Cabernet Sauvignon Reserve
Alicante Bouschet Reserve
Cabernet Franc Reserve
Grenache Reserve
Petit Verdot Reserve
Petite Sirah Reserve
Syrah Reserve
Zinfandel Reserve

Romantique
A Bordeaux blend of the very best of the property
(Cabernet Sauvignon, Cabernet Franc,
Malbec, Petit Verdot, Merlot)
(100% French Oak, 28 Months in Barrel)
Chorum Red
Nine different grapes make up this blend
(Lead by Rhone Varietals, then Bordeaux Varietals)

Pinot Gris Reserve (100% Tempranillo)
Sauvignon Blanc Estate (100% Tempranillo)
Rosé Reserve (100% Granache)

$-$$-$$$

2700 Buena Vista Drive
Paso Robles, CA 93446

+1 805 369 2500
Info@AllegrettoResort.com

AllegrettoResort.com

Wine Tasting: Every Day, 11am-5pm
Vineyard Tours: Friday-Sunday, 10am
Olive Oil Tasting: Fri/Sat 3pm-6pm, Sun 9am-12pm

Collection of Wines

Cabernet Sauvignon (Willow Creek Vineyard)
Cabernet Sauvignon (Allegretto Vineyard)
Heart of the Vibe (Petit Verdot,
Cabernet Sauvignon, Malbec, Tannat)
Cello Red (Zinfandel, Tempranillo, Tannat)
Pinot Noir Reserve (Sta. Rita Hills)
Malbec Reserve (Allegretto Vineyard)
Tannat (Allegretto Vineyard)

Cabernet Rosé (Willow Creek Vineyard)
Malbec Rosé (Allegretto Vineyard)
Tannat Rosé (Allegretto Vineyard)

Cello Grenache Blanc
Duetto (Viognier, Vermentino)
Chardonnay (Sta. Rita Hills)

A sanctuary resort of spiritual influences. Feel at peace, relaxed and inspired among the sacred energy surrounding the art and architecture here.

BIODYNAMIC VINEYARDS

Shall we begin with the wines at this resort? The Allegretto wines are as inspirational as this vineyard resort. On the following pages, you will learn the harmony and balance that has gone into every aspect of creating this property.

The vineyards and wines have also been treated with the same high level of spirituality, so it should not surprise you that the wine focus here is biodynamic.

For example, the vineyards here are planted in different directions, and with different spacing between the vines and the rows. It was sensory and metaphysical in determining what each grape variety desired. You may think this is rather esoteric; however, when you taste the wines, the magic will enlighten you in your experience.

Biodynamics applies to planting on a new moon and harvesting on a fruit day. These and other astronomical events are used here as a guide for when to perform certain tasks in the vineyard, integrating scientific understanding with a recognition of spirit in nature.

More down to earth, or shall I say in the cellar, is the extensive aging they do of their wines. Their Cabernet Sauvignon is dry farmed and aged for four years in their cellars in 60% new oak. This is extensive! Another reason why their wines are so good.

Have you ever tasted Tannat? Although its origins are from southwestern France, this grape has become the "national grape" of Uruguay. It is a big, bold, dark-red wine. I generally find this wine boring as big and bold is not enough for me.

The Allegretto Tannat has character! A special deliciousness for me. They age their Tannat in 30% new oak for sixty months. Yes, five full years! This really smooths out the wine and brings out its nice fruit. This was a wonderful surprise for me. Something you're really not going to find anywhere else.

Behind the hotel is a hill covered with their vineyards, which you can walk through, experience its spirituality, and enjoy the views. Their other vineyard is in the Willow Creek AVA on the west side of Paso Robles.

They also have eighty olive trees of nine different varietals between twenty-five to thirty years old. They make some very delicious olive oil that is available here.

$$$-$$$$-$$$$$

2700 Buena Vista Drive
Paso Robles, CA 93446

+1 805 369 2500
Info@AllegrettoResort.com

AllegrettoResort.com

Resort Open: Every Day, 24/7/365
Restaurant: Every Day, Breakfast, Lunch, Dinner
Weekend Yoga: Saturday/Sunday 9am

EXTRAORDINARY HOSPITALITY

You will feel as though you have arrived in Italy in this Tuscan-style resort of magnificence. The entrance is stunning (left page). Everything will be music to your ears as the name Allegretto describes a beautiful beat of music. You will discover that this place is all about harmony and balance. Yin and yang. Feng shui.

Everything on this property has been chosen and placed with inspiration, tapping into the non-physical realm for every pattern and shape, tapping into higher vibrations to bring forth the physical elements.

This property is the inspiration of its owner/hotelier, Doug Ayres, following his deep quest for truth and joy living with monks in monasteries around the world. You will feel his inspiration of spirituality in every moment you breathe here.

You will not want to leave the property as the spirituality will capture you, the beauty of the architecture and art will engage you and every corner of the property has continual joy to discover.

And just wait till you meet the beautiful people who work at this property. They are truly engaged in your experience. Happy. Friendly. Always engaging. The quality of hospitality is five stars.

Their guest rooms are just as special, a sanctuary of European-style elegance. Luxurious. Roomy. Very comfortable beds! Get a room on the piazza (photo above), a view, patio or balcony (photo right).

Cello Ristorante & Bar. The photos say everything about the deliciousness of this gourmet Italian food. The chef is quite inventive, regularly creating new dishes. Even if you're not staying in the hotel, the restaurant is worth your special treat.

Photos from top to bottom...
Shishito Peppers: simply prepared in sesame oil, garlic and soy sauce. Yummy.
Beet Salad: thinly sliced yellow and red beets under a mixed green salad with candied walnuts, local goat cheese and a citrus vinaigrette. Refreshing.
Mediterranean Style Shrimp: sautéed prawns, garlic, cherry tomatoes, and Kalamata olives in a white wine broth mixed with perfectly cooked Etto pasta. Succulent.
Local Seafood Soup: juicy shrimp, flavorful clams and succulent mussels cooked in a rich flavorful broth of saffron, fennel and tarragon. Divine.

F rom different cultures and faiths, every artifact here is an instrument playing the Allegretto symphony.

– Doug Ayres, Proprietor

A MUSEUM EXHIBIT

This hotel is a work of art. Literally! Walls are plastered with pulverized Israeli marble. Fireplaces are hand-carved Renaissance-style. The property is filled with original art and artifacts from multiple centuries representing different cultures, faiths and traditions.

Everywhere you turn, there is something amazing to see. An **ancient egyptian obelisk**. The *Buddha Hindu Goddess Siddhartha Gautama*. So many ancient cultures represented here.

You must experience the **Sonic Labyrinth** (photo below). As you walk through an outdoor labyrinth, motion sensors activate a series of soft, soothing tones that evolve as you walk, cultivating a sense of relaxation and focus. Think of it like a sound circle, a place for tranquility generated by wind instruments. This is the first of its kind in the world.

Visiting **Abbaye de Lerins** is very special in the early morning and late afternoon when the sun enters directly through handmade stained-glass windows and creates beautiful colored designs on the walls and floor (photo above). A beautiful place of peace and harmony, this abbey is modeled after rustic chapels of Europe and includes the *Virgin of Guadalupe*, actually blessed at the *Basilica of Our Lady of Guadalupe* in Mexico City.

Praying Buddha (left page), carved in 1856 in Rajasthan India, stands tall in front of a vast mirror along a hallway giving a reflection to eternity.

Five forces in nature (earth, fire, ether, water, and air) represented geometrically in this *Tunnel of Cosmic Creation* (photo above left) and resting together in the 800 lb rotating granite sphere; the oneness.

A Series Of Uplifting Terraces Creates Ideal Terroir For Wine Grapes Here

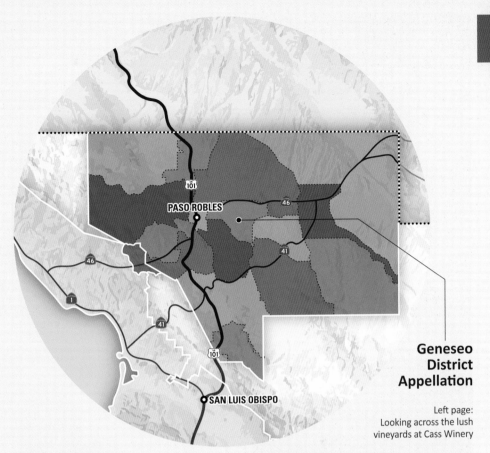

Geneseo
District
Appellation

Left page:
Looking across the lush
vineyards at Cass Winery

IDEAL TERROIR

The Geneseo District (AVA) is located immediately south of the Estrella AVA we just explored and north of the El Pomar AVA, which is the next appellation in this book. Being on the east side of Paso, Geneseo enjoys hot days and cool nights from the Templeton Gap breezes, ideal for wine grapes.

Geneseo was established by way of Geneseo Illinois, by way of Geneseo New York, by way of German descendants invited through an ad in the *Geneseo Republic* newspaper in Illinois. All this caused German immigrants to move and settle here, bringing their farming experience, traditions, faith, and the name Geneseo. Back to the beginning, "Geneseo" means "beautiful valley" in the Iroquois language of the native Indians in upstate New York.

One of those families, the Ernst family, began planting the first vineyards here in 1884 with more than twenty varieties they obtained from a UC Davis project.

Seven generations later, the Ernst family descendants continue with what is now Steinbeck Vineyards & Winery, farming 500 acres of vines that produce highly sought-after fruit purchased by wineries of names we know well.

The landscape here is valuable for wine grape growing. The Huerhuero and La Panza Faults have lifted the earth here for millions of years, uplifting most of this appellation into stair-steps of terraces with north, east, west and southern exposures, giving growers many options to maximize the grape varietal's optimal terroir needs. Further, the Estrella River runs south into Geneseo, and along with the Huerhuero Creek, they provide the natural fresh irrigation for the vines.

Here are some excellent wineries to visit here.
• Eberly Winery, page 127
• Robert Hall Winery, page 133
• Paris Valley Road Winery, page 135
• Cass Winery, page 139

GARY EBERLE
AN AMERICAN WINE LEGEND

The Pioneer of American Syrah
Making Paso Robles A Household Name

*"I don't want to be a geneticist,
I want to be an alcoholic!"*
— **Gary Eberle**

FROM PENN STATE TO WINE ESTATE

I find it interesting how so many of us think we know where we are going in life... until things happen, and courses change. Gary Eberle was a big guy and excelled at football. Penn State recruited him, and he studied biology on a football scholarship. Then, Gary discovered he actually loved college. He graduated with a Bachelor of Science in biology. He became fascinated with DNA and went to Louisiana State University to do graduate work studying cellular genetics.

While attending LSU, one of his professors introduced him to the decadent world of food and wine, which led him to change his career. Gary gave up DNA for AVA! He wanted to be a winemaker. In other words, as Gary humorously puts it: "I don't want to be a geneticist, I want to be an alcoholic!" So, Gary headed to California, where he pursued a doctorate in oenology and viticulture at the University of California Davis.

Gary happened to be at UC Davis with the opportunity to study with professors who were examining whether Paso Robles could be the next Napa Valley. Gary realized the potential and moved to Paso to start a winery. First, he co-founded the Estrella River Winery, where he changed the course of Rhône varietals in the United States. Then, a few years later, he created Eberly Winery.

Gary believed that Paso had the perfect terroir for Rhône grapes to excel. So, he went to France, the Rhône Valley, and met Michel Chapoutier, another unconventional wine lover ready to help pioneer Syrah in California. Gary left with his prized cuttings of Syrah and headed back to Paso Robles, where in two years, he propagated enough vines to plant twenty acres.

In 1978, Gary became the first to produce a 100% Syrah wine, the first 100% virus-free, clean Syrah in the United States. He shipped the vines to winemakers all over, and for decades, Gary was the only US source of Syrah vines. Today, approximately 65% of all Syrah grown in the United States is this Eberle Estrella clone, and Paso Robles has become known as the best terroir of Rhône varietals. Winemakers came. Syrah flourished. Thanks to Gary, now there is so much excellent Syrah to be had in Paso (10% of the wines here).

And other Rhône varietals as well, including Viognier. Gary was the sixth winemaker in the United States to produce Viognier. It is hard to find great Viognier, and Gary has it! Also, be sure to try his Steinbeck Vineyard Syrah, his oldest Syrah vineyard (over forty year old vines).

Gary's most valuable mentor was the great Robert Mondavi himself. Mondavi is undisputedly the most influential person in putting Napa Valley and the California wine regions on the wine map. He created the prominence. This is exactly what Mr. Mondavi taught Mr. Eberle.

"Mondavi never taught me a damn thing about winemaking," says Gary Eberle. "He taught me a whole lot about selling wine though." Gary listened. He realized that the Eberle Winery was not going to succeed if Paso Robles did not succeed. Gary led the charge. And others followed. Gary took to the skies as a pilot, and he flew his little airplane all over the country, preaching the Paso message. Today, Paso Robles is now considered one of the premier wine regions as a result of Gary and those who embraced this paragon.

In 1983, Gary co-founded the Paso Robles Appellation, the largest AVA in California history. Gary also opened his namesake winery that year, Eberle Winery, premiering his favorite wine, Cabernet Sauvignon. Gary has gone on to create seventeen different wines available at his winery. All with a premium focus, single varieties and designated vineyards. This has won him numerous awards, ranking in the top ten of gold medal award-winning wineries in the country. Year after year, Eberle Winery maintains being one of the highest award-winning wineries in the United States.

And the awards keep piling up. In 1997, Eberle was recognized by his peers when the Paso Robles Wine Country Alliance awarded him **Wine Industry Person of the Year**. In 2013, Paso Robles was awarded **Wine Region of the Year** by *Wine Enthusiast* magazine. In 2015, Eberle was honored with the **Lifetime Achievement Award** by the California State Fair. In 2019, Eberle was awarded the esteemed **Robert Mondavi Hospitality Award**. Rarely does this award go to a winemaker; typically it goes to restaurants and hotels, as they represent hospitality. In 2020, Gary Eberle was awarded the ultimate recognition when *Wine Enthusiast* honored him **American Wine Legend** during their Wine Star Awards. This is particularly impressive when you consider Gary is only the fourth person recognized with this award in *Wine Enthusiast's* forty-two year history.

Go to Eberle Winery (page 127), shake Gary's hand and thank him for all he has done for Paso Robles and the wine industry in general. Paso Robles would not be the same without Gary's forty-five years of advocacy and passion.

$$-$$$-$$$$

3810 East Highway 46
Paso Robles, CA 93446

+1 805 238 9607
TastingRoom@EberleWinery.com

EberleWinery.com

Open: Every Day, 10am-6pm
Tastings Are Always Complimentary

T he beginnings of Paso Robles and the origins of Syrah in America are found here.

ENTHUSIASTICALLY WELCOMED

The best reason to go to Eberle Winery is because of Gary Eberle (see "The Pioneer of American Syrah" on page 125). He is a Paso Robles icon. Gary is at the winery seven days a week. Typically, he is sitting out front with a bottle of Cabernet Sauvignon (his favorite wine) greeting people and sharing stories. Gary loves nothing more than greeting people at his winery with his two adorable black standard poodles, Sangiovese and Barbera.

The second-best reason to go the Eberle Winery is for the wine. Eberle Winery is one of the highest award-winning wineries and ranks in the top ten of gold medal award-winning wineries in the country. The wine here is excellent. Expect Gary's (and my) favorite, Cabernet Sauvignon, to be outstanding. The terroir here is perfect for this varietal. Plus Gary obtained the wood from Napa's BV Private Reserve vineyard to plant his Steinbeck Vineyard, in which he makes this wine. Sensational.

There is no tasting fee at Eberle Winery. Gary insists that Americans are fair people, so when they taste how good his wine is, they reciprocate and take wine home.

If you are a Syrah lover, this is also your place. This is home to the first 100% Syrah wine in America. Eberle created the Estrella Syrah clone, now representing some 65% of all Syrah grown in the United States (see more on page 125). Taste its origin, taste its perfection, taste it here.

Are you a Viognier lover? Do you know what it is? I call it the red wine drinker's white wine. Full bodied, thick viscosity, honeysuckle on the nose, and stone fruit of peaches and apricot in the mouth. I am telling you, this is a unique delicious wine. It is hard to find really good Viognier, and Eberle has it!

Imagine 16,800 square feet of underground caves. It is an amazing experience winding through the tunnels beneath the Eberle Winery. My favorite is the VIP Nook, a cubbyhole in the cave where up to six people can experience an intimate tasting, dedicated server and cheese pairing included (photo left page).

Wonder about the boar logo? It is the German translation of Eberle, meaning "small boar." The Estrella Syrah clone was born and is now planted all over Paso Robles and throughout California. Syrah is particularly excellent in the Estrella AVA, as well as in other parts of Paso Robles.

Collection of Wines

Steinbeck Vineyard Syrah (Eberle Estrella Clone)
Reserve Estate Cabernet Sauvignon
Estate Cabernet Sauvignon
Vineyard Selection Cabernet Sauvignon
Cabernet Sauvignon/Syrah Blend
Reserve Zinfandel (Sauret Vineyard)
Eberle Zinfandel
Sangiovese
Barbera
Eberle Vintage Port

Full Boar Red (Cabernet Sauvignon based blend)
Côtes-du-Rôbles Rouge (Grenache, Syrah, Mourvèdre)
Côtes-du-Rôbles Rosé (Grenache, Syrah, Viognier)

Côtes-du-Rôbles Blanc (Grenache Blanc, Roussanne, Viognier)
Eberle Viognier, Mills Road
Eberle Estate Chardonnay
Estate Muscat Canelli

FIELD OF LIGHT, AT SENSORIO

$$-$$$-$$$$

4380 Highway 46 East
Paso Robles, CA 93446

+1 (805) 226-4287
Info@SensorioPaso.com

SensorioPaso.com

Open: Thursday/Sunday, 5pm-9pm (Fri/Sat 9:30pm)

The next exit east of Eberle Winery on Hwy 46E is this spectacular nighttime experience called Sensorio. This is a *valley of lights* (see photo) of 58,800 lights across fifteen acres in which you can wander throughout, in and around. Nothing like anything I have ever seen. This is British artist Bruce Munro's largest artwork exhibit he has created to date. Don't miss it!

In addition to **general admission** tickets, they have **VIP terrace experiences**, where you get priority entry and exclusive access to their terrace that overlooks the valley of lights. Plus, you get to sit down, with guaranteed seating, fireplace tables, heaters, private restrooms, an Airstream bar, and the best views of the exhibition. They have an upgraded VIP terrace experience that comes with a platter of either a charcuterie or crudité.

SAN LUIS OBISPO **PASO ROBLES** GENESEO ■
Winery, Vineyards, Restaurant
ROBERT HALL WINERY

$$-$$$

3443 Mill Road
Paso Robles, CA 93446

+1 805 239 1616
Info@RobertHallWinery.com

RobertHallWinery.com

Open: Every Day, 10am-5pm

Collection of Cavern Select Wines

GSM (Grenache, Syrah, Mourvèdre)
Meritage (Cabernet Sauvignon, Cabernet Franc, Malbec)
Reserve Cabernet Sauvignon
Cabernet Sauvignon
Cabernet Franc
Malbec
Carbonic Carignan
Mourvèdre
Petite Sirah
Zinfandel
Tempranillo
Syrah
Syrah Rosé

Chenin Blanc
Vermentino
Chardonnay
Sparkling Grenache Blanc

R ...ure goes beyond sustainable

...mics and organics.

HIG

T...   ...operty. As
...   ...e walkways
...   ...d of quality.
...   ...d creative. The
...   ...d the artwork
...   ...l vibe for a new

...   ...on multiple patios,
...   ...and overlooking their
...   ...ve) as you relax during
...   ...re are many choices for
...   ...d they have a full kitchen,
...   ...s, and special VIP tastings.

...   ...heir advanced thinking in
...   ...ethods to their property. Their
...   ...have been Certified Sustainable
...   ...g in 1999. Currently, they have
...   ...ree-year journey into regenerative
...   ...e-third of their acreage.

...   ...e viticulture includes and goes
...   ...erging of biodynamics, organics and
...   ...and into a holistic land-management
...   ...using the power of photosynthesis to
...   ...he carbon in the soil while improving soil
...   ...op yields, water resilience, and nutrient

density. The results are already seen here in the dramatic improvement in the quality of the grapes, and the resulting wines.

Ultimately, they are creating a zero-waste environment as well, using worms to regenerate their waste water (already 85% achieved), and solar power to take them off the grid (already 90% achieved).

• **The Cavern Select Wine Experience**. A tasting flight of their Select Series wines.

• **Seasonal Reserve Wines Tastings**. A tasting flight of their Reserve Series wines.

• **Paired Culinary Experience.** Their Cavern Select wines are professionally paired by their sommelier and chef for an extraordinary pairing experience.

• **Cavern Tour & Barrel Tasting.** With a sparkling glass of wine in hand, you will be personally escorted around the estate, through the vineyards and underground into their cavern to learn about their winemaking. Taste wines directly from the barrel and finish by tasting the same wines from bottles paired with a board of charcuterie and fromage.

• **Sustainability Tour.** Their sustainability manager will take you on an interesting educational tour to understand their commitment to sustainability and how their regenerative viticulture methods are forward thinking in producing quality wines. Plus, there's a full tasting of their excellent wines.

ExploringWineRegions.com

RETURN

SUPPLY

TRIAD

TRIAD

SAN LUIS OBISPO **PASO ROBLES** GENESEO ∎
Winery, Vineyards, Restaurant
PARIS VALLEY ROAD WINERY

$-$$-$$$

5625 East Highway 46
Paso Robles, CA 93446

+1 805 727 9463
Info@ParisValleyRoad.com

ParisValleyRoad.com

Tastings & Experiences
Open: Every Day, 10am-5pm
Lunch: Thursday-Sunday, 11am-2pm

F our decades of propagating special French clones, brings forth today's wine rooted in gratitude.

A PASSION FOR BORDEAUX

It began in 1977, when the Stoller family started Sunrise Nurseries to produce the finest grape vine stock in the world. In this quest, they were granted a master ENTAV license by the French Ministry of Agriculture to propagate French clones in the United States. The success continued with exclusive French, Portuguese and Spanish relationships to propagate these original mother vines.

Three generations later, Craig Stoller started planting vineyards from these special French clones with the objective of producing their own premium Bordeaux-style wines. He has grown it to four vineyards in four central coast AVAs: San Lucas (Monterey), Edna Valley (SLO), El Pomar (Paso), and Geneseo (Paso), totaling over 500 acres of vines.

In 2020, he opened a very impressive state-of-the-art winery (photos left and above), tasting room and restaurant (next page) within their historic Geneseo vineyards. It is easily accessible, being immediately off of Highway 46 East. This is a beautiful property, and so are the wines and cuisine.

Why the name Paris Valley Road? It represents their beginning, the name of a little two-lane road on the west side of their very first vineyards in Monterey. Now they have a beautiful new home-style building in which to enjoy their foods and wines.

They have numerous tasting experiences, depending how much you would like to get involved, how much you would like to learn or just how much fun you would like to have with them.

• **The Tasting Experience**. A hand-selected flight in their tasting room or on their outdoor patio.

• **Private Seated Tastings**. A selection of five limited-production wines with your very own private table and server to share the stories behind each wine.

• **Winemaker For A Day**. A hands-on experience tasting five different Bordeaux varietals, learning about the different varietals and discovering their attributes. Once you have tasted your options and have in mind what you want to create, their wine educator will guide you through creating your own blend. They provide all the tools necessary to mix and refine your blend until you feel it's just right.

• **French Cheese & Wine Pairing.** Their wine educator will guide you through five major families of French cheeses, pairing them with their wines. This is a delicious learning experience for your palate.

• **Le Déjeuner Chef's Paired Lunch.** This is a remarkable five-course meal expertly paired with five of their Bordeaux-inspired wines. This gourmet lunch is prepared in-house by their executive chef and team.

Collection of Wines

L'Entente (Bordeaux Red Blend)
Reserve Cabernet Sauvignon
Cabernet Sauvignon
Cabernet Franc
Petit Verdot
Malbec
Merlot

Malbec Rosé
Sauvignon Blanc
Chardonnay
Paris Valley Road Sparkling (Methodé Traditionelle)

$$-$$$

5625 East Highway 46
Paso Robles, CA 93446

+1 805 727 9463
Info@ParisValleyRoad.com

ParisValleyRoad.com

Lunch, Thursday-Saturday, 11am-2pm
Sunday Brunch, 10am-2pm

CÉPAGE AT PARIS VALLEY ROAD, GASTRONOMY

The culinary experiences at Paris Valley Road are seriously delicious. Just a stop for a glass of wine and lunch is worth the visit. However, they have more. A lot more!

The most amazing offer is their **Le Déjeuner Chef's Paired Lunch.** This is a five-course meal expertly paired with five of their Bordeaux-style wines. Just look at the food all over these two pages. I loved this experience and I know you will as well. It is gourmet all the way, and the wines were perfectly paired. Their **French Cheese & Wine Pairing** is amazing as well. This is a five-course cheese pairing; the five major families of French cheeses are paired with their wines. This is a delicious learning experience for your palate.

This is a newly constructed homestyle building furnished to make you feel at home (photo above). There is an array of inside rooms and an outside patio for views across the rolling hills of vineyards. Now, let's let the food speak to us.

"Deviled" Eggs (photo left): Shoyu style. Deviled Hollandaise. Smoked trout roe.
Lobster Avocado Toast (photo below left): Lobster tail. Avocado mash. Caviar. Sprouts.
Pork Belly Bao (photo below middle): Soy. Avocado. Daikon slaw. Shoyu egg.
Duck Grilled Cheese (photo below right): Duck confit. Manchego. Orange marmalade.
Sorbet (photo right): Strawberry & Malbec Rosé.

$$-$$$-$$$$

7350 Linne Road
Paso Robles, CA 93446

+1 805 239 1730, ext 120
TastingRoom@CassWines.com

CassWines.com

Open: Every Day, 11am-5pm

The ultimate in wine tourism experiences… plan numerous experiences with excellent wines.

INDULGE

If you want to immerse yourself in everything wine imaginable, this is your place. There are no other wineries in Paso that comes close to the number of offerings at Cass Winery. The only challenge I see is deciding which activities to plan first.

This is not just a 200-acre playground for wine lovers (photo above), the 145 acres of planted vines here are all pedigree (ENTAV certified clones by the French government). The estate is on top of a large 900' elevation terrace above the Huerhuero River. The quality of grapes here is exceptional, and top-level wineries in Paso buy this fruit from Cass.

Cass keeps 40% of their estate-grown grapes for their own wines. They have planted twelve varieties of Bordeaux and Rhône vines; Cabernet Sauvignon represents 70%. I just love to indulge in their Mourvèdre; as it is off-the-charts delicious. This wine was honored **Red Wine of the Year** and the winery itself has been awarded **Winery of the Year** from the *Central Coast Wine Competition* in 2015, 2018 and 2020.

The Cass tasting room is inside their on-premises restaurant. Open seven days a week. You can either order off the menu of delicious foods (they can pair wines with what you order) or do a tasting flight paired with different foods.

Benny Burger, 1/3-lb estate-raised grass-fed beef, house bacon blue cheese, horseradish aioli, pickled onions, organic arugula, locally made brioche bun.
Alice's Crab Cakes, winery owner's California-style secret family recipe, served on a bed of dressed greens, fresh avocado, and house-made rémoulade.

Collection of Wines

Mourvèdre
Damas Noir (Reserve Mourvèdre)
Cabernet Sauvignon(Cab Sauv, Merlot, Malbec, Petite Verdot)
Reserve(Cabernet Sauvignon, Petite Sirah, Malbec, Merlot)
Backbone Syrah
Grenache
Malbec

Rockin' Ted (Mourvèdre, Grenache, Syrah, Petite Sirah)
Vintage Ted (Cabernet Sauvignon, Mourvèdre, Petit Verdot)
Rockin' One Red (Mourvèdre, Grenache, Syrah, Petite Sirah)

Oasis Rosé (Mourvèdre, Grenache)
Harlen Sparkling Oasis Rosé (Mourvèdre, Grenache)
Rockin' One Blanc (Roussanne, Viognier, Marsanne)
Viognier
Marsanne
Roussanne

CASS CAMPS • RETREATS • EDUCATION & FUN

There is almost an endless number of activities available at Cass Winery. They have an entire team dedicated to producing very fulfilling retreats as well as Cass Camps offering personal group activities and corporate team building, plus numerous individual activities in which you can indulge à la carte.

A WINEMAKER'S DUDE RANCH RETREAT

This is a real hands-on grape harvest retreat (bottom center two photos). It is an extensive three-day retreat, including accommodations at the Geneseo Inn on the property. Their iconic Chef Charlie has extraordinary culinary skills and will be preparing breakfast, lunch and dinner, along with a cooking demonstration. Owner Steve Cass will walk you through his prized vineyards and share meals with you. And share lots of his wine with you. You will be wined and dined beyond your imagination.

You'll be making wine! You will harvest grapes with the vineyard manager, stomp grapes in wine barrels and see the process through the winery with the winemaker. A guest winemaker will show you exactly how to make wine and you will go home with a winemaking kit. Their sommelier will do an extensive food and wine-pairing educational experience. And they will send you home with lots of wine. *Now that is a great retreat!*

They also offer similar retreats, like the **Hands-On Olive Harvest Retreat**, of an extensive nature. There is also the **Hands-On Beekeeping Retreat**, which will captivate you on the lives of pollinators.

And more... There is **Horseback Riding** through the vineyards, along the Huerhuero River and up the rolling hills for a beautiful sunset. For photography lovers, the **Shutterbug Scavenger Hunt** or their **Outdoor Photography Workshop** will enhance your skills. How about **Archery** or an **Archery Class with Picnic Lunch**? In the culinary department, Chef Charlie does **Garden-To-Table Cooking Demos** and **Kitchen Skills Cooking Classes**, along with a **Chef Challenge** and **Sip-Like-A-Sommelier Training**, and **Winemaker-In-Training** classes, and they have bicycles at the inn for guests, plus offer a **Bike & Picnic Package**.

If that is not enough, join them for the annual **New Year's Eve CASSino Party** or their many **Five-Course Winemaker Dinners** throughout the year. What I have to say about all this is: *indulge!*

Calendared Events and Retreats
+1 805 239 1730, x111
Events@CassWines.com

Private Events, Retreats and Camps
+1 805 239 1730, x122
PrivateEvents@CassWines.com

CassWines.com/Camp-Cass

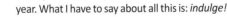

GENESEO INN – EIGHT LUXURY ROOMS

The Geneseo Inn is located on the Cass Winery property in the middle of their vineyards. Now this is the way to take in wine country!

The inn was created using commercial shipping containers. Beautiful modern architecture was produced here, inside and out (photos left and below). Luxury all the way. The containers are elevated above the vineyards so the view from your bed or balcony is magnificent across their vineyards with a backdrop of undeveloped rolling hills. Imagine enjoying a beautiful sunrise and a fresh cup of coffee (photo page 122).

The rooms are spacious, with high ceilings, modern design, luxury appointments, and refrigerators, coffee-makers, water, robes, daily surprise snacks, and a gourmet breakfast from their executive chef. Three types of breakfasts to choose from; changes daily (photo right).

Each room is named after a song. Mine was Country Road (photo right and below). When you enter the room, the Country Road song is playing to get you in the mood. Other rooms are White Rabbit, Ebony & Ivory, etc.

PRIVATE GUEST HOUSE

Located at a private corner of the Cass vineyards, with three bedrooms, two baths, a full kitchen, and front deck with vineyard views. This is definitely your get-away-from-it-all in-the-vineyards spot. It is a farmhouse described as having a shabby-chic interior. Includes telephone, Dish TV, Netflix, WiFi, and Pandora music.

SAN LUIS OBISPO **PASO ROBLES** GENESEO ■
Winery, Restaurant, Accommodations
CASS WINERY

$$$

7350 Linne Road
Paso Robles, CA 93446

+1 805 239 8969
TheInn@CassWines.com

CassWines.com/stay

Open: All Year, Everyday, 11am-5pm

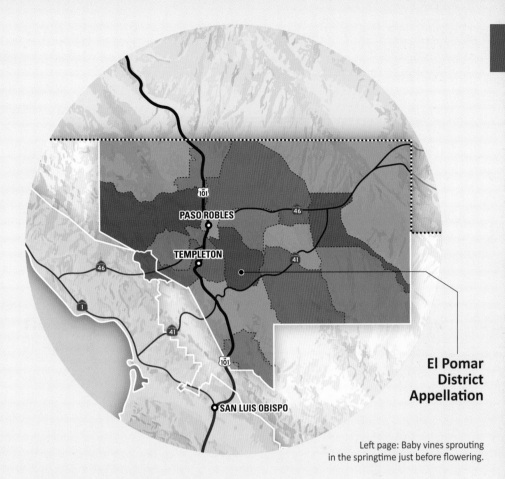

Left page: Baby vines sprouting
in the springtime just before flowering.

IN THE FACE OF TEMPLETON WINDS

The El Pomar District (AVA) is pretty much in the center of the Paso Robles AVA, just south of the Genseo AVA we explored just previously, on the east side of Paso, directly east of the Templeton Gap AVA.

East of the highway, this puts the El Pomar AVA in the hotter, drier area of the Paso Robles. Being directly east of Templeton Gap, puts El Pomar directly in the face of the cool the Templeton Gap winds that flow directly from the Pacific Ocean. Winds are typically 10-20 mph during the growing season. This creates hot days and cool nights, as much as 60° difference, ideal for wine-grape growing. As a result, some consider this AVA as having perfect terroir.

Originally, El Pomar was the almond capital of California with 1,375 acres of almond trees. Gradually the almond industry moved to the San Joaquin Valley

for easier farming. Vineyards took over. There are more than 2,000 acres of vines today.

This is a very special appellation; however, it is more of a growing region than where you will find wineries to visit. Many of the well-known wineries you know have vineyards here or purchase grapes from growers in this El Pomar AVA.

I have discovered two unique winery experiences for you here. One is a private personal tasting at the home of one of the largest growers and vineyard management families. The other is a hilltop winery where you can see the terroir, and feel the Templeton Gap winds, and enjoy lunch while tasting their wines.

Here are the two wineries to check out.

• Pomar Junction Vineyard & Winery, page 147
• Bovino Vineyards, page 149

$-$$-$$$

Merrill Family Private Wine Cellar
El Pomar AVA, Paso Robles, CA 93446

+1 805 238 9940
Info@PomarJunction.com

PomarJunction.com

Open: Private Tastings By Appointment Only

A farming family with personalized tasting in the Merrill family private wine cellar.

14,000 ACRES OF VINEYARDS

The Merrill family is a very special family. They are responsible for managing vineyards for some of the most well-known wineries to optimize the quality of their grapes. Remember, you must have high quality grapes to make high-quality wines. They also have 400 acres of vineyards on their estates in which they sell quality grapes to well-known wineries.

Here is the benefit to us. It is not just that they are highly coveted for their vineyard management expertise, which they apply to the 400 acres of vines they own themselves, they cherry-pick – or better said, grape-pick – the best of their vineyards to make their own wines. Don't be fooled by the playfulness of the train on their labels, these are actually very good wines.

Working the vineyards, the Merrills find that the diurnal effect in El Pomar is often 50° between day and night temperatures, and can be as much a 60° at times. This extreme is magical for grapes. They also credit the Templeton Gap for making the cooler years warmer in El Pomar and the hot years are cooler here.

I sat down with the Merrill family and tasted through some fifteen or so wines, and there were some real gems. For me, their Zinfandel Reserve was the rock star. Paso Robles is known for excellent Zinfandel, and who should know best, the Merrill family has one to impress.

Collection of Wines

<u>Reserve Wines</u>
Train Wreck (A Blend of the Winemaker's Favorite Barrels)
Cab Forward (Cabernet Sauvignon, Merlot, Petit Verdot)
The Crossing - GSM (Grenache, Syrah, Mourvèdre)
GSM Magnum (Grenache, Syrah, Mourvèdre)

Reserve Cabernet Sauvignon
Reserve Tempranillo
Reserve Zinfandel
Reserve Pinot Noir

<u>Estate Series</u>
Cabernet Sauvignon, Merlot, Petit Verdot
Syrah, Mourvèdre, Grenache Noir, Roussanne
Syrah Rose, Petit Sirah, Zinfandel

<u>White & Sweet Wines</u>
Cotes de Pomar Blanc (Roussanne, Granache Blanc, Viognier)
Viognier, Grenache Blanc
Muscat, Reserve Late Harvest Viognier

SAN LUIS OBISPO **PASO ROBLES** EL POMAR ■
Winery, Vineyards, Restaurant
BOVINO VINEYARDS

$$-$$$

5685 El Pomar Drive
Templeton, CA 93465

+1 805 238 2007
Info@BovinoVineyards.com

BovinoVineyards.com

Open: Friday-Monday, 11am-5pm
Reservations available on their website

A mazing views west, into the face of the Templeton Gap winds, and gorgeous sunsets.

A CATTLEMAN'S DREAM

This property is what I call a hobby vineyard, whereby the previous owner planted the ultimate selection of vines. Actually, this is thirty-two different hobby vineyards. Seventeen different grape varieties, planted in three different soil types, using four different root stocks to align the soil perfectly to the clones chosen for the vineyards above ground.

And the clones chosen make this a very exciting property as well. For example, the well-desired clones 4, 191 and 337 for Cabernet Sauvignon were grafted. Clone 467 for Sauvignon Blanc was used as well. For each grape variety, the best clones were matched with the best root stocks and married into each soil type and vineyard location. You only spend this much money on a perfect vineyard when it is a hobby, as how can you ever expect a return on this kind of investment?

Guess who benefits from all this? You and I, and the cattle rancher who purchased this eighty-three acre estate. And then he named the property and wines Bovino after the cattle. He has gone on to expand the winery, hire a very talented winemaker, and create a restaurant on top of the winery ... so all of us can enjoy this property.

I am a Bordeaux wine lover, as you have discovered in my *Exploring Wine Regions – Bordeaux France* book. The Cabernet Sauvignon here is excellent, as well as the other Bordeaux varietals. They make both Left Bank and Right Bank Bordeaux blends. *Joludi* (Joe-Lu-Dee) is the label, and they are getting 90-point scores.

Now, the best part of this property is the rooftop restaurant (photo above), open for lunch, and the best way to taste their wines. Get a bottle or glass of your favorite wine, or do a flight and discover their many wines as you enjoy lunch and the amazing views.

The Grenache here is totally awesome! And try the Albariño, its uniqueness is interestingly delightful. The Devilish Eggs (below) are topped with pickled mustard seeds and cornichons. Wow! The cheese and charcuterie plate pretty much shows all its yumminess.

Collection of Wines

Joludi - Left Bank Reserve
(Cabernet Sauvignon, Merlot, Cabernet Franc)
Joludi - Right Bank Reserve
(Petite Verdot, Merlot, Cabernet Franc)
Joludi - Cabernet Sauvignon

Joludi - Syrah
Joludi - Grenache
Joludi - GSM (Grenache, Syrah, Mourvèdre)

Joludi - Tempranillo
Joludi - Zinfandel
Joludi - Zinfandel OPA Reserve
Joludi - Sangiovese Reserve

Joludi - Arneis
Joludi - Albariño
Generosity (Sauvignon Blanc)
gen.er.os.i.ty - Rosé (Grenache, Syrah, Mourvèdre)

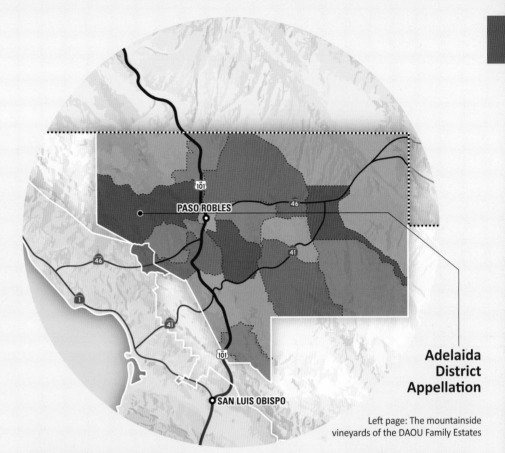

Adelaida District Appellation

Left page: The mountainside vineyards of the DAOU Family Estates

MOUNTAINOUS TERRAIN

The Adelaida District (AVA) is Paso Robles' northwest district, literally into the foothills of the Santa Lucia Mountains. The terrain here is more rugged, with greater elevations and steep slopes for the vines to struggle. Struggling is a good thing for vines.

The roads are wonderfully curvy meandering the mountainous terrain. It is also wetter here, with particularly clean air. Sounds perfect for viticulture. Indeed. And perfect for people too. It is beautiful in nature and clean blue skies. And there are places to stay the night as well.

The terroir in Adelaida AVA is expressively unique from the other AVAs. Not just in mountainous terrain; the soil contains ancient marine sediment with streaks of crystallized calcite and limestone. You will see the limestone blocks stacked for walls like you would see in Bordeaux France. See the resemblance coming? This AVA is idea for Bordeaux varietals.

With the highest elevation (2,300') in Paso Robles, the cool maritime influence of the Pacific Ocean in the mornings and the desert heat from the east in the afternoons, the diurnal effect here well exceeds 40°, ever so valuable to optimize grape quality.

This is obviously a very special place. With special wineries too. I have uncovered several unique, interesting and innovative wineries here to share with you. Great wines too and excellent culinary experiences, food and wine pairings, plus overnight accommodations at wineries.

- Adelaida Vineyards & Winery, page 153
- JUSTIN Vineyards & Winery, page 155
- Tablas Creek Vineyard, page 161
- Daou Vineyards, page 163
- La Cuvier Winery, page 165
- McPrice Myers Winery, page 167
- Alta Colina, page 171
- Six Mile Bridge, page 173
- LAW Estate Wines, page 175

ADELAIDA

ADELAIDA
VINEYARDS & WINERY

Michael Higgins

Signature Tasting

Sparkling Wine Signature 2017
HMR Estate Vineyard
Aged in French oak puncheons - 4 months

Anna's Red Signature 2018
Anna's Estate Vineyard
Aged in French oak 18% new - 18 months

93pts - Jeb Dunnuck

Syrah Signature 2014
Viking Estate Vineyard | Library Release
Aged in French oak 40% new - 18 months

92pts - Robert Parker's Wine Advocate

Cabernet Sauvignon Signature 2018
Viking Estate Vineyard

$$-$$$

5805 Adelaida Road
Paso Robles, CA 93446

+1 805 239 8980
Visit@Adelaida.com

Adelaida.com

Open: Wednesday-Monday, 10am-5pm

A large ranch comprised of numerous vineyards of different grapes chosen perfectly for each terroir.

EXTENSIVE HISTORY

Five decades ago, the Van Steenwyk family started investing here by acquiring a 500-acre ranch growing walnuts and almonds. They named it Hilltop Ranch, as the highest elevation property in the region at 2,320'.

A few years later, they acquired 400 more acres of neighboring HMR Ranch and Viking Ranch, with very steep slopes from 1,900' peaks and growing Cabernet Sauvignon. Now that is a stressed-out environment for grapes, which we know produces excellent wines.

This attracted John Munch (page 165) as their first winemaker. John was a wine Négociant at the time and created the Adelaida Cellars label that later became the name of the winery on this property. And, much later, became the name of the appellation for which they and thirty plus other wineries now reside.

Most surprising to me is the Pinot Noir vineyards on the HMR Ranch. Pinot Noir in Paso? That makes no sense! This is a warm climate growing Bordeaux and Rhone varietals, not Burgundian. Looking at this in further depth, these vineyards are planted in a unique microclimate at high elevation and in a north facing bowl within an east/west valley that invites fog, all

providing a colder environment for this cool-climate grape. Plus, these vineyards were planted in 1964. Imagine the quality of these sixty-year-old vines! I had to taste. Magnificent! An impressively beautiful wine.

The ranch is now over 2,000 acres, containing a culmination of strategically planted vineyards to take advantage of the terroir perfectly suited for each grape. As you can now imagine, the wines here are excellent.

The **Standard Tasting** is in the recently renovated and spacious winery with both indoor and outdoor spaces where reservations are not necessary.

The **Food & Wine Tasting** has a curated meal of expertly paired small bites with each Signature wine and is hosted in their private Library Room.

The **Signature Tasting** focuses on their Signature wines presented in their elegant Signature Room (photo above) and complimented with artisanal cheeses and charcuterie.

The **Hilltop Tasting** (photo left) is my favorite. They take you to the top of one of their mountain peaks for a stunning view of the valley while you taste through their best wines; with a **Signature Wine & Cheese Pairing** while relaxing on the shaded deck under a beautiful oak tree. This is a very romantic spot!

Collection of Wines

Cabernet Sauvignon Signature Series
Syrah Signature Series
Mourvèdre Signature Series

Viking Estate Cabernet Sauvignon
Michael's Estate Zinfandel
Anna's Estate Syrah
Anna's Estate Red (Grenache, Mourvèdre,
Petite Sirah, Syrah, Alicante Bouschet)
Anna's Estate Counoise

HMR Estate Vineyard Pinto Noir
HMR Estate Vineyard Chardonnay
Anna's Estate White (Roussanne, Grenache Blanc, Picpoul Blanc)
Adelaida Estate The Don (fortified sweet wine)

$-$$-$$$

11680 Chimney Rock Road
Paso Robles, CA 93446

+1 805 238 6932
Concierge@JUSTINWine.com

JUSTINWine.com

Tastings & Tours Open:
Every Day, 11am-4pm
Lunch: Seven Days, 11am-3pm
Dinner: Thursday-Saturday, from 6:30pm

A winery after your Bordeaux heart, that is making authentic blends of the Left and Right Banks.

BIG. BOLD. DELICIOUS.

The origins of this property date back to 1981. The vineyards have expanded quite a bit since they grew to better understand the Adelaida AVA terroir; however, their mission has always been to produce world-class Bordeaux blends. And that they do very well.

ISOSCELES is what we know to be their top wine. And it is great, if you have not tried it. ISOSCELES is a Left Bank Bordeaux blend, think Grand Cru Classé and the Médoc. If you have read my Bordeaux France book, you are up to speed on the qualities of this wine. Cabernet Sauvignon leads the way here. It is big, bold and rich with the Cabernet Sauvignon flavors we love so much.

JUSTIFICATION is their second wine, and really should not be considered a second wine. It is their first wine of Right Bank Bordeaux blend. It is Merlot and Cabernet Franc, just as they do it in Bordeaux. A softer wine because of the Merlot, yet still rich and full-bodied.

They have several tastings and tours. I am partial to the **Private Cave Tour & Tasting** (see cave entrance left page). This is both an indoor (winery and cave) and outdoor tour (vineyards and terroir) followed by a tasting of their signature wines.

Enjoy their large tasting bar inside with an extensive gift shop (photo next page). Outside are multiple tiers of open and spacious lounge areas to do tasting experiences. Or enjoy a glass of wine and relax as you take in the beautiful view of rolling hills of vineyards.

They also have a tasting room downtown across from the central park and offer shuttle service to the winery to dine. Speaking of dining, they have a very nice à la carte lunch menu and a fixed seven-course dinner of extraordinary cuisine (see next page).

Collection of Wines

ISOSCELES
(Bordeaux, Left Bank, First-Growth Style)
(Cabernet Sauvignon, Cabernet Franc, Merlot)
JUSTIFICATION
(Bordeaux, Right-Bank Style)
(Cabernet Franc and Merlot)
TRILATERAL (GSM: Grenache, Syrah, Mourvèdre)
SAVANT (Syrah, Cabernet Sauvignon)
RIGHT ANGLE (Cabernet, Malbec, Petite Sirah, Petit Verdot)
TRIAL (GSM: Grenache, Syrah, Mourvèdre)

Reserve Cabernet Sauvignon, Reserve Malbec,
Reserve Tempranillo, Cabernet Sauvignon,
Zinfandel, Merlot, Syrah

Chardonnay, Sauvignon Blanc, Viognier, Rosé

Sunny's Block (Orange Muscat Desert Wine)

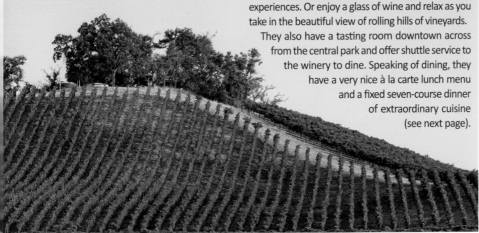

MICHELIN STAR RESTAURANT AT JUSTIN

SAN LUIS OBISPO **PASO ROBLES** ADELAIDA ■
Winery, Vineyards, Restaurant, Lodging
JUSTIN VINEYARDS & WINERY

$$-$$$-$$$$-$$$$$

+1 805 238 6932
Concierge@JUSTINWine.com

JUSTINWine.com

*The Restaurant at JUSTIN: Open All Year
Reservations are a must (lunch and dinner)!*

*Light Lunch: Seven Days, 11am-3pm
Extensive Lunch: Thursday-Sunday, 11am-3pm*

*Pre-Fixe Dinner Experience: Thursday-Saturday
Seatings: 6:30pm, 7:00pm, 7:30pm, and 8:00pm*

Michelin has discovered JUSTIN and Executive Chef Rachel Haggstrom hit the marks with both a star and green star awards. The food is imaginative, beautiful, deliciously captivating, and creatively presented. If you are into the very best of gourmet cuisine, and love fresh, locally inspired ingredients, you really must spend an evening here. They use artisan ingredients from local purveyors, with a kitchen team who is quite passionate about excellence. The evening is a seven-course fixed menu, paired with their wines and delivered with exceptional service. They also have a great lunch menu, which is à la carte with some very delicious choices. If you are into burgers, they are very impressive here (photo right). Both indoor and outdoor dining.

This is the ultimate way to experience the JUSTIN wines; in a well-crafted food and wine pairing experience. How can you possibly enjoy great wines without yummy foods involved. For lunch, they will suggest the right pairing based on each dish you order. For dinner, they orchestrate the perfect pairing and each wine is described as it's presented with each serving. They will also bring out their library wines to pair with dinner if you desire.

Ocean Trout Tartar-Stuffed Squash Blossom (photo left page): gazpacho vinaigrette, basil oil, Armenian cucumber, chive, opal basil, tomatoes, and tomato skin.

Sturia Caviar (photo below): sturia oscietra caviar, buckwheat pancake, poached onion, crème fraiche, egg crémeux, onion flower, chive baton, and society garlic.

Maine Lobster Tail (photo below right): Tahitian vanilla bean-poached lobster tail, cream of spinach, ravioli filled with lobster, ricotta, zucchini lobster powder, lobster jus (made with JUSTIFICATION), nasturtium flower, and nasturtium leaf.

JUST INN – FOUR VILLAS AND A CHÂTEAU

JUST INN is four very luxurious villas, three of which are in a private area behind the JUSTIN Hospitality Center. Private, yet close to everything, including the amazing restaurant. The fourth villa is located above the winery (imagine seeing the activity at harvest time). It is the largest and most spacious of the villas. It has a full-size chef's kitchen as well. All villas have fireplaces and separate bedrooms. Photos left and bottom left are of the upstairs **JUSTIFICATION Suite**, which has amazing views (see cover photo). Photo below and lower right are of the downstairs 1,200 sq' **ISOSCELES Suite**. All rooms come with a gourmet breakfast, either in-suite or outside on the patio overlooking the gardens (photo upper right): **Breakfast hash**: potatoes, mojo picon, estate vegetables, poached egg, filet, and avocado.

The **Château at JUSTIN** is a hilltop castle very much like you would see in Bordeaux France. It is a massive 29,000 sq' castle, plus an additional 15,000 sq' of outdoor space. It has four bedrooms and eight baths, along with everything that you would expect in a castle home. Includes a gourmet chef. Pricey, yet one-of a-kind amazing!

$$$$-$$$$$

+1 805 591 3224
Concierge@JUSTINWine.com

JUSTINWine.com

JUST INN: Open All Year
Call, Email or Room Bookings On Their Website

$$-$$$-$$$$

9339 Adelaida Road
Paso Robles, CA 93446

+1 805 237 1231
Visit@TablasCreek.com

TablasCreek.com

Open: Every Day, 10am-4pm

A partnership of Châteauneuf-du-Pape vines to produce authentic Rhône varietals in Paso.

EXPERIENCE RHÔNE EXCELLENCE

If it isn't the Bordeaux grapes that do well in Paso Robles, it is the Rhône varietals that excel here in a big way. And Tablas Creek Vineyard is leading the way. In partnership with Château de Beaucastel, a winery located in the southern part of the Rhône valley in France known for its excellent Châteauneuf du Pape wines, Tablas Creek is importing and propagating cuttings from their estate. To the tune of over a million vines! Tablas Creek has become the best source for Rhône vines in America.

At the helm is Jason Haas, Partner and General Manager, taking over from his father Robert Haas, an icon in the wine business who started Tablas Creek in his sixties as a second childhood. Robert was a well-known importer of French wines. For me, he is famous for buying most of Château Lafite and Pétrus' 1961 vintage when the British wine merchants balked at this stellar year's big price. The wine came to America. How lucky were we?!

As a notable wine importer, this is how Robert got to know the owners of Château de Beaucastel, and developed a relationship which ultimately brought their precious vines to Paso Robles. Today, more than 600 vineyards around the United States use these Tablas Creek cuttings. Remarkable!

The Mediterranean climate and limestone soil on their property is ideal for Rhône varietals. The way Jason sees it, they have rainforest winters (43" of rain in six months) and desert summers (2" of rain). With nearly half of their vines head-trained and no irrigation from their inception (photo left page), their vineyards are all organic, moving to biodynamic over the next ten years.

Tours can be any way you want them. Vineyard walks, history lessons, a petting zoo (they have animals). As much or as little as you want. They produce numerous and interesting blends, with grapes you know and love, and with grapes you have never heard of before (look right). I highly suggest a visit to see which blends meet your fancy.

Collection of Wines (Exclusively Rhône)

Flagship Wines (Chateau Beaucastel Estate)
Esprit de Tablas (Mourvèdre, Syrah, Grenache, Counoise)
Esprit de Tablas Blanc (Roussanne, Grenache Blanc, Picpoul Blanc, Picardan, Clairette Blanche)
Dianthus Rosé (Mourvèdre, Grenache, Counoise)

Special Rhône Blends
Patelin de Tablas (Grenache, Syrah, Counoise, Mourvèdre)
Patelin de Tablas Blanc (Viognier, Grenache Blanc, Marsanne, Roussanne)

Cotes de Tablas (Syrah, Grenache, Mourvèdre, Counoise, Terret Noir)
Cotes de Tablas Blanc (Grenache Blanc, Roussanne, Viognier, Marsanne, Clairette Blanche)
Cotes de Tablas Rosé (Grenache, Mourvèdre, Counoise)

Varietal Wines
Syrah, Grenache, Mourvèdre, Counoise, Tannat, Viognier, Grenache Blanc, Clairette Blanche, Marsanne, Bourboulenc, Roussanne, Picpoul Blanc, Vermentino

Sweet Wines
Petit Manseng, Vin de Paille (Roussanne), Vin de Paille Quintessence (Roussanne), Vin de Paille Sacrérouge (Mourvèdre)

$$-$$$-$$$$-$$$$$

2777 Hidden Mountain Road
Paso Robles, CA 93446

+1 805 226 5460
Visit@DaouVineyards.com

**DaouVineyards.com
PatrimonyEstate.com**

Open: Every Day, 10am-5pm

The Daou Mountain of very special terroir.

A PASSION FOR CABERNET

This is a wonderful success story. Two Lebanese brothers, while growing up in southern France, developed a passion for wine. This dream incubated for decades. After selling their stock in DAOU Systems, a networking technology company in San Diego California, that they founded and took public, Daniel and George Daou moved to Paso Robles to buy a mountain in the Adelaida District. I know that sounds like a mouthful, and it is.

DAOU Mountain is not just a beautiful piece of the Santa Lucia Mountain Range sitting at 2,200 feet elevation, it has very special terroir. Most notable is delineated by one of America's most influential winemakers, André Tchelistcheff (most known for defining the style of California's best wines, especially Cabernet Sauvignon), when he said **"this mountain is a jewel of ecological elements."**

This is a brand-new-everything endeavor! And recent! They purchased this property in 2007. And they only purchased dirt. No vines, no winery, not even a well or power. They started from scratch believing they had the ultimate terroir for Bordeaux varietals. This was a lot of imagination, a great deal of hard work and endless passion for greatness. Their attention to detail is obsessive. In the vineyard, every vine is cultivated for its purest expression. Daniel Daou is the winemaker, educated as a scientist, expressive as an artist. The perfect combination for a great winemaker.

Everything here is thought of in its perfect state and optimal opportunity. In the vineyard, for example, they harvest at night to optimize the grapes' perfect moment for harvest. In the winery, they purchased a very expensive optical sorter to precisely sort the grapes perfectly for each style of wine. The optics analyze each individual grape according to the specifications they define, removing every grape that does not meet their standards of excellence.

I could go on and on; rather, it is time to taste the results. The Cabernet Sauvignon here is to-die-for. You know I am a Cabernet lover, and this is a place to fall in love. Simply a bottle of Estate Cabernet Sauvignon, relaxing on top of their mountain, enjoying the view, and pondering... Happy!

You must try **Soul Of A Lion**, a Bordeaux blend of epic deliciousness! Cabernet Sauvignon dominant. And **PATRIMONY**, their Cabernet Sauvignon that achieved 100 points from Robert Parker. It is so profound, a new winery tasting room is being constructed to present and taste this masterwork.

Go visit their mountain. They have in-depth food and wine experiences, well-appointed indoor spaces, and massive outdoor grounds with many private tasting areas (photo left) and spectacular views from the mountaintop. More so, do their **Hidden Mountain Experience**; this is what is special here, it includes barrel tasting and their premium wines. They are warm, inviting people, so the connection and conversation on the walk will be particularly memorable.

Collection of Wines

Soul Of A Lion (Cabernet Sauvignon, Cabernet Franc, Petit Verdot)
Estate Mayote (Syrah, Cabernet Sauvignon, Petit Verdot)
Estate Micho (Merlot, Cabernet Sauvignon)
Reserve Eye Of The Falcon (Cabernet Sauvignon, Petit Verdot)
Unbound (Petite Sirah, Tannat, Tempranillo)
Reserve Seventeen Forty (Cabernet Franc, Merlot)
Pessimist (Petite Sirah, Zinfandel, Syrah, Lagrein)

PATRIMONY (98 Points, Cabernet Sauvignon)
Estate Cabernet Sauvignon
Cabernet Sauvignon
Pinot Noir

Estate Chardonnay
Daou Reserve Chardonnay
Chemin de Fleurs (Grenache Blanc, Roussanne, Viognier)
Reserve Rosé (Grenache)
Discovery Rosé (Grenache, Sauvignon Blanc.)
Sauvignon Blanc

John Munch, Owner, Le Cuvier Winery

$$$

23333 Vine Hill Lane
Paso Robles, CA 93446

+1 805 238 5706
Club@LCWine.com

LCWine.com

Open: Friday-Monday, 11am-5pm

Y east and other wine pathogens die of boredom unless given an interesting environment within which to practice their art.

– John Munch

INTERESTING GENTLEMAN

John Munch is clearly in a class by himself. To sit down with him for a glass of wine, as I did, and to ponder the meaning of wine, hmmm, another sip is needed. I discovered that John is as esoteric as he is logically understood. He just has a very different approach to making great wine. I suggest you check him out.

All of his wines spend thirty-three months in neutral oak barrels, and some wines far exceed the dance of three years in barrel. When the wine speaks to him, he knows it is great.

Yeast is not bored here! John really does create an environment for yeast to practice its art. It is a natural approach. Vineyards are not irrigated. Grapes sit in open vats with yeast dancing to the tune of its desire. Not a pretty sight to see, yet the magic created in this artistic endeavor is worth the patience. The supernatural really happens here.

Imagine his Cabernet Sauvignon aged in neutral oak barrels for five years! With 8% evaporation loss each year (fumes enjoyed by angels), this becomes a 40% wine-loss concentration. Imagine just how rich and smooth this wine has become. Magnifique!

John also uses the Solera Style of winemaking for his **Pentimento** Bordeaux blend. He breeds multi-year vintages together. Solera means "on the ground" in Spanish, referring to the lower level of barrels where the wine is transferred from barrel to barrel, top to bottom, the oldest mixtures being in the barrel right *on the ground*. This wine is a beautiful mix of the rich caramel of old wines and the fresh fruit of a new wine.

John comes from illustrious achievements. He created the iconic Adelaida Cellars (see page 153) as a Négociant to the outstanding winery it is today.

Make reservations for a food-and-wine-pairing lunch. It's a small place with a very talented chef. The cuisine above is for the wine pairing experience. An example of lunch is their duck breast over red wine and mushroom black pearl rice risotto, parsnip purée, parsley and basil foam, and raspberry dust with a chervil to provide the perfect garnish. Enjoy!

Collection of Wines
(all wines spend a minimum of 33 months in neutral oak)

La Veuve du Pape XLB (Syrah, Grenache, Petite Sirah)
Littoral (Bordeaux Blend)
Pentimento (Multi-Vintage, Solera Style, Bordeaux Blend)
L'enfant du Pape (Rhône Blend)
Veuve du Pape XLB (Rhône Blend)
Cabernet Sauvignon
Syrah XLB
Syrah
Malbec
Red Bat Cuvée (Petite Sirah, Zinfandel, Syrah)

NV Chardonnay XLB (Blend of 2006-2017 Vintages)

$$-$$$

3525 Adelaida Road
Paso Robles, CA 93446

+1 805 237 1245
VIP@McPriceMyers.com

McPriceMyers.com

Open: Every Day, 11am-5pm

GSM Rhône Valley wines you will never forget. The quality is extraordinary!

PASSION FOR FOOD AND WINE

This was one of the most amazing GSM experiences I've ever had (Grenache, Syrah, Mourvèdre). I don't know where you are in loving this classic Rhône blend. I have mixed feelings, as sometimes I love them, and sometimes I don't. I tasted through four of the GSMs here at McPrice Myers; each of them had different ratios of the three grapes, and I love them all. Love them!

Why? Why were they all extraordinary GSMs, even though the ratio of the grapes changed? My theory, as I got to know the owner and winemaker Mac Myers, is it's because he passionately loves these wines. He is in love with France's Rhône Valley and everything it represents in wine and food. He has made it his mission and passion to know these grapes and how to make extraordinary Rhône wines. We sure are the happy recipients of his devotion.

In talking with Mac, I realized he knows almost as much about the Rhône Valley as the people who live there. He goes often! Takes his wines. Does blind wine tastings with them. Eats at their extraordinary restaurants, and does numerous food and wine pairings. Mac has become an expert in making Rhône style wines.

Here in Paso Robles, Mac is particular in his choice of vineyards for the quality of grapes he demands. Fermentation is well thought-through as well; like when I was there, they were stomping grapes with their feet in the old style to get the profile he wanted from the grapes. He has his own vineyards above the winery on steep hillside property. They are stunningly beautiful while tasting outdoors (photo above). On top of the hill is a beautiful house they rent (see next page).

Let me tell you a little bit about why the GSM is a great blend. First of all, GSM is the name of the blend, not the order of the dominant grape. It could be an SGM or GMS; however, the trade name stays the same. It all depends on the winemaker and the quality and expression of each grape that vintage.

GSM is a full-bodied red wine blend of the southern Rhône Valley, particularly Châteauneuf-du-Pape. Of the three main varietals used to make this wine, Grenache tends to be the most dominant grape used, providing the softness, spiced-berry flavors, red fruits, and a round mouthfeel to the wine. Syrah brings structure to the wine, lots of dark fruit flavors and aromas such as blackberries, plums, black pepper, bacon, and leather. Mourvèdre brings a floral and herbaceous aroma, and the tannins bring color pigments and length to the wine.

Collection of Wines

Proprietary Series
Cuvée Kristina (Syrah, Grenache, Viognier)
Altas Viñas (Mourvèdre, Syrah, Grenache)
L'Ange Rouge (Grenache, Syrah, Mourvèdre)
Sel De La Terre (Grenache)
Brave Fortune (Syrah)
Fait Accompli (Syrah, Cabernet Sauvignon, Petit Verdot)

Single Vineyard Series
Hommage A Stevan Larner (Syrah, Grenache)
Estate Cuvée (Syrah, Grenache, Mourvèdre, Viognier)
Paper Street Cuvée (Syrah, Grenache, Mourvèdre, Petite Sirah, Graciano)
The Brightest Star (Zinfandel, Petite Sirah, Grenache)
Clariette Blanche (Paper Street Vineyard)
Viognier (Ballard Canyon, Santa Ynez Valley)

Three - Beautiful Earth Series Wines
Four - Hard Working Wine Series

HILLTOP HOME – ABOVE THE VINEYARDS

The McPrice Myers Winery is located at the base of a pretty steep hillside that they have covered with beautiful vineyards. They carved a road circling around through the vineyards and winding around the hills until you get to the very top. Hilltop is a beautifully renovated luxury-modern home overlooking the valley of vineyards (photo below left). *And the home is available to rent!*

The living area is spectacular, a huge open space of tall ceilings, open through the living room, dining room and kitchen, facing the amazing views (photo left page). The full kitchen has everything you would need.

The master bedroom suite is beautiful and romantic. Check out the two photos below. You gotta love the bathroom, with the big tub in the walk-in glass shower. So sexy!

This is a full three-bedroom home, with the other two bedrooms (and their own separate bathrooms) on the opposite side of the house for master suite privacy.

The massive outdoor patio has an infinity swimming pool, gas grill and insane views. Dinner with sunsets and coffee for the sunrise are a beautiful aspect of staying here.

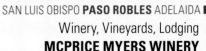

SAN LUIS OBISPO **PASO ROBLES** ADELAIDA

Winery, Vineyards, Lodging
MCPRICE MYERS WINERY

$$$$$

3525 Adelaida Road
Paso Robles, CA 93446

+1 805 237 1245
VIP@McPriceMyers.com

McPriceMyers.com/stay

SAN LUIS OBISPO **PASO ROBLES** ADELAIDA ■
Winery, Vineyards, Cuisine
ALTA COLINA

$$-$$$

2825 Adelaida Road
Paso Robles, CA 93446

+1 805 227 4191
Visit@AltaColina.com

AltaColina.com

Open: Thursday-Monday, 10am-4pm

Whether you like Syrah or not, you must visit this winery and experience their wines.

RHÔNE EXPERTS HERE

There I was, visiting a winery that specializes in Syrah wines. Syrah is really not my cup of tea or glass of wine. I know others who love this grape. How will I write good things about Alta Colina? Once in a while I taste a Syrah that blows me away in deliciousness. So maybe I need to be open-minded, and learn something from these Rhône/Syrah experts.

There I was, standing on top of their 1,800-foot mountain – and let me tell you, it was a very steep climb up that mountain – now looking across vineyards on varying slopes (photo above). I was with the owner, Bob Tillman, and the winemaker, Molly Lonborg. They were pointing out the various Rhône varietals they were growing, mostly Syrah. Then the bottles came open. I had not yet informed them of my dilemma.

Sure enough, the Syrah was not very exciting. And I was honest with them. No problem, they were not flustered at all. They simply poured me a new glass from a different bottle. This was a totally different experience. This was an exciting wine. Big with soft tannins and beautiful black fruit! Delicious! This was a Syrah from a different clone from a different hillside.

Now it was time to talk dirty. What was I drinking? I needed to know. And how can I pick my kind of Syrah in the future? The simple answer was: **Old 900** is their label, and if I stuck with them, I would always be happy. You may prefer their other Syrahs. They have many.

I was sitting with the two experts: this was an opportunity. My eyes were opened. First was the clone, which they were able to obtain from the famed Rhône producer John Alban, who snuck in this noteworthy clone from France, along with an extra-special Viognier. Today, it is growing in a different location at Alta Colina, a north-facing, cool slope (photo left) in this warm region. These grapes are getting the best of both the warm and cool expressions in the wine. Now I have found an excellent Syrah to stick with drinking.

The winery is a modern building right off Adelaida Road. It is a canyon here, with a steep hillside behind the winery. This is where they had to carve a road into the hill to get to the top. Only fifty yards per year is all the county would let them cut. At the top are the vineyards and where you can have an amazing tasting experience. This is what you can enjoy at the winery.

• **The Tasting Room**. Personalized tastings of their Rhône wines in the winery tasting room.
• **Taste Behind The Cellar Door**. This is an educational tasting experience among the oak barrels inside their barrel room.
• **Taste On The Vineyard**. This is where I was: on top of their mountain with stunning views. Sit under a massive oak tree and learn about their vineyards, organic farming, and the varying terroir and clones that make each wine special as you drink them.

Collection of Wines

Old 900 (Syrah)
Keystone (Syrah)
Toasted Slope (Syrah)
Downslope Red (Syrah, Grenache)
Carbonic (Grenache)
Petillant Natural (Grenache)
GSM (Grenache, Syrah, Mourvèdre)
Sun Worshipper (Mourvèdre)
Ann's Block (Petit Sirah)

Model Citizen (Roussanne)
Claude Cuveé (Marsanne)
12 O'Clock High (Viognier)
Grenache Blanc
Rosé (Grenache)
Vin De Paille (Viognier Desert Wine)

$$-$$$

5120 Peachy Canyon Road
Paso Robles, CA 93446

+1 805 239 5844
Contact@Sixmilebridge.com

Sixmilebridge.com

Open: Every Day, 10am-3:45pm

Collection of Wines

Cabernet Sauvignon
Cabernet Franc

Shannon (Left Bank) (Cabernet Sauvignon, Merlot,
Malbec, Cabernet Franc, Petit Verdot)
Shannon Extended Aging (36 months in French oak)

Limerick (Right Bank) (Merlot, Petit Verdot,
Cabernet Sauvignon, Cabernet Franc)

Incantation (Malbec, Cabernet Sauvignon, Petit Verdot)

Paladin (Zinfandel, Cabernet Sauvignon, Merlot,
Petit Verdot, Cabernet Franc, Malbec)

Rosé (Cabernet Franc)
Sauvignon Blanc (Sauvignon Blanc)

When you love Cabernet Sauvignon wines so much, you acquire an excellent property to cultivate excellent Bordeaux blends.

DREAM COME TRUE

You might be wondering, where is the bridge? Six miles is a very long crossing. What could possibly need that expansiveness in Paso? Well, Sixmilebridge is actually the name of a little town in Ireland once home to this winery's owner, James Moroney, and his family. There is a very interesting history about this town if you want to look it up. Today, the name represents the full circle of Jim's passion for wine.

On his journey to Paso Robles, Jim was in the publishing business in Texas. You just gotta love those publishing people :). Jim and his wife, Barbara, are very nice people, and they have created a very friendly hospitable environment visiting the winery.

The property has unusually steep slopes planted to grapes. I can attest to a wild ride down the slopes better than an amusement park ride (photo left page). These slope-stressed vines are in soils of limestone and clay. Sounds like Bordeaux to me.

The first vineyards were planted on the limestone in 2013, and the second planting was on clay in 2018.

The goal here is to produce the kind of wines that people who seek outstanding wines look to find. While the vineyards are still young here, the rich qualities are already pronounced. This is a winery to put on your watch list and start collecting.

The focus here is very straight forward, with only a few wines, and all Bordeaux blends. A little Zinfandel though. Why? Well, because it is Paso and things are creatively different here.

My favorite is their Shannon. This is a classic Bordeaux Left Bank blend, utilizing all five Bordeaux varietals with Cabernet Sauvignon predominant.

• **The Sixmilebridge Flight**. A standard flight of their wines in the main tastings room.

• **The Sixmilebridge Reserve Flight**. An educational experience exploring barrel selections and vintage offerings in their Reserve Room.

• **The Sixmilebridge Deck**. Beautiful wooden decks have been created under large oak trees alongside a towering sloped vineyard. Here you purchase bottles of wine (no tasting flights) and bring lunch to enjoy a picnic in this peaceful setting.

SAN LUIS OBISPO **PASO ROBLES** ADELAIDA ■
Winery, Vineyards, Cuisine
LAW ESTATE WINES

$$$-$$$$

3885 Peachy Canyon Road
Paso Robles, CA 93446

+1 805 226 9200
Info@LAWEstateWines.com

LAWEstateWines.com

Open: Thursday-Tuesday, 10am-4pm

H ave you fallen in love with Grenache wines yet? This is a premier winery to discover the very best in Grenache and interesting Grenache blends.

EARTH'S EXPLORATION

The owners of LAW Estate Wines, Don and Susie Law, have devoted a career to exploring Earth in search of oil and gas. In following their wine passion, for years they exhaustingly scoured California's soil in search of the perfect location to produce ultra-premium Rhône style wines. And you guessed it, they dug soil pits to analyze the earth to know the best terroir to plant their favorite grapes. They dug forty-two pits on the property alone to find the limestone and low-vigor soil they needed for the best Grenache you will experience.

If you have not fallen in love with Grenache yet, this place will spoil you. Try their Black Label of 100% Grenache and discover their concentration of the rich flavors of this delicate wine. Knowing Grenache, you would not expect it to be a full-bodied wine. This is truly an amazing wine. It has the complexity and boldness of a Bordeaux wine, yet keeps the fresh ripe-fruit flavors to love about Grenache. This wine received a 99-point score!

Now onto their White Label wines. These are their blends. I am particularly fond of the Audacious. The name fits my personality. Plus, the blend has two of my favorite grapes: Grenache and Cabernet Sauvignon. Imagine a bold Grenache as I described earlier, and now add the big bold grape of Cabernet Sauvignon. Add a touch of Carignan and Syrah and this is an awesome blend. Like I said, they are focused on ultra-premium, and you will be spoiled.

To go with these beautifully opulent wines is an atmosphere of elegance when you visit. Modern architecture with a warm homey feel. Choose the living-room setting in front of the fireplace, as I did (photo above), and you have the ultimate visiting experience.

Every tasting is by reservation only in this seated atmosphere. You receive a dedicated host to create a personalized relationship with you and their wines. Both indoor and outdoor seating has amazing views of the rolling hillside of vineyards.

Collection of Wines

The Nines (Grenache)
Prima (Mourvèdre)
Intrepid (Syrah)

Beguiling (Grenache, Syrah)
Aspire (Syrah, Grenache)
Audacious (Grenache, Carignan, Cabernet Sauvignon, Syrah)
Sagacious (Grenache, Syrah, Mourvèdre)
Beyond Category (Tempranillo, Grenache, Graciano, Carignan)
First Tracks (Petit Verdot, Cabernet Sauvignon, Syrah)

Rosé (Grenache, Mourvedre, Syrah, Carignan)
Soph (Roussanne, Marsanne, Clairette Blanche)

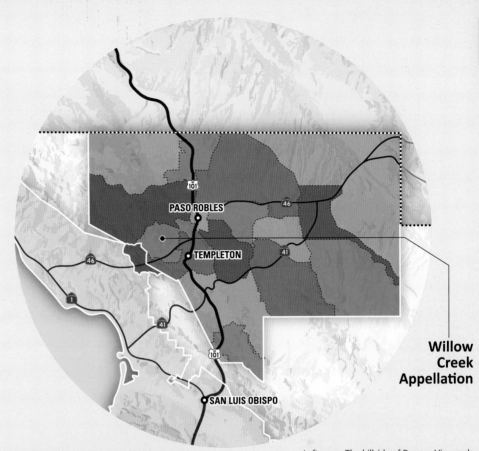

Willow Creek Appellation

Left page: The hillside of Denner Vineyards

COOLEST & WETTEST AVA

The Willow Creek District (AVA) is adjacent south of the Adelaida AVA in the foothills of the Santa Lucia Mountain and shares many of the same characteristics, primarily the mountainous terrain and coastal weather influences.

Willow Creek is the wettest and coolest AVA in Paso Robles. Agriculture began here because of the high quantities of rainfall for dry farming prior to irrigation. The AVA gets its name from the Willow Creek that runs through the middle of the AVA, as well as the willow trees that prosper along the streams and riverbanks here. The oldest vineyard in Paso Robles is here, the Ueberroth Vineyard, farmed by **Turley Wine Cellars** as a single-vineyard wine.

Since a winery, and an AVA elsewhere, already use the Willow Creek name, the official name here to distinguish the unique qualities of this terroir is: The Paso Robles Willow Creek District.

I feel it is important to distinguish the northern part of this AVA, which shares the very similar mountainous terroir and is adjacent to Adelaida's AVA, and the southern tip of this AVA, adjacent the Templeton Gap AVA and fully exposed to the benefits of the strong Templeton Gap winds.

There are many great wineries here, and I separate the central and southern tip (along Highway 46 West) wineries for you.

----Willow Creek AVA (CENTRAL)----
• Opolo Vineyards, page 179
• Denner Vineyards, page 183
----Willow Creek AVA (SOUTHERN TIP)----
• Booker Vineyard, page 185
• Niner Wine Estate, page 187
• Barton Family Wines, page 191
• Hunt Cellars, page 195
• Turley Wine Cellars, page 197

$-$$

7110 Vineyard Drive
Paso Robles, CA 93446

+1 805 238 9593
Info@Opolo.com

Opolo.com

Open: Every Day, 10am-5pm

Collection of Wines

Mountain Zinfandel
Reserve Zinfandel
Cabernet Sauvignon
Reserve Cabernet Sauvignon
Fusion (Cabernet Sauvignon, Syrah)
Serenade (Cabernet Sauvignon, Malbec)
Concerto (Merlot, Cab Franc, Cab Sauv, Petit Verdot)
Grand Rouge (Grenache, Syrah, Counoise, Mourvèdre)
Sangiovese

Albarino
Viognier
Rosé (Grenache, Syrah, Viognier)
Flirtations (Muscat Cannelli, Sweet Wine)
Blanc De Blancs (Sparkling Methode Champenoise)

Collection of Distilled Spirits

Chamomile Liqueur, Coffee Liqueur,
Walnut Liqueur, Chocolate Mint Liqueur

Cherry Brandy, Fig Brandy, Pear Brandy, VS Brandy,
Malt 'n Oats, and Grappa

W ine and spirits tastings, and pairings, plus wood-fired pizza, in a large open-air patio.

FLAGSHIP MOUNTAIN ZINFANDEL

You may know the Opolo name because of their widely distributed Mountain Zinfandel. This is the most planted grape on their 300 acres of vineyards. This is a big beautiful property of rolling hills of vineyards and oak trees in the mountainous region of the Willow Creek AVA.

Opolo's vineyards were first planted in 1995, and now, today, they have a full line up of what works great in Paso Robles... Rhône and Bordeaux varietals, and Zinfandel. When you visit the winery, you must also taste their Reserve Zinfandel, the very best barrels of their Mountain Zinfandel.

A visit here is filled with so much to experience. Consider staying the night as well (next page). Their original winery has been converted into a very cool open-air patio. Here you can do tastings, and I recommend their very well-orchestrated pairing experience. The wine comes with a large platter of artisan cheeses, fruits, nuts, and specialty meats aligned with each wine they serve. And add lunch, too, to enjoy the afternoon. They cook creatively delicious pizza in their wood-fired oven on the patio. Plus, they serve a couple of inspiring salads and an assortment of delicious sausages.

WILLOW CREEK DISTILLERY

Opolo has built an entire distillery on premises in the original winery and beside the large patio tasting area. You must go in and visit. They are making some really interesting spirits.

I particularly love their fruit brandies. Maybe because I am a fruit lover, these are very good. The fruit flavors were so pronounced, sipping was endlessly delicious. My favorite was the pear brandy (see photo right).

THE INN AT OPOLO & THE NUT HOUSE

Here is an opportunity to enjoy accommodations in the vineyards. Away from the winery activities, and amongst large oak trees and vineyards, The Inn at Opolo Vineyards has three unique luxury suites (photo below top). These rooms are comfy and spacious, complete with fireplaces (a great place in the winter) and big soaking tubs. They also have an outdoor balcony and romantic sitting spots under the trees.

The food is excellent as well. Breakfast comes with the rooms, and it's hot made-to-order cuisine (see photo left page) with fresh orange juice, sparkling wine, mixed fruit and fresh coffee. The eggs benedict is a real treat here. Every afternoon, they bring you wine and appetizers. This is a classy place with many extras you will love in the room.

Opolo Vineyards also has walnut orchards on the property. Atop a hill in one of the orchards is The Nut House, where I thought the recommendation was because of my personality. This is a huge one-bedroom home for rent (see the three photos bottom and right) and comes with all the same services and cuisine as The Inn at Opolo. This is a spacious executive-style home with a full kitchen, dining room, living room, and huge master bedroom suite complete with whirlpool tub. The outside patio overlooks the orchards and vineyards, perfect for breakfast (photo left).

SAN LUIS OBISPO **PASO ROBLES** WILLOW CREEK
Winery, Vineyards, Restaurant, Lodging
OPOLO VINEYARDS

$$$-$$$$

7110 Vineyard Drive
Paso Robles, CA 93446

+1 805 238 9593
Info@Opolo.com

Opolo.com

$$$

5414 Vineyard Drive
Paso Robles, CA 93446

+1 805 239 4287
TastingRoom@DennerVineyards.com

DennerVineyards.com

Open: Every Day, 10am-4pm

Making wines to cause sensory experiences, reflecting the specific vineyard property.

BEAUTIFUL VIOGNIER

This was a dream for Ron Denner, previously of the Ditch Witch, to find the perfect piece of dirt to make world-class wines. While Ron certainly has a career in knowing dirt, he enlisted the expertise of John Crossland of the famous Beckstoffer Vineyards in Napa Valley to design and plant his vineyards. The best way to world-class wine is by planting world-class vineyards. This, Ron has been serious about.

Next, Denner consulted with Justin Smith, the talented winemaker/owner of Saxum Vineyards (wines scoring 99 points), to implement sustainable farming practices with the aim to allow the wines to reflect the vineyard.

We can see how Denner has set up their course for success. As Justin Smith would say: "If a wine can show the best possible expression of where it came from and what season it was grown in, as well as please the senses, you have a great bottle."

Denner wants the wines to express the fabulous vineyards, and in so doing, they avoid foreign elements like commercial yeast or enzymes or other winemaking products they feel blur the essence of the vineyards terroir. Their end goal with all their wines is to cause another sensory experience other than just the act of drinking the wine, all an expression of the this beautiful place.

And with all this, great bottles of wine are emerging! I am a Viognier fan, especially Condrieu France, and overly critical of California Viognier wines. So, when Denner's winemaker Anthony Yont told me that he is tasting the best white wines off this property, it was time to open a bottle of his Viognier.

Let's understand the unique elements that go into making this wine. It is aged exclusively in oak Cigar Barrels (long 600-litre cigar-shaped vessels) to provide greater contact with its lees (the heavy sediment). This builds creaminess in the wine. His Viognier is beautifully rich and elegant, with nice acidity, texture and flavors. I will be back for more!

You will love the beautiful environment here for tastings. The indoor design is modern, with large high-ceiling expansive windows. The outdoor patio overlooks the valley, rolling hills and vineyards. And there is a cozier, romantic fireside setting as well.

Collection of Wines

Cabernet Sauvignon (Cabernet Sauvignon, Petit Verdot)
Mother of Exile (Cabernet Sauvignon, Petit Verdot, Merlot, Cabernet Franc)
Grenache (Grenache, Cinsaut, Mourvèdre)
Ditch Digger (Grenache, Mourvèdre, Syrah, Cinsaut, Counoise, Graciano)
Syrah (Syrah, Roussanne, Grenache)
Dirt Worshipper (Syrah, Viognier, Roussanne)
Sacred Burro (Carignan, Cabernet Sauvignon, Grenache)
Zinfandel (Zinfandel, Tempranillo)

Viognier (100% Viognier)
Theresa (Roussanne, Grenache Blanc, Marsanne, Picpoul, Vermentino)
Rosé (Cinsaut, Grenache, Carignan, Mourvèdre)

$$-$$$-$$$$

2644 Anderson Road
Paso Robles, CA 93446

+1 805 237 7367
Info@BookerWines.com

BookerWines.com

Open: Every Day, 10am-5pm

A n extravagant encounter of beautiful elegance, opulence and refinement.

SIMPLE • ELEGANT • DIVINE

When you arrive at this property, you will quickly notice the simplicity of design. Modern, inviting lines, and elegance in the interior and architecture. It will put you in the mood for desiring exceptionally well-crafted wines. Wines of elegance and rich beauty. And Booker delivers in every way imaginable. Even the wine list is simple. Just eight straightforward labels. Mostly Rhône and mostly single varietal.

After seven years of working for legendary winemakers Justin Smith (Saxum) and Stephan Asseo (L'Aventure), Eric and Lisa Jensen wanted to purchase an extraordinary vineyard to grow the very best fruit for the very best winemaking. They ultimately acquired a special parcel of a hundred acres of the 1,200-acre Booker Estate donated to charity after the Booker brothers' deaths.

Four years later though, the Jensens decided to bottle their own wine, wines that they believed would be considered world-class. Perfect farming. On extreme vertical slopes (photo left). Organic.

Biodynamically inspired. Then using a very soft touch in winemaking to allow the extraordinary fruit to manifest into remarkable wines. Success might best be revealed by Robert Parker's multiple 99- and 100-point scores!

They have five very nice visiting options...

• **Classic Tasting**. A seated tasting of current releases. Music included.

• **Cave Experience**. A private guide drives you throughout the property, then into the barrel room to an elegant living room in a cave for tasting library wines and listing to vinyl records.

• **Terrace Tasting**. Enjoy a special terrace tucked into the hillside vineyard. Taste member exclusives, newest releases and highly sought-after wines (photo above).

• **Bocce & Bottles**. Buy bottles and get exclusive use of their outdoor lounge and bocce ball court. Perfect for a larger group.

• **Private Event**. Intimate or group, fully customized, including dinners. A totally VIP experience in their private indoor and outdoor areas. Enjoy their most sought-after wines in a specially created occasion.

Collection of Wines

ONES Syrah (100% Cabernet Sauvignon)

Fracture (100% Syrah)
Ripper (100% Grenache)
Tempranillo (100% Tempranillo)

Oublié (Grenache, Syrah, Mourvèdre)
Vertigo (Syrah, Mourvèdre, Grenache, Viognier)

White (Viognier, Roussanne, Chardonnay, Marsanne)
Pink (Rosé of Grenache)

$$-$$$

2400 Highway 46 West
Paso Robles, CA 93446

+1 805 239 2233
Info@NinerWine.com

NinerWine.com

Open: Every Day, 10am-5pm

Collection of Wines

Fog Catcher
(Cabernet Sauvignon, Petit Verdot, Cabernet Franc, Malbec, Carménère)
Reserve Twisted Spur
(Petit Verdot, Syrah, Cabernet Sauvignon)
Reserve Cabernet Sauvignon - Bootjack Ranch
(Cabernet Sauvignon, Petit Verdot, Malbec)
Reserve Cabernet Sauvignon - Heart Hill Vineyard
(Cabernet Sauvignon)
Reserve Cabernet Franc
(Cabernet Franc, Malbec, Cabernet Sauvignon)
Reserve Syrah (Syrah)
Reserve Grenache (Grenache, Syrah)

Syrah
Malbec
Pinot Noir
Sangiovese
Cabernet Sauvignon

Chardonnay and Reserve Chardonnay
Blanc de Noirs (Pinot Noir Méthode Traditionnelle)

N umerous tours, wine and food experiences, all to plan the best afternoon of your life.

FOOD AND WINE

You will love this place. It is all about food and wine experiences, and there are many to choose from. I suggest indulging!

Almost everything here brings both food and wine together in experiences. For me, this is the only way to drink wine (with food) or to eat food (wine is a must). Here, it all happens in a very delicious way.

"We believe that the most memorable experiences happen at the intersection of fantastic food and wine." — Niner Wine Estate

Niner focuses on Bordeaux wines, and they do them well (their Reserve Cabernet Sauvignon is outstanding!). They also own a vineyard to the south in the cool climate of the Edna Valley (San Luis Obispo). There, they grow Pinot Noir and Chardonnay, in which they produce, and make available here at the winery in Paso Robles.

An abundance of experiences and tours...
• **Estate Tasting**. Tasting of a flight of four wines.
• **Lunch & Estate Tasting**. A delicious lunch paired with a flight of four wines.
• **Fog Catcher Tasting**. An elevated experience in their special tank room with a flight of reserve and library wines. This is a more in-depth service if you want to talk wine with an educated server. Lunch can be served as well.
• **Hillside Picnic Tour & Tasting**. Tour of their hillside vineyard with an impressive picnic and wine tasting at the top of the hill overlooking the vineyards.
• **Vineyard & Winery Tour**. Tour of both vineyards and the impressive winery (photo left).
• **Vineyard Progressive Tour & Tasting**. A tour of three different locations in their vineyards. You will hear the story of each vineyard and taste wines made from the grapes of these vineyards, all paired with small bites.
• **Garden Tasting**. A three-course structured food-and-wine-pairing experience in the half-acre Chef's Garden.

THE NINER RESTAURANT

$-$$-$$$

2400 Highway 46 West
Paso Robles, CA 93446

+1 805 239 2233
Info@NinerWine.com

NinerWine.com

Niner Restaurant: Open All Year
Available with wine tasting reservations!

Lunch: Seven Days, 10am-4pm

A great feature of the Niner Wine Estates is their gourmet restaurant. As you saw on the previous page, there are many food aspects to the experiences here, and this is a real restaurant with full meals. Wine is best experienced with foods paired well with them.

Jacob Burrell is their Executive Chef. He comes to Niner with experience from many well-known restaurants around the world, including the Michelin three-star Manresa Restaurant, Sierra Mar at Post Ranch Inn and the Big Sur Bakery. And he is an Iron Chef winner! Are you getting the idea that the food here is really good?

They serve meat, fish, chicken, salads, and pasta meals, along with other creative dishes. And the fresh-baked bread is out-of-this-world decadently delicious. Niner maintains a half-acre Chef's Garden to provide fresh fruits, vegetables, herbs, and edible flowers for their lunch menu. Lunch is served seven days a week. They create one or two public dinners every month (call for the schedule). Every Friday night during the summer is Niner Nights, a casual setting for club members to drink wine and enjoy delicious bites while watching the sunset.

Winter Salad With Garden Beets (photo below): beets from their garden, Rogue River blue cheese (Oregon), winter greens (endive is pictured).

Farmers Cheese With Focaccia (photo right): fromage Blanc from Stepladder Ranch & Creamery, herbs from their garden, sourdough focaccia that they bake fresh each morning. And I am telling you, this bread is out-of-this-world delicious.

Fava Bean Pasta (photo below right): simple winter/spring pasta with fava beans from their garden, pork sausage from JR Meats, locally handmade Etto pasta.

$$-$$$

2174 Highway 46 West
Paso Robles, CA 93446

+1 805 237 0771
Howl@GreyWolfCellars.com

BartonFamilyWines.com

Open: Every Day, 11am-5pm

Long-established winery adds a delicious restaurant and a small-batch distillery.

TERROIR-FOCUSED WINES

Barton Family Wines is a family-owned-and-operated business that has three labels of wines, a restaurant and a distillery, all on the same property. It's the husband-wife team of Joe and Jenny Barton, along with their two daughters and Joe's mother.

Joe suddenly stepped into this business when his father tragically passed away when Joe was only twenty-three years old. Reminds me of Baron Philippe Rothschild, who took over the family business Château Mouton Rothschild at age twenty. Just like the Baron, Joe has made this his lifelong passion: over two decades already (since 1998) of producing award-winning wines. Joe was recognized by his peers as San Luis Obispo County's **Winemaker of the Year** in 2020 for his outstanding achievements and contributions to the industry.

Barton's success comes from his focus on vineyards. Joe is a farmer; he loves tractors and bud breaks. He is a Cal Poly fruit science major who puts his focus on finding and cultivating the best vineyards, particularly dry-farmed vineyards.

Joe has been able to understand the distinct microclimates within several of the Paso Robles AVAs. This has led him to create wines which characterize each unique terroir. You must taste his wines. You will appreciate how he has brought out the best expression of each varietal, and to really recognize this, most wines are single varietal (see below right).

You will also discover some hard-to-find varietals on the wine list here. Counoise anyone? How about Picpoul Blanc or Clairette Blanc? Check out their Bitter Sweet Apéritif (left page). Most of his wines are dipped in wax, giving the extra-nice touch of a luxury wine.

The visits here are straightforward. Come for a tasting. Have a food and wine pairing. Have lunch. Enjoy a bottle on the patio for the afternoon. Taste the spirits. Enjoy a unique cocktail. You can really enjoy the day here.

Collection of Wines

Paradise City (Syrah)
Purple Rain (Pinot Noir)
Simple Man (Zinfandel)
Danger Zone (Mourvèdre)
The Dance (Cabernet Sauvignon)
Hot Blooded (Counoise)
Mr. Jones (Grenache)
Stayin' Alive (Merlot)
California Love (Grenache, Counoise)
Watchtower (Syrah, Grenache, Mourvèdre)

Sweet Garden (Chardonnay)
Broken Road (Viognier)
Tiny Dancer (Picpoul Blanc)
Summertime (Grenache Blanc)
Holiday (Clairette Blanc)
Pet-Nat (Sparkling Clairette Blanc)
Bittersweet Symphony (Apertife - Grenache Blanc, Viognier)

GREY Label (eight additional wines)
Grey Wolf Label (four additional wines)

Winery, Vineyards, Restaurant, Distillery
BARTON FAMILY WINES

KROBAR CRAFT DISTILLERY

2174 Highway 46 West
Paso Robles, CA 93446

+1 (833) 576-2271
Steve@KrobarDistillery.com

KrobarDistillery.com

Open: Thursday-Monday, 11am-5pm

DISTILLERY TASTING ROOM

The distillery is located immediately behind the Barton Family Winery. It has a very cool vibe, with a full open bar for tastings and purchases (photo top). Indoor and outdoor spaces. These are high-quality, small-batch, craft spirits.

What makes this place amazing is that they have a mixologist on premise to create cocktails for you. You can try a traditional cocktail, like an Old Fashioned, or try some new interesting ideas of the mixologist. You will leave with more than just some delicious bottles, you will have ideas for cocktails to make at home.

Collection of Spirits

Barrel Select Bourbon Whiskey (cask strength)
Bourbon Whiskey (cask strength)
Bourbon Whiskey
American Bourbon Whiskey
Rye Whiskey (cask strength)
Rye Whiskey

Original Recipe Gin
Barrel-Aged Gin (photo right)
Pink Gin
Orange Gin

Navy Strength Golden Rum
Brandy
Botanical Brandy
Vodka
Lime Vodka
Bitter Liqueur

S mall-batch,
craft distillery.

A casual lunch spot with great outdoor spaces to enjoy wine and foods.

$-$$

BARTON'S KITCHEN
2174 Highway 46 West
Paso Robles, CA 93446

+1 805 237 0771
Howl@GreyWolfCellars.com

BartonFamilyWines.com

Open: Every Day, 11am-4:30pm

FULL MEAL OR PAIRING MENU

This is a wonderful setting to have lunch. They create a quarterly menu based on seasonality from local farmers and other purveyors. The cuisine is focused on freshness, seasonality and creativity. Choose from a full meal or their quarterly pairing menu. Food with wine is a marriage not to miss.

Burrata & Basil (upper left): heirloom tomatoes, summer berries, plum vinaigrette, crostini.
Wedge Salad (lower left): little gem, stone fruit, sweet peppers, smoked trout, orange-buttermilk dressing.
Grilled Shrimp & Vegetables (photo left): Spanish romesco sauce, peppers, potatoes, green beans.
Charcuterie (below): meats, cheeses, fruits, nuts.

$$-$$$-$$$$

2875 Oakdale Road
Paso Robles, CA 93446

+1 805 237 1600
HuntCellars@HuntCellars.com

HuntCellars.com

Open: Every Day, 10:30am-5:30pm

Collection of Wines

Encore Plus (Cabernet Sauvignon, Cabernet Franc)
Cabovation (Cabernet Sauvignon)
Cloud 9 (Cabernet Sauvignon)
Benchmark (Cabernet Sauvignon)
Bon Vivant (Cabernet Sauvignon)
Opulance (Cabernet Franc)
Unforgettable (Merlot)

Outlaw Ridge (Zinfandel)
Rocketman (Zinfandel)
Vinovation (Zinfandel)
Serenade (Syrah)
Irresistable (Petit Sirah)
Imagine (Pinot Noir)
Starving Artist (Barbera)

Rhapsody (Sangiovese)
Rhapsody In Red (Bordeaux Blend)
Que Syrah Sirah (GSM Mourvèdre, Grenache)
Maestro Super Tuscan (Sangiovese, Merlot, Cabernet
Sauvignon, Cabernet Franc, Petite Sirah)

White Wines (four additional wines)
Port Wines (four additional wines)

Winemaking inspired by senses and passion.

SENSORY MAGIC

We all have gifts. And when we lose one, we appreciate more of what we have. Sometimes what we are left with is magnified, as with Stevie Wonder, who lost his eyesight and gained a great sense of hearing. Also David Hunt, winemaker of Hunt Cellars, who also lost his eyesight and gained a palate many of us dream we had.

Stevie Wonder produced over thirty top-ten hits and was awarded twenty-two Grammy awards; David Hunt has produced over **200 90+ score wines** from top critics like Robert Parker, and many **96-point scores**.

I have known David Hunt for a very long time and have been fortunate to be invited to his private blind-tasting events. Hunt Cellars wines are considered more like expensive Napa wines, and David proudly pairs his wines against Napa super-greats, such as Harlan, Lokoya and Bond wines. That is a lot of confidence! David says: "The truth always comes out." It's hard to believe; however, I am there to witness the results. Most of the tasters choose the Hunt wines as the best. These are wines you must be tasting.

Hunt Cellars has 550 acres of vines in the Creston AVA (left page), and an intimate stone cottage tasting room right off Hwy 46 in the Willow Creek District.

And now for the best part. Hunt's tastings always include vintage wines every day of the year. Even their standard wine club delivers vintage wine in every shipment. These are big red wines, and aging makes an important difference. This might be the only winery that regularly serves vintages.

Speaking of vintages, Hunt created a twenty-year project of adding vintage after vintage of Cabernet Sauvignon into barrels to continue aging together. He releases a hundred cases per year so his fans can experience and enjoy the process. I tasted eight years into this blend; *Time In The Bottle* is an extraordinary experience of the best of young and old wine flavors together.

Common criticism that you cannot age white wine caused David to send a thirteen-year-old bottle of Sauvignon Blanc to *Wine Enthusiast* to see what is possible. The wine became an **editor's favorite**.

I forget that David is blind, as he always shakes my hand, looks me in the eyes when he talks to me, and pours me glasses of wine, never spilling a drop. David is an inspiration in rising above a handicap and producing extraordinary things in life.

David also has great senses for music, producing many albums of romantic and inspirational songs; notice that Hunt wines are named after songs.

$$$

2900 Vineyard Drive
Paso Robles, CA 93446

+1 805 434 1030
PasoRobles@TurleyWineCellars.com

TurleyWineCellars.com

Open: Thursday-Monday, 10am-3pm

V ery old vines, dry-farmed, and organic, make the most amazing Zinfandel wines.

OLD VINE ZINS

It was the year 1993 when emergency room doctor Larry Turley began his passion for old Zinfandel vineyards in California. Larry believes he can resuscitate any old vineyard back to health. Of course he would think that way; any doctor in the emergency room better think that way. And he has succeeded in a big way. He now has over fifty vineyards in twelve counties throughout California, four of which are in Paso Robles.

Brought back to life, these vineyards thrive very much on their own. The vineyards are dry-farmed (no irrigation), organically (no synthetic fertilizers or pesticides), and there is almost no intervention in the winery either: all native yeast for fermentation and no enzymes or acids added. We get to truly taste the special nuances of each vineyards and vines, which are often over a hundred years old.

For example, let's take the Old Vine Zins from their Ueberroth Vineyard in Paso, and yes, this is the well-known Olympic Ueberroth. Planted in 1885, this vineyard is as cool looking as it is strategically functional. The rows look to go in every direction because the vines are head-trained and perfectly panted the same distance in all directions (see the visual left page). The vines are planted on very steep limestone slopes (I felt the climb, and my boots left white with lime) around a 270° exposure sloping contiguously to the east, south and west for optimum sun exposure throughout the day. This vineyard is brilliant. It has never been watered, is certified organic, and being roughly 140 years old, the grapes and resulting wine are extraordinarily delicious (photo right).

With fifty vineyards in twelve counties, Turley Wine Cellars still only has two tasting rooms: Paso Robles and Plymouth (in the foothills of the California Sierra Nevada mountain range). What this means is that we can taste their different wines from vineyards all over California.

The visit here is a straightforward tasting. Reservations gets you a table inside the tasting room or outside on the patio.

Collection of Paso Robles Wines

Ueberroth Vineyard (1885 Old Vines Zinfandel)
Amadeo's Vineyard (1920s Old Vines Zinfandel)
Pesenti Vineyard (1920s Old Vines Zinfandel)
Dusi Vineyard (1945 Old Vines Zinfandel)

Tecolote Red Wine (1920s Old Vines Grenache, Carignan)

Pesenti Vineyard (1920s Old Vines Petite Sirah)

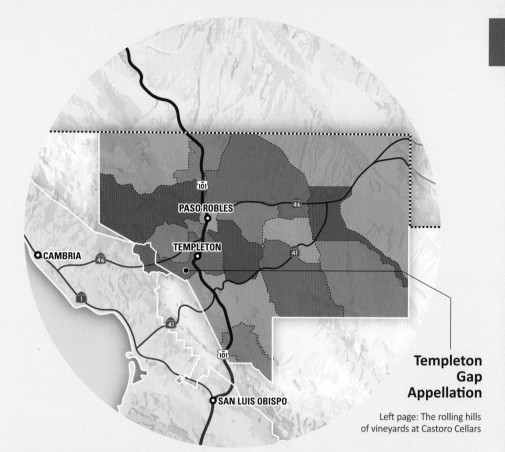

Templeton Gap Appellation

Left page: The rolling hills of vineyards at Castoro Cellars

WINDS BRING THE COLD OCEAN

The name Templeton Gap is a modern name by winemakers to describe the weather effect that benefit their grapes. The name caught on by many throughout Paso Robles because the Templeton Gap winds affect numerous AVAs. Maps later began to use the name to describe the gap in the mountain range that allowed the cool air to enter Paso Robles. Without the Templeton Gap, wine grapes in Paso Robles would not be possible.

As a pilot, I had to study weather and learned how this phenomenon works. In the summer and fall when the inland valleys get hot, this heat literally sucks the cold out of the Pacific Ocean to itself. This is why it gets windy and the wind carries fog and cold air towards the heated valleys. The same thing happens in San Francisco with the cold, fog and winds in the summer. As Mark Twain put it: "The coldest winter I ever spent was the summer in San Francisco."

This occurs during an optimal time of the year for the grapes, when they are maturing and ripening. This weather phenomenon creates a huge temperature difference between the day and night. This is known as the diurnal effect which can be as much as a 50° swing here, ideal for the grapes. Warmer daytime temperatures help foster sugar development, and cool nights help to preserve aromas, freshness and acidity.

In 2014, the Templeton Gap District (AVA) became an official area describing the appellation where this weather begins and has its greatest effect. It is located directly south of the Willow Creek AVA, and the town of Templeton is located on its eastern edge.

Here are four wineries you should experience.
- Castoro Cellars, page 201
- Hope Family Wines, page 203
- SummerWood Winery & Inn, page 205
- Peachy Canyon Winery, page 209

$$-$$$

1315 North Bethel Road
Templeton, CA 93465

+1 805 238 0725
Events@CastoroCellars.com

CastoroCellars.com

Open: Every Day, 10am-5pm

Collection of Wines

Bethel Road Lane 2 (Cabernet Sauvignon,
Tannat, Petit Verdot, Malbec, Alicante Bouschet)
Pasofusion (Tempranillo, Malbec, Tannat, Petite Sirah)
East Meets West (Syrah)
Zinfandel (Zinfandel, Petit Sirah)
Petit Sirah
Charbono
Primitivo

Bethel Road Grenache Rosé
Grenache Rosé
Whale Rock Chardonnay
Chardonnay
Tango (Viognier, Chardonnay)
Pinot Grigio
Falanghina

Méthode Champenoise (Blanc de Blanc Sparkling)
Muscat Canelli (Late Harvest Muscat)
Zinfandel (Late Harvest Zinfandel)

B
eautiful outdoor tasting, surrounded by organic vineyards and live music.

PIONEERS

Meet Niels Udsen. A true pioneer in Paso Robles, he established Castoro Cellars in 1983, the year Paso Robles became an AVA, which put him at the beginning of the exciting growth that was to happen here. There were only twelve wineries at the time he started.

As Neils explained it to me, he worked backwards. Neils and his wife, Bimmer, started, not by planting vineyards but by making some wine, five-gallon jugs at a time. Then they sold a few. After they had a little business, they purchased their own equipment, then a winery, then a tasting room. Lastly, they purchased and planted vineyards.

Today, Castoro Cellars has grown to over 1,400 acres of estate vineyards, which are 100% certified organic and SIP certified for sustainable farming. They are growing twenty-nine varieties of grapes, possibly more than anyone else in Paso Robles.

Beyond the wine, Castoro Cellars has **live music** all year. During the summer, shows are outside, with the vineyard and sunset as the backdrop. In the winter, shows are held indoors in their events gallery.

In September, they produce the massive and annual **Whale Rock Music & Arts Festival**. In March is the **Zinfandel Festival**. May is the **Paso Robles Wine Festival**, and in October is their **Harvest Festival**.

They also have **Yoga Brunch & Bubbles** on Sunday mornings, plus an eithteen-hole **Disc Golf Course** open all year (except for muddy days). The course is near the tasting room and is a great way to get out in the vineyards and rolling hills of big beautiful oaks trees. It is both fun and challenging (official disk tournaments are held here). **Whale Rock Disc Golf Course** is designed to be enjoyable for kids and beginners while challenging the experts. Course map, disc rental and play information is available. Family friendly. No pets though.

$$-$$$-$$$$

1585 Live Oak Road
Paso Robles, CA 93446

+1 805 238 4112
TastingRoom@HFWines.com

HopeFamilyWines.com

Open: Every Day, 10am-5pm

A farming family obsessed with high-quality grapes, and the results are quite delicious.

SEVENTH-BEST WINE IN THE WORLD

The Hope family have been farmers in Paso Robles for over thirty years, initially planting apple orchards. I can just imagine the great quality of their apples from the Templeton Gap's cool winds. As the wine industry blossomed, the Hopes started planting grapes. The orchards have since disappeared.

The Hope vineyards planted on their estate are Rhône varietals, as they see the microclimate here (the coldest in Paso Robles) to bring about the true varietal characteristics of the Old World in France. They saw the unique microclimate of warm sunny days and cool coastal nights closely aligning with the climate of the Rhône Valley.

They have developed five labels: Liberty School, Treana, Quest, Troublemaker, and Austin Hope (their premium line). I have listed the Austin Hope wines to the right. The flagship, in my opinion, is the Cabernet Sauvignon. And this is not just my opinion, as *Wine Enthusiast* has placed this wine on their **Top 100 Wines of the Year** list, placing it tenth in 2019 and seventh in 2020. And this is not the reserve either.

I am a Cabernet lover and this wine is beautifully structured. Austin Hope has gone to great lengths to

make this wine extraordinary. He has painstakingly sought the best vineyards throughout Paso Robles to make this wine. From five appellations: Creston, Estrella, Adelaida, El Pomar, Geneseo, all certified sustainable and managed to his specification of very low yield for the richest fruit. Further, he demands the coopers age the oak staves longer before constructing the barrels.

And in aging, he is further unconventional. After eleven months in 10% new, 25% once used, and 65% two-to-three-times-used French Oak, he ages the blend for another three months in 75% new and 25% once-used French Oak. If you are a Cabernet lover, you cannot miss this one!

They have wonderful tasting areas. Inside are comfortable living-room-type areas among the tanks (photo left) and outside are private sectioned-off areas overlooking the vineyards. This is for their regular **Legacy Tasting** of five wines. You will love their **Grenache Vineyard Experience** that takes you into the vineyards (immediately below the outside tasting area) with a glass of Grenache to talk about the vines which produced the wine that you are tasting (photo above). And you can taste the grapes if it is that time of year.

Collection of Aston Hope Wines

GSM (Grenache, Syrah, Mourvèdre)
Lagrein/Petit Sirah
Mourvèdre/Syrah

Cabernet Sauvignon
Reserve Cabernet Sauvignon
Syrah
Graciano
Grenache
Mourvèdre

Sauvignon Blanc
Chenin Blanc
Chardonnay

$$-$$$-$$$$

2175 Arbor Road
Paso Robles, CA 93446

Winery: +1 805 227 1365
Info@SummerWoodWine.com

SummerWoodWine.com

Open: Every Day, 10am-5pm

Collection of Wines

Private Reserve
(Syrah, Cabernet Sauvignon, Merlot, Malbec, Cabernet Franc)
Reserve Cabernet
Cabernet Sauvignon
Reserve Syrah
Syrah

GSM (Grenache, Syrah, Mourvèdre)
Diosa (Syrah, Mourvèdre, Grenache)
Vin Rouge (Syrah, Cabernet Sauvignon, Merlot,
Malbec, Mourvèdre, Petite Sirah)

Viognier
Marsanne
Grenache Blanc
Sparkling Grenache Blanc

Rosé (Grenache)
Diosa Blanc
(Viognier, Marsanne, Roussanne, Grenache Blanc)
Blanc Vin
(Roussanne, Marsanne, Viognier, Grenache Blanc)

G ive joy to all our customers by providing them with truly genuine high-quality products and our friendly hospitality. — Mr. Fukae, founder

OMOTENASHI

The winery and inn have a very special owner, the Fukae family from Osaka Japan. Starting in 1964, they built a multibillion-dollar empire through the Japanese concept of Omotenashi.

Omotenashi translates to *hospitality*; however, it means so much more. The word represents a deep-rooted cultural mindset that stems from a traditional tea ceremony first performed by a man named Sen-no Rikyu; it represents wholeheartedly looking after guests so they can relax and enjoy a memorable experience.

This is exactly what you can expect at SummerWood. The people here, from management to staff, all share a genuine enthusiasm for food, wine and hospitality.

SummerWood Winery & Inn is particularly special to Mr. Fukae, as he named it after his oldest son's first name, Natsuki (Natsuki translates to "summer wood" in Japanese).

The winemaker here, South American Mauricio Marchant, has been at SummerWood Winery now since 2010. He is responsible for embracing these qualities in all aspects of the winemaking process, from the vineyards to the winery to the finished bottle. Mauricio is a Chilean winemaker who worked at two of Chile's most admired wineries: Viña Santa Rita and Concha y Toro SA, where he was a member of the renowned Don Melchor winemaking team.

Surrounding the winery, inn and tasting room are their white-wine grapes. The white Rhône wines here are quite exceptional. And if you are a Cabernet fan like I am, you must ask for a bottle of their Reserve Cabernet Sauvignon.

They have an outside park-like setting with a lawn and gazebo where you can bring a picnic and a glass of SummerWood wine. They also have a large boutique of unique wine accessories, local specialty foods and gift items.

Mauricio personally invites all of you to drop by.

A BEAUTIFUL INN WITH GOURMET BREAKFASTS

I really like this place. And the way to my heart is through their breakfasts. I love a good breakfast. Fresh orange juice. Fresh coffee. Real cream. Fresh fruits and nuts on top of delicious yogurt (photo top right). And hot cooked-to-order breakfast, delivered in style (photo middle right), by the well-known chef of a local steakhouse. What else would he be doing in the morning?

The location is ideal, less than a mile from Highway 101, on Highway 46 West, five minutes south of downtown Paso Robles. And the property is in the middle of the vineyards. It is beautiful here. Serene. The inn was extensively renovated in 2013 to very high standards that you will notice. Rooms are spacious. The beds are super comfy. Just look at that bed in the photo (lower right). It really is as good as it looks! And if Wi-Fi and cellular are important to you, this is a place you can count on for both. Remember, this is an agricultural region, so services are not always the best. You can count on SummerWood Inn.

Don't forget their late-afternoon appetizers and cheeses, served with SummerWood wines. Relax after the day on their back patio and enjoy the view across the vineyards (photo below). Dessert and coffee are served later in the evening. Turn down service with a handmade confection is also provided.

When you arrive, they welcome you with a bottle of their wine in your room. And the winery is next door to indulge further. Complimentary for guests of the inn. All rooms have fireplaces, cable television, and patios or balconies.

I am thinking you are really going to like this place as well.

$$$

2175 Arbor Road
Paso Robles, CA 93446

Inn: +1 805 227 1111
Reservations@SummerWoodWine.com

SummerWoodWine.com

Open: Every Day

$$-$$$

1480 N Bethel Road
Templeton, CA 93465

+1 805 239 1918
TastingRoom@PeachyCanyon.com

PeachyCanyon.com

Open: Every Day, 10am-5pm

Collection of Wines

Zinfandel Series
D Block Zinfandel (Original Heritage Clones)
Old Schoolhouse (18 Heritage Clones)
Bailey (Adelaida Appellation)
Willow (Willow Creek Appellation)
Mustard Creek (Zinfandel, Petite Sirah)
Nancy's View Zin (Zinfandel, Petite Sirah)
Westside (Zinfandel, Petite Sirah)
Vortex (Zinfandel, Petite Sirah, Grenache)
Especial (Zinfandel, Carignan, Petite Sirah, Grenache)
The Odd One (Zinfandel, Counoise, Carignan, Syrah,
Petite Sirah, Mourvedre, Grenache)
Incredible Red (Zinfandel, Syrah, Mourvedre)

Bordeaux and Rhône Series
Para Siempre (Cabernet Sauvignon, Cabernet Franc, Malbec)
Devine (Cabernet Sauvignon, Malbec, Syrah)
Cirque Du Vin (Cabernet Sauvignon, Petit Verdot,
Malbec, Cabernet Franc)
Ms Behave Malbec
GSM (Grenache, Syrah, Mourvèdre)
Petite Sirah

Rosé (Counoise, Grenache, Cinsault)
Pêche Blanche (Grenache Blanc, Picpoul Blanc, Viognier)

An exclusive and uniquely special Zinfandel, deemed California's Heritage Grape.

EXCEPTIONAL ZINFANDEL HERE

In 1995, **University of California, Davis**, the renowned college for oenology and viticulture, embarked on a special program to find and isolate heritage Zinfandel vines in California.

The search parameters were simple, yet difficult: find Zinfandel vines at vineyards over a hundred years old. They collected these vines and isolated them to protect only those plants that had no diseases. They also ran DNA analysis so they could separate the different Zinfandel clones, ultimately having a group of eighteen unique vines that became known as **Heritage Zinfandel Vines**.

UC Davis propagated these vines and enlisted three wineries in 2010 to plant one-acre vineyards with the purpose of making wines from these notable grapes. Peachy Canyon Winery was one of these special chosen wineries. After the UC Davis program was completed, the other two wineries abandoned these vineyards. Today, Peachy Canyon is the only winery to have these eighteen Zinfandel clones in one vineyard block, making this Heritage Zinfandel Wine. They call it **D-Block Zinfandel**.

Peachy Canyon sees this as a hundred-year project. They want their vineyard to surpass a hundred years from these special hundred-year-old clones. I can't wait to drink their 2110 vintage!

The vineyard is dry-farmed (no irrigation). All eighteen clones from this single block are harvested and fermented together in new French oak barrels. Aging is eighteen months in the same oak barrels of which they were fermented. Imagine aromas of violets and roses, and flavors of ripe cherries covered in rich chocolate. Yum!

They can only make fifty cases of wine from this special one-acre vineyard. Wait until you taste it; it's extraordinary Zinfandel. Don't worry though, Peachy Canyon specializes in Zinfandel, and they have several different types of marvelous Zinfandel, wines. Further, they have taken these eighteen heritage clones and propagated them into new vineyards. The legend is expanding. I tasted several impressive Zinfandel wines here.

Tasting is inside a historic schoolhouse or outside on their beautiful patio in the park amongst their vineyards. Bring a lunch and do a tasting, or enjoy a bottle of their wine under the trees.

TIN CITY TEMPLETON, CA

Tin City is a little industrial park at the north edge of the town of Templeton, right off Highway 101, a few minutes south of downtown Paso Robles. The buildings are made of, you guessed it, corrugated tin (see it in the photo right). The warehouses are occupied by artisan winemakers, brewers, distillers, a creamery, and olive oil producers. Everyone makes what they sell. The first winery showed up in 2013 and quickly became the stomping grounds for Paso's boutique winemakers, with more than twenty-five wineries here now, less than a decade later. This is a great place to park your car and walk around to so many good places.

What made this all happen? Cheap industrial park rent. Up-and-coming winemakers had a place to get started. And they stayed when this became the coolest plate in town as a creative winemaking community. When you visit these wineries, chances are you will be meeting the winemaker and have interesting conversations.

Giornata Wines (Winery)
+1 805 434 3075 • 470 Marquita Avenue
Open: Every Day, By Appointment

GiornataWines.com

Gioranata is an inspiration of Italian wines. They exclusively work with Italian varietals, specifically the clones of the best producers in Italy. They farm their own vineyards in Paso Robles, using Italian viticultural methods. They grow well-known as well as hard-to-find reds: Nebbiolo, Sangiovese, Aglianico, Barbera; and whites: Fiano, Ribolla Gialla, Friulano, Trebbiano.

The grapes are brought to their Tin City industrial park facility where they hand make the wines in Italian winemaking traditions. Make reservations to see their facility and taste their wines. They have so many interesting and different shapes, sizes and materials for vessels to make these special wines. Everything is by hand and the wines are uniquely Italian. If you love Italian wines, this is a must visit winery.

Field Recordings Winery (Winery)
+1 805 503 9660 • 3070 Limestone Way
Open: Every Day, 11am-5pm (Fri/Sat 8pm)

FieldRecordingsWine.com

Orange wine specialist here. After perfecting orange wines in various of their labels, they wanted to elevate the box version of wine with orange. They call it Boxíe. It was one of the best tasting wines I tried there. Chardonnay, Pinot Gris, Riesling and Albariño.

Orange wine is white wine grapes produce like red wine grapes, fermented on the skins. Here they ferment on the skins for thirty full days. Hence the orange color derived from the skins.

I have a long-running joke with a friend of mine teasing him about box wines. Field Recordings has dampened my jokes with the quality of Boxíe. My friend is very happy now.

Upstairs is a fun space, a high school gym, complete with hoop and lockers. Very affordable.

Onx Wines (Winery)
+1 805 434 5607 • 2910 Limestone Way
Open: Every Day, 10am-5pm

OnxWine.com

Here in Tin City, this is the production facility (winery) and tasting room for Onx Wines. Grapes are grown on their estate vineyards (127 acres) in the Templeton Gap AVA, growing eighteen different varietals, with a philosophy of concentrated and highly expressive fruit.

This results in big delicious wines. My favorite is Mad Crush (below), a rich Grenache as result of the five bigger grapes blend in. Check out the artistically meaningful label. All wines come with these interesting collage labels. Spacious tasting room. Gourmet charcuterie boxes or gourmet cheese-only boxes are available.

They also offer vineyards experiences. This is an off-road vehicle adventure through their vineyards, with wine, education and discovery.

ETTO Pasta Bar (Restaurant)

+1 805 369 2787 • 3070 Limestone Way, Suite B
Open: Every Day, 10am-9pm

EttoPastaBar.com

The most amazing pasta you will ever taste. Fresh Bianco DiNapoli tomatoes simmered in the juices of pork cheeks that were quickly sautéed, creating a crispy exterior and tender, juicy center. Bucatini pasta (hallow center), perfectly prepared; the texture of this delicious dish was everything to the enjoyment. This is the Etto Factory's (below) evolution into a restaurant. Italian recipes, Paso Robles ingredients.

Barrelhouse Brewing Company

+1 805 296 1128 • 3055 Limestone Way
Open: Every Day, 11am-9pm

BarrelHouseBrewing.com

Winemakers say... to make a barrel of wine, you drink a case of beer. A nice way to end a day of wine tasting might be to enjoy a fresh micro-brew. Here, their live beer menu continuously updates their latest fresh brew. I counted sixteen beers on tap and another twelve cans and bottles. They have a large beer garden with picnic tables to hangout, listen to live bands, and enjoy the daily food truck.

Tin City Cider Company

+1 805 293 6349 • 3005 Limestone Way
Open: Every Day, 11am-6pm (8pm Ths-Sat)

TinCityCider.com

Have you ever had a freshly made cider? This was my first. They do cider flights so you can taste through the collection. The ciders are carefully crafted with fresh California apples and fermented and aged in oak barrels. Seven ciders on tap when I was there. I had some favorites.

ETTO Pastificio (Pasta Factory)

+1 805 400 3193 • 3070 Limestone Way
Open: Every Day, 10am-6pm

EttoPastificio.com

This pasta is out-of-this-world delicious. It's organic, made on site, fresh or dried, in a huge array of shapes. Plus, they have everything needed to create amazing meals: fresh local meats and produce, fresh sauces, Italian pantry staples, wine, desserts, and gift items to inspire any culinary enthusiast.

Olivas de Oro (Olive Oil Mill)

+1 805 227 4223 • 2989 B Limestone Way
Open: Every Day, 11am-5pm (6:30pm Sat/Sun)

OlivasDeOro.com

Locally grown and milled olives in the Paso Robles Creston AVA. In Tin City, they have a big tasting room (yes, tastings!). Plus, other delectables. How about a white truffle aged balsamic. Decadent! Other artisan vinegars, sauces, condiments, sea salts, and very interesting blends with their fresh olive oils.

Negranti Creamery (Ice Cream)

+1 805 369 2663 • 2989 A Limestone Way
Open: Every Day, 11:30am-7pm (9pm Sat/Sun)

NegrantiCreamery.com

Freshly made and wholesome, sheep's-milk ice cream. Handcrafted by the Negranti family, who hand-milks their ewes, adding local organic ingredients into sixteen fresh-churned, seasonal, artisan flavors. Besides being super yummy, it is lactose-intolerant friendly, gluten free and higher in protein. And they ship nationwide.

Roasted Duck (left page)
dry-aged duck, roasted chestnuts, honey parsnips,
pine nuts, with sous vide steak water.

Grassy Bar Oyster (top)
seaweed salsa verde and lemon soy sauce.

Winter Fruit Salad (second)
pineapple guava, blood orange, tangerine, pistachio,
yogurt, fennel, vadouvan, and champagne pairing.

Japanese Egg Custard (third)
chawanmushi with pork belly, mushrooms
roasted in preserved lime oil, cauliflower, and shoyu.

Aged Pork Loin (bottom)
baby pork aged thirty days, sunchoke potatoes,
chanterelle mushrooms, onion, parsley,
with foie gras truffle sauce.

$$$$$

3075 Blue Rock Road, Unit B
Paso Robles (Tin City), CA 93446

No Phone Number
Info@SixTestKitchen.com

SixTestKitchen.com

Pre-Fixe Dinner Experience Only
Wednesday-Saturday Evenings
Seatings: 6:00 and 6:30pm

Reservations are required and difficult to get.
The Secret: on the first day of the month,
at 9:00am, their calendar opens
for the subsequent month

Michelin Star Awarded

MICHELIN STAR RESTAURANT IN TIN CITY

What in the world is a Michelin-star restaurant doing in a corrugated tin building in an industrial park? Well, Tin City is coming alive with wineries and other restaurants.

Would you like the backstory? The owner/executive chef Ricky Odbert, started this restaurant concept as a "test kitchen" in a home garage. He could only serve six customers; hence, Six Test Kitchen. With his success came the attention of the health department and Ricky quickly needed to move to a commercial space. Today, he only serves twelve customers per evening, four nights per week.

On a concrete floor, tall high-top stools and a beautifully designed bar facing the open kitchen. It actually feels very intimate, warm and cozy (photo above). This is a very creative, prefix dining experience. Menu changes every evening. Actually, there is no menu. It is an experience created daily by Ricky and his sommelier wine steward based on fresh ingredients and creativity. They will pair all of the courses with delicious wines. The night I was there, I experienced fourteen courses and amazing wine pairings!

This is an adult experience. No children. An experience where you accept the imaginative and progressive cuisine of the evening. The recipes are complex and they do not accommodate vegan, vegetarian, pescatarian, dairy-free or gluten-free diets.

One of my favorite flavors of the evening was lime oil. They quarter limes and vacuum pack them in salt and sugar for one month. An incredible flavor with the pork belly.

CALIFORNIA · SLO · PASO ROBLES **SANTA MARGARITA RANCH AVA**

Southernmost AVA in Paso Robles, Close to San Luis Obispo City

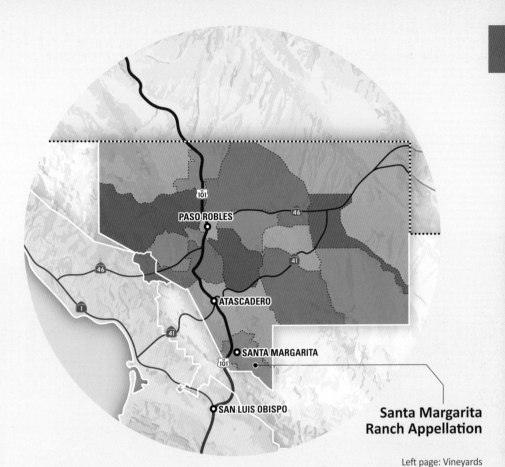

Santa Margarita Ranch Appellation

Left page: Vineyards of the Ancient Peaks Winery

AN 18,300 ACRE AVA RANCH

Santa Margarita Ranch District is the southernmost AVA in Paso Robles. It is only ten miles north of the city of San Luis Obispo, twenty-three miles south of the city of Paso Robles. Santa Margarita is a little town of just 1,100 people where you will find the tasting room for **Ancient Peaks Winery**, the only winery in this AVA.

Santa Margarita is named after the mission built here: **Santa Margarita de Cortona Asistencia**. With the missionaries came livestock, farming and grapevines. Santa Margarita became a Wells Fargo Stagecoach stop, then a train stop for the Southern Pacific Railroad. From this, a new planned-community was created adjacent the train stop.

It was not until 200 years later that the **Robert Mondavi Winery** leased a 1,000 acres here and vineyards were planted.

The Santa Margarita Ranch AVA is quite different than any of the Paso Robles AVAs, or any of the San Luis Obispo AVAs for that matter, most specifically in the type and diversity of soils. Santa Margarita Ranch is a narrow valley surrounded by mountains on three sides affecting the maritime influence, bringing more rainfall, higher daytime and lower nighttime temperatures. Soils consist of marine sediment, granitic rock, loam, sandy loam, gravelly loam, and as an ancient seabed, there are areas with an abundance of fossilized oysters.

The Santa Margarita Ranch AVA is 18,300 acres large, with Ancient Peaks representing 14,000 of these acres. No wonder there is just one big ranch winery operation here.

Here is the winery of Santa Margarita Ranch.
• Ancient Peaks Winery, page 217

$$-$$$

22720 El Camino Real
Santa Margarita, CA 93453

+1 805 365 7045
Info@APWinery.com

AncientPeaks.com

Open: Every Day, 11am-5:30pm

I magine vineyards planted on ancient seabeds, with oysters spewing out of the soil.

Collection of Wines

Oyster Ridge
(Cabernet Sauvignon, Merlot, Syrah, Petite Sirah, Malbec)

The Pearl Collection (Reserve Wines)
Cabernet Sauvignon
Cabernet Franc
Petit Verdot
Petit Sirah
Chardonnay

Renegade (Syrah, Petit Verdot)
Cabernet Sauvignon
Pinot Noir
Merlot
Zinfandel

Chardonnay
Sauvignon Blanc
Rosé (Pinot Noir)
Sparkling Rosé (Pinot Noir, Chardonnay)

ANCIENT FOSSILIZED OYSTERS

Now let's explore the only winery in the Santa Margarita Ranch AVA, Ancient Peaks Winery. They occupy a whopping 14,000 acres of this 18,300-acre AVA. One of the key attributes to the quality of the wines at Ancient Peaks are from the diverse soil types.

Robert Mondavi knew this. Robert is known for being a forward thinker, a visionary with a passion for making the finest wines in the world. The fact that he chose this location to plant vineyards speaks loudly of the qualities of this terroir.

In 1999, the Robert Mondavi Winery leased a large portion of the land here and planted vineyards. They were very strategic in making use of the different soil types. When the Mondavi family sold the winery, the new company did not have the vision for this property and let the lease go.

And Ancient Peaks Winery was then born.

As you can imagine, Ancient Peaks was overjoyed with the opportunity to have these vineyards, abandoned by the new Mondavi owner.

The vineyards were strategically planted with different varietals on the five diverse soil types: ancient seabed, granite, volcanic, shale, and alluvium. The actual soil types are on display in the tasting room where you can see just how dramatically they are different (photo above).

The ancient seabed, which they call Oyster Ridge, literally has large fossilized oysters spewing out of the ground. As a result, this soil has super-high calcium content, which produces beautiful aromatics and superior flavors in the wine. As you could easily imagine, their top premium wine is called Oyster Ridge (photo right).

The Ancient Peaks tasting room (photo next page) is located in the little historic town of Santa Margarita. Tastings include the Pearl Collection and limited-edition reserve wines. Reservations or walk-ins are acceptable. They have a café with light fare and locally made artisan cheese & charcuterie boards. This tasting room is also where you can schedule activities as described on the next page.

$-$$-$$$

22720 El Camino Real
Santa Margarita, CA 93453

+1 805 365 7045
Info@APWinery.com

AncientPeaks.com

Open: Every Day, 11am-5:30pm

THE CINNAMON ROOM CAFÉ

Adjacent the tasting room (photo above) is a nice little café with very nice soups, salads and sandwiches. Plus, they have charcuterie boards with locally made artisan cheese (see photos to the right). Enjoy with your tasting flight, a glass or a bottle of your favorite wine. The Cinnamon Room is named after their beloved cow who roamed the ranch for three decades. With her unusual oppositional horns, she was easily recognizable and loved by everyone.

ZIPLINE OVER OAK TREES AND VINEYARDS

This is a must-do thrilling experience. Within this massive ranch are six spans of ziplines meandering more than 7,500 total feet. You will soar over the mountainsides, across the valleys, over the massive oak trees and across the vineyards (photo left page). The views are amazing. The thrill is invigorating. It is totally awesome! And night ziplining too.

WILDLIFE RANCH TOURS

Explore this 14,000-acre ranch and learn about its history: the geography dating back millions of years; how the mountains, hills and valley were formed; why the terroir is unique and ideal for viticulture. Also learn about the amazing wildlife on this property. You never know what animals you might see. They have wild turkeys, red-tailed hawks, bald eagles, owls, bobcats, raccoons, and bears. This is a two-and-a-half-hour adventure to totally enjoy.

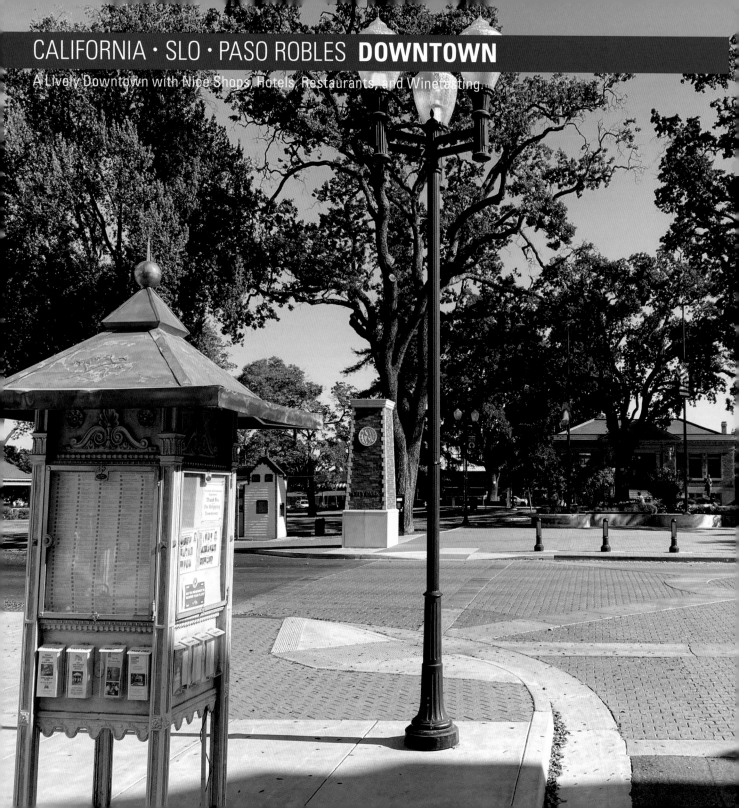

CALIFORNIA · SLO · PASO ROBLES **DOWNTOWN**

A Lively Downtown with Nice Shops, Hotels, Restaurants, and Winetasting.

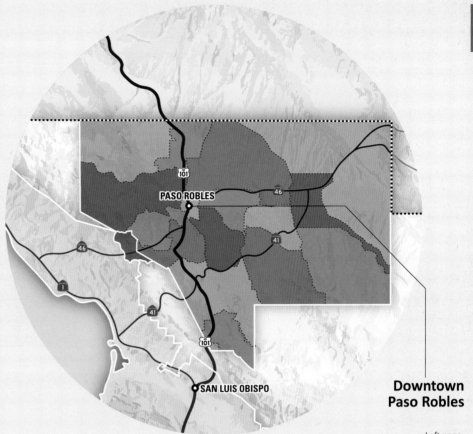

**Downtown
Paso Robles**

Left page:
Downtown City Park, Paso Robles

LIVELY DOWNTOWN PASO

Historic downtown Paso Robles makes for a great walking city for the day or a nice stroll in the evening. There are numerous restaurants, bars and wine tasting rooms (I counted fifteen), plus art galleries, museums, shopping, a movie theater, and hotels.

Outlaw Jesse James spent some time here with his nephew, Drury James, a rancher and one of the founders of Paso Robles who had the vision to turn Paso Robles into a health resort. In 1890, Drury also designed the square block of **Downtown City Park**, central to this four by five block downtown area. There are numerous architectural building here, including the **Carnegie Library,** a Classical Revival building that opened in 1908 and today houses the **Historical Society & History Museum** (photo left page) exhibiting an interesting **Wine History Gallery.**

Numerous events and festivals and are held in this central green space with an impressive hexagonal gazebo; which presents the **Concerts in the Park** series. This town loves to party, and this park is home to celebrating their numerous local holiday events as well as national holidays.

The restaurant scene here is excellent. This once sleepy town is now bustling with creative food experiences. When I think of Paso, I think of excellent red wines and now to indulge in their delicious restaurants. Even Michelin has taken notice and awarded very deserving stars to **Six Test Kitchen** in Tin City and to **Restaurant at JUSTIN** at the winery. The food seen here is awesome. In the downtown area there are many excellent restaurants and numerous wine-tasting rooms.

DOWNTOWN **PASO ROBLES** TASTING ROOMS

Downtown Paso Robles has become a mecca of tasting rooms. The number keeps growing. Last I counted they topped fifteen tasting rooms.

Some wineries that already have tasting rooms at the winery, also have a location here downtown (for example, JUSTIN Winery is here).

For other wineries, they make the downtown Paso scene their primary tasting facility.

And for very small wineries, whose individual winemakers make handcrafted wines, this is their opportunity to be able to have a tasting room so you can discover them.

TRENDY FRENCH CUISINE

Les Petites Canailles, also known as simply LPC, is translated from French as "The Little Rascals." This is in honor of the owners', Courtney and Julien Asseo, three kids.

While this place looks like a simple casual restaurant, it is in disguise of seriously creative French cuisine. It is trendy and upscale though. They even got Michelin's attention. The dishes are unique, with surprising flavors, and presented with such artistry. Just check out the photos below.

They are located downtown kitty-corner to the Downtown City Park (previous spread). It's a small restaurant, so you definitely want to make reservations. They do have space at their bar on a first-come basis.

The wine list is very exciting. They have plenty of good wines by the glass and an extensive array of wines by the bottle. Primarily local and French wines (Burgundy and Bordeaux).

$$$-$$$$-$$$$$

1215 Spring Street
Paso Robles, CA 93446

+1 805 296 3754
Info@LPSRestaurant.com

LPCRestaurant.com

Open: Thursday-Monday, 5pm-9pm (Fri/Sat 10pm)
Advanced Reservations Are Needed

Burgundy Escargot Risotto (photo top left): delicious escargot in a carnaroli rice and light-green parsley-juice garlic butter risotto, accented with dark green parsley juice, and decorated with edible yellow flowers.

Leeks à la Plancha (photo center left): leeks standing upright, topped with a rustic vinaigrette of chopped herbs, parsley, onions, tarragon, chervil, garlic, espelette pepper, and pinenuts with extra-virgin olive oil.

Roasted Monkfish (photo below left): firm and sweetly succulent fish with mighty cap mushrooms; decadent in a rich mushroom sauce made from a stock of the fish bones and mushrooms.

Northern Italian Cuisine
BUONA TAVOLA
+1 805 237 0600 • 943 Spring Street, Downtown
Open: Every Day, 5:30pm-9pm (Mon-Fri 11am lunch)

BTSLO.com

Many years ago, I stumbled into this restaurant without any recommendations. I ordered their *Fettuccine Al Sugo Di Carni Miste* — a fettuccine pasta with slowly braised chicken, duck, veal, and beef, and herbs, as an amazing meat sauce.

Life changed in that moment. The complex and mouthwatering flavors overtook me. My date kept wanting bites of my dish. My taste buds had beautiful dreams that night. And the next.

At home, I acquired the four meats, slowly cooked them separately, with herbs I felt made each of them special. Then I merged the meats into a beautiful tomato sauce I created. You have no idea how hungry I'm becoming writing this for you. This dish makes me very happy. Here is the catch. Time! It is time-consuming work to create this amazing dish. Best to leave it to the chef of the restaurant.

Need I say more? Book your reservations.

Rotisserie & Bar
THE HATCH
+1 805 221 5727 • 835 13th Street, Downtown
Open: Every Day, 4:30pm-9pm (Fri/Sat 11pm)

HatchPasoRobles.com

Classic cocktails here. Like you see below. This was an ever so delicious *Barrel-Aged Old Fashioned*, using the ultra-premium *Four Roses Yellow Label Bourbon*, adding bitters, a beautifully square luxury ice cube and an orange skin twirl. You can sit at the bar and watch all cocktail excellence happen and have dinner.

I would call this comfort food here. They have a wood-fired rotisserie, and the food is delicious. The chicken below was recommended and it was out-of-this-world succulent, as great chicken should be. The chicken is sprayed with sweet soy sauce while on the rotisserie. The aioli sauce you see in the photo was super good (olive oil and rosemary emulsified into mashed garlic). Yet the chicken was excellent without it. I just had to split bites.

This is a lively atmosphere of locals and visitors. If you bring a bottle of wine purchased at one of the downtown tasting rooms, they waive the corkage fee.

Barbeque Restaurant
JEFFRY'S WINE COUNTRY BBQ
+1 805 369 2132 • 819 12th Street, Downtown
Open: Thursday-Monday, 11am-8pm

JeffrysWineCountryBBQ.com

Down a back alley (Norma's Way Alley) in downtown Paso Robles, nestled in-between building on all sides, is a courtyard with an outdoor barbeque smoking so flavorful you must take a seat. And eat! This is some of the most amazing BBQ!

Porkbelly ribs, tri-tip, pulled pork, pulled chicken, pork loin, and brisket, all with their own signature dry rub. Their mouthwatering BBQ sauce is homemade from scratch. And so is their jalapeno-citrus aioli, horseradish cream sauce, roasted tomato salsa, lime sour cream, siracha aioli, hoisin BBQ sauce, red wine vinaigrette, balsamic vinaigrette, and buttermilk ranch. Are you getting hungry yet?

They have numerous craft beers on draft, and lots of local Paso Robles wines, all meant to compliment the meats. It's okay to bring your vegetarian friends, as they have great non-meat choices so good you may want skip the meat yourself. For a half second!

THE FARM IS AT YOUR TABLE

It has become so commonplace now to hear restaurants say their concept is "farm to table" that it hardly makes it special anymore. This restaurant is so serious about it though, they go on to reveal all the local farmers they are so proud to source their organic wholesome foods.

Loo Loo Farms, Oleo Farms Gracious Greens, Back Porch Bakery, Leo Leo Gelato, Etto Pasta (page 211), Magnolia Farms, La Migliore Bakery, and Speedy Berries. They are as proud of the farmers as they are of their cuisine. It shows. Just look at the photographs.

I have dined at this restaurant several times. It is always excellent, and there is always a fresh new menu. Of course, these are real farms providing the freshest organic produce and natural grass-fed meats for the cuisine here daily.

The photographs say it all. I am getting hungry just looking at them again. Counterclockwise from top left...

Burrata. An Italian cow milk cheese made from mozzarella and cream. Garnished with beets, delicata squash, Tuscan kale, pumpkin seeds, olive oil, balsamic reduction, pickled tarragon, and blueberries.

Watermelon Feta Salad. Arugula, cucumber, fresh lemon and lightly sprinkled with Tajin Clásico chili salt.

Lamb Meatballs. Sherry, foie gras, and créme.

Pan Roasted Sablefish. Black cod with complex flavors and textures of white cauliflower and crushed English pees, topped with a pistachio aillade.

Pan-Seared Diver Scallops. Duck bacon lardon, cauliflower pureé, and basil oil.

Coconut Bread Pudding. Topped with a rich Italian mascarponi creme cheese and blueberry.

$$$

1313 Park Street
Downtown Paso Robles, CA 93446

+1 805 226 5888
EventsTHO@gmail.com

ThomasHillOrganics.com

Open: All Year,
Monday, Tuesday, Thursday
11am-3pm & 5pm-9pm

Friday, Saturday
11am-3pm & 5pm-9:30pm

Sunday Brunch
10am-2pm & 5pm-9pm

Make reservations by telephone

MIXED-USE CULINARY EXTRAVAGANZA

Paso Market Walk is a brand new mixed-use development, contemporary and chic, that has a whole host of diverse merchants. Everything here conjures up food and wine.

Early morning **coffee house** (photo right) and **on-site bakery** for pastries and more (bottom photo). Everything is baked from scratch! The afternoon opens up **Japanese ramen**, **grilled sandwiches** and **authentic Italian pizza** from a handmade brick oven from Naples Italy.

There is a **wine merchant** on the scene. Every Wednesday night is **wine wednesdays**, hosting a winemaker – and his wines, of course – with a special farm-to-table menu from their kitchen to pair with the wines.

Taste some **homemade beer** (they even grow the grains and hops). An **organic produce stand**, a **vegan cheese shop** (photo below), **handcrafted gelato**, and a food-focused **mercantile**.

This property runs a full block, and on each end are full restaurants: **Finca** and **In Bloom** (next page).

Stay upstairs in **The Lofts**, rooms and suites (next page).

SAN LUIS OBISPO **PASO ROBLES** DOWNTOWN ■
Shopping, Restaurants, Lodging
PASO MARKET WALK

$-$$-$$$

1803 Spring Street
Paso Robles, CA 93446

+1 805 720 1255
Jill@PasoMarketWalk.com

PasoMarketWalk.com/stay

Open: Every Day, 6:30am-8pm

Six blocks North of The Downtown City Park

IN BLOOM RESTAURANT

$$-$$$ -$$$$

Paso Market Walk
1845 Spring Street
Paso Robles, CA 93446

+1 805 286 4344
InBloomPasoRobles.com

Open: Tuesday-Sunday, 5pm-9pm

Snake River Farms Wagyu New York (top): Perfectly grilled and deliciously tender Wagyu steak on top of a pear and caramelized onion puree with horseradish.

Beets (below left): crispy dehydrated beet leaf with braised and raw beets, toasted almonds, lightly topped with an apple gel and beet dressing.

Mushrooms (below center): Shiitake and Black Pearl oyster mushrooms, chestnuts, arugula pesto, and mushroom aioli.

Semifreddo (below right): a decadently light raspberry and thyme frozen mousse, with raspberries and homemade whipped cream.

R elationships with local farmers is how they created this restaurant.

EVERYTHING IS MADE ON THE PREMISES, EXCEPT THE SALT

In Bloom is an upscale restaurant in a casual environment. They are located on the north corner of Paso Market Walk. Open for dinner only. Indoor and outdoor dining along with a lively bar.

The owners, Chris & Nicole Haisma, are restaurateurs from Chicago. After visiting Paso Robles for fifteen years, and collecting the amazing wines of the area, they always wanted to live here and create relationships with local farmers that Paso Robles offered them differently than Chicago. And they are very proud of their partnerships: Bautisa Family Farms, Templeton Valley Farms, Mighty Cap Mushrooms, Loo Loo Farms, Morro Bay Mushrooms, Babe Farms, Half Moon Herbary, and Oliveto Ranch.

UPSTAIRS LOFTS, ROOMS AND SUITES

The Lofts are stunning, new and contemporary lodgings that were just build above the new **Paso Market Walk** (see previous pages). Beyond the atmosphere of modern beauty (see the photographs), they have also thought a lot about the practicalities of visitors. Not just complimentary Wi-Fi, they have a wine refrigerator in the room (they know we are going to collect wine being in the wine region), microwave so we can heat foods easily, and a Keurig coffee machine (with many coffee pods and cream too). The kitchen has lots of counter space, plus a nice little dining room table. The beds are amazing. You can feel the luxurious sheets (Egyptian cotton sheets). How about a forty-eight inch flat-screen television, with login for Netflix, Hulu and HBO.

The Lofts have their own private entrance completely separate from the Paso Market Walk. Private parking also provided. They have six unique lofts (four of the lofts are in the photographs below). A nice feature of staying in The Lofts is that the Paso Market Walk has coffee and pastries in the morning, many different food choices for lunch and dinner, wine and beer purveyors, and two full restaurants on the property.

$$$-$$$$

1803 Spring Street
Paso Robles, CA 93446

+1 805 720 1255
Jill@PasoMarketWalk.com

TheLoftsAtTheMarket.com

Open: Every Day
Six blocks North of The Downtown City Park
Reservations On Their Website

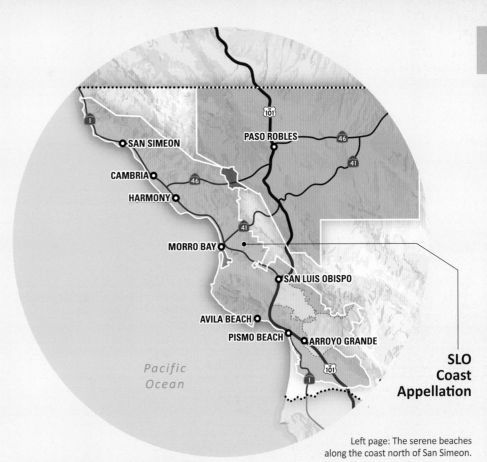

SLO
Coast
Appellation

Left page: The serene beaches
along the coast north of San Simeon.

NEW COASTAL APPELLATION

Set your eyes on the sandy beaches and rugged seaside cliffs that characterize the dramatic landscape here. See lush forests of **Monterey Pines**, one of only five native groves left in the world today, holding sway over the magnificent **Santa Lucia Mountains**. Coastal black-tail deer, brush rabbits and the rare red-legged frog inhabit the pristine wilderness along this northern coast of San Luis Obispo County.

Northernmost is San Simeon, where there are miles of pristine empty beaches, the **Monterey Pine Forest** that you can hike in for hours, the **Elephant Seals** where you can watch thousands of seals sleep, play and fight all year. Most notable is experiencing the glitz, glamour and grandeur of the magnificent **Hearst Castle**.

Cambria is a cute little beach town here that has captivated so many hearts. Just south is **Harmony**, a tiny privately owned town worth visiting. And

farther south is **Morro Bay,** with the famous **Morro Rock**, a state historical landmark.

South county sports the **Avila Beach** community of natural hot mineral springs, nude-sunbathing, world-class massages, and a host of personal rejuvenation therapies. The beautiful sandy beaches here have a uniquely sunny and warm microclimate.

This coastal area embraces a new appellation designated on March 9, 2022, as the **SLO Coast AVA**. It's a long narrow strip of land along the coast, with 97% of the vineyards within six miles of the ocean. It includes **Edna Valley AVA** and **Arroyo Grande AVA** as its sub-appellations. From the cold Pacific Ocean, this AVA creates the coldest wine region in California perfect for the varietals of Pinot Noir and Chardonnay grown here.

I uncover this area, the cities and towns, the wineries and restaurants, from north to south.

SAN LUIS OBISPO WINERIES

	Number of Wines	Red Wines	White Wines	Rosé Wines	Sweet Wines	Sparkling Wines	Wine Shop	Boutique	Lodging	Restaurant	Food Options	Food & Wine Pairings	Tours	Educational Workshops	Fun Activities	Pinot Noir	Chardonnay	Syrah	Other
SLO Coast AVA (north)																			
Hearst Ranch Winery	14	✓	✓	✓			✓	✓		✓						✓	✓		✓
Stolo Vineyards	8	✓	✓	✓			✓	✓		✓				✓	✓	✓	✓	✓	✓
Harmony Cellars	12	✓	✓	✓	✓		✓	✓			✓	✓		✓	✓		✓		✓
Absolution Cellars	15	✓	✓	✓			✓	✓									✓	✓	✓
SLO Coast AVA (south)																			
Sinor-LaVallee	10	✓					✓			✓	✓					✓		✓	
Alapay Cellars	13	✓	✓	✓	✓	✓	✓	✓		✓	✓					✓		✓	
Peloton Vineyards	13	✓	✓	✓			✓	✓								✓		✓	
Timbre Winery	16	✓	✓	✓			✓									✓		✓	
Verdad Wines, Lindquist Wines	36	✓	✓	✓			✓	✓							✓		✓	✓	✓	✓
Edna Valley AVA																			
La Lomita Ranch	7	✓	✓				✓		✓	✓			✓	✓		✓	✓	✓	✓
Tolosa Winery	18	✓	✓				✓						✓	✓	✓	✓	✓	✓	✓
Wolff Vineyards	9	✓	✓	✓	✓		✓								✓	✓	✓	✓	✓
Chamisal Vineyards	13	✓	✓			✓	✓			✓						✓	✓	✓	✓
Claiborne & Churchill Winery	18	✓	✓	✓	✓		✓				✓		✓	✓		✓	✓	✓	✓
Kynsi Winery	18	✓	✓	✓			✓									✓	✓		
Center of Effort	9	✓	✓		✓	✓	✓				✓		✓	✓					
Saucelito Canyon Tasting Room	19	✓	✓	✓			✓			✓									✓
Arroyo Grande Valley AVA																			
Saucelito Canyon Winery	19	✓	✓	✓			✓			✓								✓	
Talley Vineyards	19	✓	✓	✓	✓		✓			✓			✓		✓	✓	✓	✓	✓
Laetitia Vineyard & Winery	20	✓	✓	✓	✓		✓			✓					✓	✓	✓		✓
Downtown Industrial Park																			
Stephan Ross Wine Cellars	18	✓	✓	✓			✓	✓							✓	✓	✓	✓	
El Lugar Wines	6	✓	✓	✓			✓									✓	✓		
Downtown San Luis Obispo																			
Ragtag Wine Company	9	✓	✓	✓			✓									✓	✓	✓	✓
Dunites Wine Company	9	✓	✓	✓			✓									✓	✓		✓

Guardian of the vineyards

SAN SIMEON, VILLAGE & BEYOND

San Simeon is located on the ocean directly west of Paso Robles. This is the northernmost coastal area of San Luis Obispo County. Drive CA-46 West twenty-five miles from Paso Robles to Hwy 1 (CA-1), then fifteen miles north and you are there.

Old San Simeon Village was once a thriving place with saloons, a blacksmith, a livery stable, a butcher, a school, a depot for a stagecoach travelers, a telegraph line, and hotels, including the first-class Bay View Hotel that was frequented by famous guests (Thomas Edison, Winston Churchill, Calvin Coolidge, and Cary Grant). The only business to survive is **Sebastian's General Store**. The Sebastian Brothers provided goods and services to whalers, fishermen, miners, and neighboring ranches. The Sebastian family still owns and operates as a general merchandise store for over 150 years. The **Hearst Ranch Winery** and their tasting room is now located in one of the ocean-front warehouses where Hearst received his building materials and the furniture he stored for his **Hearst Castle** located directly above on the hill.

There are miles and miles of vast beaches that you can hike endlessly and not see anyone. Quiet. Serene. Just the purr of the ocean. Some beaches are sandy and others are rocky with lots of sea creatures in the crevices.

Monterey Pine Forest

Immediately north of the Old San Simeon Village is a natural forest of the Monterey Pine. It is a small forest right on the ocean in which you can hike and enjoy this rare and endangered tree native to only three very limited areas: Santa Cruz, Monterey Peninsula and San Luis Obispo County in California.

Piedras Blancas Light Station
+1 805 927 7361 • 15950 Cabrillo Hwy
Open: All Year, 9:45am Tours, RSVP Required
PiedrasBlancas.org

Explore inside a historic lighthouse and see how they served a critical role in maritime navigation on the coasts of the United States.

This is a **California Coastal National Monument** including the tower and some of the support buildings, all considered historic, listed on the National Register of Historic Places.

Located right off the highway (CA-1), just six miles north of the Old San Simeon Village.

Elephant Seals

Have you ever seen elephant seals up close? They love the San Simeon beaches where you can watch them play, fight, swim, sleep, throw sand on themselves, and do a lot more sleeping, all year long. Open 24/7.

Most spectacular though is when upwards of 18,000 elephant seals converge onto the beaches here for mating and birthing from November through March each year. To see a dominant 5,000 lb giant bull fight for the right to carve out his females is quite the experience.

The California State Park has created a special overlook to make it easy to view the seals. It is called **Elephant Seal Vista Point** and it is located right off the highway (CA-1) just five miles north of Old San Simeon Village.

William Randolph Hearst (Hearst Castle)

As a publisher, I have a great respect for the massive success Randolph Hearst achieved in publishing. Second homes are something that come with success, then and today. Consider this though. To build the Hearst Castle *today*, it would cost you $5 billion dollars. To put that in perspective, can you imagine any of the super-wealthy people of today spending anything near that amount on a second home? Rarely does the primary home exceed $50 million, a far cry from a $5 billion second-home estate. For me, it shows the magnitude of what this media mogul created (the nation's largest newspaper chain and magazine empire). Still in the family today, Hearst Communications generates $11.5 billion a year in revenues, and the Hearst family is worth $21 billion.

As a wine lover, I am delighted Hearst was also a passionate connoisseur of fine wines, serving only the best to his guests, even during prohibition. As an advocate of freedom and personal liberties, Hearst conducted a nationwide contest in his newspapers with a $25,000 award for the best plan for the repeal of Prohibition. You just gotta love this guy.

As a fellow aviator, Hearst also made airplanes a big part of his personal and business life. He sought to further the cause of aviation by offering $50,000 to the first aviator to cross the United States in an airplane under thirty days. Hard to imagine thirty days today. This was the beginnings of what makes airplanes so valuable to us today. Hearst put a runway on the ranch in San Simeon (photo below) so he could easily fly to the Castle, and to get editorials flown in for his approval prior to publishing (imagine no fax, email, or FedEx existed at that time). His distinguished guests could also arrive by private airplane, including such aviators as Howard Hughes, Amelia Earhart and Charles Lindbergh.

THE CASTLE ON THE ENCHANTED HILL

In that day and age, publishing a major newspaper created great wealth. For Randolph Hearst, it was the *San Francisco Examiner* and others that made him one of the most powerful media magnates of all time.

With such great wealth, Hearst and his family still loved to camp out on their 250,000-acre ranch in San Simeon overlooking the Pacific Ocean. Eventually, in 1919, Hearst enlisted the famous architect Julia Morgan to "build a little something here."

Three decades later the little project was yet to be completed. Morgan and Hearst had created a 90,080-square-foot estate that housed 165 rooms and 127 acres of gardens, terraces, pools and walkways (estate aerial photo below). This "little something" was first called *Camp Hill*, then *The Enchanted Hill* and ultimately *The Hearst Castle*, one of the most magnificent architectural masterpieces that would cost nearly $5 billion to build today.

The main house was Mediterranean Revival style, and its facade suggests a Spanish cathedral with its bell towers and ornate decorations. Three guesthouses of mighty proportions were also constructed, blending the same architectural style with the land's natural beauty.

Inside, Hearst decorated the palace with his priceless European and Mediterranean art collections, adding to an out-of-this-world elegance only the glamour of the 1930s can bestow. They never failed to incorporate art into all parts of the construction, in particular, using many priceless objects that Hearst acquired, borrowing design elements from different art forms and replicating them in modern materials throughout the castle.

The grandeur and glory of the castle didn't just encompass its grandiose size and priceless artifacts. Hearst regularly hosted lavish parties attended by the luminaries of the day, including such silver screen greats as Lionel and John Barrymore, Greta Garbo, David Niven, and Marion Davies, purported to be Hearst's mistress; famous politicians, such as Winston Churchill and Calvin Coolidge; and the literati set, such as Hedda Hopper, Louella Parsons and George Bernard Shaw. This A-List of Who's Who most certainly added to the enchantment of Hearst Castle during the 1930s heyday.

My castle favorites are the swimming pools. Their clean fresh colorful grandeur just begs me to jump in. The **Neptune Pool** (photo left) is a magnificent Greco-Roman-style outdoor pool of 345,000 gallons of water that features unparalleled coastline views of the Pacific Ocean. The **Roman Pool** (photo below left) is a 1,665-square-foot indoor work of art. Decorated from ceiling to floor with colorful one-inch square mosaic tiles and a statue of *Diana and the Stag*, a replica of the original classic sculpture called *Diana of Ephesus* that lives in the Louvre.

Ah, to be transported back in time to the thirties to strategize with luminaries in the library (photo below) and sip a cocktail with Mr. Hearst in his den (photo right).

750 Hearst Castle Road
San Simeon, CA 93452

+1 805 444 4445
VisitorInfo@HearstCastle.com

HearstCastle.org

Five different tours, plus an evening tour.

See the **Hearst Wine Cellar** on the **Cottages & Kitchens Tour**. Two rooms underground with double vault doors protecting the wine he served his guests during prohibition. Hearst's favorite wine was the Bordeaux Château Cheval Blanc.

Open: All Year, Every Day, Starting at 9am

SAN LUIS OBISPO **SLO COAST** SAN SIMEON ■
Winery, Oceanfront Tasting
HEARST RANCH WINERY

$$-$$$-$$$$

442 Slo San Simeon Road
San Simeon, CA 93452

+1 805 927 4100
Info@HearstRanchWinery.com

HearstRanchWinery.com

Open: Every Day, 11am-4pm
RSVP Available On Their Website

The only winery tasting room on the beach along the Central Coast of California.

FOOD, WINE AND OCEAN VIEWS

So where are the grapes? Don't see any along the San Simeon hillsides? Me neither! That is because Hearst Ranch owns ninety acres of vineyards in the noteworthy Estrella appellation of Paso Robles. This is where great wine grapes should be grown.

While you can visit the winery in Paso Robles, the tasting room in the **Old San Simeon Village** is a very unique experience. The village makes you feel like you are back in the gold rush days. The tasting room is in one of the large warehouses Randolph Hearst used to receive art, furniture and construction materials from Europe for his castle.

Hearst Ranch has a huge indoor tasting (in the warehouse) with historical photos of Randolph Hearst, his massive ranch and construction of the castle, plus a wine shop and gift shop as well.

Tasting outside is the most unique experience ever, as this is the only beach-front tasting along the Central Coast, right on the water. It is a large beautiful outdoor space of picnic tables and umbrellas overlooking the San Simeon Bay, beach, pier, and Monterey Pine Forest peninsula.

Being a wine club member goes way beyond the discount for wines and free tastings. Take a look at the comfy couches and lounges in the photo on the left page. This is the outdoor tasting setting for club members. How cool is this! Almost makes you feel like you are Randolph Hearst.

Another member benefit is tasting the Proprietor's Reserve wines. While they have an excellent lineup of wines as winemaker Soren Christensen is consistent in producing solid wines. However, the Proprietor's Reserve wines are knock-your-socks-off wines. I carried a bottle with me on my trip, drank a little bit every day, and watched the quality develop beautifully each day. You will absolutely love this wine!

This is the perfect place to get a bottle of wine and enjoy the view and fresh ocean air. When Paso Robles becomes 100° during a hot summer day, the Hearst Ranch San Simeon Tasting is a refreshing alternative, and only a half an hour away.

Thursday through Monday, they have a gourmet food truck (see photo above for some extra delicious tacos). Plus, their deli has cheese and charcuterie everyday of the week.

Collection of Wines

Proprietor's Reserve Cabernet Sauvignon
Proprietor's Reserve The Point (Petit Verdot, Cabernet
Sauvignon, Cabernet Franc, Malbec, Merlot)
Proprietor's Reserve Chardonnay

Lone Tree Cabernet Franc
GSM Reserve Red Wine (Grenache, Syrah,
Petite Sirah, Mourvedre, Viognier)
Pancho Petit Verdot
Carpoforo Zinfandel
Chileno Tempranillo
Pico Creek Merlot
The Pergola Petite Sirah
Bunkhouse Cabernet Sauvignon
Babicora Malbec
Randolph Red Cuvée (Cabernet Sauvignon, Grenache,
Cabernet Franc, Syrah, Mourvèdre, Malbec)
Three Sisters Red Cuvée (Syrah, Mourvèdre,
Grenache, Petite Sirah)

CAMBRIA VILLAGE

Cambria is a seaside village in the far northwest of San Luis Obispo County along the ocean in the Monterey Pine Forest. Cambria is just south of San Simeon on Hwy 1 bordered to the east by the Santa Lucia Mountains. On the other side of the mountains is Paso Robles, just twenty-five miles on CA-46.

We think of Cambria as the cute little artist village with nice cool weather in the summer. So many people have summer homes here.

The town has many artist shops, an eclectic assortment of restaurants, and numerous outdoor activities. For me, I love exploring the beaches. Some are sandy, others with rocks and tidepools. They are all beautiful.

There is no shortage of wildlife here. Eagles in the sky. Little crabs in the crevices. And 1,000 lb seals sleeping in the sand. They all seem to smile at me.

Cambria resides in the new SLO Coast AVA and has vineyards. Yes, you can visit a winery here and taste good wines (see next page).

Cambria Coffee Roasting Company
+1 805 927 0670 • 761 Main Street
Open: Every Day, 7am-5:30pm

CambriaCoffeeSales.com

I have learned that the best coffee comes from places that actually roast the beans themselves – and quality beans. It is not just enough to have fresh ground.

At home, my favorite coffee house roasts their own beans. Such a difference. Whenever I am headed to Cambria, I crave this coffee.

Cambria Coffee is so delicious that I go overboard... starting with a breakfast **caffè latté**, then one at noon, and a craving for one more in the afternoon. How addictive is that?!

Friday through Sunday, they make, *fresh to order,* **French beignets**. To die for! This is the place to be.

Robin's Restaurant (Mexican, Thai, Indian)
+1 805 927 5007 • 4095 Burton Drive
Open: Every Day, 11am-3pm, 4:30pm-9pm

RobinsRestaurant.com

This restaurant's reputation runs far and wide. I was in downtown San Luis Obispo telling someone that I was traveling to Cambria. Robin's was the first thing he thought of. Then someone else chimed in saying he grew up in Cambria and he told me about two dished that were his craving favorites.

Robin's Salmon Bisque was his ultimate choice. Secret ingredients. Totally awesome. Richly and savory.

Rogan Josh was the other favorite (photo below). Northern Indian lamb, curry, yogurt, tomatoes, green beans, almonds, cilantro-mint chutney, pineapple chutney, chapati, and basmati brown rice.

Sea Chest Oyster Bar
+1 805 927 4514 • 6216 Moonstone Beach Drive
Open: Wednesday-Monday, 5:30pm-9pm

SeaChestOysterBar.com

So, they open at 5:30pm. Be there by 5:00pm I was emphatically advised! When I arrived, there was already a line of twenty-five plus people. Some brought their own lawn chairs and had been there for an hour. Well, clearly, Sea Chest has a great reputation.

Finally inside, this place is hopping. Those who came later, were waiting for the second shift. Several choices of oysters. Look below. You could taste the freshness as if they just came out of the water.

There is a board on the wall of their fresh fish. Six great choices. Hard to choose. Mahi mahi was my selection. Unbelievable fresh. I will be back – earlier.

$$-$$$

2905 Burton Drive
Cambria, CA 93428

+1 805 927 4200
Concierge@CambriaPinesLodge.com

CambriaPinesLodge.com

RUSTIC LODGE WITH MODERN STYLE

While the first thing we think of with Cambria is a very cool beach community, I never realized in previous visits that Cambria had pine forests until I came to this lodge. And the Cambria Pines Lodge is every flavor of a mountain lodge.

The outside is an old lodge wood feeling and inside the rooms have been update modern style. The living room has an appropriate fireplace to keep you warm and cozy in the woods. So does the bedroom, separate and romantic, burning flames while snuggling in bed (photo above). The outside deck has wooden lounge chairs to enjoy the view of the pine forest across the rolling hills (photo below).

Morning comes with a hot breakfast buffet. Evening arrives with live music in the lounge (photo right page). The daytime offers pool, spa and an incredible array of gardens (photo right). Elaborate gardens are all around the hotel, plus a nursery with an abundance of plants to purchase.

$$-$$$

3776 Santa Rosa Creek Road
Cambria, CA 93428

+1 (805) 924-3131
Info@StoloFamilyVineyards.com

StoloFamilyVineyards.com

Open: Every Day, 12pm-5pm
RSVP Available On Their Website

I magine vineyards along the north coast, in Cambria, making nice wines.

COLD CLIMATE SYRAH

Who would've ever thought that you could plant vineyards in Cambria. It's this cool little town that has no sense of being a wine region. Yet, into the hills, less than three miles from the beach, there are vineyards planted on a hillside and also in a meadow. And when you taste the wines here, you will be pleasantly surprised.

Back in 1998, the famous Rhône winemaker John Alban planted Syrah grapes on this property. He was also being very smart with the cold environment to also plant the Burgundian grapes of Pinot Noir and Chardonnay. Today, these well-established vineyards are producing wines of unbelievable quality. You must taste them.

Stolo Vineyards recently brought on a new winemaker to elevate the wines even further. Rajat "Raj" Parr is an accomplished wine grape-grower with thirty years experience. He is also a sommelier, perfect for making wines conducive for foods. He is the author of two wine books. Raj has also received several prestigious James Beard Awards.

If you love cold-weather Syrah, this is the ultimate cold terroir, and I must admit, the Syrah is very good. Wine Enthusiast loves their cold-weather Syrah, honoring them with 97 points for their Creekside Estate Syrah. I agree that the creekside vineyard is definitely their best terroir for Syrah. I love their hillside vineyards for Pinot Noir. Everyone has their favorites, mine is their Hillside Reserve Pinot Noir. This wine really showed me that Cambria has awesomely capable terroir.

By the way, Cambria and Stolo Vineyards are included in the new SLO Coast AVA. I wondered why the new appellation came this far up the coast; however, Stolo Vineyards proves the value of the AVA including this north coast.

Plus, this is Cambria! Spend some time in Cambria and enjoy winery tasting while you are here. You get both.

This winery has an excellent park environment (photo above) to enjoy their wines. Wine tasting is available indoors or in the park. You can bring a picnic or they have charcuterie plates available.

Stolo has a variety of entertainment. They host live musicians in what they call their **Music in the Meadow** series on Thursday afternoons. They also have a **Health & Wellness** program on Tuesday and Thursday mornings with Pilates.

Collection of Wines

Hillside Reserve Syrah
Hillside Reserve Pinot Noir
Hillside Reserve Chardonnay

Creekside Estate Syrah
Creekside Estate Pinot Noir

Sauvignon Blanc
Dry Gewürztraminer
Rosé of Pinot Noir

HARMONY TINY ARTISAN TOWN

Located five miles south of Cambria on Hwy 1, the town of Harmony is a most unusual town to discover. It is a one-block town, 2.5 acres, three businesses (below), a population of eighteen people, and an official post office of 93435, established in 1914.

Harmony was originally established in 1869 with the boom of the dairy industry. The Harmony Valley Creamery served the area with high-quality milk, cream, butter and cheese. Randolph Hearst and his guests would make this an important stop on the way to the castle. They became famous for their buttermilk served to motorists as they drove through on Hwy 1.

When the dairy business moved from the central coast to the central valley, the town was abandoned. Recently, a successful Texan Dairyman purchased the entire town and has restored its businesses and character. And Harmony Valley Creamery is back, now producing super-delicious hand-crafted ice cream.

Harmony Glass Works
+1 805 927 4248 • 2180 Old Creamery Road
Open: Every Day, 9am-5pm

HarmonyGlassworks.com

Contemporary glassblowing, working studio and school on premises. An extensive gallery of sculptures, ornaments, vases, jewelry, and wine stoppers!

Harmony Pottery Studio & Gallery
+1 805 927 4293 • 2191 Old Creamery Road
Open: Every Day, 10am-5pm

HarmonyTown.com

A remarkable assemblage of the Central Coast's most unique gallery and studio of ceramic art and porcelain. It is an extensive collection of beautiful works from 150 different artists. Since 1973.

Harmony Valley Creamery
+1 805 927 1028 • 2177 Old Creamery Road
Open: Every Day, 11am-5pm

HarmonyValleyCreamery.com

Fifty years of handcrafted small-batch ice cream. Udderly awesome! Pints available all week and scoops from the Creamery Scoop truck on the weekends.

$$

3255 Harmony Valley Road
Harmony, CA 93435

+1 805 927 1625
Info@HarmonyCellars.com

HarmonyCellars.com

Open: Thursday-Monday, 10am-5pm

Beautiful hillside views for tasting very good wines at great prices.

HISTORY OF HARMONY WINE

Harmony Cellars is located on the hillside overlooking the town of Harmony. This is the ultimate view of this picturesque little town. Especially now that the winery has built a large deck over the slope as a great place to sit out with a glass of wine and enjoy the view.

The winery officially started in 1989 by Chuck and Kim Mulligan. Kim's great grandfather is a founder of the old Harmony Creamery. Winemaking started way back then as her great-grandfather Giacomo Barlogio made wine in his basement. This is even before Prohibition required basements for winemaking.

The property is a beautifully undeveloped rolling hillside with their 150 acres as part of Giacomo's original land holdings in their family now for four generations. Their winery is in its historic barn. The grapes come from Paso Robles and Monterey.

Chuck is the winemaker and has thirty years experience creating these wines. He has generated a reputation of producing quality wines at great prices. This winery is one of the best overall price/quality combinations of any of the wineries I have visited throughout the central coast.

I was happily surprised with their Chardonnay. I am primarily a red wine drinker. The full and rich flavors, plus big viscosity like red wine, got my attention. The Chardonnay grapes are fermented in American oak barrels and then aged for fourteen months in these barrels.

This Chardonnay is complex. Possible too much for a delicate fish. This wine has body and can pair with substantive cheeses and meats. It is truly a red wine drinkers white wine. I promise you that you will be happily surprised.

There are many events going on here. Lots of music. Live concerts on Friday nights! Winemaker dinners on the property, pairing delicious foods with their wines while watching the sunset. Workshops too. Create beautiful sea glass wine charms in a workshop led by a local artist. Sip wine, of course.

On their property is the original Harmony Creamery, now their winery, still standing today. You can wander the old brick pathways surrounding the property and see the history of this old building. This is a nice day to explore the historic town of Harmony and make your way to the Harmony Cellars to finish a beautiful day.

Collection of Wines

Reserve Aria (Cabernet Sauvignon, Malbec)
Robusto (Sangiovese, Petite Sirah, Cabernet Sauvignon, Malbec)
Que Sirah Syrah (Petite Sirah, Syrah, Cabernet Sauvignon)

Grandpa Barlogio Zinfandel
Treble (Syrah)
Petite Sirah
Cabernet Sauvignon
Repertoire (Zinfandel, Petite Sirah, Cabernet Sauvignon, Syrah, Malbec, Merlot, Petit Verdot, Tannat)

Rosa Riserva (Rosé of, Syrah)
Chardonnay
Reserve Pinot Gris

Huzzah! (Sparkling Chardonnay)

MORRO BAY EMBARCADERO

Morro Bay is a coastal city twenty miles west of downtown San Luis Obispo on CA-1. It is famous for its **Morro Rock**, a twenty-five-million-year-old volcanic plug that has become a natural preserve and a state historical landmark (see next page).

Morro's Bay is protected by a large stretch of sand dunes to keep it calm from the ocean. The wildlife is abundant. The Morro Bay Estuary has been identified as an Important bird area by the Audubon Society. In the bay are many fishing and sailing boats, kayaks (you can rent), sea otters, and seal lions.

With fisherman bringing in fish catches every day, the Morro Bay Embarcadero village has many fresh fish restaurants. Below are two very different choices. Both are excellent.

There is wine tasting in the village too. We cannot miss out on wine tasting. Absolution Cellars in located right in the village for tasting and sales (right page).

Galley Seafood Grill
+1 805 772 7777 • 899 Embarcadero
Open: Wednesday-Monday, 11:30am-8:30pm

GalleyMorroBay.com

The view is almost as good as the fresh fish. Right on the bay, overlooking the Morrow Rock (photo below). Indoor and outdoor dining.

Below is fresh **Shrimp Louis Salad** with avocado, tomato and hard-boiled egg on a bed of crisp greens.

Giovanni's Fish Market
+1 805 772 2025 • 1001 Front Street
Open: Every Day, 9am-6pm

GiosFish.com

Super casual dining at this fish market that will cook you anything fish. And a to-go market. Fillets. Shellfish. Crustacean. Sushi grade fish. Smoked fish. Oysters.

Below is a very yummy **Tuna & Salmon Poke Bowl** with seaweed, wasabi and avocado. It was so fresh!

SAN LUIS OBISPO **SLO COAST** MORRO BAY ▮
Winery
ABSOLUTION CELLARS

$$-$$$

845 Embarcadero #H
Morro Bay, CA 93442

+1 805 242 6362
Info@AbsolutionCellars.com

AbsolutionCellars.com

Open: Thursday-Monday, 12pm-5pm

A wine enthusiast is now making single-variety, single-vineyard, small-batch wines.

DREAM COME TRUE

Have you ever thought about making your own wine? I have. And I did it twice. And the results were extraordinarily good wines. I still have some in my cellar continuing to age.

Absolution sellers is a dream come true for a Florida-based real estate building consultant who fell in love enough with wine that he came to California in 2012 to blend one bottle of his own wine. Dirk Neumann now had a little taste of what it's like to make his own wine. So, he came back next year and did it again. The following year, though, he arranged to make an entire barrel of wine, and he did so again the next year. As he shared the wine he made, people were absolutely loving what he was making.

What do you do when people love the wine you're making, you make more, of course. And Dirk did. The next year he made eight barrels, then twelve barrels, Then twenty-two barrels, and by 2019 he was making 36 barrels of wine. Do the math: 25 cases per barrel of wine. Dirk now had an abundance of wine. Fortunately, really great wine.

Dirk discovered that he could consult living anywhere in the country. So, he moved to California where he could be close to the grapes and wines

he was making. Dirk has an important focus: only choose extraordinary vineyards with excellent growers. He makes single vineyard, single varietals, in small-batch, handmade wines. It is important to note, great wines are made in the vineyard, and this is what Dirk is focused upon.

Here is an example. Dirk has a special three-quarter acre vineyard to himself in the Chalone Valley in Monterey County. Chalone is the special appellation that placed third in the famous 1976 Paris competition when Napa Valley beat French wines in a blind tasting.

If you did the math, adding up the number of bottles that have accumulated over the years, a tasting room was becoming an absolute necessity. In February 2020, Absolution Cellars opened its tasting room in the village of Morro Bay. What a great place to enjoy fish and drink great wines.

Considering they opened one month prior to the pandemic close-down, wine continued to be made until they finally opened a full five days a week for tasting. We benefit from tasting older vintages as current releases.

Dirk is on premises for the tastings, so you get to hear the interesting stories surrounding each wine and the beautiful artwork that goes on the bottles.

Collection of Wines

Granache
Tannat
Wicked Sensation (Grenache, Tannat,)
Syrah
Pinot Noir (Pommard 5 Clone)
Pinot Noir (Old Chalone Clones)

Malbec
Petit Verdot
Cabernet Savignon
Consonance (Cabernet Savignon, Zinfandel)
Grenache (Colburn Vineyard)
Tempranillo
Zinfandel

Rosé of Sangiovese
Albariño

On the peak of Cerro San Luis viewing west across three additional Morros. Inset: hiking trail on Cerro San Luis

Above the clouds on top of Bishop Peak

TWENTY-FIVE MILLION YEARS AGO...

You may be familiar with the famous **Morro Rock** standing proud against the ocean in Morro Bay. This is just one of nine volcanic plugs that formed twenty-five million years ago, together they are called the Nine Morro Sisters.

It all started in what is today the Edna Valley wine region with **Islay Hill** being the first volcano to erupt here. There was not much of an eruption though, as these volcanoes were formed when volcanic plugs of magma welled up and solidified into softer rock. The softer rocks eroded away during the millions of years that followed, leaving dramatic, steep rocky buttes we see today. In this order, these nine sisters were formed from southeast **Islay Hill** to northwest **Morro Rock**. This is now a wealth of geologic discovery that provides the area with a unique natural skyline. And awesome hiking!

Islay Hill is at the entrance to the Edna Valley wine region, with vineyards planted right up to its base. Hike to the top and see an amazing view of Edna Valley with vineyards rolling across valley's landscape (photo right top).

Cerra San Lucas is a challenging long hike, and with steep trails to feel your leg and butt muscles work. The views are amazing like you see in the left-page photos.

The tallest Sister is **Bishop Peak** (the first Morro you see in the landscape photo left page). This is easily a four-hour adventure; three hours of hiking and one hour enjoying the view. It gains strenuousness as you reach the top with boulders to navigate. Go up during a foggy morning and be above the clouds with the soaring birds (photo above).

The next three Morros are not available for public access. The last three Morros are located in the Morro Bay State Park.

Cerro Cabrillo may look like an innocent climb (photo below right). Don't be mislead: the trails are extremely steep at points. I almost made it to the top; however, the massive boulders were prevalent with lively poison oak, so I thought I would stay safe.

Black Hill is the easiest climb. In ten minutes, you are at the top with a beautiful view of **Morro Rock**, the bay and the Pacific Ocean (photo below).

Morro Rock is considered the treasure of the Morros. It's a domed-shaped rock standing proud in Morro Bay, right at the ocean, as a natural preserve and state historical landmark. You can walk right up to its base cliffs, yet no climbing allowed.

Five of Nine Morro Sisters are *Hikeable
from southeast to northwest, plus elevation

*1) Islay Hill - 775'
*2) Cerro San Luis - 1,292'
*3) Bishop Peak - 1,559'
4) Chumash Peak - 1,257'
5) Cerro Romauldo - 1,306'
6) Hollister Peak - 1,404'
*7) Cerro Cabrillo - 911'
*8) Black Hill - 665'
9) Morro Rock - 576'

To find the trailhead of each Morro, type into Maps: "morro name" trailhead

On top of Islay Hill viewing southeast into the Edna Valley Wine Region

Cerro Cabrillo

The view of the famous Morro Rock from on Black Hill

AVILA BEACH VILLAGE

Avila Beach is the most northern beach in southern San Luis Obispo county, and the closest beach to downtown San Luis Obispo (ten miles). The beaches from north to south are Avila Beach, Shell Beach, Pismo Beach, Grover Beach, and Oceano (seventeen miles from San Luis Obispo). Lots of white sand along the coast here! And Sand dunes in Oceano.

Avila Beach is the coziest beach town along here, with a quaint village, white sand beach and a pier. Avila Beach is in a bay protected from the ocean waves and winds off the sea, making it warmer here during non-summer days.

Avila Beach Village has a large walking boardwalk along the beach with numerous restaurants and shops to enjoy. Three wine tasting places here, one with fresh oysters to pair with Chardonnay (see review next page).

Alapay Cellars (Winery)
+1 805 595 2632 • 415 1st Street
Open: Every Day, 10:30am-6:30pm

AlapayCellars.com

One block off the Avila Boardwalk, Alapay is 2,000 sq' of sit-at-the-bar or bar tops or comfortable couch tastings in a hip lounge vibe, all surrounding an extensive gift shop of everything wine (photo below).

The wines here are aged in French Oak barrels for fourteen months. Grapes are sources from well-known vineyards located along the central coast. There is definitely a French style to the wines here, blending with the California terroir influence. They started in 2001 with grapes from the famous Bien Nacido Vineyards in Santa Maria. Today they are producing thirteen wines, all are small-lot terroir-driven wines.

This is a place of fun and events. Morro Bay Sunset Cruise, Winemaker Dinners, Christmas Cruise on the Rhine River in Basel, Switzerland and Amsterdam.

Peloton Vineyards (Winery)
+1 805 627 1080 • 470 Front Street
Open: Thursday-Monday, 11am-5pm

PelotonCellars.com

A half block off the Avila Boardwalk, Peloton is tucked in the back of a beautiful corridor with a wonderful outdoor seating (photo below). It is a quiet little place to enjoy tasting wines and enjoying the afternoon.

The style of wines here are the rich, fully ripe fruit, higher in alcohol, bold flavors, in both red and white wines. They contract with vineyards in SLO Coast and Paso Robles and manage the vines themselves to create their style.

Peloton was created by four longtime friends in 2005 and opened this tasting room in 2010. They are cyclists and named the winery after this French word meaning "group," and more specifically the dynamic main pack of riders in a cycling race. They feel that their wines embody the color and spirit of cycling.

Blue Moon Over Avila (French Bistro)
+1 805 595 2583 • 460 Front Street
Open: Every Day, 11:30am-8:30pm

BlueMoonOverAvila.com

Located directly on the Avila Boardwalk, with outdoor seating facing the sandy beach, waves and pier setting off into the bay. And once in a while, a beautiful moon sitting in the sky.

With this European setting comes a delicious French lunch or dinner paired with excellent wines from around the world. It is such a European feel here, you could easily think you are sitting in Southern France along the Mediterranean Sea.

Blue Moon also has an indoor wine bar, with a wine Maître D' from France to enlighten you on interesting European wines. I counted thirty-three wines by the glass! They also engage guest chefs from France to create in the kitchen bringing their magical flavors to the French cuisine here.

SAN LUIS OBISPO **AVILA BEACH** ◼
Winery, Vineyards, Oysters
SINOR-LAVALLEE WINERY

$$-$$$

550 First Street
Avila Beach, CA 93424

+1 805 459 9595
WineClub@SinorLaVallee.com

SinorLaVallee.com

Open: Every Day, Noon-6pm

O ysters and Chardonnay: a perfect pairing for wine tasting at the beach.

WINETASTING AT THE BEACH

When was the last time you discovered a winery's tasting room at the beach? I have never seen one. This was a real treat to find. And not just a tasting room, great wines as well, plus fresh oysters!

Sinor-LaVallee is just one block from the sand at Avila Beach with both indoor (photo above) and outdoor tasting areas. They bring in fresh oysters every day, which pairs perfectly with their Chardonnay wines. I am salivating right now just thinking of **oysters and chardonnay** (photo right)!

Now you might be thinking, Avila Beach is not a wine region, that cannot be good terroir. You are correct. Make no mistake though, these wines are excellent. The vineyards are located strategically just 1.2 miles from the ocean in the rolling hills between Edna Valley and Avila Beach. The vineyards are named Bassi Vineyard.

Bassi Vineyard has extreme coastal influence, morning fogs, briny air currents and steep oceanic weathered soils of tierra loam, soft sandstone and fine sandy loam with limited clay. The underlying bedrock is hard marine sandstone through which the vine roots can barely penetrate, making the

yields extremely low, which we all know produces intense rich fruit. The Bassi Vineyard definitely expresses its terroir in each bottle. You will love it.

Without a great winemaker, what is a great vineyard? Winemaker Mike Sinor has decades of experience working for some of the best wineries in Edna Valley. One of his big successes is the Ancient Peaks Winery (page 217), in the Santa Margarita Ranch AVA of Paso Robles, where he is the Founding Winemaker.

When Mike discovered and acquired the Bassi Vineyard, and started showing great wines from the vineyards, he immediately had followers. Some of the best winemakers in SLO started purchasing fruit from Mike. I saw this first hand when I was invited to Mike's Winemakers BBQ at Bassi Vineyard where there was a Whos Who in attendance.

For Sinor, he keeps his favorite fruit, of course. Mike's Chardonnay is his most expensive wine. And it shows. I am not a Chardonnay fan, and yet this wine pleases my palate very much. Add some oysters for the perfect pairing.

Collection of Wines

Pinot Noir Black Label

Chardonnay White Label
Pinot Noir White Label
Syrah White Label

Pinot Noir Whole Cluster
Carbonic Pinot Noir - Bassi Vineyard
Pinot Noir Estate
Chardonnay Estate
Syrah Estate
Syrah Whole Cluster

PIRATES COVE NUDE BEACH

Pirates Cove is a secluded beach between Avila and Pismo. From Highway 101, exit Avila Beach Drive west to Cave Landing Drive. Continue on the dirt road to the parking lot. There is a sign to the cliff trail hiking down. Pirates Cove is a private south-facing cove for plenty of warm sun and protection from the winds and big swells.

You have to love the San Luis Obispo County for embracing a legal nude beach in a cove that has sported lawlessness for centuries. This is where Sir Francis Drake of the British Navy, acting as a pirate, stole $500 million in treasure from a Spanish ship in 1579. Booze runners used this cove during Prohibition, keeping the locals happy and maintaining its illicit reputation.

Pirates Cove is still a lawless sort of beach. You can drink, smoke, bring your pets, and be totally naked in public. Note, this is not a clothing-optional beach, it is a nude beach. When you arrive, you are expected to be naked.

Today, a group of regular users call themselves pirates and self-manage the beach in cooperation with the sheriff's department, Coastal Commission and the Port San Luis Harbor District (the owners of the beach). The pirates insist on everyone keeping the beach clean, no clothed voyagers, and a harmonious environment. This beach is beautiful, and the people are nice and welcoming.

AVILA BEACH A SPECIAL PLACE

Avila Beach is a very special place. It is located in a sheltered bay where the beach is spared from ocean winds that scrape away beaches and make them bald, cold and uncomfortable. The waves are calm here, the air beautifully warm. Avila Beach is the ultimate swimming and sunbathing beach. Pirates Cove (left page) has its own sheltered bay at the south of this bay with double protection from the harsh ocean. Here you don't even need a bathing suit!

Looking at Avila Beach Village though, it seems brand new. And it kind of is. The history here is that Avila was the primary pier for goods to reach San Luis Obispo and beyond. Santa Fe Railroad built tracks into the harbor and ultimately Avila's Port San Luis became the largest crude oil shipping point in the world. Until an oil pipe broke and the mess needed to be cleaned up.

This became an entire removal of the town, all commercial and residences! Removal of all the contaminated soil. A complete restoration of the property. Then a ground-up construction of a brand-new town. This is definitely turning a lemon into lemonade, a new village emerged.

When the community chose their style of a new town, they wanted it to be funky and eclectic. Someone even described tidied-up funky. Today this New England style exterior represents a brand-new Avila Beach Village. Everything is new from the early 2000s. Unlikely that there is any other endeavor undertaken like this in the world.

And the seagulls, they witnessed it all and love it here.

PISMO BEACH HIP BEACH TOWN

Pismo Beach is the classic cool, hip beach town. Expansive sandy beaches, surfers riding the waves, sexy swimwear, beautifully restored pier, all in a flipflop shorts town filled with beachy shops. Lots of neon everywhere. The neon signs are part of the coolness here! You can indulge in cafés, coffeehouses, pubs, night clubs, and restaurants.

Along the coast, north of town, are large cliffs and rocky beaches (see coastline photos next page). It is a great place to explore sealife in the tidepools. Check out the crab that discovered me. We examined each other for quite a while. He outstared me!

Also on these cliffs are some amazing resorts. I shot the photo on the next page from the **Dolphin Bay Resort** (right page). The views are spectacular from the rooms.

Pismo Beach is located south of Avila Beach off Hwy 101 (CA-101). Here is the magic. The vineyards in Edna Valley (see page 259) are only ten minutes away. You can stay on the beach and get to the wine regions faster than staying in downtown San Luis Obispo.

Lido Restaurant (at Dolphin Bay Resort)
+1 805 773 8900 • 2727 Shell Beach Road
Open: Every Day, 8am-9pm

TheDolphinBay.com/Lido

The cuisine here is amazing. Just look at the scallops below and the steak to the right. Delicious. Let's get to something even more special here, their wines.

They cellar over 800 different wines from all over the world. From Bordeaux first-growths to local and boutique producers. Their Wine Director, sommelier, is on premises to help you choose through this extensive array of wines. They do not markup the typical double and triple prices of restaurants. They sell their wines at normal wine shop retail prices served at the table. Some wines are less than retail, so you might want to consider taking some home.

They have an inside lounge, a beautiful dining room and outdoors dining with views of the Pacific Ocean (photo right).

THE ULTIMATE HOTEL ROOM • OPTIMUM LOCATION

You are going to love this hotel. You will probably think, as I did, that these were condominiums converted into a hotel. Not the case. The owner is an avid traveler and wants many basic luxuries while he is traveling. So, he decided to build this hotel to represent all the special things that he likes traveling.

The rooms are to die for! Everything has been thought through. Large spacious living room with a fireplace and big-screen TV. And a luxurious sofa and arm chairs to enjoy it all. Full-size gourmet kitchen and dining room. Laundry facilities inside the space. Separate bedroom. To me, it is the little things that make a difference, like double sinks and his-and-hers walk-in closets. My favorite though is the outdoor spacious patio overlooking the cliffs and the beautiful Pacific Ocean (photo left). Everything is stylish.

Consider this special treat, their location. You can enjoy being at the beach, breathing the fresh ocean breeze and staying in this wonderful hotel, yet you are close to the wineries in Edna Valley (only ten minutes). The ocean here is spectacular with the cliffs and rocky tidepools full of sealife (see photo next page taken at Dolphin Bay Resort).

$$$-$$$$-$$$$$

2727 Shell Beach Road
Cambria, CA 93449

+1 805 773 4300
Info@TheDolphinBay.com

TheDolphinBay.com

PISMO BEACH COASTLINE

The view from Dolphin Bay Resort

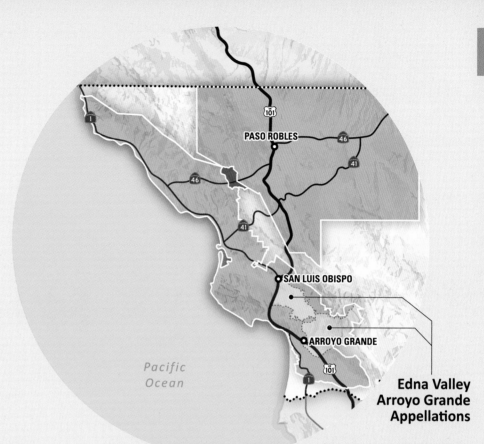

Edna Valley
Arroyo Grande
Appellations

Left page: The landscape of Edna Valley

CALIFORNIA'S COLDEST AVA

Edna Valley is the coldest appellation in all of California. It's comparable to cold Burgundy. I found the Chardonnay and Pinot Noir here reflects the flavors of France more than other cooler wine regions in California.

Edna Valley is a northwest-southeast running valley of volcanic hills in San Luis Obispo County. The SLO Airport is adjacent to Edna Valley at its western edge. The city of San Luis Obispo is just ten minutes northwest of Edna Valley. Everything is so close and accessible.

The Arroyo Grande Valley is adjacent to Edna Valley at its southern border. Both valleys share the cool climate terroir conducive to producing Pinot Noir and Chardonnay. You will also find cool climate Syrah being grown and bottled here.

Edna Valley is actually an extension of the sea with cold Pacific Ocean wind blowing directly into the valley into the vineyards. Oscillations of warm and cold air caused by a venturi effect brings in and clears the fog. This creates a microclimate ideal for ripening delicate Pinot Noir and Chardonnay.

I am not a California Chardonnay fan. I much prefer Burgundy. However, I found the extra cold growing area here, like Burgundy, producing Chardonnay wines I loved very much.

You should definitely experience these wineries.

- Sinor-LaVallee, page 251
- La Lomita Ranch, page 261
- Tolosa Winery, page 265
- Wolff Vineyards, page 267
- Chamisal Vineyards, page 269
- Claiborne & Churchill, page 271
- Kynsi Winery, page 273
- Center of Effort, page 275
- Saucelito Canyon, page 277
- Talley Vineyards, page 279
- Laetitia Vineyard & Winery, page 281

$$-$$$

1985 La Lomita Way
San Luis Obispo, CA 93401

+1 805 706 8034
Info@LaLomitaWines.com

LaLomitaWines.com

Open: Thursday-Sunday, 11am-4pm

Collection of Wines

Estate Islay Hill Grenache
Estate Islay Hill Albariño

Spanish Springs Vineyard Grenache
Slide Hill Vineyard Syrah
Greengate Vineyard Pinot Noir
Chene Vineyard Pinot Noir
Rosemary's Vineyard Chardonnay

V ineyards planted on an ancient volcanic hill are showing some deliciously different wines.

VOLCANIC VINEYARDS

Islay Hill is the first in the volcanic chain of the Nine Morro Sisters (see page 249), located right at the entrance to Edna Valley. La Lomita Ranch is on Islay Hill and has planted the only vineyards on one of these 20-million-year-old ancient volcanic cones.

This is a new project, with the vineyards planted in 2015 and 2016. Most of their wines in the beginning are from fruit sourced from their neighbors. They have very good neighbors! Don't be afraid to come taste what they have now, and see the quality and style of their winemaker. Native yeasts, open one-ton fermentation vats, aged on lees, basket pressed, no filtering or fining, all organic practices.

Islay Hill is planted with the Edna Valley classics of Chardonnay, Pinot Noir and Syrah, plus Albariño and Grenache. Grenache is planted the highest on the volcanic cone and is already showing fruit to make wine. Might seem a bit early; however, I tasted their 2019 Grenache from just three-year-old fruit. It was way more sophisticated than I expected.

It had the nice Grenache fruit we come to love as well. I can just imagine how good this fruit will become as the vineyard matures.

Albariño is the first wine they produced from their vineyards on Islay Hill. This wine made me thinking about a seafood risotto with lots of rich butter and cheese.

In addition to their standard tasting, La Lomita Ranch has created the **Aromas of Wine Sensory Experience** to immerse yourself in the discovery of the aromas of wine, which aromas are prevalent in each wine varietal, and how terroir and winemaking affects the aromas.

If you would like to do some hiking into their hillside vineyards on Islay Hill, their **Vineyard Tour Experience** will get you up close to see the terroir. And for a bonus, you will see some great views into the Edna Valley.

And if you are extra energetic, you can hike to the very top of Islay Hill for some amazing views in all directions. The entrance to the trailhead is in the neighborhood on the west side of the hill.

BED & BREAKFAST EQUESTRIAN RANCH

La Lomita Ranch was once a famous Arabian horse breeding ranch. Horses still live there today. The hacienda you see below is where the famed Arabian horses would be displayed to their suited buyers. It is a beautiful environment made for beautiful horses, and now ready for your beautiful getaway. There is much outdoor space to relax by the fountain or overlooking the small lake. Or take a nice walk around the 700-acre ranch and enjoy the outdoors or visit the equestrian barn to say hello to the horses.

The fancy horse stalls along the sides in the photo below have been converted into one-room suites with private baths. Each pair of horse stalls (photo top right) is a bedroom and adjoining bath (photos lower right). These stalls have been renovated into very luxurious quarters. The bedding is ultra-comfy. The baths are spaciously very nice. And enjoy the small gift basket they provide of locally made products.

The bed and breakfast provides for a large display of fruits, fresh baked breads and pastries, and homemade jams each morning, plus hot egg dishes. Fresh orange juice and French press coffee. The hospitality is very good here.

$$$

1985 La Lomita Way
San Luis Obispo, CA 93401

+1 805 706 8010
Info@LaLomitaWines.com

LaLomitaWines.com

Open: All Year, Every Day

$$$-$$$$

4910 Edna Road
San Luis Obispo, CA 93401

+1 805 782 0500
Concierge@TolosaWinery.com

TolosaWinery.com

Open: Every Day, 11am-6pm

P inot Noir specialists allowing you to taste Pinot Noir from all over California's AVAs.

SIDE-BY-SIDE TASTINGS

If you are a Pinot Noir lover, like I am, you are familiar with the exceptionally great appellations in which this grape excels in California. Namely, Sta. Rita Hills, Russian River, Santa Lucia Highlands, Santa Maria Valley, Sonoma Coast, and here in Edna Valley. Tolosa Winery goes way beyond specializing in Pinot Noir from their Edna Ranch, they have contracted for fruit from choice vineyards in these renowned appellations.

Have you ever tasted side-by-side six Pinot Noir wines from these appellations to discover the differences. Sounds like a fun idea, doesn't it? Even if you already have, the difficulty is having six different winemakers involved. As we all know, winemakers have their own techniques and style.

At Tolosa, the tasting comes from one winemaker, with the same techniques and winery equipment used for all six wines from these six appellations. This is a true comparison of appellations, the terroir. I did the tasting, and the results were surprising to me. I thought I knew the appellations better. And my

favorites did not score as well as I expected. My eyes were opened, my palate expanded and new wines discovered.

This is no small winery, and what comes with that, is sophistication in analyzing the soils and planting the right rootstock for each specialized terroir. This is a 720-acre ranch, of which one hundred acres are used exclusively for the Tolosa Wines. Within these hundred acres they have named six specifically defined vineyards that have a multitude of soil types and compositions. Deliberate rootstock has been chosen for each micro-plot of land to bring out the very best character for their wines. The results show in their wines.

Tolosa is the first winery you reach when you head into Edna Valley on Hwy 227. They are almost adjacent to the SLO Airport, and just five miles from the ocean putting their vineyards in the face of the marine influence.

They have beautiful outdoor space to enjoy tasting under mature olive trees.

Collection of Wines

Primera (Flagship Pinot Noir)

Pinot Noir - Single Vineyards
Hollister - Edna Ranch, Edna Valley
El Coro - Petaluma Gap, Sonoma Coast
Gunsalus - Green Valley, Russian River
Apex - Santa Lucia Highlands
Drum Canyon - Sta. Rita Hills
Solomon Hills - Santa Maria Valley

Edna Ranch Vineyard Wines - Edna Valley
1772 (Pinot Noir)
Stone Lion (Pinot Noir)
Pacific Wind (Pinot Noir)
Cuvée (Pinot Noir)
1772 (Syrah)
1772 (Petite Sirah)
1772 (Chardonnay)
Pacific Wind (Chardonnay)
Stone Lion (Chardonnay)
Pure (Chardonnay)
1772 (Sauvignon Blanc)

$$

6238 Orcutt Road
San Luis Obispo, CA 93401

+1 805 781 0448
Info@WolffVineyards.com

WolffVineyards.com

Open: Every Day, 11am-5pm

T he Oldest Chardonnay vines in the Edna Valley were planted here in 1976.

ENGINEERING & OENOLOGY

This is a special place to enjoy Chardonnay wine because the grapes are grown on vines from the 1970s. One of the original pioneers of this region planted fifty-five acres of Chardonnay vines in 1976 on this property of the historically famous Wente Clone. Planted on its own rootstock, these vines have matured with deep roots in the soil. Today these vines are the oldest Chardonnay vines in Edna Valley and are producing delicious wines.

Old vines notoriously have very small yields, and this is exactly what is happing in these vineyards. If you have not tasted Chardonnay from old vines, this is a great opportunity to experience the complexity, richness and well-balanced nature of this wine. And, you will love the tropical fruit on the nose.

In 1999, the Wolff family purchased this property with these old vines. Up until then, all the fruit was sold to ultra-premium wineries, who made fantastic wines that won awards and received high scores. When Wolff purchased the property, he implemented organic and biodynamic techniques to dramatically improve the health of the vineyards. This led to the creation of the sustainable certification for wineries (SIP Certified). Wolff

planted more vineyards (Pinot Noir, Syrah, Petite Sirah, Riesling, and Teroldego, an unusual varietal from northern Italy) to expand the property to a 125-acre estate. All SIP Certified.

Jean-Pierre Wolff, PhD, a Belgian born scientist with a doctoral degree in applied engineering, continues to better engineer his vineyards. Jean-Pierre walked me through his vineyards to show me what I consider absolutely brilliant. It makes me wonder why no one else has ever thought about or implemented this irrigation system previously.

Jean-Pierre plants his new vines with their roots three feet below the surface and adds a three-foot pipe to bring the water down to these roots. A drip system is placed at the top of the pipe, irrigating the roots three feet below (photo left page). No evaporation. Imagine that! Brilliant. He immediately cut his water consumption by 50%. No wonder he was elected chairman of the Central Coast Regional Water Quality Control Board.

At the tasting room, you can enjoy a beautiful outdoor space overlooking the vineyards (photo above). On Friday nights, June through September, they have **Sunset in the Vineyard**, with a live band, wines by the glass or bottle and a food truck serving tri-tip sandwiches and lasagna squares.

Collection of Wines

Chardonnay Old Vines
Sparkling Wine (Chardonnay Methode Champenoise)

White Wolff (Albarino, Roussanne,
Grenache Blanc, Marsanne)
Red Wolff (Merlot, Cabernet Sauvignon, Grenache)

Pinot Noir
Rosé Wolff (Pinot Noir)
Syrah
Petite Sirah
Teroldego

SAN LUIS OBISPO **EDNA VALLEY** ■
Winery, Vineyards
CHAMISAL VINEYARDS

$$-$$$

7525 Orcutt Road
San Luis Obispo, CA 93401

+1 805 541 9463
Info@ChamisalVineyards.com

ChamisalVineyards.com

Open: Thursday-Sunday, 10am-5pm

I n 1973, the first vineyards here were planted at Chamisal, drawing much acclaim for the wines.

WHY CHARDONNAY IS SO GOOD

This became the perfect stop for me after visiting wineries for a week in Edna Valley. My palate has always favored California Pinot Noir and Burgundy Chardonnay. And definitely not the other way around. So here I was, winery after winery, loving the Chardonnay I was tasting. And wondering why? I needed to understand.

Terroir was my analysis. Was the soil different here? Was it the east/west valley allowing a direct flow from the ocean? Better fog? Cooler longer growing seasons? Winemaker techniques?

Spending the day with Chamisal's winemaker, Fintan du Fresne (Fin), a geologist from New Zealand, was a valuable experience. Fin began his career studying the relationship of land and how it affected grape growing, essentially the concept of how geology affects terroir. This fascination led Fin to go on and obtain postgraduate degrees in viticulture and oenology.

Right from the beginning of our conversation, Fin tells me that the Edna Valley is the coldest appellation in all of California. We spoke in cold Burgundian terms and that would indicate why I love Edna Valley Chardonnay.

Fin is fortunate to be working at Chamisal, this is the land where the first vineyard was planted in Edna Valley in 1973. With such deep history of this property, he is working with both old-vine Pinot Noir as well as old-vine Chardonnay. And a great reputation to continue and expand.

The Chamise Chardonnay was the star for me. The wine is both rich and fresh at the same time. Caramel rich and lemon fresh on the nose. Toasted almond rich and ocean salinity fresh in the mouth. And it lingers long and beautifully. The Chamise Vineyard has the most devigorating soil on their property. This results in small berries of rich intense fruit (photo left page). A special wine, indeed.

The tasting room has cheese and charcuterie plates to enjoy with their wines. The beautiful patio has nice views across the Pinot Noir vineyards (photo above).

Collection of Wines

Pinot Noir Wines
Morrito
Soberanes
Califa
Radian Vineyard
Edna Valley

Chardonnay Wines
Chamise
Califa
Monterey County
Stainless
Edna Valley
Sta. Rita Hills
San Luis Obispo

Chamisal Estate Sparkling Wine

$$-$$$

2649 Carpenter Canyon Road
San Luis Obispo, CA 93401

+1 805 544 4066
Info@ClaiborneChurchill.com

ClaiborneChurchill.com

Open: Every Day, 12pm-5pm

Imagine Dry Riesling and Dry Gewürztraminer in the Edna Valley.

A CHANGE OF WINES TO TASTE

The Claiborne & Churchill brand began with Dry Riesling and Dry Gewürztraminer. Founders Claiborne Thompson and Fredericka Churchill were backpacking through the wine regions of Alsace France. They would hike ten to twelve miles a day through vineyards, stopping at wineries to taste their wines. They fell in love with Riesling and Gewürztraminer.

They came back to California passionate about making these wines. The Edna Valley appellation is cold, just like the Alsace appellation. They were convinced they could make great wines.

One little detail, they were not winemakers. They were educators, Clay holding a PhD from Harvard. So, the first step was to work at a winery to learn winemaking from the ground up. It started with hard labor. He learned. He gave up his tenured professorship and never looked back. Two years later, in 1983, they made their first harvest and launched the winery.

Clay jokes that he is now making wine that nobody drinks and nobody can pronounce.

Over the next forty years, people discovered their wines, and liked them. A lot. And not without hard work. They would load up their truck with wine and head to Los Angeles and San Francisco to sell their wines to restaurants. Their name was getting out.

One of their most successful wines is named after Fredericka. It is a blend of Riesling, Gewürztraminer and Chardonnay. You must taste it. It is different from any wine you have tasted. Super delicious. Cuvée Fredericka is now their best-selling wine.

They have gone on to add other varietals. Particularly Pinot Noir, which thrives in Edna Valley. They established relationships with excellent Pinot growers, and the wines are stellar.

Live Music here on Fridays and Sundays. You can taste wine outside on their patio in the garden (photo above), or in their cellar, the world's first **Straw Bale Winery**. The walls are solely composed of stacked straw bales. Insulation is so good that the cellar stays cold without AC. Bring a picnic lunch or they have charcuterie and cheese boards.

They have **Blind Tasting Experiences**, **Vineyard & Winery Tours**, or a **Private Tastings** with the owners and/or winemaker.

Collection of Wines

Dry Gewürztraminer
Dry Riesling (Estate)
Dry Riesling (Central Coast)
Cuvée Fredericka (Dry Gewürztraminer,
Dry Riesling, Chardonnay)
Chardonnay (Spanish Springs)
Chardonnay (Greengate Ranch)

Runestone Pinot Noir
Pinot Noir (Greengate Ranch)
Twin Creeks Pinot Noir
Classic Pinot Noir
Grenache
Syrah/Grenache
Syrah (Spanish Springs Vineyard)
Syrah (Edna Valley)

Cuvée Elizabeth (Dry Rosé of Pinto Noir)
PortObispo (Fortified Port)
Nektar (Late Harvest Estate Riesling)

$$-$$$

2212 Corbett Canyon Road
San Luis Obispo, CA 93401

+1 805 544 8461
TastingRoom@Kynsi.com

Kynsi.com

Open: Every Day, 11am-5pm

L ocated on the site of the famous Stone Corral Vineyard of Pinot Noir.

BARN OWLS AND BULLDOG PUP

Have you heard of **Stone Corral Vineyard** in Edna Valley? It is twenty-eight acres of the most highly acclaimed Pinot Noir here. This is a very special property for several reasons. First, the soil is extremely sandy, making it excessively well-drained and causing the vineyard to dry out quickly. This soil is producing a distinctly dark and plush style Pinot Noir.

Second, the vineyard is planted with a special Pinot Noir clone. The Dijon Clone. This clone is considered a perfect Pinot Noir as the result of blending several Pinot Noir clones. In 1987, the first legal (not hidden in a suitcase) Pinot Noir clones came to America from the University of Dijon in Burgundy France. The clones were named Dijon after the return address on the shipping container. In Latin, it means "divine". Further, the blending of these clones has brought about the perfection from the attributes each one contributes.

Third, the ownership of these vines is a collaboration of three winemakers who share in the harvest: Talley Vineyards (page 279),

Stephen Ross Winery (page page 294) and Kynsi Winery. The opportunity for different winemakers to collaborate has brought forward a very unique commitment to excellence.

And fourth, Kynsi Winery is located at the Stone Corral Vineyard. Go to Kynsi and see the vineyard, and taste this special wine (photo right).

The owners of Kynsi winery have another special place in winemaking. In 1986, Don Othman invented the **Bulldog Pup** (photo left page) which became a top-quality racking device for the wine industry because it more gently transfers wine between vessels than a conventional pump and it keeps out oxygen, a big enemy to wine.

Kynsi means *"talon"* in Finnish. At a time of a serious plague of gophers on the property, **barn owls** decided to inhabit the old abandoned barn that was once used when there was a dairy here. As their new home even today, the owls keep nature in balance on this land, and have become the mascot to the winery.

They have seated tastings on a beautiful patio under trees, surrounded by vineyards and the iconic barn home to barn owls.

Collection of Wines

Pinot Noir (Precious Stone)
Pinot Noir (Stone Corral Vineyard)
Pinot Noir (Edna Valley)
Pinot Noir (Solomon Hills Vineyard)
Pinot Noir (Clone 2A)
Pinot Noir (Clone 115)
Pinot Noir (Clone 667)
Pinot Noir (Clone 777)
Pinot Noir (Clone 2A)
Pinot Noir (Clone 2A)
Pinot Noir Rosé (Barn Owl Blush)

Syrah (Edna Valley)
Syrah (Bien Nacido Vineyard)
Syrah (Kalanna)
Nocturnum (Grenache, Syrah)
Grenache (Jespersen Vineyard)

Pinot Blanc (Bien Nacido Vineyard)
Chardonnay (Bien Nacido Vineyard)

$$-$$$

2195 Corbett Canyon Road
San Luis Obispo, CA 93401

+1 805 782 9463
Reservations@CenterOfEffortWine.com

COEWine.com

Open: Thursday-Monday, 11am-4pm
By Appointment Only

A vision for savoring the world's finest wines and delivering the best hospitality.

DREAMS

After growing up in San Luis Obispo, high school sweethearts Bill and Cheryl Swanson ended up traveling the world extensively as Bill was the CEO of Raytheon Aerospace Company. Now retired, they have come back home and purchased a property where they had been tasting wine for thirty years. They have completely re-developed the property and built new buildings to take on a new dream: Center of Effort.

The new dream is to produce exceptionally great wines, the finest Pinot Noir and Chardonnay possible. And to do this in an environment of outstanding hospitality. In one of the new buildings is a commercial kitchen (photo right) and beautiful dining areas. This has become a hospitality center for savoring the finest of food and wine.

Every quarter they invite a prominent chef to produce an amazing evening of culinary delights. Of course, paired with amazing wines. They call it their **Chefs Series**. It's pricey, and only for eight people. First choice to buy the evening goes to their members before the general public. How's

that for a great reason to become a member. They also do a **Chefs Counter Dinner** for thirty people for the evening. At this event you can buy one seat; however, it is still the members' first choice.

All visits are by appointment only. They want to know you're coming so they can give you first-class very-attentive hospitality. And food should be very much a part of your experience. Yes, you can do just a wine tasting; however, they have so much more to offer in food and wine pairings.

You can choose a simple platter of meats, cheeses and fruits (photo above). Or they can create an entire lunch for you. Or just a sandwich. Or an extensive three-course meal. It's all a matter of how much you would like to indulge.

There are elegant indoor dining areas (photo above) and a comfortable outdoor patio with many places to lounge and view their vineyards and the rolling hills.

And another new building I feel very appreciative to have viewed inside. As a sports car lover and owner of a new Aston Martin, I was able to see Bill's Ferrari collection and an amazing Bugatti, plus other antique sports cars (photo right).

Collection of Wines

Rosso Corsa (Pinot Noir)
Andare (Pinot Noir)
Pinot Noir
Effort Pinot Noir

Giallo Solare (Chardonnay)
Chardonnay
Effort Chardonnay

Effortvesence (Sparkling Chardonnay, Pinot Noir)
Dolcezza (Sweet Wine of Chenin Blanc, Chardonnay)

$$-$$$

3080 Biddle Ranch Road
San Luis Obispo, CA 93401

+1 805 543 2111
WineClub@SaucelitoCanyon.com

SaucelitoCanyon.com

Open: Every Day, 11am-5pm

Collection of Wines

The Zinfandel Classics
1880 (100% Old Vine Estate Zinfandel)
Heritage (Old Vines and Cuttings from Old Vines)
Estate Zin (100% Estate Zinfandel)
Dos Ranchos Zin (50% Estate, 50% Neighbor Zinfandel)
Backroad Zin (Paso and Arroyo Grande AVAs Zinfandel)

Zinfandel Appellation Series
Dry Creek Zinfandel (Dry Creek AVA)
Peterson Family Zinfandel (Lodi AVA)
Enz Vineyard Zinfandel (Lime Kiln Valley AVA)

Zinfandel Blends
Rabble Rouser (Zinfandel, Petite Sirah)
Dos Mas (Zinfandel, Grenache, Petite Sirah)
Muchacho (Zinfandel, Tempranillo, Petite Sirah)
Elodie (Zinfandel, Cabernet Sauvignon, Cabernet Franc)

Non-Zinfandel Wines
Sauvage (Cabernet Sauvignon, Cabernet Franc)
Grenache (Morrow View Vineyard, Edna Valley AVA)
Tempranillo (Arroyo Grande Valley AVA)

Rosé Series
Dry Rosé (Zinfandel, Grenache, Tempranillo)
White Label Rosé (Grenache, Counoise)

White Wine Series
Grenache Blanc (Edna Valley AVA)
Cote de Blanc (Viognier, Grenache Blanc)

Z infandel specialists, producing very special grapes from vines that were planted in 1880.

UNIQUE IN EDNA VALLEY

You must be thinking, Edna Valley is way too cold to be growing Zinfandel grapes. Michael would not possibly show us a winery that is using the wrong terroir for this varietal. If these are your thoughts, your thinking-cap is working very well.

Saucelito Canyon chose to base their tasting room central in the Edna Valley to make it easy for us to visit and taste. Their vineyards are in the next appellation to the south. And even more so, they are in a distant back canyon in a very remote area of the Arroyo Grande AVA. They would never expect you to find this place. It was not until my second trip did I make the two-hour trek to these vineyards.

These Zinfandel vines were planted in 1880 here, a site 20° hotter, of sand and oyster shells, and no electricity. Prohibition caused this land to be abandoned. Nearly one hundred years later, Bill Greenough, an English major from Santa Barbara, discovered this remote rugged area. He had this wild idea he could resuscitate the vines. So he bought the land, and with just a pick and a shovel, he went at this endeavor all by himself until the vines came back to life. His friends and family knew he was crazy.

It is true that unconventional people accomplish some of the most amazing feats. And here, Bill has brought back to life and created one of the most remarkable Zinfandel wines in California (photos left page). It is now the oldest commercial vineyard in the county.

Bill went on to plant more Zinfandel vineyards on the property in the 1970s and 1980s, and then again in 2014. In 2009, Bill's son Tom Greenough took over as winemaker continuing the historic tradition of Zinfandel as well as bringing a new vision of adding other vineyards and making blends.

At the tasting room, you can taste these different Zinfandel wines and blends. The addition of the **Zinfandel Appellation Series** brings extraordinary grapes from other notable Zinfandel AVAs around California to their lineup of great Zinfandel wines. This is an excellent way to taste the unique nuances of these different notable appellations side-by-side.

Here in the land of Chardonnay and Pinot Noir, experience the difference from these Zinfandel experts. They have an array of tapas boxes, cheese platters and charcuterie to pair with their wines in a beautiful setting under the trees (photo above).

$$-$$$-$$$$

3031 Lopez Drive
Arroyo Grande, CA 93420

+1 805 489 0446
Hospitality@TalleyVineyards.com

TalleyVineyards.com

Open: Thursday-Sunday, 11am-4:30pm

A beautiful hillside property with wines as great as their stunning views.

98-POINT WINES

In Arroyo Grande Valley there are only a couple of wineries to visit, and Talley Vineyards is the most convenient one. Literally just outside of Edna Valley on a beautiful property worth an afternoon visit.

The Talley family are farmers first. Since 1948, they have been growing twenty different crops of vegetables, plus lemon and avocado orchards. The tasting room has a great view overlooking a pepper field. In 1982, they added viticulture and planted their first vineyard (photo left page), with the first vintage being 1986.

This first vineyard property is known as Rincon Vineyard, in which they built the winery and tasting room. This steep hillside property gives us great views, and provides these vines added warmth and struggle. A good thing in my view, and I much prefer their Single Vineyard Rincon Pinot Noir. This is a really delicious wine. I am particularly fond of the wine's savory aromas, and delicious raspberries and other rich red fruit flavors. If you like richness in your Pinot Noir, you are going to like this wine.

While the Rincon Vineyard Pinot Noir favors my palate, I must recognize Rosemary's Vineyard for producing excellent Pinot Noir and Chardonnay. These wines have received very high scores, as high as 98 points from Robert Parker. Both the Rosemary's Vineyard wines have been served at the White House on numerous occasions. And the 2002 Rosemary's Vineyard Chardonnay was judged **Best California Chardonnay** on the thirtieth anniversary of the *Judgment of Paris Tasting*.

As you can now imagine, there are wines here for everyone's palate. They offer an **Estate Seated Tasting**, where you can choose indoors in their floor-to-ceiling windowed tasting room or outdoors on the beautiful patio (photo above). I particularly like their **Single Vineyard Tasting**, where you can taste all three Pinot Noirs from each of three different vineyards. Same with Chardonnay; three different Chardonnays from three different vineyards. This is a great experience to taste the terroir differences between vineyards of the same appellation.

Collection of Wines

The Adobe (Flagship Blend of Pinot Noir)
Estate Pinot Noir
Estate Chardonnay

Single Vineyard Selections
Rosemary's (Pinot Noir)
Rincon (Pinot Noir)
Stone Corral (Pinot Noir)
Rosemary's (Chardonnay)
Rincon (Chardonnay)
Oliver's (Chardonnay)

Tasting Room/Wine Club Exclusives
Syrah
Grenache
Pinot Noir Rosé
Sauvignon Blanc
Grüner Veltliner
Riesling

$$-$$$

453 Laetitia Vineyard Drive
Arroyo Grande, CA 93420

+1 805 474 7651
Info@LaetitiaWine.com

LaetitiaWine.com

Open: Every Day, 10am-5:30pm

A beautiful setting under the oak trees; sipping sparkling wines and snacking on goodies.

SPARKLING WINES

Are you a lover of French Champagne or Crémant or Spanish Cava, or Italian Prosecco? Then come to the Laetitia Winery here in the Arroyo Grande Valley, which specializes in sparkling wines. Laetitia is the largest winery in the Arroyo Grande Valley with over 2,000 acres; 913 acres are planted with vines. Now that is a lot of grapes!

Located at the west edge of the Arroyo Grande Valley, closest to the ocean and adjacent to Highway 101 with their own highway exit, Laetitia is a beautiful property of rolling hills. As you enter the property (photo left) you get to meander around the hills of vineyards and oak trees until you reach the hilltop tasting room. The outdoor patio has beautiful views across the vineyards.

At the winery there are many choices of their bubbly treats. And, they have assembled a delicious cheese board with some of San Luis Obispo's finest purveyors (photo above). It is a really good collection of different animal cheeses along with some dried fruits and figs, Marcona almonds, olives, and rosemary. It is served with baguette slices from the Black Porch Bakery drizzled with red wine and herbs. This includes goat cheese from *Central Coast Creamery*, cow and goat cheddar from *Seascape Cheese*, sheep cheese from *Shooting Star*, and a sheep and cow cheese from *Sagittarius*.

Speaking of goats, Laetitia uses goats for weed control instead of poisons. The property is sustainably farmed (SIP Certified) including water and energy conservation, such as the re-use of compost and water reclamation, plus a cutting-edge weather station and soil moisture technology.

Their outside patio is a beautiful place to enjoy the **Daily Wine Flight Experience**. They also offer a unique **Campfire and S'mores on the Coast**, where you actually sit around a campfire, roast s'mores, and pair them with some of their single-vineyard Pinot Noirs. Also enjoy their **Picnic Areas**, either nestled under several large oak trees, or up with their Bocce Ball courts and walking trails. Here you can bring a lunch and get a bottle of one of their sparkling or still wines.

In addition to their specialty of sparkling wines, Laetitia also has a big **Single Vineyard Pinot Noir** program. Remember, this is the Arroyo Grande Valley AVA, so Pinot Noir does extremely well here. They have nine interesting single-vineyard wines.

Collection of Wines

Sparkling Wines
Brut Coquard
Brut de Blancs
Brut de Noirs
Cuvée M
Brut Rosé
Non-Vintage Brut Cuvée
Non-Vintage XD

Single Vineyard Pinot Noir
La Colline, La Coupelle, Les Galets
Block Y Clone 115, Block Z Clone 828
Clone 459, Clone 667, Clone 777, Clone 2A
Reserve du Domaine Pinot Noir
Whole Cluster Pinot Noir

Chardonnay
Clone 17 Single Vineyard Chardonnay
Estate Chardonnay
Reserve du Domaine Chardonnay

ARROYO GRANDE, VILLAGE

Arroyo Grande is adjacent inland from Grover Beach, northeast of Oceano and southeast of Pismo Beach. Arroyo Grande is a small city, an agricultural valley, an appellation for spectacular wine grapes (see page 259), and also a very nice little village with many shops, excellent restaurants and wine-tasting rooms. Hwy 101 (CA-101) goes directly past the village.

This village is a turn-of-the-century downtown with its main street (Branch Street) lined with historic buildings from the late 1800s and early 1900s. Apparently, the last **swinging bridge** in California resides here, crossing the Arroyo Grande Creek into the village. This forty feet suspended swinging bridge is a landmark, circa 1875 (photo right).

If you love museums, this village has six museums: **Heritage House** (South County Historical Society), **Santa Manuela Schoolhouse** (circa 1901), **IOOF Hall** (circa 1902), **The Barn Museum** (antique vehicles and agricultural artifacts), **Paulding History House** (circa 1891), and **The Patricia Loomis History Library and Research Center** (circa late 1800s). This is currently an active research and reference library with artifacts dating back to the days of the early settlers.

Gina's Italian Cuisine
+1 805 481 3266 • 138 East Branch Street
Open: Every Day, 11am-9pm (Sunday 4pm-9pm)

GinasItalianCuisine.com

Authentic Italian. Everything homemade. Fresh pastas and sauces daily. **Shrimp & Lobster Ravioli** (photo below) was extraordinary. Delicate, yet rich flavors, and you could taste the texture of the fresh pasta. Garnished with garlic, basil and diced tomatoes.

Verdad Wines, Lindquist Wines
+1 805 270 4900 • 134 A West Branch Street
Open: Every Day, Noon-5pm (Fri-Sat 6pm)

VerdadAndLindquistFamilyWines.com

This is a husband-and-wife collaboration. Their farming is organic, biodynamic and certified sustainable.

Louisa is focused on her love of Spanish varietals with Verdad Wine Cellars. The Tempranillo she poured for me was truly remarkable.

Bob specializes in Rhône varietals with his Lindquist Family Wines label.

Together they are exploring Burgundian varietals.

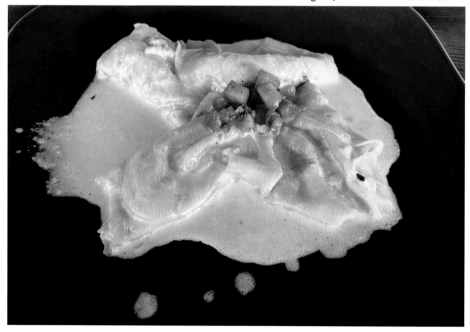

Mason Bar & Kitchen

+1 805 202 8918 • 307 East Branch Street
Open: Every Day, 11:30am-10pm (Fri-Sat 12am)
MasonBarAG.com

This is not bar food. This is gourmet, farm-fresh ingredients, served with style.

Imagine **Duo of Yellowfin** (top photo). Tartare: avocado, sesame, citrus, Fresno and Shishito peppers. Tataki: sesame crust, soy glaze, baby herbs, wasabi aioli.

Now **Salmon Belly Tempura Tacos** (bottom photo). Wild king salmon belly, tempura batter, corn tortillas, citrus slaw, pickled peppers, avocado, tartar sauce.

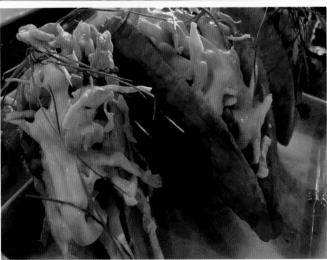

Timbre Winery

+1 805 270 4308 • 225 East Branch Street
Open: Every Day, Noon-5pm (Fri-Sat 6pm)
TimbreWinery.com

The winemaker/proprietor here, Joshua Klapper, is a sommelier from noted restaurants in Los Angeles. He was recognized with *Wine Spectator's* Grand Award for the wine list he created at Sona Restaurant. An important skill of a sommelier is to know the vineyard locations and vintages of wines. This is terroir, ever important in creating great wines.

Josh took his sommelier/terroir skills to the central coast, exploring great vineyard locations, and launched into the winemaking business, creating wines that represent extraordinary places.

I had the pleasure to taste through several of his Pinot Noir wines. Each was great in its own way. I could taste the unique places and the varying vintages as I enjoyed his exceptionally well-crafted wines.

A Youthful Happening City

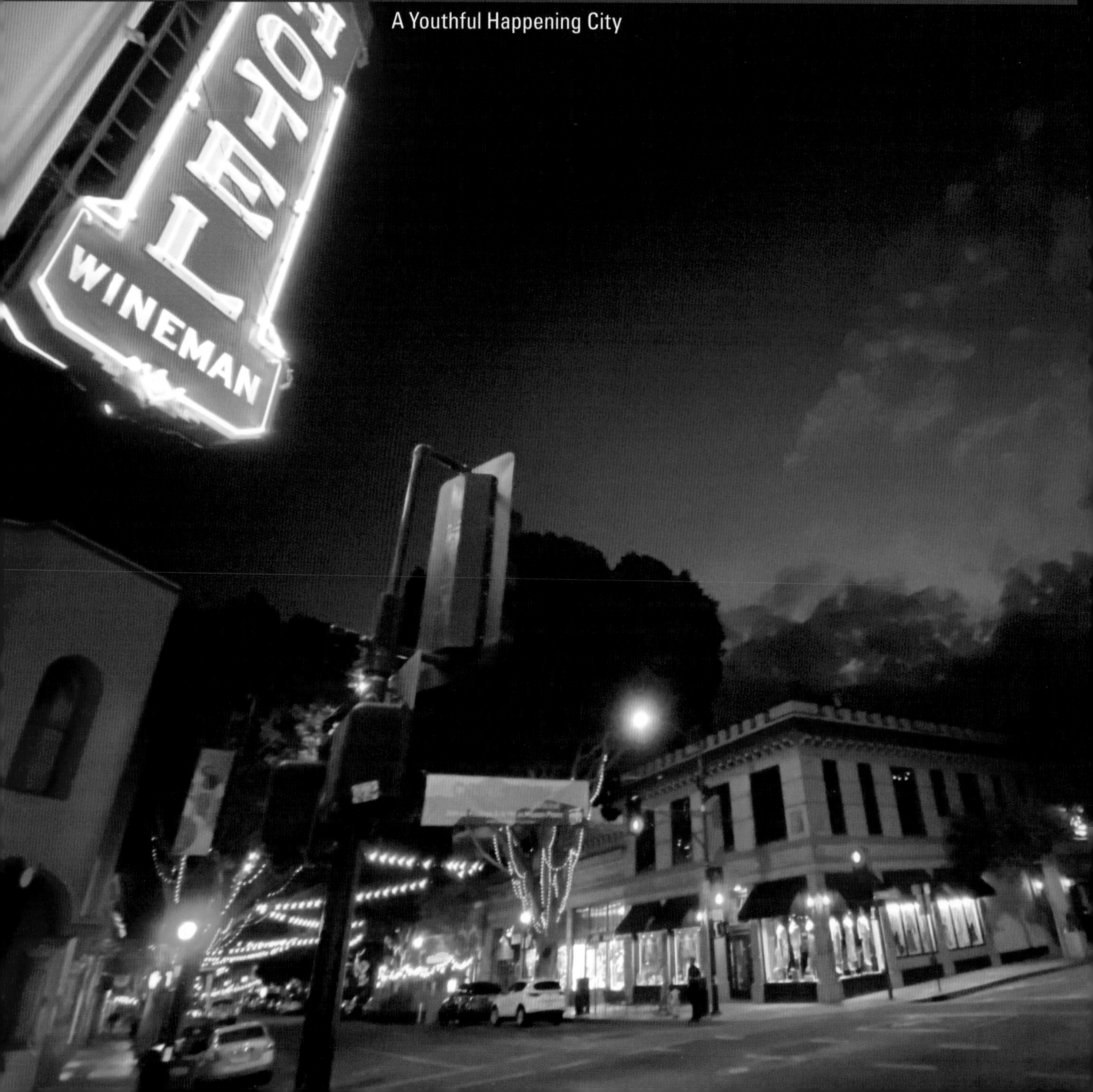

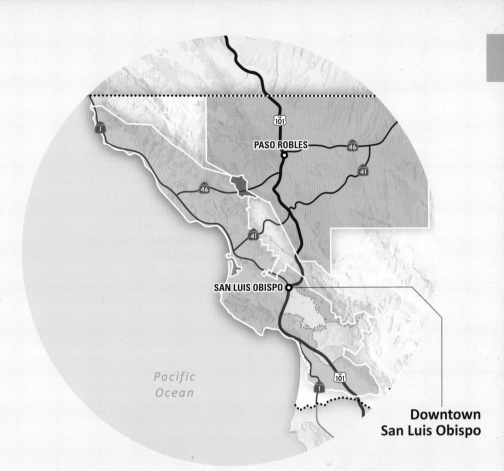

PASO ROBLES

SAN LUIS OBISPO

Pacific
Ocean

**Downtown
San Luis Obispo**

Left page: Downtown San Luis Obispo

LIVELY DOWNTOWN SLO

Downtown San Luis Obispo is a lively happening place. This renovated historic spot crosses several blocks in all directions. You will find big names here like **Apple Computers** and **Victoria's Secret**, as well as little unique shops, like **Moon Doggies** surf shop and **Lokum** Turkish coffee and pastries. This is a walk-around city with lots to do. Don't miss Thursday nights' **Farmers Market**. It is a big to-do with lots of locals and visitors having fun (photo page 293).

The **Mission San Luis Obispo de Tolosa** is right in the middle of town and open to the public for historical visits and worship. In fact, the mission is the reason San Luis Obispo exists. The Spanish missionaries came here and got things started in 1772 as the fifth of twenty-one California Missions. Today it is a California Registered Historical Landmark.

SLO is a college town (over 22,000 students), so lots of young energy and things to do here.

The **restaurant scene** here is as diverse as it is casual to gourmet. And many! Numerous lounges for cocktails, local beer and wine, and some wine tasting too. I tasted quite a few and have given you some of my favorite reviews to follow. If you love beef jerky, then you must visit **Cattaneo Brothers Jerky**, and eat the finest handcrafted jerky imaginable.

The **Railroad District** is six blocks from downtown where the train brings in 20,000 passengers annually. This is a wonderful residential neighborhood with a few super great restaurants you must check out.

The **Industrial District** is south of town, west of the airport, and where winemakers find low rent, make high quality wines, and give us great prices. **Stephen Ross Wine Cellar** and **El Lugar Wines** are a couple of wineries you must check out.

Northern Italian Cuisine	Italy's Puglia Region (The Boot Heel)	Peruvian Modern Gastronomy

BUONA TAVOLA

+1 805 545 8000 • 1037 Monterey Street, Downtown
Open: Every Day, 5:30pm-9pm (Mon-Fri 11am lunch)

BTSLO.com

GIUSEPPE'S CUCINA RUSTICA

+1 805 541 9922 • 849 Monterey Street, Downtown
Open: Every Day, 11:30am-3:30pm, 4:30-Close

GiuseppesRestaurant.com

MISTURA

+1 805 439 3292 • 570 Higuera Street, Downtown
Open: Tuesday-Sunday, 11am-9pm (Fri/Sat 10pm)

MisturaRestaurants.com

This is the original restaurant that I found in downtown Paso Robles a decade ago, and I fell in love with their *Fettuccine Al Sugo Di Carni Miste* – a fettuccine pasta with slowly braised chicken, duck, veal, pork, and beef in an herbed meat sauce. Here they have five meats, adding the pork. Either way, this sauce is a mouthful of savory flavors. Every time I think of this dish, I get hungry, like right now!

This original location is thirty years old now. It is easy to see why they endure. Great food. Unique recipes. Excellent service. Superb ambiance. At this location, it is not uncommon that one of the partners is enjoying waiting on tables. It adds to the authentic atmosphere.

Fresh fish on the special daily menu is extra delicious as well (photo below). It shows I really need to get off my favorite pasta habit, and try more. Wednesdays is half price on bottles of wine. Great list.

In 1988, Cal Poly student Giuseppe DiFronzo had an idea to create a farm and establish a restaurant to serve farm-to-fork wholesome foods. His school project came true! Not just an early adopter of farm-to-table, he is rather unique in creating his own DiFronzo Farm in Edna Valley (with vineyards) and his Guiseppi's Cucina Rustica restaurant downtown to serve fresh Puglia Region Italian cuisine.

It has been a while since I have seen Sand Dabs. Ever tried them? They are little tiny fish; white, delicate and delicious. Here (photo below), the Sand Dabs are a specialty, fished locally in Morro Bay and prepared alla piccata, meaning, the fish is sliced and sautéed in a sauce of lemon, white wine, capers, garlic, and some secret spices. It's served with Israeli couscous and topped with fresh arugula. It was light, yet full of savory flavors.

They have a large bar; indoor and outdoor dining.

This is a creative restaurant serving Peruvian culture and cuisine. Mistura captures the multicultural spirit of Peru by combining its native Incan and pre-Columbian culinary heritage along with Italian, Spanish, Japanese, and Chinese influences, which embodies the country's flavorful cuisine.

Each dish is a unique creation, using traditional elements of Peruvian cuisine and Andean native ingredient. Dishes are small so you can discover.

Olivar Causa (photo below) octopus and Alaskan king crab, avocado, botija (an olive aioli), and tobiko (Japanese flying fish roe) served with seasoned, cold whipped potatoes with lime and ajies.

You must try a Peruvian cocktail. **Chilcano** (photo below) is a classic Peruvian cocktail that combines the snap of cold-pressed lime juice and house-distilled Pisco (a type of brandy from Peru) with the refreshing fizz of ginger ale. You will want a second!

GASTRONOMIC CENTER OF WINE, CHEESE AND DINING

This is a very sophisticated shop of extraordinary wines, cheeses, accessories, and gastronomy. The team is amazing. The chef comes from celebrated restaurants in Los Angeles. The wine director is both a chef and sommelier. The owner is passionate about delivering the ultimate culinary experiences. The cuisine is as delicious as their beautiful presentations (photos below). They have a large collection of big names and hard-to-find wines from twenty-seven countries. They search for unique wines, like Morrocan Sauvignon Blanc (photo right), a 1985 Château Latour, and over 2,000 other wines in inventory. When do you ever see anything like this in a big city, let alone in this small wine regions city? This is a reason to travel to San Luis Obispo.

Tomato Salad (below top): a variety of Finley Farms heirloom tomatoes over whipped ricotta and decadent juices of barrel-aged ponzu and Fromage Blanc. Served with freshly baked sourdough bread.

Niman Ranch Pork Belly (below left): German-style confit pork belly with sweet peppers, Swiss chard, and a delicious olallieberry agrodolce.

Corn Fritter (below center): covered with sliced Iberico ham, pickled Fresno chilis, and sweet baby bells.

Basque Cheesecake (below right), a La Viña inspired crème fraîche creamy with caramelized top.

$$-$$$-$$$$-$$$$$

1039 Chorro Street
Downtown San Luis Obispo, CA 93401

+1 805 439 4185
Experience@Park1039.com

Park1039.com

Open: Wednesday-Sunday, 11am-6pm
Friday & Saturday, 11am-Close

$$$-$$$$-$$$$$

877 Palm Street
Downtown San Luis Obispo, CA 93401

+1 805 235 0700
Info@Hotel-SLO.com

Hotel-SLO.com

MODERN LUXURY

Hotel SLO, as the insiders know it, is a spectacularly beautiful hotel. Super modern. Exceptional design. And its location is optimal in downtown San Luis Obispo, walkable to the many shops and amazing restaurants. And they have their own restaurant, **Ox + Anchor** (next page), which is worth your culinary exploration even if you do not stay at the hotel.

The rooms are bright and spacious with tall ceilings, many windows and balconies to sit out and enjoy the views of the city and beautiful hillsides. Simple, yet they have thought of everything you will need in the room. Quality everywhere: natural woods, handmade rugs, original artwork, and the beds are ever-so comfortable.

This is a place to stay and hang out. Live music every night. A rooftop lounge to enjoy the sunsets. Multiple restaurants. Wine tasting. A spa. And just so many beautiful places to sit and relax and enjoy.

BEAUTIFUL FOOD FROM A MASTERFUL CHEF

While this restaurant considers itself a steakhouse, it is way more than steak, with many interesting and creative dishes to experience. The seafood was amazing. Creative and inventive. As you look at these pictures, I hope you are beginning to see how much fun this chef has with his recipes. This is not your typical hotel restaurant. Plus, access is from outside the hotel so you can enjoy this experience even if you're not staying in the hotel. And you should.

Speaking of the chef, **Executive Chef Ryan Fancher** claims it is his *innovative and intellectual approach to cooking* that makes this restaurant shine. It makes sense knowing his highly regarded past at extraordinary restaurants. El Dorado Kitchen in Sonoma and Barndiva in Healdsburg begin to paint the picture. Chef Ryan feels he gained his culinary skills working with two exceptionally talented chefs... Richard Reddington at Auberge de Soleil, Thomas Keller at The French Laundry, and ultimately opening Per Se in New York, the famed restaurant of Thomas Keller that earned three Michelin stars.

This is a chef you want to visit. Let me share with you a few of the delights you can experience.

Lobster Stuffed Avocado (photo left page): a beautifully peeled avocado half, sitting on top of a delicious chive crème fraiche, is stacked with a generous amounts of chilled lobster salad, and garnished with a gaufrette potato chip.

Yellowfin Ahi Tuna Tartare (photo below left): yellowfin is a leaner tuna, which is perfect for a tuna tartare, and is chopped beautifully here and placed on top of a deliciously creamy avocado mound in ponzu sauce. Topped with scallions and garnished with jalapeño, tomatoes, carrots, radish, mint, and basil. Wonton utensils provided.

Grilled Pacific Swordfish (photo right center): grilled with an olive tapenade, capers, herbs and spices, and a cabernet sauvignon reduction and chives for a delicious dipping.

Ribeye (photo right below): grilled to perfection with an ever-so-flavorful grill-butter they make with butter, olive oil, garlic, thyme, rosemary, sage, shallots, and liquid smoke. The dipping sauce is chive oil and chives.

$$$-$$$$-$$$$$

877 Palm Street
Downtown San Luis Obispo, CA 93401

+1 805 234-9968

OxAndAnchor.com

Open: Wednesday-Sunday, 5pm-Close

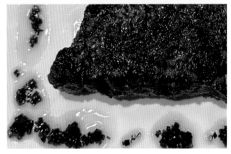

Restaurant, Lounge
Novo Restaurant & Lounge

$-$$-$$$

726 Higuera Street
Downtown San Luis Obispo, CA 93401

+1 805 543 3986
NovoRestaurant.com

Open: Every Day, 11am-9pm (Sun 10am)

Rack of Lamb (below right): grilled New Zealand rack of lamb served over a puree of root vegetables of carrots, Yukon golds, turnip, and garlic. Topped with roasted baby onion, grilled asparagus and a house mustard and thyme vinaigrette.

Duck Breast (below center): pan-seared Maple Leaf Farms duck breast served with spicy Panang curry sauce, glazed local peas, baby carrots and onions, and forbidden black rice. Forbidden rice is also known as "Emperor's Rice," having very high levels of antioxidants and was historically reserved only for the emperor and used as a tribute food in ancient China.

Lemon Cheesecake (below left): is light, fluffy and gluten free. Served on a graham cracker crust with fresh berry coulis and topped with local raspberries and blackberries.

O one person. Full-time. Every Day. Shopping at local farmers markets for fresh ingredients.

TRADITIONAL FOODS OF THE WORLD

The front of this place may look like a lounge and bar. It is. However, walk through and, in the back, are three levels of patios (photo above) along the San Luis Obispo Creek. The frogs will sing to you in the evening.

The cuisine here is very impressive. I call it traditional foods from around the world. For example, traditional Thai curries and authentic Korean short ribs. The portions are generous and the pricing very fair. The place is popular so be sure to make reservations.

As a healthy eater, I was impressed and surprised that this restaurant hires a full-time person who goes everyday to the various farmers' markets that occur daily here. The foods are fresh, and you can taste it. Being in an agricultural area, this restaurant takes full advantage of local freshness.

Mission San Luis Obispo de Tolosa (Landmark Attraction)
+1 805 781 8220 • 751 Palm Street
Open: Every Day, Opening at 7am

MissionSanLuisObispo.org

The mission started San Luis Obispo in 1772 when Father Junipero Serra arrived and established the fifth California mission here. It is named after Saint Louis, Bishop of Toulouse, France. This is how San Luis Obispo derived its name.

Today, the mission is a California Registered Historical Landmark and open everyday for visitors to roam and enjoy the property. Find a bench, enjoy the beautiful gardens and listen to the five bells be hand-rung in the tower to call parishioners to mass as they have for over 200 years.

The mission is an active parish with daily masses. Monday-Friday: 7:00am and 12:10pm. Saturday: 7:00am and 5:30pm. Sunday: 7:00am, 9:00am and 11:00am. Reconciliation, Saturday: 4:00pm-5:00pm.

It's located right in the middle of town amongst the activity of restaurants and shops. Docent tours are everyday, Monday-Saturday: 1:15pm, Sunday: 2:00pm. They have an elementary and high school, a museum and a gift shop.

Downtown Farmers Market (Five Blocks of The Street)
+1 805 541 0286 • Higuera Street
Open: All Year, Every Thursday Evening, 6:00pm-9:00pm

DowntownSLO.com/Farmers-Market

Every Thursday night, the City of San Luis Obispo closes off five blocks of Higuera Street, the primary road in downtown. At 6:00pm, the street comes alive with locals and visitors (photo lower right) in a big shopping, eating and drinking party.

This open-air market is worth attending. Enjoy fresh produce from local farmers, indulge in several famous BBQ vendors (photo upper right) and other delicious foods, interesting local crafts, entertainment, live music, and much more!

This is a reason to plan your visit to downtown on a Thursday night.

San Luis Obispo Museum of Art
+1 805 543 8562 • 1010 Broad Street
Open: Every Day, 11am-5pm

SLOMA.org

SLOMA is located in downtown San Luis Obispo and focuses on exhibitions of contemporary California artists. The work displayed is stunning. Open to all, free admission. They also offer youth and adult art classes, lectures, film nights, trips, concerts, and art events throughout the year.

Public Art Program (City Art)
+1 805 541 0286 • 989 Chorro Street
Open: All Year, Every Day

DowntownSLO.com/Explore/Public-Art

The city has an amazing Public Art Program, with more than seventy unique pieces around the city. There are murals, mosaics, paintings, utility box art, stained glass, benches, bridge railings, cow trail sculptures, and some interesting sculptures, like the one below: **Tequski Wa Suwa, Qiqsmu, Yach Ka**

Lokum (Turkish Café)
+1 805 550 6622 • 715 Higuera Street
Open: Every Day, 10am-9pm

Lokum.com

This is a gorgeous Turkish café, with extravagant chandeliers, and a delightful tasting space for Turkish coffee and other delights. Everything is served on beautiful china in a very classy environment. They have numerous Turkish Delights, directly from Turkey, with flavors beyond your imagination.

SLO INDUSTRIAL PARK WINERIES

What is an industrial park winery? In short, it is where winemakers can find low rent, make high-quality wines, and give us great prices. Think about it. An industrial park offers winemakers a large space for a great price compared to buying numerous acres of vineyards and building large facilities for winemaking and visitors. One big industrial space offers room for vinification, aging, bottling, and storing, as well as space for receiving guests. A little industrial park flavor adds to the ambiance with the niceties that can be added to make guests comfortable (photos below).

The San Luis Obispo Industrial Park wineries are located south of downtown and immediately west of the airport. There are already several wineries there, and growing. These are well-experienced winemakers making excellent wines. Photo right is of winemaker/proprietor Steve Dooley tasting wine from his barrels at Stephen Ross Wines.

Stephen Ross Wine Cellars (Winery)
+1 805 594 1318 • 178 Suburban Road
Open: Every Day, 11am-3pm (Fri/Mon 5pm)

StephenRossWine.com

It was a natural endeavor for Steve Dooley to obtain his oenology degree from UC Davis after his teenage years of making rhubarb and apple wines in his parents basement. Steve went on to work for prestigious wineries in Napa Valley and Edna Valley before starting his own wines in 1994.

Steve is the winemaker/proprietor of Stephen Ross Wine Cellars, consults and makes wines for other area wineries, plus he is the president of the SLO Coast Wine Collective (photo above).

His focus is to work only with quality vineyards and handcrafting the best wines possible. Steve planted his estate vineyard, exclusively Pinot Noir in 2001. He contracts with top-level vineyards in three counties of the Central Coast. He is making a lot of great wines.

El Lugar Wines (Winery)
+1 805 801 0119 • 710 Fiero Lane #23
Open: Every Day, By Appointment

ElLugarWines.com

After fifteen years as winemaker for a prominent winery in Edna Valley, Coby Parker Garcia and his wife Katie, pursued their dream of creating the very best Pinot Noir from amazing vineyards they have come to know. El Lugar means "the place" in Spanish. For them, it defines a small lot, vineyard designate Pinot Noirs, defined by its place of origin. The wines are consistently being awarded scores in the mid '90s. These are delicious Pinot Noir wines you must try.

SLO Cider Company (Cider)
+1 805 439 0865 • 3419 Roberto Court, Suite C
Open: Every Day, 4pm-9pm (Sat/Sun 12pm-9pm)

SLOCiderCo.com

This is a draft-style apple cider, not orchard based. The apples come from the Pacific Northwest. The beginning here is a longtime experimentation in making a great tasting cider. I think they have perfected a magical cider. It is delicious.

All the ciders are made from this magical base. And you can drink it pure, either unfiltered or filtered. I must be a purest, as I loved the nice clean and unfiltered clear fresh cider the best. They also create some delicious flavors.

Tropical (passion fruit, bitter-sweet orange and pink guava pulp)
Rosé (red raspberry and hibiscus flower)
Hops (fresh citra hops for bold notes of resinous pine and bright citrus)
Holiday Spice (maple, date nectar, organic cinnamon, organic nutmeg)
Strawberry, Watermelon, Lemon Ginger

SLO DOWNTOWN WINERIES

Two wineries have already set up shop in downtown San Luis Obispo. Ragtag and Dunites (see below). I believe there will be more soon. Also, Region SLO is now in Downtown SLO with a tasting room for twenty-six different SLO wineries all in one place (photo right). All three of these tasting facilities are right in the middle of town within a few blocks from each other. Easy walking.

I love the idea of going for a glass of wine prior to dinner. Any one of these three places will serve you a full glass of wine. And their hours are perfect for a pre-dinner drink. You could also make it a full-day wine tasting, and visit all three tasting rooms. And do a little shopping in between. And enjoy the great restaurants that are everywhere.

Ragtag Wine Company (Winery)
+1 805 439 0774 • 779 Higuera Street
Open: Every Day, Noon-9pm

RagtagWineCo.com

The Ragtag winery very much fits its name. It is a hodgepodge mix of people with their own philosophies with an equally diverse mix of interesting vineyards. Their goal is to hand make small batch wines which represent their unique locations. They choose interesting vineyards which will produce unique wines representing their terroir!

The tasting room is right on the main street in the middle of it all. They are open every day and have live music Thursdays through Sundays 6pm-9pm. A little music. A little wine. Then a beautiful dinner. I like that kind of evening.

I also like their Malbec. It is hard to find a good Malbec in California. They have a special vineyard in the Santa Margarita Ranch AVA (Paso Robles).

Dunites Wines Company (Winery)
+1 805 858 8488 • 1133 Garden Street
Open: Thursday-Saturday, 1pm-8pm (Wed/Sun 6pm)

DunitesWineCo.com

Do you know the Dunites? They were hermits who created a secret utopia in the sand dunes of Oceano (southern SLO) a hundred years ago. They lived naturally, non-traditional, creative thinkers, not bound by norms.

This is exactly how the Dunites wines are created. Beyond rules. Creative. Not traditional. Their wines are unique and worth your try. I really liked their ancestral méthode of Sparkling Petillant Natural.

Region SLO (26 Wineries)
+1 805 329 3855 • 979 Morro Street
Open: Every Day, Noon-8pm (Ths-Sat 10pm)

DrinkRegion.com

Region SLO is located in the back of the Hotel SLO building, facing downtown SLOs primary district. This is an amazing place you must visit. They showcase twenty-six different wines in the San Luis Obispo *Region* (including Paso Robles).

Twenty six wineries have fifty-two wines on tap for small and large wine tasting. Each of these wineries get two weeks a year to be on the premises, hold events, have parties, make special offers, do special tastings, meet the winemaker, etc., as they choose.

This is an upscale tasting environment (check out the beautiful couches above). They have spacious inside and outside seating and provide full menu service from the Hotel SLO excellent restaurants.

This is a place to discover, just hang out, or to indulge!

Winter flowers at Edna Valley Vineyards

Three Distinctive Viticultural Areas Here, Representing Three Different French Wine Regions

The plateau vineyards at the Fess Parker Winery estate in Santa Ynez Valley

The Fiddlestix Vineyard in the Sta. Rita Hills AVA

Wild Diver Scallops with corn puree, roasted corn, popped corn, and watercress at First & Oak in Solvang

I magine a wine region filled with creative restaurants interspersed in cute little towns throughout a region that sports hot to cold weather grapes conducive for making a huge variety of wines.

SANTA BARBARA COUNTY

Now let's explore the Santa Barbara County wine regions. Santa Barbara is the name of both the county and its oceanfront city located on the southern edge of the county. The city of Santa Barbara is completely separate from the wine region. There is a mountain range in between. The largest city in Santa Barbara County is Santa Maria at the northern most edge of the county.

Santa Barbara County is most southern within the Central Coast wine regions, with San Luis Obispo County to its north, followed by Monterey County farthest north. Its wine regions encompass the western half of the county, north of the Santa Ynez Mountains and west of the San Rafael Mountain Range and Los Padres National Forest. The wine regions are completely open to the Pacific Ocean for an excellent maritime influence conducive for a variety of wine grapes.

Highway 101 is the north/south highway traversing through the Santa Barbara wine regions, from Los Angeles to the south, north into San Luis Obispo County and on to San Francisco.

The **San Barbara Airport** (SBA) has direct flights from six major airports, including Los Angeles and San Francisco, and is a forty-minute drive over the Santa Ynez Mountains into the wine regions.

The **Santa Maria Airport** (SMX) has some commercial flights and is trying to grow its access. Check what they have for your travel dates. Santa Maria is already located in the wine regions.

You might expect the lavish Santa Barbara city to have the best restaurants in the county; however, the little towns in the wine regions here have extraordinary restaurants that will impress you greatly. In fact, the Michelin star restaurant here is in the remote tiny town of Los Alamos, with other exceptional restaurants within blocks! And numerous other great restaurants in the other towns too.

For distance directions, I use the centerpoint of Buellton as it is located at the crossing of Highway 101 and Highway 246, which criss-crosses through the wine regions. Here are some helpful driving distances and times to make it easier to get around.

Driving Distance to Buellton from...
- **Los Angeles**   150 mi (3 hrs, 0 min)
- **Santa Barbara**   40 mi (0 hr, 40 min)
- **Santa Maria**   30 mi (0 hr, 25 min)
- **San Luis Obispo**   60 mi (1 hr,   0 min)
- **Monterey**   200 mi (3 hrs, 15 min)
- **San Francisco**   300 mi (4 hrs, 30 min)

Driving Distance from Buellton to...
- **Lompoc** (west)   16 mi (20 min)
- **Solvang** (east)   2 mi (5 min)
- **Los Olivos** (east)   10 mi (13 min)
- **Santa Ynez** (east)   13 mi (20 min)
- **Las Alamos** (north)   14 mi (14 min)
- **Santa Maria** (north)   30 mi (25 min)

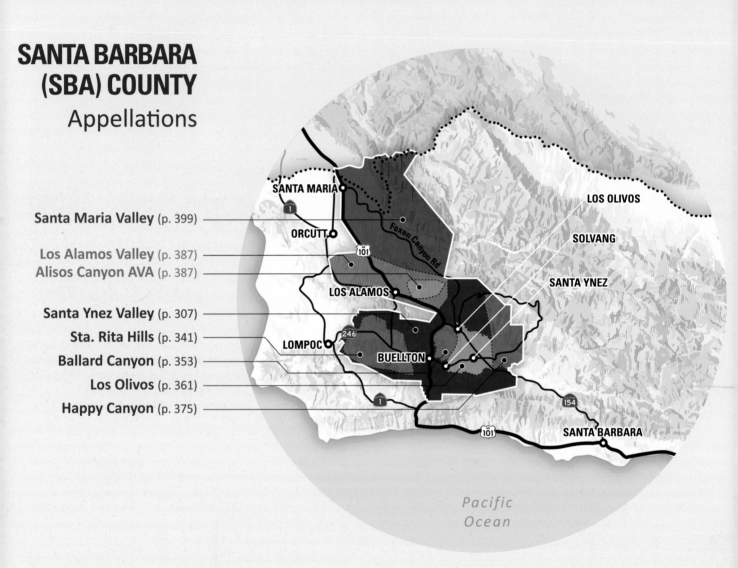

SANTA BARBARA (SBA) COUNTY
Appellations

Santa Maria Valley (p. 399)

Los Alamos Valley (p. 387)
Alisos Canyon AVA (p. 387)

Santa Ynez Valley (p. 307)

Sta. Rita Hills (p. 341)

Ballard Canyon (p. 353)

Los Olivos (p. 361)

Happy Canyon (p. 375)

SANTA MARIA
ORCUTT
LOS ALAMOS
LOMPOC
BUELLTON
Foxen Canyon Rd
LOS OLIVOS
SOLVANG
SANTA YNEZ
SANTA BARBARA
Pacific Ocean

CITIES AND TOWNS ⭕
Appellations ——————•
County limits ············

The Hilt Estate vineyards in the Sta. Rita Hills AVA

B urgundy grapes grow to the west, Rhône grapes in the middle and Bordeaux grapes to the east, plus more Burgundian grapes to the north.

APPELLATIONS OF SBA COUNTY

Santa Barbara County (SBA) has seven appellations, three of which are primary appellations, four are sub-appellations.

The **Santa Maria Valley AVA** is the northern most appellation in Santa Barbara County and is the region's first officially approved American Viticultural Area (AVA) in 1981. Santa Maria Valley is the second coldest appellation in California. Just fifteen miles from the ocean, it allows cool winds and fog to flow freely from the Pacific Ocean making it perfect terroir for Pinot Noir and Chardonnay, its two primary wines.

Notice the large **Los Alamos Valley** on the map just south of the Santa Maria Valley AVA. This valley is not an official appellation; however, it is filled with large expansive vineyards. No tasting rooms as most of the grapes are exported outside the county to wineries who know the quality here.

Inside Los Alamos Valley is a special appellation **Alisos Canyon AVA** that became the newest appellation in Santa Barbara in 2020. Renowned for its high-quality fruit, it warranted the special attention of its own appellation. What seems to

excel here most is Grenache, Viognier, Syrah, and Cabernet Franc. I was only able to find one winery here with a tasting room. Their property is beautiful, tasting is lakeside, wines are excellent, and they can provide gourmet food with reservations.

The largest and most well-known of the appellations in Santa Barbara is the **Santa Ynez Valley AVA**. It covers over 76,000 acres of land and contains a variety of microclimates as it extends twenty-five miles west to east across the valley, creating a huge difference in climate from one side to the other. In order to accurately define the differences of this terroir, four sub appellations emerged.

The west end of the valley is closest to the ocean and has cold climate perfectly conducive for Burgundian wines. The central area grows primarily Rhône varietals. The east end of the valley gets the heat perfectly suited for Bordeaux varietals.

Before diving into the sub-appellations, there are excellent wineries in the primary Santa Ynez Valley AVA. They are all located in the center of the valley, growing primarily Rhône and Bordeaux varietals.

The western region of the Santa Ynez Valley has the cooler sub-appellation **Sta. Rita Hills AVA** between Lompoc and Buellton. The valley starts just twelve

miles from the ocean and runs west between the Santa Rosa Hills and the Purisima Hills. This distinct region specializes in Pinot Noir and Chardonnay.

Just a few miles east of Buellton is the **Ballard Canyon AVA**. It's the Syrah canyon of love! A long narrow canyon running north to south, bordered by smaller canyons and dry rugged hills all set for the terroir of perfect Syrah.

Adjacent east is the **Los Olivos District AVA**, a large flat terrace that sits above the Santa Ynez River. This terroir is good for the Rhône varietals like Syrah, Grenache and Viognier, plus the Bordeaux varietals of Cabernet Sauvignon and Merlot can be found here. With flat terrain and rich soils, many wineries enjoy this easier farming.

On the far east of the valley, in the foothills of the San Rafael Mountain Range is **Happy Canyon AVA**. This is the warmest appellation in Santa Barbara. Because of the climate and soil, Happy Canyon's terroir has turned out to be excellent for Bordeaux varietals. The Cabernet Sauvignon is beautifully fruit forward, elegant and rich. The wine is opulent, standing strong with any competitors in California. The wineries are required to be by appointment here. And you definitely want to an appointment.

The 250-year storage cave at Star Lane Vineyards in the Happy Canyon AVA

SANTA BARBARA WINERIES

	Number of Wines	Red Wines	White Wines	Rosé Wines	Sweet Wines	Sparkling Wines	Wine Shop	Boutique	Lodging	Restaurant	Food Options	Food & Wine Pairings	Tours	Educational Workshops	Fun Activities	Burgundy Varietals	Rhône Varietals	Bordeaux Varietals	Other
Santa Ynez Valley AVA																			
Folded Hills Ranch Winery	14	√	√	√			√	√		√	√		√	√	√	√			
Fess Parker Winery	60	√	√	√		√	√	√		√			√		√	√	√		
Zaca Mesa Winery	34	√	√	√			√	√		√			√			√	√		
Margerum Wine Company	30	√	√	√	√	√	√	√		√	√		√	√	√	√	√		
Sta Rita Hills AVA																			
Dierberg Estate Vineyards	2	√	√				√	√					√			√			
The Hilt Estate	15	√	√		√		√	√								√			
Alma Rosa Winery	18	√	√		√		√			√			√			√	√		
Peake Ranch	9	√	√				√	√								√	√		√
Ballard Canyon AVA																			
Rusack Vineyards	15	√	√		√		√	√		√						√	√		√
Stolpman Vineyards	15	√	√	√			√	√					√			√	√		√
Beckmen Vineyards	27	√	√	√	√		√	√		√	√		√			√	√	√	√
Los Olivos AVA																			
Brave & Maiden Estate	15	√	√	√			√	√		√			√	√	√	√	√		
Roblar Winery & Vineyards	18	√	√	√		√	√	√	√	√	√					√	√	√	√
Gainey Vineyard	20	√	√	√			√	√		√	√		√			√	√	√	√
Sunstone Winery	23	√	√	√			√	√	√	√			√		√	√	√	√	√
Happy Canyon AVA																			
Crown Point Vineyards	5	√	√				√			√	√		√					√	
Happy Canyon Vineyard	8	√	√	√			√			√			√					√	
Grimm's Bluff	7	√	√	√			√						√		√			√	
Star Lane Vineyard	4	√	√	√			√	√		√	√		√					√	
Alisos Canyon AVA																			
Dovecote Estate Winery	4	√	√	√	√	√	√	√	√	√			√	√	√		√		
Lumen Wines	8	√	√				√		√	√	√	√				√	√		
Santa Maria Valley AVA																			
Bien Nacido Estate	9	√	√	√			√			√						√	√		
Foxen Vineyard & Winery	25	√	√	√	√		√	√								√	√	√	√
Presqu'ile Vineyard	25	√	√	√		√	√	√	√	√	√		√	√	√	√	√	√	√

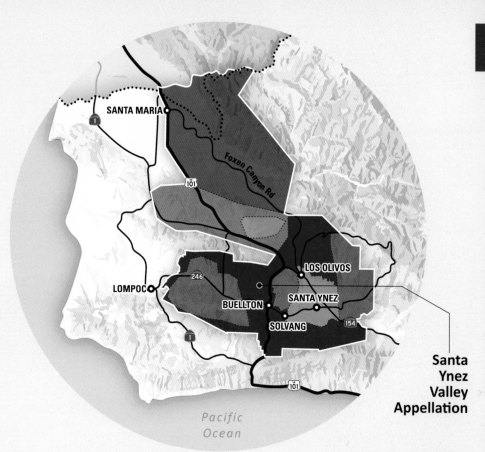

Santa Ynez Valley Appellation

Left page: The rolling hills of vineyards at Folded Hills Ranch.

THE PRIMARY APPELLATION

When you think of the Santa Barbara Wine Regions, you will most likely think of the Santa Ynez Valley AVA as this is the primary appellation that covers most of the Santa Barbara County's wine region. Most of the wineries in Santa Barbara, and in this book, are located in the Santa Ynez Valley AVA

While the Santa Ynez Valley AVA has four sub-appellations, this section only covers wineries that are located directly in the Santa Ynez Valley AVA and not in any of the sub-appellations. I have detailed those sub-appellations in their own chapters to follow. Keep in mind though, with the successful visibility of the Santa Ynez Valley name, some wineries in the sub-appellations will still label their bottles with the Santa Ynez Valley AVA name.

When you drive in from the south on Highway 101, the Santa Ynez Valley AVA is the first appellation you arrive, so these are the properties I present first.

The north part of the Santa Ynez Valley AVA has quite a few wineries located along the Foxen Canyon Road. Here I give you a couple of great wineries that are worth your visit.

From west (at Hwy 101) to east, the towns of Buellton, Solvang and Santa Ynez and are located in the Santa Ynez Valley, and they have some excellent restaurants to enjoy. I give you numerous reviews to choose.

Here are some wineries of Santa Ynez Valley AVA.
• Folded Hills Ranch Winery, page 309
• Fess Parker Winery, page 323
• Zaca Mesa Winery, page 325
• Margerum Wine Company, page 327

$$-$$$

2323 Old Coast Highway
Gaviota, CA 93117

+1 805 694 8086
Reservations@FoldedHills.com

FoldedHills.com

Open: Every Day, 11am-4pm

A 600-acre ranch of farms, vineyards and animals, and a winery producing Rhône wines.

BIODYNAMIC FARMED PROPERTY

Folded Hills Ranch is easily hidden from our scope of wineries. Not in a typical Santa Inez Valley location, they are four miles south of Buellton, five miles from the ocean. As you drive into the Santa Ynez Valley on Highway 101, just entering the appellation, the very first winery is Folded Hills. You must turn east off Highway 101 onto the Old Coast Highway in order to find it. It is 600 acres worth discovering.

Folded Hills Ranch was originally created by the Morton Salt family and later purchased by the Anheuser Busch family in 2004. The vineyards were planted in 2014 of Grenache and Syrah on the hillsides (photo previous pages), and Marsanne, Grenache Blanc and Clairette Blanc planted by the Nojoqui Creek.

Andy Busch, the great-grandson of Lilly Anheuser and Adolphus Busch who started the largest brewing company in the world, was a professional polo player. As captain of the USA polo team for the World Cup, Andy came to Santa Barbara for tournaments. Andy and his wife, Kim, fell in love with Santa Barbara, move there, and ultimately bought the Folded Hills Ranch to raise their three sons and daughter in this beautiful outdoor environment.

The property is filled with ranch and exotic animals, including Budweiser Clydesdale horses. Not just vineyards, row crops and fruit orchards in abundance. The entire property is organic, and biodynamically farmed. Learn more on the following to four pages.

Their wine tasting is right off the highway in a restored historic farmhouse. You have a choice of wine tasting in a beautiful living room, up against the wine bar, outside on the patio, or under the beautiful trees.

Here is the ultimate experience on the ranch: **Escape to the Lake**. You'll be escorted into a private part of the ranch where are you will taste wines on their exclusive lake. You will have your own wine steward to guide you through their wines and share with you the amazing details of this ranch. Tasting is on the lakeside dock, overlooking the lake and mountains in all directions. This is a super romantic experience (sunset lake photo on left page).

I highly recommend their **Wine & Cheese Pairing** (photo above). This is one of the best pairings I have experienced. Each wine and cheese is described in detail, along with the notes about why it is an excellent pairing. Very professional.

Collection of Rhône Wines

Santa Ynez Reserve Syrah
Adolphus Syrah
Polo Reserve Syrah
Clydesdale Syrah
"00" Syrah
August Red (Syrah, Grenache)
Estate Reserve Grenache
Estate Grenache
Grant Grenache
Cluster Grenache
Cluster Carbonic Grenache

Lilly Rosé Grenache
August White (Viognier, Grenache Blanc,
Roussanne, Clairette Blanche)
Estate White (Grenache Blanc, Clariette Blanche, Marssanne)
Estate Marsanne

WANT TO SAY HI TO GEORGE THE CAMEL?

Folded Hills is truly a ranch with a huge variety of animals. To see the entire 600-acre ranch, choose **The Whole Shebang** experience. You'll be escorted around the property in an off-road Polaris tour of the owner's private ranch. This is a VIP tour. You will go up into the vineyards, stop at the private lake, see the professional polo field, get a glance at the beautiful plantation home that was built by the Morton Salt family, and stop for a great number of animals along the way. And feed some of them. And not to miss, an extraordinary wine tasting experience is included of course.

Ranch animals everywhere. Sheep, goats, chickens, horses, miniature donkeys, llamas, mini-horses, etc.

Exotic animals live here, like a beautiful zebra, athletic polo horses, Budweiser Clydesdale horses, Nigerian dwarf goats, and George the camel who protects the other animals from the carnivores who visit from the mountains.

Rescued animals are loved here. Peaches is their rescue mini jersey cow. They raise Kunekune pigs that were almost extinct thirty years ago.

Wild animals live in and around the ranch. You might see wild pigs, mule deers, peacocks, golden eagles, and the ferruginous hawks. Sometimes a bear or mountain lion might show up in the middle of the night (when you are not there). George addresses that issue!

2323 Old Coast Highway
Gaviota, CA 93117

+1 805 694 8086
Reservations@FoldedHills.com

FoldedHills.com

Open: Every Day, 11am-4pm

THE FARMSTEAD OF PRODUCE AND ANIMALS

Across the Old Highway Road from the Folded Hills tasting room is their **Folded Hills Farmstead** barn and extensive animal corral. The Farmstead is where people, farmers, food, animals, and nature can intertwine. An experience to get away from city life and enjoy this peaceful ranch.

The Farmstead barn is open on the weekends and is filled with organic fruits and vegetables grown on the property, plus small-batch staples made by local artisans, and homemade baked goods made by the owner, Kim Busch, and her chef, Mark, from family recipes that have been handed down through generations.

We can either shop for their freshly harvested produce in the barn, or we can go into their fields and harvest ourself these organic foods in their **U-Pick Fields**. Everything is focused on quality. This is a family-owned ranch that focuses on health and sustainability. In fact, the ranch is 100% self-sustainable.

Folded Hills Ranch has the closest property to the ocean than any other winery here. Much closer than the westward most vineyards in Sta. Rita Hills appellation. They are only five miles from the crashing waves. This gives them the cool Pacific Ocean influence and warmer days for optimal viticulture. They hired experts to determine what would be the best grapes to grow on this property. The decision was Rhône varietals, of which they now grow exclusively.

2323 Old Coast Highway
Gaviota, CA 93117

+1 805 694 8086, x3
Farmstead@FoldedHills.com

FoldedHills.com

Open: Saturday/Sunday, 10:30am-4:30pm

$$$$$

1054 Alisal Road
Solvang, CA 93463

+1 805 693 4208
Reservations@AlisalRanch.com

AlisalRanch.com

Open: All Year, Every Day, 24 hours

T he Alisal Ranch is the ultimate outdoor playground with everything you could imagine in hospitality, gourmet cuisine and extensive activities.

A DUDE RANCH GETAWAY

And not just for dudes. It is as much a romantic escape as a family affair. Perfect for retreats or just to get away from the city to get back to nature, or to find oneself, or simply to unwind and relax.

Originally a successful cattle ranch beginning in 1810 as Rancho Nojoqui. In 1946, this 10,500-acre ranch in the Santa Ynez Mountains (south of Solvang), became Alisal Ranch open to the public for hospitality. Alisal is still a cattle ranch with over 1,500 head of cattle naturally grazing across the ranch, raising black angus grass fed beef. And over a 110 quality horses for both guests and wranglers.

The ranch is adjacent west of Folded Hills Ranch and directly southwest is President Reagan's Ranch.

The property is a natural wildlife habitat. You will see the cattle happily grazing all over the ranch. You will frequently see black-tailed deer wandering the property, sometimes relaxing hilltop checking you

out (photo below). It is not uncommon to see foxes and coyotes moving through the property during the day (photo below right).

More elusive are bobcats, black bears and mountain lions deeper into the mountains. Alisal Ranch has become a wonderful refuge for wildlife as no hunting is allowed on the property.

Birds congregate here. There is a huge lake where you will see many species of ducks, geese, herons, egrets, osprey, and much more. The skies are filled with predatory birds, such as the beautiful bald eagle, golden eagle, cooper hawks, red-tail hawks (photo upper right), barn owls, and the majestic great horned owl. And wild turkeys running in large flocks (photo center right).

Alisal Ranch is a beautiful place to get connected with nature. And all these beautiful animals help to connect. If you love horses, there is an abundance of horseback riding, which can take you out to see so much of the landscape and wildlife.

EXTENSIVE OUTDOOR EXPERIENCES

Horseback Riding. From beginner to advanced, to not ever sitting on a horse previously, Alisal Ranch is ready for you. Their wranglers can teach you all about horses and horseback riding. First timers to advanced riding techniques. **Group rides** and **private rides** are available for beginners, intermediate and advance riding. They have fifty miles of trails to ride in the 10,500-acre ranch. Ride amongst 300-year-old oak trees, spectacular sycamores and along their beautiful lake and mountain setting. Once a week they have a **breakfast group ride**, or hayride, up to their lake for a big delicious breakfast lakeside with the cowboys. And an exciting **rodeo** takes place every week during the summer.

Lake Activities. Alisal Ranch has a large natural lake inside their property. **Fly fishing** in the spring-fed lake, many **watercrafts** available (paddleboards, pedal boats, canoes, kayaks, and motorized boats). **Archery** and **air rifles** are available at the lake as well.

Have you tried **pickleball**? In playing tennis and racquetball, I would describe this as a combination of both sports. Excellent game; I cannot wait to play again. They also have **tennis** and **sand volleyball**.

Ride into Solvang on **street bicycles** or explore the ranch trails on **motorized mountain bikes**. Or stay on your feet, **hiking** extensive trails into the ranch. Or do their **rope course**, climbing trees, walls and poles.

They also have two eighteen-hole **golf courses** (a public course and a private course only for ranch guests). Love animals? They have a **petting zoo**, and you can jump in and do a real **hog wash** (yes, bathe the big hogs!).

The skies are painted with a lot more stars at the ranch. This is the place to stargaze. I saw a nice flow of meteor showers when I was there.

1054 Alisal Road
Solvang, CA 93463

+1 805 693 4208
Reservations@AlisalRanch.com

AlisalRanch.com

Open: All Year, Every Day, 24 hours

RANCH-STYLE DINING

Breakfast and dinner are included with your accommodations at Alisal Ranch. You really do not need to leave the ranch, and why would you want to? There are so many amazing activities here, Alisal has made it easy so you do not have to leave the ranch. And the food is excellent, you won't be desiring finding an outside restaurant. The menu is created daily, so you won't get bored choosing what's next of the chef's creations.

Alisal Ranch takes the culinary experience seriously. Their chef, a graduate of the California School of Culinary Arts' Le Cordon Bleu, has had award-winning participation at both Michelin-star restaurants and at five-star-hotel restaurants. He brings creativity and elegance to the dining here.

Their Ranch House Dining Room takes on a beautiful western theme. A big roaring fireplace, and candles at the tables. They also have a big lounge for before or after cocktails, also with a big roaring fireplace. They have additional restaurants poolside and at the golf course.

Let's get to the good stuff. Here are the chef's delicious descriptions.

Braised Short Ribs (photo left): the short ribs are slowly braised for forty-eight hours and glazed with a rich red wine demi-glace, served upon a Weiser Farms carrot puree.

Huevos Rancheros (photo below left): a local classic breakfast dish of pinquito beans, avocado, lime crema, handmade tortilla, and salsa ranchera.

Alisal Ranch Filet Mignon (photo below center): a classic Alisal Ranch dish with Yukon gold potatoes, haricot vert and red wine butter.

Goat Cheese Stuffed Piquillo Peppers (photo right center): a tip of the hat to Santa Barbara Spanish heritage of piquillo peppers, cypress grove goat cheese, golden raisins, pine nuts, and aged Pedro Ximénez vinegar.

Campfire Duo (photo below right): the chef's childhood favorites: s'mores panna cotta (left), graham cracker crumble and marshmallow fluff. Fire roasted banana shake (right): McConnell's vanilla ice cream, caramelized bananas, salted caramel, and toasted meringue.

1054 Alisal Road
Solvang, CA 93463

+1 805 693 4208
Reservations@AlisalRanch.com

AlisalRanch.com

Open: Breakfast, Lunch and Dinner

WESTERN STYLE LUXURY ACCOMMODATIONS

Where is John Wayne? It just seems like he should be here, somewhere, as the Alisal Ranch feels like a western celebrity's hangout. Actually, Clark Gable married Lady Silvia in the Alisal Library.

They have a huge variety of places to stay, all with inclusive pricing (dining, laundry, housekeeping with evening turndown, and so much more). All rooms have wood-burning fireplaces and refrigerators. They have luxury suites and cottages, studios if you want something smaller, and homes that can hold your entire family. Everything is luxury with western style motif. And a well-heated swimming pool and spa.

You must stay on the property in order to have access to the activities of the ranch. It is nice because it is not crowded. And you can make reservations for just about any activity.

$$$$

1054 Alisal Road
Solvang, CA 93463

+1 805 693 4208
Reservations@AlisalRanch.com

AlisalRanch.com

Open: All Year, Every Day, 24 hours

RODNEY'S VINEYARD

$-$$-$$$-$$$$

6200 Foxen Canyon Road
Los Olivos, CA 93441

+1 805 688 1545
Info@FessParker.com

FessParker.com

Open: Every Day, 10am-5pm

A
cting to flying to real estate, Fess Parker has created a wine legacy three generations strong.

RHÔNE & BURGUNDY

Remember Fess Parker? I was fortunate to know him personally. We had flying airplanes in common, both pilots with airplanes. Fess was the American Frontier Icon who played the television rolls of Davy Crockett and Daniel Boone for Walt Disney Studios.

While flying brought us together, I remember, having so much fun with Fess as he drove us around the Santa Ynez Valley in his Hummer showing me the different land he acquired, and wanted to acquire. Fess saw this frontier, and the future of the wine regions of Santa Ynez Valley.

Fess brought his acting money to Santa Barbara to invest in real estate. He purchased land to build resorts, and lots of land to plant vineyards. He started the Fess Parker Winery in 1989 and built a beautiful facility to welcome guests with great hospitality. His children have continued the family business, and recently modernized (stunningly) the tasting room (photo above).

The Fess Parker Winery is located in the far north of the Santa Ynez Valley AVA on a beautiful country drive on Foxen Canyon Road.

One of Fess Parker's most famous vineyards is Rodney's Vineyard (photo left page). It is located on the plateau above and behind the winery on their 714-acre Foxen Canyon Ranch where they specialize in Rhône varietals. Fess Parker also has vineyards in Sta. Rita Hills AVA and Santa Maria Valley AVA for their cooler Burgundian varietals. In all, I count at least sixty-six different wines from Fess Parker Winery.

They have three tastings.
• The **Classic Tasting** is either a standard tasting or a single-vineyard list of wines served out on their spacious patio.
• The **Barrel Room Tasting** is a customizable flight of five single-vineyard wines. There is nothing like a barrel tasting to see, and taste, the future.
• Their **Library Wine Room Tasting** is led by one of their sommeliers in one of their brand-new, private wine library rooms (photo above).

I have some favorite wines I can't wait to try every time I am there. Their *Fiddelstix Vineyard Pinot Noir* is extraordinary (photo right). Fiddelstix is a special vineyard in the southern part of Sta. Rita Hills AVA (photo page 300).

My other favorite is their *Rodney's Vineyard Viognier*. It is difficult to find excellent Viognier in California and I find the Foxen Canyon is ideal terroir for this grape. Fess Parker does an excellent job with this wine.

Collection of Wines

Rodney's Vineyard (Syrah)
Rodney's Vineyard (Viognier)

Ashley's Vineyard (Pinot Noir)
Bien Nacido (Pinot Noir)
Clone 115 (Pinot Noir)
Parker West (Pinot Noir)
Pommard (Pinot Noir)

Ashley's Vineyard (Chardonnay)
Parker West (Chardonnay)
Sanford & Benedict (Chardonnay)

SANTA BARBARA **SANTA YNEZ VALLEY** ■
Winery, Vineyards
ZACA MESA WINERY

$$-$$$

6905 Foxen Canyon Road
Los Olivos, CA 93441

+1 805 688 9339
Info@ZacaMesa.com

ZacaMesa.com

Open: Every Day, 10am-4pm

S anta Barbara's first (1978) and oldest Syrah vineyards bringing stunningly rich wines.

RHÔNE SPECIALISTS

What comes to mind when I think of the Zaca Mesa wines is their Viognier. I am a big fan of Condrieu France, creating my love for Viognier as my white wine choice. It is difficult to find a great Viognier in California and the Zaca Mesa Winery does it extremely well.

Do you know Viognier (*Vee-own-yay*)? I think of it as the red wine drinker's white wine. It is full bodied with rich flavors like a red wine. Think of creamy mango and honeysuckle with a beautiful vanilla nose. If anything, go to Zaca Mesa for this wine.

The Zaca Mesa Winery is fifty years old (1973), the third winery established in Santa Barbara county. And the first to grow Syrah in Santa Barbara. In the beginning, they experimented with many different varietals to see what worked best. Ultimately, Rhône grapes thrived here, and the property became 100% focused on Rhône varietals.

Don't let me lead you away from Syrah wines. They make a lot of them. Single-vineyard and single-clone wines, as well as Syrah blends (GSMs).

Zaca Mesa Winery is located at the very far north of the Santa Ynez Valley AVA on the Foxen Canyon Road. Their famous vineyard, the Black Bear Block on Mesa Vineyard (*yes, bears love this grape too!*), sits at 1,400' elevation above the morning fog, giving rise to rich character and natural acidity. This was the first (1978) and now the oldest Syrah vineyard in Santa Barbara County, and own-root planted with the famous Heritage Estrella Clone.

They have many tasting experiences with your choice of their **lounge**, **terrace** or **courtyard**. They have a **mixed flight** or **red-only flight**, a **reserve flight**, or their new Burgundian **TREAD Flight**. Dogs, families, cyclists and picnics are welcomed. They also have **the vineyard oak tree** for a private and tailored tasting experience under a big oak tree.

The best though is their **private winery tour,** walking the vineyards and learning about their grape-growing methods, through the winery, stopping and learning about each step of the winemaking process. It concludes with an elegant gastronomical experience, pairing their wines with a gourmet cheese and charcuterie board.

Collection of Rhône Wines

Black Bear Block Syrah
Estrella Syrah
Chapel G Syrah
Eight Barrel Syrah
Clydesdale Syrah
Grenache
Mourvèdre
Petite Sirah
Inceptive (Syrah, Grenache, Mourvèdre)
Z Cuvée (Mourvèdre, Grenache, Cinsault, Syrah)

Roussanne
Grenache Blanc
Rosé of Grenache
Cushman Block Viognier
Z Cuvée Blanc (Grenache Blanc, Roussanne)

BUELLTON CITY

Buellton is the first city when arriving to the Santa Barbara Wine Regions from the south on Highway 101. It is located at the intersection of Hwy 101 (north/south) and Hwy 246 (east/west). To the west on Hwy 246 is the **Sta. Rita Hills AVA** wine region. To the east on Hwy 246 is Solvang, Santa Ynez and the **Santa Ynez Valley AVA** wine region. To the north is Los Alamos, Santa Maria and **Santa Maria Valley AVA** wine region. There are numerous gas stations at this intersection, and the lowest prices around.

Buellton is famous for the Anderson split-pea soup, and also the Hitching Post II restaurant that was the central spot in the movie *Sideways*, plus other good restaurants, a couple of which you will find below. Buellton is a mecca of standard hotels.

Photo right is the Graffiti Wall of Industrial Eats restaurant.

Ostrichland USA (Big Bird Ranch)
+1 805 686 9696 • 610 E Highway 246
Open: Every Day, 9am-5pm

OstrichlandUSA.com

Visit and feed over a hundred ostriches and emus on this ranch where these big birds roam freely. They will come right up to you and smile face to face. You can buy fresh ostrich eggs here all year (the size of twenty-five chicken eggs, and they taste the same), and fresh emu eggs during the winter and spring (the size of eight chicken eggs, tasting like creamy duck eggs).

Hitching Post II (Steakhouse)
+1 805 688 0676 • 406 E Highway 246
Open: Wednesday-Sunday, 11:30am-8:30pm

HitchingPost2.com

After the Sideways movie fame as the hitching spot for Miles and Jack to hook up with Maya and Stephanie, the Hitching Post II is known for its grilled meats and seafood barbecued on red oak wood. It is known as a Santa Maria style barbecue, as the first Hitching Post was, and still is, in Santa Maria (Casmalia, to be exact, pop 138).

Industrial Eats (Restaurant)
+1 805 688 8807 • 181 B Industrial Way
Open: Every Day, 12pm-8pm

IndustrialEats.com

This is a hip and trendy place. A cool eatery in an industrial park, with grocery graffiti all over it's exterior walls (above). They want a community and bring people together with their communal tables. Great prices. Wholesome foods. The cuisine is extra creative, with recipes from all over the world. And numerous pizzas cooked in their wood-fired ovens.

$-$$-$$$-$$$$

59 Industrial Way
Buellton, CA 93427

+1 805 686 8500
Info@MargerumWines.com

MargerumWines.com

Buellton Winery Private Experiences
Open: By Reservation Only

Collection of Wines

Margerum Über Syrah (35 Vineyard Blocks)
M5 Red Reserve (5 Rhône Grapes, 12 Vineyards)
M5 Red (5 Rhône Grapes, 12 Vineyards)
(Grenache, Syrah, Mourvèdre, Counoise, Cinsault)

Margerum Helena Red (Syrah, Grenache)
Margerum Estate Grenache
Margerum SBC Grenache
Margerum Estate Syrah Block Three
Margerum Estate Syrah
Margerum Syrah
Margerum Mason Street (Syrah)
Margerum Estate Cinsault

Margerum Riviera Rosé (Grenache, Syrah)
M5 White (Grenache Blanc, Marsanne, Roussanne, Viognier, Picpoul Blanc)
Estate Trois Blondes (Marsanne, Viognier, Roussanne)
Margerum Sybarite Sauvignon Blanc
Margerum Estate Picpoul Blanc
Margerum Estate Viognier
Margerum Riesling

F inalist, Winemaker of the Year, creating unique Rhône wines worth your attention.

CREATIVITY & INNOVATION

First thing I noticed walking through the Margerum winery, tasting from tanks and barrels with Doug Margerum, was the creativity going into making his wines. Wines we know; however, with innovative ideas to make them better.

Most notable is their *Margerum Über Syrah*. 100% Syrah; not from one vineyard though. The Syrah grapes come from thirty-five different vineyard blocks which ripen at various different times over a month and a half. So, co-fermentation is for forty-five days as each Syrah bock is harvested and added to the tank. What a concept!

In special barrels, Ermitage French oak barriques, still aging, the wine had the qualities of a ten year old wine. The complexities of delicious fresh fruit with aged wine elegance combined. Extraordinary. In the bottle, magnificent. I kept the bottle and tasted it every day as I watched it mature. This is one of those wines to buy a case, and open a bottle every now and then to experience its development.

The winery and aging facilities are in an industrial park in Buellton. They also have a tasting room in downtown Santa Barbara; however, in Buellton they provide **private experiences** by reservation.

Private Deep-Dive Tasting occurs in their barrel room where you will taste numerous wines right out of the barrels as they are aging (see photo above of Doug Margerum contemplating his M5 Blend out of the barrel). After tasting from the barrels, bottles of the same wines will be open so you can see how the wine develops. Cheeses, charcuterie and accoutrements included.

Private Food & Wine Pairing is curated by their chef and sommelier for a very articulate and detailed wine experience oriented around the art of matching food and wine. Tasty and educational.

Private Library Tasting explore historic vintages from Doug Margerum's twenty-one years creating wine.

Private M5 Red or M5 White Blending Seminar is a hands-on experience tasting all five varietals individually, then tasting how they come together while you blend them into an M5 wine.

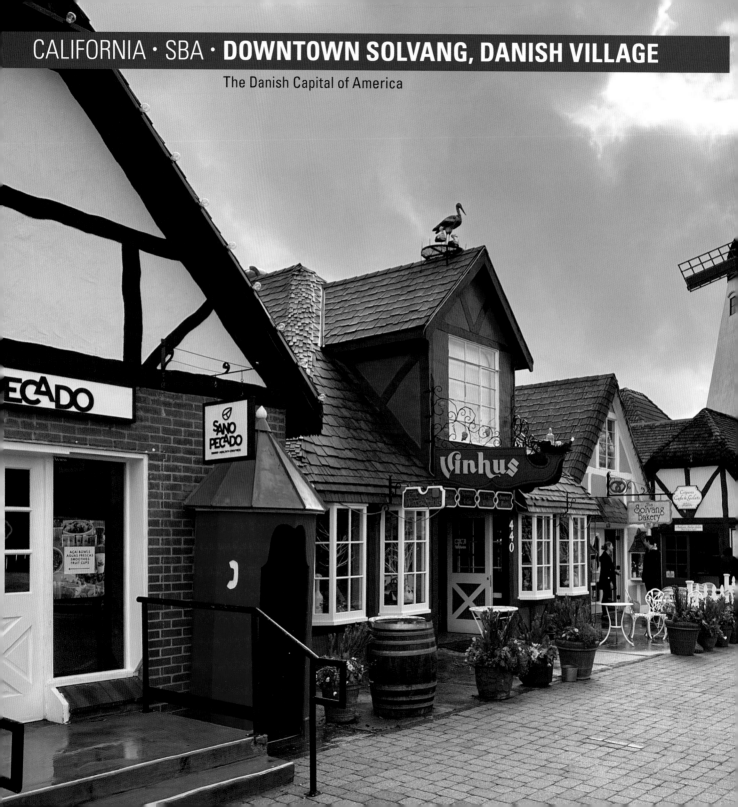

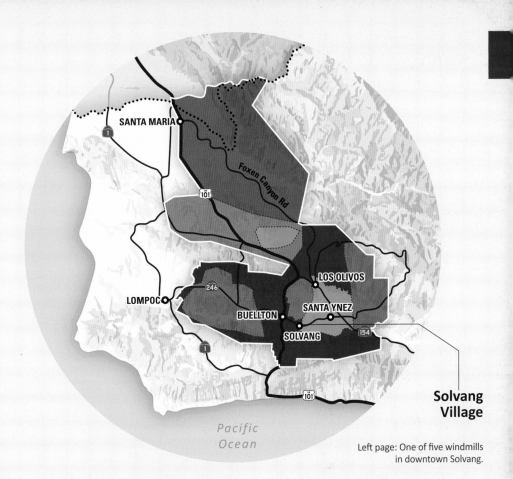

Solvang Village

Left page: One of five windmills in downtown Solvang.

AN AUTHENTIC DANISH VILLAGE

In 1850, Demark suffered an economic crisis. Danes began migrating to the United States, mostly to the Midwest. By the turn of the twentieth century, those who settled in these areas were looking to get away from the harsh winters and find viable land for a new Danish community. In 1911, three Danish immigrants purchased 9,000 acres of land from the Mission Santa Inéz to establish the new Danish community. The new settlement was named Solvang, meaning "sunny field" in Danish. It was what they wanted, 300 days of sunshine all year.

This California Danish village is now known as the **Danish Capital of America**. Just take a walk down Copenhagen Drive, their classic shopping street, and you will feel like you are in Denmark. Ever had a Danish pancake, a thin crêpe ever so tasty. I want one now just thinking about it. Be sure to ride the horse drawn trolley for a tour of the town.

Solvang is located right in the middle of the wine regions. It has nice hotels and great restaurants, plus all the fun of the Danish style community. It is located just two miles east of Buellton on Highway 246, in the southwest corner of the Los Olivos AVA and at the southern edge of the Ballard Canyon AVA.

Apparently, the modernization of Denmark has removed so much of the classic Danish architecture and replaced it with modern buildings. Differently, Solvang has retained this authentic architecture and the Danes come to Solvang to see how their country originally looked.

Leonardo's Cucina Italiana

+1 805 686 0846 • 632 Alamo Pintado Road, Solvang
Open: Monday-Saturday, 11am-9pm

LeonardosCucina.com

Authentic Italian recipes from Cariati Italy, a small town of a few thousand people, mostly fishermen and carpenters. Leonardo will personally welcome you in an enthusiastic Italian style to his restaurant to experience the warm atmosphere of his childhood when getting together at the dinner table was always a delicious feast.

Paula's Pancake House

+1 805 688 2867 • 1531 Mission Drive, Solvang
Open: Every Day, 7am-3pm

PaulasPancakeHouse.com

Danish Pancake. Did I say Danish pancakes?!! I come to this restaurant every time I am in town just for the Danish pancake. It is a large, very thin, delicious crêpe served with their homemade whipped cream and fresh fruit. I love egg breakfasts, and Paula is famous for eggs benedict; however, I crave this special treat every time I am here.

S. Y. Kitchen, Cucina Rustica

+1 805 691 9794 • 1110 Faraday Street, Santa Ynez
Open: Every Day, 4:30pm-9pm (Fri-Sun +11:30am-2pm)

SYKitchen.com

Executive Chef Luca Crestanelli was born, raised and educated in gastronomy and culinary arts in Verona, Italy. He spent his career as a chef in fancy restaurants in big cities (he is talented!). Now, he's in a rustic farmhouse creating great cuisine in a casual atmosphere. Excellent cocktails. Ask if he has fresh truffles, as I did, and see what he makes (below).

Copenhagen Sausage Garden
+1 805 697 7354 • 1660 Copenhagen Drive, Solvang
Open: Every Day, 11am-8pm (Fri-Sat 9pm)

CSG-Solvang.com

An outdoor beer garden in the heart of the Solvang Village. They focus on just beer and sausage. Enjoy a famous **Danish Rød Pølse** with a **Danish Red Lager** (actually very good beer). This is a family business where they hand-make all eleven high-quality sausages (and two vegan sausages). There are also numerous family made toppings to experiment with yourself.

Old Mission Santa Inés
+1 805 688 4815 • 1760 Mission Drive, Solvang
Open: Every Day, 9am-4pm (Sun 10am)

MissionSantaInes.org

Built in 1804, Mission Santa Inés became the 19th of the twenty-one missions in California, and the first Seminary in California (1844) to train young men to become priests. The mission has been completely restored to its original beauty and has an extensive museum of many of the original artifacts from 200 years ago. As an active church, mass is every weekend.

LUXURY HOTEL IN THE MIDDLE OF THE WINE REGION

The Landsby is the perfect hotel centrally located in the Santa Barbara Wine Region. Being in Solvang puts this property right in the middle of the Santa Ynez Valley appellation, and extremely close to each of the sub-appellations.

The Landsby is also central within the Solvang Village. In the front is the village's primary road, Mission Drive (Hwy 246). From the side of the hotel, it opens to Copenhagen Drive, the most nostalgic street in Solvang, filled with shops and restaurants. The entire village is walkable, especially considering The Landsby is central.

Speaking of restaurants, Solvang has numerous amazing restaurants. It has become a mecca of deliciousness (see the following pages). And the Landsby has its own gourmet restaurant on premises. Mad & Vin is also open to the public (see next page). They also have a happening bar/lounge, with appetizers.

The hotel has been completed remodeled and modernized. Still with Danish aesthetics, yet a clean and modern motif. The rooms are luxurious, spacious and very interesting with their multi-level bedroom/living room design (photo below left). They have both showers and large bathtubs, with bath salts for the ultimate enjoyment. Many of the rooms open into their gardens (photo left page) with beautiful bay windows and Dutch doors.

$$$-$$$$

1576 Mission Drive
Solvang, CA 93463

+1 805 688 3121
Reservations@TheLandsby.com

TheLandsby.com

Reservations On Their Website

SEASONAL GOURMET CUISINE

This is not your typical hotel restaurant. They hired an executive chef with great talent to create the menu and experience of a gourmet restaurant. Chef Daniel Milian (photo right) brings decades experience to Mad & Vin.

Daniel is a Santa Ynez Valley native, raised here and always worked here. He started as a dishwasher and earned his way to executive chef. This led him to become chef de cuisine at the amazing Alisal Guest Ranch where he earned employee of the year (see page 315).

Chef Daniel has a great passion for farm-to-table ingredients which he learned from his mother's cooking. He feels this has led him to his culinary accomplishments. Now, at Mad & Vin, Daniel has embarked on what he calls "Eat with Your Eyes" ornamentation techniques. He is now taking his polished skills of making delicious food and adding the visual elements, which makes food taste even better. We do eat with our eyes, just look at the beautiful presentations in the photos of these two pages. The taste was as spectacular as the look.

Pork Tomahawk (photo left), standing on their ends, this grilled 14oz Niman Ranch pork tomahawk chop was marinated in brine for twenty-four hours and served with garlic mashed potatoes, sautéed broccolini and a seasonal fruit chutney. The crusty outside texture and flavors are deliciously unique and holds in the juice tender meat inside. Using your fingers are acceptable here, and appropriate.

Short Ribs (photo below left), seared and braised in Lucas & Lewellen Pinot Noir and their own natural juices, then served with applewood lardon, garlic mashed potatoes, sautéed baby heirloom carrots, and green beans.

Cedar Plank Salmon (photo right below), Ora salmon prepared on a cedar plank with bourbon whole grain honey mustard. Unbelievably juicy and tender, served on a purple beet puree glaze, baby potatoes, baby carrots, and green goddess.

SANTA BARBARA **SOLVANG** VILLAGE

Restaurant
MAD & VIN

$$-$$$-$$$$

1576 Mission Drive
Solvang, CA 93463

+1 805 697 7048
TheLandsby.com/dining

Open: Every Day, 7:30am-9pm
Breakfast, Lunch And Dinner
Reservations On Their Website

STUNNING PRESENTATIONS OF DELICIOUS FOOD

First & Oak is located in the beautiful Mirabelle Inn on a quiet street in downtown Solvang. It is an upscale French-style restaurant focused on sustainable and organic ingredients. Everything is fresh and homemade.

While focused on fresh local ingredients, the actual ingredients are prepared and presented in very creative ways. A tomato tea soup on top of a colorful salad for example (left page). Their chef comes from excellent pedigree. Chef Steven Snook indulged eight years working with Gordon Ramsay at several of his restaurants, including his flagship destination, Restaurant Gordon Ramsay in Chelsea, a three-star Michelin restaurant. First & Oak has already achieved Michelin's Plate award.

Dining is both indoors, and in the outside patio along the sidewalk. Their indoor dining room is beautiful with antiques and paintings along the walls. The dining room centerpiece is an antique French table covered with open bottles of wine. They have a huge selection of excellent wines by the glass, and a food and wine pairing is certainly appropriate with their sommelier pairing each dish.

Here are some of the beauties here...

Tomato Tea (photo left page): the tea is actually an organic tomato soup with numerous ingredients simmered for two days, then strained and clarified into a tea. The bowl is filled with thinly shaved colorful vegetables and the magic occurs when the tomato tea is poured from a tea pot into the bowl right in front of you at the table.

Prime Mignon (photo below): a tender, flavorful and perfectly cooked filet of beef from the narrow front part of the tenderloin with Tokyo turnups in a Béarnaise sauce.

Roasted Cauliflower (photo right): truffle and chive vinaigrette, crisp quinoa, Marcona almonds, and golden raisins.

Chocolate & Honey (photo below right): a chocolate mousse, honeycomb crumble and bee pollen.

$$$-$$$$

409 1st Street
Solvang, CA 93463

+1 805 688 1703
Info@FirstAndOak.com

FirstAndOak.com

Open: Every Day, 5pm-8:30pm

Michelin Plate Awarded

Restaurant
Peasants FEAST

$-$$-$$$-$$$$

487 Atterdag Road
Solvang, CA 93463

+1 805 686 4555
Info@PeasantsFeast.com

PeasantsFeast.com

Open: Wednesday-Sunday, 11am-6pm

C reativity in abundance here. Even their basic salad goes wildly gourmet.

CASUAL GOURMET

You might wonder how a casual restaurant of soups, salads, burgers, tacos, and sandwiches could impress a fine dining connoisseur. This is a casual little place for lunch and dinner. Yet, somebody really knows what they are doing in the kitchen.

Executive Chef Michael Cherney comes from Michelin three-star restaurant experience. Plus, he lived on a forty-acre sustainable and organic farm in northern California. Imagine bringing wholesome foods to a simple casual restaurant, and adding the creativity of a Michelin-star cuisine. You get Peasants FEAST, a restaurant created by Michael and his wife, Sarah, with twenty-five years in the hospitality industry managing restaurants. As you can imagine, new creative dishes show up on the menu everyday at specials.

Baby Gem Salad (top): a gem of a salad it is to see and experience. Starting with local baby gem lettuce, adding radish, carrots, beets, toasted almonds, and a shallot thyme vinaigrette dressing.

Fig Grilled Cheese (below right): the most amazing flavors of aged Manchego cheese, mozzarella cheese, fig jam, wilted arugula, and parmesan crisps. Served melted between pain au levain artisan bread.

Bowl of Carrot Ginger Soup (below left): a deliciously rich soup, hosting Calabrian chili oil, fresh croutons, and chives.

$$-$$$-$$$$-$$$$$

1635 Mission Drive
Solvang, CA 93463

+1 805 624 5420
Information@CoastRange.restaurant

CoastRange.restaurant

Open: Wednesday-Monday, 10am-10pm
Vaquero Bar: Wednesday-Monday, 10am-Midnight

A steakhouse extraordinaire. This is a creation from five food and wine professionals.

THE DREAM OF FIVE FRIENDS

Five long-time friends, having numerous celebrated careers in both the food and wine industries, had talked about doing something together over the many years of their friendship. The pandemic came. Things changed. Now they had the time to create the most amazing restaurant with all their talents combined.

Coast Range was born a steakhouse, famous for their enormous **Cape Grim Tomahawk Steaks**. But there is more. **Grilled Bone Marrow** (photo above) of generous proportions, topped with pickled shallots vinaigrette and red onion jam. Ever so delicious! And an extraordinary **Creekstone Bone-In Ribeye** (photo below middle). Flavoricious!

All their meats enjoy a homemade *Range Rub*, a blend of herbs and seasonings designed by the partners. Once you taste this rub, you are going to want to have it at home. Good news, they sell the **Coast Range, Range Rub** at the restaurant to take with you.

Beyond steakhouse, they have numerous interesting dishes. They have **rock crab claws**, **jumbo prawns** and **Oysters** on the half shell (with a tequila sauce). I loved the **Hamachi Crudo**, beautiful raw yellowtail soaked in a delicious shiro dashi and topped with a habanero yuzu kosho (photo below left).

The interior is a work of spectacular design (photo right center). Exclusively booths. It was built by the hands of the partners. What else are you going to do during the pandemic? *Magnificent!*

At night, their **Vaquero Bar** (photo top right) is the happening spot in town. And the only late-night place open. They spin real vinyl. Pick your tunes and the bartender will rock your world.

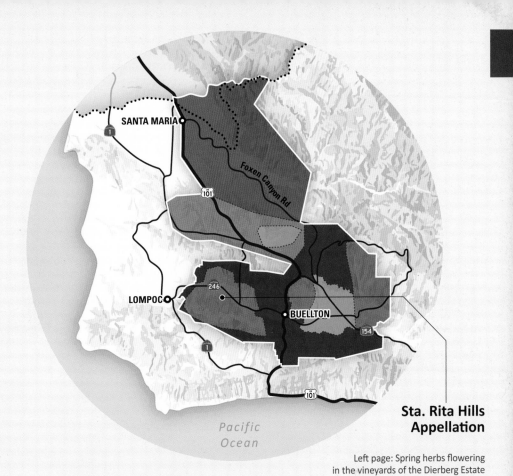

**Sta. Rita Hills
Appellation**

Pacific
Ocean

Left page: Spring herbs flowering
in the vineyards of the Dierberg Estate

BURGUNDIAN TERROIR

The Sta. Rita Hills Appellation is located in the far west region of the Santa Ynez Valley nearest the ocean. This is a very special appellation as the mountain range traverses east/west. Normally mountain ranges go north/south. Here, this east/west range allows the ocean influence to enter the valley directly without any obstructions.

Here is the magic. The rising heat in the eastern Santa Ynez Valley literally sucks the cold and moisture out of the ocean and into the valley, directly into the Sta. Rita Hills AVA. This inhaling of the ocean hits the Santa Rita Hill lying directly in the middle of the valley. This hill creates the venturi effect: $p1 - p2 = p\backslash2 \ (v\,2/2 - v\,2/1)$, which increases the wind speed on each side of the hill further adding to the terroir of the appellation. Because

of all this, the Sta. Rita Hills AVA is a cold windy place, perfect for growing the Burgundian grapes of Pinot Noir and Chardonnay.

This east/west valley has two roads crossing it. On the north side is Highway 246, and on the south is Santa Rosa Road. You will many find wineries along both these roads. The Santa Rosa Road is a much smaller winding two-lane road that makes you feel like you are in a more historic countryside setting. Note, there are no roads to cross north and south, this must be done at the far east and west sides at Hwy 101 or Hwy 1, respectively.

Here is a diverse group of wineries within the Sta. Rita Hills Appellation to visit and discover.
• Dierberg Estate Vineyards, page 343
• The Hilt Estate, page 345
• Alma Rosa Winery, page 347
• Peake Ranch, page 349

$$-$$$

1280 Drum Canyon Road
Sta. Rita Hills, CA 93436

+1 805 697 1452
Reservations@DierbergVineyard.com

DierbergVineyard.com

Open: Every Day, 11am-5pm

Bergundian apprenticed winemaker is making excellent Pinot Noir and Chardonnay here.

BEAUTIFUL TERROIR

The Dierberg family came to the Sta. Rita Hills, AVA in 2008, and acquired the Drum Canyon Vineyards to cultivate excellence in Burgundian wines. They focus exclusively on Pinot Noir and Chardonnay.

They are devoted to a sustainable approach to their business, including viticulture where they achieved the official California Certified Sustainable Certification. The Dierbergs believe that growing the highest quality grapes and crafting delicious wines can only be achieved by taking care of the land and their people. The vineyards feel wholesome, the vines healthy, the terroir moist and radiant (photo left page).

The Dierbergs hired their winemaker quite strategically. Tyler Thomas, UC Davis Viticulture and Oenology, had the amazing opportunity to apprentice with Aubert de Villaine of Domaine de la Romanée-Conti in Burgundy, France.

Domaine de la Romanée-Conti (often known as DRC) is considered one of the greatest wine producers in the world. Their price reflects such quality with an average price per bottle at $26,000. DRC is the ultimate Pinot Noir (red Burgundy) if you so choose to splurge!

Tyler says the most important thing he learned from Aubert is to "Stay out of the way in winemaking." Meaning, allow the wines to express their terroir. Tyler is also a plant physiologist with degrees in botany and plant molecular biology, so focusing on the vineyard and terroir is in his nature. Taste his wines and see how this technique is working deliciously!

The Drum Canyon Vineyards is located in the northeast corner of the Sta. Rita Hills AVA along Hwy 246. The canyon and hillside vineyards are beautiful (photo on previous spread). They restored a historic barn on the property and turned into a tasting room (photo above).

In the Dierberg Estate Barn you can enjoy a regular **tasting experience** or a **private tasting**, which includes wines from their other winery, Star Lane Vineyards in Happy Canyon AVA (page 383). I suggest their **Drum Canyon Hike & Taste**, where you hike to the vineyards top slopes and see the views.

Collection of Wines

Estate Pinot Noir (Drum Canyon Vineyard)
Pinot Noir (Drum Canyon Vineyard, Sta. Rita Hills AVA)
Pinot Noir (Ty Block, Drum Canyon Vineyard)
Pinot Noir (Sta. Rita Hills AVA)

Syrah (Happy Canyon AVA)

Estate Chardonnay (Drum Canyon Vineyard)
Chardonnay (Drum Canyon Vineyard, Sta. Rita Hills)
Chardonnay (Sta. Rita Hills)

$$-$$$

2240 Santa Rosa Road
Lompoc, CA 93436

+1 805 564 8581
info@TheHiltEstate.com

TheHiltEstate.com

Open: Thursday-Monday, 11am-5pm

Vineyards sharing an extremely rugged ranch property with poison oak and rattlesnakes.

SOUTHWEST CORNER OF THE AVA

In 2014, The Hilt Estate began its estate wines by purchasing the 3,600-acre Rancho Salsipuedes, a land grant that translates from Spanish: Get out if you can. This ranch is a steep, aggressive property in the southwest corner of the Sta. Rita Hills Appellation. The property itself marks the border of the appellation in its hilltop ridgelines. This wild rugged property is a jungle of poison oak and rattlesnakes.

"Get out if you can" was probably very good advice. Except, imagine having vineyards on the ridges and the steep hillsides of this property, with diatomaceous earth, sandy loam, and clay soils to mix with an extensive selection of clonal traits. Add the climate conditions of heavy fog mornings and extensive afternoon winds to create long growing seasons from this windblown, refrigerated sunshine.

This is not a very good place for people to survive; however, it's exceptionally great terroir for Pinot Noir and Chardonnay.

I really like how their winemaker Matt Dees expressed his wines. For the Chardonnay, he is looking for electricity. He wants lime-pit quality and fresh salty brininess. For the Pinot Noir, he looks to the dark side. He wants a hint of corruption. Sultry, sensual and supple.

This was a great wine tasting. Matt makes wines from each individual vineyard, giving the opportunity to taste the nuances of each site. He also makes an estate wine for both varietals, blending together the best of the different parts of the property. While the single-vineyard wines are quite coveted, I personally loved the estate blends the most, also realizing they represent what The Hilt Estate property taste likes.

This is a very serious property. Adults only. No pets. No food. No member discounts. It is a beautiful luxurious environment in an old barn-style building (photo left page). Enjoy a tasting in an opulent living room. Or sit around a wood-burning stove in lavish comfort (photo above). The wines and the environment are both elegant and stylish.

Collection of Wines

Bentrock Pinot Noir
Radian Vineyards Pinot Noir
Vanguard Pinot Noir
Old Guard Pinot Noir
Puerto Del Mar Pinot Noir
Estate Pinot Noir

Bentrock Chardonnay
Radian Vineyards Chardonnay
Vanguard Chardonnay
Old Guard Chardonnay
Puerto Del Mar Chardonnay
Estate Chardonnay

The Hilt Sparkling (Chardonnay, Pinot Noir)
The Hilt Rosé (Pinot Noir)
The Hilt Pétillant Natural (Pinot Noir)

$$$-$$$$

7250 Santa Rosa Road
Buellton, CA 93427

+1 805 691 9395
Info@AlmaRosaWinery.com

AlmaRosaWinery.com

Open: Every Day
Private Ranch Tours - By Appointment Only
Solvang Tasting Room, 11am-6pm (Ths-Sat 7:30pm)

Solvang Tasting Room
1623 Mission Drive, Solvang

Collection of Wines

Pinot Noir (El Jabali Vineyards, SRH)
Pinot Noir (La Encantada Vineyards, SRH)
Pinot Noir (Bentrock Vineyards, SRH)
Pinot Noir (Rancho La Viña Vineyards, SRH)
Barrel Select Pinot Noir (All Four SRH Vineyards)
Pinto Noir (Sta. Rita Hills)
Vin Gris of Pinto Noir (Sta. Rita Hills)

Chardonnay (El Jabali Vineyards, SRH)
Chardonnay (Inoks Vineyards, SRH)
Chardonnay (Sta. Rita Hills)
Pinot Blanc (La Encantada Vineyards, SRH)
Pinot Gris (La Encantada Vineyards, SRH)

Brut (Pinot Noir Sparkling)
Blanc de Blancs (Chardonnay, Pinot Blanc Sparkling)

The origins of the Sta. Rita Hills Appellation began here with Richard Sanford.

PINOT NOIR EXCELLENCE

Richard Sanford is the pioneer of winemaking in this valley. He was first, planting vineyards in 1971, with his initial vintage in 1976 of Pinot Noir. Richard has created three wineries here, including the Sanford Winery and its distinguished Sanford & Benedict Vineyard. Most recently is Alma Rosa Winery that he started in 2005. It is a beautiful 628-acre ranch in the southeastern part of the Sta. Rita Hills appellation. It is worth a ranch visit.

After returning from the Vietnam war and gaining a degree in geology, Richard wanted to live in nature and found himself interested in viticulture. Discovering a love for wine, he started reading every book he could obtain from the UC Davis Oenology Library. He was self-trained in winemaking and looking for the perfect place to grow grapes. He looked all up and down the Central Coast. No one had yet planted vineyards in Sta. Rita Hills, Edna Valley or Santa Lucia Highlands, all stellar locations for Pinot Noir. In fact, none of those names even existed yet in 1971 when Richard planted his first vineyard in what has become the famous Sta. Rita Hills appellation for extraordinary Pinot Noir.

In 2015, Richard planted what might be his very last vineyard, a very special vineyard, hilltop on the Alma Rosa Ranch (photo left page with Richard). He named the vineyard *El Caracol* ("the snail" in Spanish) as the vineyard is a Fibonacci Spiral. It is an azimuth circle in an exact spiral with all the vineyard rows facing the center of the top of the hill. There are 36 rows of vines all 10° apart in the circle. They begin at 6 feet apart. As they spread down the hill expanding to 12 feet, new rows begin as the spiral continues down the slopes. It's stunning. Look on aerial maps and you will see this magnificent design.

This is also Richard's center of spirituality. A place for tai chi. And when you taste the delicious wines from this vineyard, you will believe the vines have taken on this ethereal energy as well.

While Alma Rosa has a nice tasting room in downtown Solvang (indoor and outdoor spaces), I recommend you visit the ranch. They have a **Private Ranch House Wine Tasting** where you can tour the ranch and have a private tasting in their Ranch House or under the massive oak trees in a beautiful garden (photo above).

$$-$$$

7290 Santa Rosa Road
Buellton, CA 93427

+1 805 688 7093
Info@PeakeRanch.com

PeakeRanch.com

Open: Every Day, 11am-5pm

The most stunning vineyards in the Central Coast Wine Regions.

BEAUTIFUL PINOT NOIR

This has to be one of the most beautiful vineyard properties in the Central Coast. Winding along Santa Rosa Road westbound from Buellton you pass over a knoll to arrive at Peake Ranch. Like magic, the countryside opens up to a landscape of spectacular vineyards. This is one of the most beautiful sites to be surprised. You don't know it's coming, and the beauty will take your breath away (photo next page). This is your arrival introduction to the Peake Ranch property.

Look closer (photo left page) and you will see vineyard designs so meticulously composed you imagine a painter in your midst. Whenever I have a moment, I come back to this place, just to take in the awe. These photos are from mid-autumn after harvest when vines begin to shut down for the winter and the leaves begin to change color.

With the stunning picturesque view, you must still enter Peake Ranch. It is forty-eight acres in the south east corner of the Sta. Rita Hills AVA. And history. Do you remember the original tasting room for the Sanford Winery? It is here on this property. This is also where Richard Sanford and other winemakers met to define the Sta. Rita Hills special appellation.

As you would expect, Peake Ranch is growing Pinot Noir and Chardonnay, plus Grenache and Syrah. They also have vineyards on the north side of Sta. Rita Hills AVA, and in Santa Maria Valley AVA. They focus on these cool-weather varietals. It is a educational experience to taste the differences in Pinot Noir from these three cool yet different properties. This helps in deciding what you love best in Pinot Noir. It is great to have the choices, and to have the experience.

You have most likely seen the **John Sebastiano Vineyard** specified on other Pinot Noir labels. This is Peake Ranch's other vineyard in Sta. Rita Hills appellation, in which they sell some of their grapes to discerning winemakers who mark this special vineyard on their labels.

Their tasting areas are beautiful. Inside, you can enjoy wine by the fireplace (photo above). Their outside patio is spacious, overlooking the vineyards and the Santa Rosa Hills.

Collection of Wines

Pinot Noir, John Sebastiano Vineyard
Pinot Noir, Peake Ranch Vineyard
Pinot Noir, Sta. Rita Hills (Both Vineyards)

Chardonnay, Sierra Madre Vineyard (Santa Maria)
Chardonnay, Peake Ranch Vineyard
Chardonnay, Santa Barbara County (SRH, Santa Maria)
Grüner Veltliner (Sta. Rita Hills)

Bellis Noir (Grenache, Syrah, Pinot Noir)
Syrah, John Sebastiano Vineyard

The golden vineyards of autumn at Peake Ranch in Sta. Rita Hills AVA

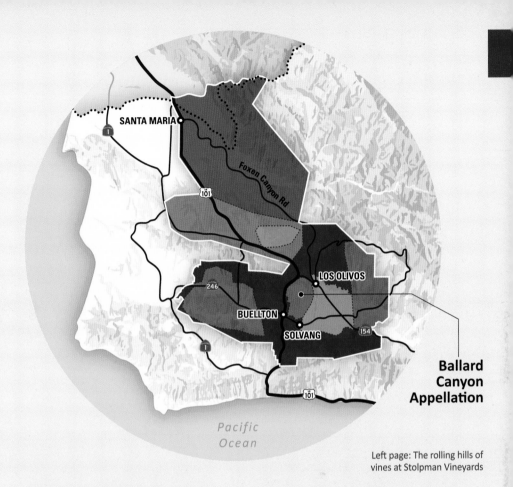

Ballard
Canyon
Appellation

*Pacific
Ocean*

Left page: The rolling hills of
vines at Stolpman Vineyards

THE LOVE CANYON OF SYRAH

In the middle of the Santa Ynez Valley is the Ballard Canyon AVA. This little canyon appellation produces some super amazing Syrah. It is almost as if the winemakers can cover their eyes and tie up their hands and they still make the great Syrah because the terroir is so good. The truth though is there are very talented winemakers here because they want to make top-level Syrah. And they do.

Remember that the Santa Ynez Valley is already ideal for Rhône varietals (including Syrah), so there are distinctions about the Syrah from the Ballard Canyon AVA. To the west of Ballard Canyon, the Syrah tends to be greener and more peppery in its flavors. Some people like this style. And to the east of Ballard Canyon, the fruit tends to be more ripe and higher alcohol, which is also a loved

quality. This is an just a generalization though as every viticulturist and winemaker has their style and methods. For my taste, this appellation really delivers a top-level outstanding Syrah.

This is a small appellation with just one onsight winery tasting room, **Rusack Vineyards**. For **Stolpman Vineyards**, their winery is in Lompoc, tasting room in Los Alamos Village, and their beautiful vineyards are in Ballard Canyon (they have vineyard tours experiences). **Beckmen Vineyards** has vineyards in both the Ballard Canyon and Los Olivos AVAs, with their winery and tasting room amongst their Los Olivos vineyards.

Here are three Ballard Canyon AVA wineries that have amazing Syrah.
• Rusnack Vineyards, page 355
• Stolpman Vineyards, page 357
• Beckmen Vineyards, page 359

$$-$$$

1819 Ballard Canyon Road
Solvang, CA 93463

+1 805 688 1278
Reservations@Rusack.com

Rusack.com

Open: Thursday-Monday, 11am-5pm

First winery in Ballard Canyon replants its vines to maximize quality and environment.

EXTRAORDINARY SYRAH

It was November 2002, when I met Geoff Rusack, and his winemaker, John Falconi, in the freshly plowed fields at Rusack Vineyards (photo left page). Geoff had a dream. He saw the future of greatness in Ballard Canyon. Later, Ballard Canyon became its own appellation, signifying the exceptional terroir here for Syrah.

This was the first winery in Ballard Canyon (Ballard Canyon Winery, est. 1974), and following Rusack's purchase he wanted to optimize the vineyards so he replanted them. Geoff was obsessed with quality to produce world-class wines.

He realigned the rows to precisely follow the hillside contours allowing for better drainage, reduced soil erosion and optimal sun exposure for even ripening of the fruit. Plus a new state-of-the art irrigation system provided precise moisture control with enhanced water conservation.

Now, twenty years later to the month, I'm here seeing the beautiful vineyards Geoff planted and tasting the results. Extraordinary Syrah!

Meeting Geoff's current winemaker, Steven Gerbac, I wanted to know his take on why Ballard Canyon was exceptional great terroir for Syrah. He felt the canyon was perfectly centered in the middle of the Santa Ynez Valley, avoiding too much underdeveloped greenness or over ripening alcohol easily found elsewhere. We discussed it further, and in depth. And in all, the Ballard Canyon AVA is magical for Syrah, and here is a winery that is obsessed with its highest quality.

I tasted through all of their Syrah wines and took an extra special liking to their *Reserve Syrah, Ballard Canyon Estate*. There is a richness, an extra bold silky smoothness to absolutely love. And the price is very fair.

Tasting is on a beautiful **terrace deck, garden or lounge**, under huge oak trees, overlooking the special vineyards planted in 2001 (see photo above). The furniture it's extra comfy, and there is knowledgeable table service. Charcuterie plates are available with advanced notice.

Geoff is currently living on Catalina Island where he has planted vineyards and is experimenting with the direct ocean influence on Chardonnay and Pinot Noir. The wines are available to taste and purchase. They are unique, and it is worth seeing what island viticulture can produce.

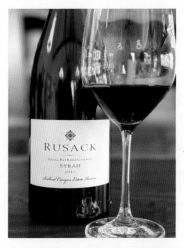

Collection of Wines

Icon Syrah, Ballard Canyon Estate
Reserve Syrah, Ballard Canyon Estate
Syrah, Ballard Canyon Estate

Zinfandel, Ballard Canyon Estate
Zinfandel, Santa Catalina Island Vineyards

Pinot Noir, Mt. Carmel Vineyard
Pinot Noir, Solomon Hills Vineyard
Reserve Pinot Noir, Sta. Rita Hills

Icon Sauvignon Blanc, Ballard Canyon Estate
Sauvignon Blanc, Ballard Canyon Estate
Chardonnay, Santa Barbara County
Chardonnay, Bien Nacido Vineyard
Chardonnay, Mt. Carmel Vineyard
Soul of the Vine (Desert Wine Of Sémillon)

A rare hill of limestone covered with clay, an amazing terroir for Rhône varietals.

$$-$$$

2001 Ballard Canyon Road
Solvang, CA 93463

Tasting Room - Los Olivos Village
2434 Alamo Pintado Avenue
Los Olivos, CA 93441

+1 805 688 0400
Info@StolpmanVineyards.com

StolpmanVineyards.com

Open: Every Day, 11am-4pm

STUNNING SYRAH

Knowing of my visit to Stolpman Vineyards, I had to look in my cellar, I knew I had some, several bottles of 2005 and 2006. I called a friend and we went out for steaks, took the '05 Syrah, and, wow, we were both blown away. This meant meeting Peter Stolpman, and his father ,Tom, was an extra special experience to understand the greatness here.

Originally, Tom purchased this unique hillside property of limestone and clay topsoil in 1990. They withheld irrigation from the vines to force the roots to grow deep into the terroir. Today, they can dry farm or at most a couple of irrigations a year when necessary. They only irrigate on a new moon, descending moon, as they are biodynamic farmers. Tom believed the terroir would be magical and winemakers would come flocking to him for grapes. And he was right.

Pete, on the other hand, has taken this business to a whole new level. His creativity in growing, blending, winemaking, and management are admirable and very impressive. To begin with, he employs his vineyard workers full-time, year-round. This is a passionate and dedicated team about the optimum health and success of the vineyards. Pete created a unique employee benefit program, a special wine called *La Cuadrilla*, in which all of the profits of this wine goes to the vineyard workers.

I witnessed a new vineyard of Petite Sirah and Roussanne, co-planted 75/25. They manage these red and white vines so they mature at the same time to co-harvest and co-ferment them. Taste it, *Hair of the Bear*, and see how this creativity unfolds to a very delicious wine. They also co-ferment Sangiovese and Syrah (50/50), It's called *La Croce*, the only cofermentation of Sangiovese and Syrah in the world.

In 2013, they planted a single pre-clonal Syrah vine from Domaine Auguste Clape's Reynard Parcel in Cornas France. They put live shoots of this mother vine underground around the mother to start new vines, all connected to the mother (left page with Peter). By 2022, they achieved 800 vines and expect a full vineyard of 2,000 heads by 2030. This will make one barrel (300 bottles) of this *Mother Vine Syrah*.

Visiting Stolpman Vineyards has several options. They have a tasting room, **Los Olivos Patio**, in the downtown Los Olivos Village. Open every day. Adjacent, is **Fresh Garage Patio** to taste their new label of young; natively fermented; uncrushed, whole clusters; and served-chilled, wines.

To visit the **Vineyards On Your Own**, they have a permanent picnic table under an oak tree right along Ballard Canyon Road. Bring a picnic, a bottle of Stolpman wine, and enjoy the afternoon with this amazing vineyard view (photo above).

Every month they do a **vineyard hike** through the property for an educational experience through their Ballard Canyon vineyards. Expand on this with their **Private Appointments On The Vineyard** where you will end the hike tasting underneath an 800 year old oak tree surrounded by the vineyards.

Collection of Wines

Angeli Syrah (oldest own-rooted Syrah)
Hilltops Syrah
Estate Syrah

La Croce (Syrah, Sangiovese)
Hair of the Bear (Petite Sirah, Roussanne)
Pliocene (Mourvèdre)
L'Avion (Roussanne)
Sangiovese
Grenache

Viognier
Sauvignon Blanc
Uni White (Roussanne)
Estate Rosé (Grenache, Mourvèdre, Syrah)

$$-$$$

2670 Ontiveros Road
Los Olivos, CA 93441

+1 805 688 8664
Info@BeckmenVineyards.com

BeckmenVineyards.com

Open: Every Day, 11am-5pm

In two appellations, Ballard Canyon AVA and Los Olivos AVA, with Rhône and Bordeaux wines.

SENSATIONAL SYRAH

It was a beautiful spring morning. I was wandering through vineyards during bud-break, seeing the delicate new green shoots emerging. It's a perfect time for close-up photography. The vines were starting a new year, it was the birth of the next vintage. I wanted to capture it.

Then a car passed along side the vineyards. It stopped, and a stately looking gentleman stepped out and asked if he could help. He introduced himself as Tom Beckmen. I quickly realized I was invading his vineyards, so I told him what I was doing. We talked about the seasons of the vineyards and how springtime can be so beautiful. He informed me I was photographing Cabernet Sauvignon, and he helped me find some really good vines to shoot. I captured some wonderful spring beauty that day (see page 6). Six months later, I was standing in his vineyards again seeing the beauty of the harvest (photo left page).

The Beckmen winery and tasting room is located in the Los Olivos AVA. They are in a bit of a remote area, making it interesting to find their little oasis. On this property, the vineyards are primarily Cabernet Sauvignon. This is also where you can see up close the activities in the winery. The tasting room is right there too. They have two lakes and gazebos for beautiful tasting and picnicking.

The **Private Tour & Wine Tasting** is the ultimate experience where you walk the vineyards and have a reserve level tasting on the covered vineyard pond dock (photo above), including cheese and charcuterie platter or boxed lunch.

Beckmen Vineyards is most known for their other property in the Ballard Canyon AVA, the Purisima Mountain Vineyard (PMV). This property is primarily Syrah and other Rhône varietals. It is a mountain ranging from 500 feet of elevation to its peak at 1,150 feet. The subsoil is limestone, very unique to this area, substantially adding to the flavors and quality of the grapes.

PMV was planted in 1994 and became fully biodynamically farmed as of 2002. Not just officially certified biodynamic, the property is self-sustainable. For example, they have cows, pigs and chickens that feed off the farm and provide manure for their organic compost pile to feed the vines.

Now, you must taste their PMV Block Six Syrah, it is sensational. Also, their PMV Grenache is extraordinary. This is a place to love the environment as much as the great wines.

Collection of Rhône Wines

Purisima Red Wine (Syrah)
PMV Block Six Syrah
PMV Syrah Own(own-rooted vines)
PMV Clone #1 Syrah
PMV Syrah
Barrel Select Cuvée (Syrah, Grenache, Mourvèdre)
Cuvée Le Bec (Syrah, Grenache, Mourvèdre, Counoise)

PMV Grenache Libre
PMV Block Eight Grenache
PMV Grenache
Estate Grenache
Grenache
PMV Grenache Rosé

PMV Grenache Blanc
PMV Viognier
Late Harvest VDP White Wine (Roussanne, Marsanne)

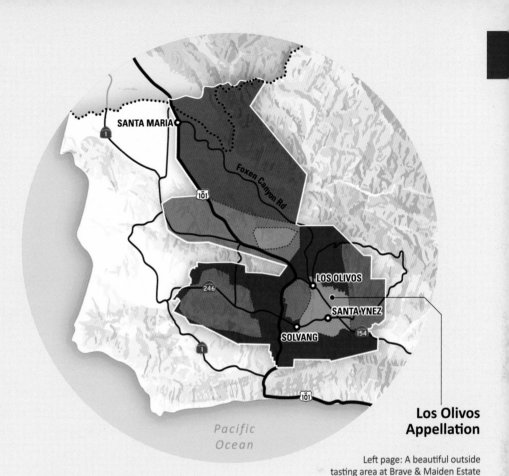

**Los Olivos
Appellation**

Left page: A beautiful outside
tasting area at Brave & Maiden Estate

RHÔNE & BORDEAUX VARIETALS

The Los Olivos District Appellation is located in the central eastern side of the Santa Ynez Valley AVA. It is adjacent to the east of Ballard Canyon AVA and adjacent west of the Happy Canyon AVA.

This is a very attractive appellation for farmers as the region is flat and the soil is rich, making this a much easier area to farm. The Los Olivos neighboring appellations are hilly with steep cliffs and poor soil. While this makes for excellent terroir for viticulture, a flat rich soil appellation is more conducive for tractors, workers and vineyard growth. As a result, many wineries are located here and have tasting rooms to visit them.

The Los Olivos District also has a cute little village to stroll around. The **Los Olivos Village** is filled with tasting rooms from both small

handcrafted winemakers wanting a low-cost tasting room to introduce us to their wines, and several of the large wineries have their tasting rooms in the village for easy access to their wines. This is the perfect day trip to enjoy a plethora of wines all in one place. Other shops and restaurants are in the village as well.

And another thought: this is the perfect winter escape. Book a room in one of the beautiful luxury hotels in the village and spend your days walking around eating amazing foods and drinking delicious wines. Back at the room, start a warm cozy fire and enjoy the winter away in the wine region.

Here are several excellent wineries to visit.
• Brave & Maiden Estate, page 363
• Roblar Winery & Vineyards, page 365
• Gainey Vineyard, page 367
• Sunstone Winery, page 369

U pscale luxurious environment to enjoy a private and reserved intimate experience.

BEAUTIFUL TASTING

The original owners bought this property to build their 12,000 sq' castle home and to plant forty-six acres of vineyards to beautify their estate. Look across these vineyards on the left-page photo with the castle in the distance.

All the grapes were grown to be sold to outside winemakers. Until, the new owners came along in 2010. Jason Djang and Rizal Risjadhad had a new objective. To create the finest estate-grown wines they could from this singular estate. The wines here are beautiful and elegant.

Tastings are also beautiful and elegant. This is an upscale luxurious environment (see photo above), by reservations only, where they customize your experience with a dedicated person. The outside tasting area (photo left page) is beautiful as well. The architecture and design are quite inviting, and sets the stage for a relaxed, intimate experience.

They want their memberships here to be an interaction with their passionate customers, not just another subscription to a wine club.

They put on interesting educational events. For example, a **Build The Perfect Cheeseboard Class** with a cheesemonger where you will learn wine pairings. Cheese platters have become a mainstay in entertaining, so this course is quite useful. They show how to easily assemble excellent cheeses, and accompanying fruits, nuts and charcuteries, without spending much time in the kitchen.

• **Private Seated Tastings** at a reserved private table in one of their beautiful tasting spaces, indoors or out. And they will share with you some of their limited production, at the winery only, wines. Outdoors, you have views of their vineyards where you can take a nice stroll on a path inside the vineyard to see the vines up close.

• **Private Winery Tour and Seated Tastings** includes a fully educational experience getting a behind-the-scenes look at their working winery. It is a walking tour taking you into the vineyard, winemaking tank room, barrel-aging room, and of course, a private tasting of their wines.

Collection of Wines

Limited Cabernet Sauvignon
Cabernet Sauvignon
Limited Cabernet Franc
Cabernet Franc
Limited Merlot
Merlot
Limited Syrah
Syrah

Rule of Thirds (Grenache, Mourvèdre, Syrah)
Bequest (Cabernet Franc, Merlot, Cabernet Sauvignon, Petit Verdot)
Union (Syrah, Merlot, Cabernet Franc)

Limited Rosé (Grenache, Syrah, Mourvèdre)
Pride Rosé (Sauvignon Blanc, Cabernet Sauvignon, Cabernet Franc, Syrah, Merlot)

Limited Sauvignon Blanc
Sauvignon Blanc

$$-$$$

3010 Roblar Avenue
Santa Ynez, CA 93460

+1 805 686 2603
TastingRoom@RoblarWinery.com

RoblarWinery.com

Open: Every Day, 11am-5pm

Collection of Wines

Cabernet Sauvignon Reserve
Estate Cabernet Franc
Estate Grenache
Estate Grassetto (Sangiovese,
Cabernet Sauvignon, Cabernet Franc)
Estate Ottimo (Cabernet Sauvignon, Petit Verdot, Syrah)
GSM (Syrah, Grenache, Mourvèdre)
Petit Verdot
Petite Sirah
Estate Rosé (Grenache, Syrah, Graciano, Sangiovese)

Vinador White (Viognier)
Estate Sauvignon Blanc
Sauvignon Blanc (Gleason Family Vineyards)
Cuvée Blanc (Sauvignon Blanc, Sémillon,
Malvasia Bianca, Roussanne)
Platinum Chardonnay
Estate Fume Blanc

Sparkling Brut (Pinot Noir, Chardonnay, Pinot Meunier)
Sparkling Blanc de Blanc (Chardonnay)
Sparkling Rosé (Pinot Noir, Chardonnay, Merlot)

F
rom the Roblar Farm direct to their restaurant, served with delicious Roblar wines.

WINERY RESTAURANT

Look at the beautiful environment (photo above). This is the perfect outdoor restaurant experience, and yet you are at a winery. It is so nice to have a restaurant at a winery. It's the best for food and wine pairings, that is for sure.

The outdoor dining is expansive. Large pergolas everywhere. Umbrella tables by the vineyards. A big beautiful fountain in the center. A romantic fireplace to stay warm. All with full-service wine tasting and a full-service restaurant.

Roblar also has an extensive farm where they grow the foods for their restaurant. Fruits, vegetables and meats fresh off the farm. So, the menu changes frequently in order to accommodate

the freshest off the farm. Aside the winery, they also have an extensive produce stand where you can buy the goods off their farm.

In the restaurant, they have a variety of creative salads (a bounty of fresh vegetable from their farm, below right) and yummy pizzas (wood-fired Italian sausage and peppers, below left), plus, spicy garlic scrimp, lamb meatballs, and branzino with little neck clams, just to get you salivating. On Thursdays, they do dinner, **Birds & Bubbles**, fried chicken and sparkling wines.

As you might expect, the Syrah here is very good. They are also doing Bordeaux style wines. I came across a Cabernet Franc that was extraordinary. The left page photo is of beautiful Cabernet Sauvignon leaves in the fall, turning yellow, orange and red.

$$-$$$

3950 East Highway 246
Santa Ynez, CA 93460

+1 805 688 0558
Info@GaineyVineyard.com

GaineyVineyard.com

Open: Every Day, 11am-5pm

Sixty years, four generations, three ranches, creating Rhône, Burgundy and Bordeaux wines.

WINEMAKING ORIGINS

It all began more than sixty years ago when the Gainey family acquired 1,800 acres of undeveloped land in the Santa Ynez Valley. They started as ranchers with cattle and horses. And farmers with fruits, vegetables, flowers, and hay. Ultimately, there was a vision for vineyards and wine.

It was 1984, when they started with their first fifty acres of vineyards. When you think of this date, Mr. Gainey was truly one of the original visionaries of Santa Ynez Valley being a wine region. The Gainey's continue to expand their vineyards on this estate in this southeastern corner of the Los Olivos AVA. This is where they built their winery and beautiful tasting rooms.

Being at the eastern part of the Los Olivos AVA, this puts Gainey Vineyards very close to the Happy Canyon AVA. As a result of their warmer location and south facing vineyards, plus rocky soils, this terroir is ideal for Bordeaux varietals. Gainey is producing excellent Cabernet Sauvignon, Merlot, etc. This ranch is also where they are growing their Rhône grapes in different appropriate terroir.

I had the pleasure to meet Dan Gainey at his Evans Ranch in the Sta. Rita Hills AVA. Yes, they have expanded to two more ranches now in the Sta. Rita Hills. Here they are growing their Burgundian grapes for their Evan's Ranch wines as beautiful as these vineyards (photo left page).

In spending the day with Dan, I discovered two very impressive components to the Gainey success. First were the extraordinary locations of vineyards. They have the right terroir for Bordeaux, Rhône and Burgundian varietals. Second was his team. He treats them like family. It is a special environment here that you will feel when you arrive.

At the **Gainey Tasting Room** (on the winery property) you can taste all wines, and chartcuterie platters are available.

The **Evan's Ranch Tasting Room** is located in the Los Olivos Village. All wines available here as well.

Their **Private Tasting Experience** is a more luxurious tasting journey (with a dedicated wine specialist) at your choice of four special settings: indoors in their private cellar or their club lounge, which is a living room setting with fireplace (photo above), or outside in their Syrah vineyard or demonstration vineyard. This private tasting is also available at the Evan's Ranch Tasting Room.

Collection of Wines

Patrick's Vineyard Selection (Cabernet Sauvignon, Merlot, Petit Verdot)
Limited Selection Cabernet Sauvignon
Limited Selection Cabernet Franc
Limited Selection Merlot
Estate Merlot
Evan's Ranch Las Brisas Syrah
Evan's Ranch Lone Oak Syrah
Limited Selection Syrah
Evan's Ranch Lone Oak Pinot Noir
Evan's Ranch Morgan's Pinot Noir
Limited Selection Pinot Noir
Estate Pinot Noir

Diane's Rosé (Estate Pinot Noir)
Limited Selection Sauvignon Blanc
Limited Selection Riesling
Evan's Ranch Las Brisas Chardonnay
Evan's Ranch Caitlin's Chardonnay
Limited Selection Chardonnay
Estate Sauvignon Blanc
Estate Chardonnay

$$-$$$

125 North Refugio Road
Santa Ynez, CA 93460

+1 805 688 9463
Taste@SunstoneWinery.com

SunstoneWinery.com

Open: Every Day, 11am-5pm

Collection of Wines

Eros (Merlot, Cabernet Franc, Cabernet Sauvignon)
Founder's Reserve (Merlot, Cabernet Franc)
Fred's Red Reserve (Merlot, Cabernet Franc)
Villa Reserve (Merlot, Syrah, Cabernet Franc)
Soleil Rouge (Sangiovese, Cabernet Sauvignon,
Cabernet Franc, Merlot)
Zephyr (Cabernet Sauvignon, Cabernet Franc,
Grenache, Syrah)
Estate Cabernet Franc, Petit Verdot Reserve
Cabernet Sauvignon (Santa Ynez Valley)
Malbec Reserve, Grenache, Estate Syrah
Syrah (Santa Ynez Valley)
Rapsodie (Grenache, Syrah, Mourvedre)
Pinot Noir Reserve (Sta. Rita Hills)
Pinot Noir (Santa Barbara County)
Syrah Rosé, Grenache Rosé

Linda's Estate Viognier,
Viognier Grenache Blanc, Reserve Chardonnay,
Symphonie du Soleil (Viognier, Roussanne, Grenache Blanc, Marsanne)

S anta Barbara's first organic vineyards. Now the first winery in California to receive permits for cannabis land use.

WINE AND CANNABIS

This property was a dream for the Rice family in 1989 to bring their family to the Santa Barbara Wine Region, to a peaceful fifty-two-acre ranch in the Santa Ynez Valley. They planted vineyards immediately the next year. Little did they know then, that they would be creating the very first organic vineyard estate in Santa Barbara County.

They chose this property because of its terraced south-sloping exposure to the sun, its rocky soil, plus a perfect microclimate of early morning fog, warm breezy afternoons and cool evenings, all overlooking the Santa Ynez River.

Sadly, Linda passed and Fred needed to move on. It was hard to stay on an estate he created so special with Linda.

The new owners, Teddy and Djamila Cabugos, bring an exciting new energy to this property. They have big plans and have already dramatically improved and expanded the outdoor tasting area. Food is now available. And lots of special things for members, for example, opening up the castle for tastings, events and accommodations (next page).

Brittany Rice, Fred and Linda's daughter, was there in the very beginning learning winemaking. She helped plant the first Merlot vines when she was sixteen years old and has worked alongside the winemaking team since. She also became a Cordon Bleu trained chef. Today she is the director of winemaking here at Sunstone Winery carrying on the legend.

A big attraction to Teddy and Djamila is the thirty-year reputation of high-quality wines of Sunstone. An even further attraction to them is a 6.5-acre plot that was once a vineyard, now dormant and waiting to be replanted. They will now replant it with cannabis as they are introducing **Sunstone Spritz**, a delicious cannabis-infused sparkling beverage. Imagine watermelon, grapefruit orange, pineapple coconut, or, my favorite, peach passion fruit. I'm getting thirsty!

The Cabugos are making huge progress in creating new regulations that allow them to make this spritzer and other cannabis products. They have become the first vineyard estate in California to receive cannabis land use permit. Now you can visit the Sunstone Winery, tour the beautiful property and caves, and tour the cannabis farm.

They have an app for delivery at Sunstone, and they can also deliver a case of the Sunstone Spritz directly to your home in California.

A LUXURY WINERY CASTLE

I had the great pleasure of knowing Jim and Linda Rice, original owners of Sunstone Winery in 1989. Little did I know they were planning to build a castle on the property as their home. Jim is a contractor and Linda a designer, so it was the perfect match to go to Italy and get great design inspiration, and then to France to bring back forty-two containers of salvage materials to build the castle. Linda has passed and Jim has moved on. The new owners have made the castle available as unique luxury lodging. Just look at the pictures on these pages and you will want to be there.

In order to get into this castle, you first must be a Sunstone Wine Club member. Also, you need to have some type of wine event, even as small as a private tasting or a dinner. The castle comes complete with a large kitchen (photo below right), dining and living area, and five self-contained bedrooms/baths. Four of the bedrooms are full scale suites. Just look at the amazing suite on the left page. It is 8,500 square feet of luxury! You can rent the entire castle (perfect for an event) or just a single suite. Inquire on their website.

The castle is in pristine condition. It overlooks their vineyards with spectacular sunset views (see page 430). It took five years to build and was constructed entirely from artifacts and materials recovered from reclamations in rural villages in France. It is built from limestone salvaged from chateaus of Aix Provence, Normandy, and Loire Valley. The wood beams, rafters, and roof tiles were reclaimed from a nineteenth century Queen Victorian Era lavender factory that burned down.

$$$

125 North Refugio Road
Santa Ynez, CA 93460

+1 805 688 9463
Info@SunstoneWinery.com

SunstoneWinery.com

Open: All Year, Every Day

Newly renovated patio at Sunstone Winery

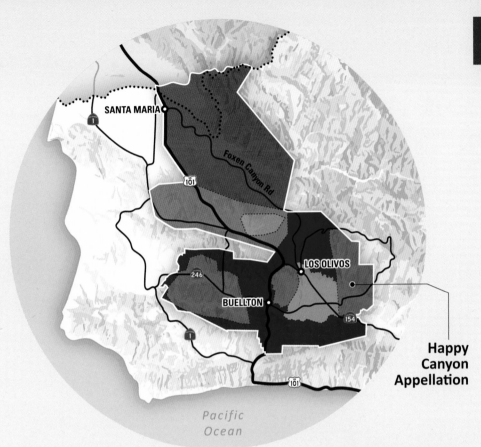

Happy
Canyon
Appellation

*Pacific
Ocean*

Left page: Stony hillside vineyards at
Crown Point Vineyards in the Happy Canyon AVA

CABERNET SAUVIGNON!!!

The Happy Canyon appellation's terroir is so remarkable for Bordeaux varietals that you will taste some of the very best Cabernet Sauvignon in all of California right here.

Happy Canyon AVA is located at the far east edge of the Santa Ynez Valley AVA. It is in the foothills of the Los Padres National Forest. The vineyards are in canyons with steep hills, sharp terrain, and an abundance of stones. This is a spectacularly beautiful region, and extraordinary terroir for growing Cabernet Sauvignon.

If you are a Cabernet Sauvignon lover, as I am, you will be shocked and totally impressed, with the seriously high-quality wines here. I could not believe the stellar quality I was tasting. Vintners

here have been hiring the very best winemakers out of Napa Valley to come here. The results are impressive.

The wineries here are not allowed by the county to accept walk-in visitors, so you must make an appointment. And it is better with a reservation anyway because they can plan for you and provide a curated experience. Tours of the vineyards, wineries, a lake and a cave are all possible.

Here are three extraordinary wineries to visit.
• Crown Point Vineyards, page 377
• Happy Canyon Vineyard, page 379
• Grimm's Bluff, page 381
• Star Lane Vineyard, page 383

$$$$

1733 Fletcher Way
Santa Ynez, CA 93460

+1 805 693 9300
Info@CrownPointVineyards.com

CrownPointVineyards.com

Open: Monday-Saturday, 8:30am-4pm
By Appointment Only

Taste an amazing Cabernet Sauvignon you will not believe comes from Santa Barbara.

PHENOMENAL CABERNET

This is the winery that opened my eyes to Happy Canyon. I had no idea how remarkable the Cabernet Sauvignon wines were being created here. This experience reinforced why Happy Canyon AVA is a unique appellation perfect for spectacular Cabernet Sauvignon wines.

So, my eyes were open, I was inspired, and yet I was standing amongst some of the best Cabernet Sauvignon wines I have ever tasted. Meeting the French winemaker, Simon Faury, further emphasized why the wines were so noticeable.

Simon worked for some of the very best wineries in the world... Château Pichon-Longueville Baron, Domaine de Chevalier, Robert Mondavi Winery, and Harlan Estate. And a master's degree in oenology and viticulture from the University of Bordeaux France. Simon also had the incredible opportunity to work with Michel Rolland at Bodega Rolland, and has now brought him in as the primary consultant at Crown Point Vineyards. Michel is considered one of the most influential oenologists in the industry.

Simon took me off-roading through his vineyards, showing me the incredible terroir, and I witnessed gravel and stones like you would see in Bordeaux vineyards (photo previous page). I was beginning to understand how he was making phenomenal wines in these foothills of the San Rafael Mountains.

It was time. Simon and I joined their estate director, AJ Fairbanks, in their luxurious tasting facility. The space is stunningly beautiful (photo above). Accompanied by very nice cheeses. They are by appointment only so they can plan ahead of time for an incredible experience when you arrive.

They offer three experiences. **Taste of Crown Point** is a tasting in the luxurious tasting room. The **Discover Crown Point** is an off-road experience to the apex of the estate, where you can look down through the valley and see their forty-five acres of exclusively Bordeaux varietals (Cabernet Sauvignon, Merlot, Cabernet Franc, Malbec, Petit Verdot, and Sauvignon Blanc). **Past, Present & Future** is their ultimate experience, where you get to taste library wines, current releases, and go into the cellar to taste the future out of their barrels.

Collection of Wines

Reserve Cabernet Sauvignon
Cabernet Sauvignon

Estate Selection (Cabernet Sauvignon,
Merlot, Cabernet France, Petit Verdot, Malbec)
Relevant Red (Cabernet Sauvignon,
Cabernet Franc, Petit Verdot, Malbec, Merlot)

Estate White (Sauvignon Blanc)

$$-$$$

1100 Secretariat Drive
Santa Ynez, CA 93460

+1 805 203 0749
WineExperience@HappyCanyonVineyard.com

HappyCanyonVineyard.com

Open: Every Day
Estate Vineyard Experience - By Appointment Only
Santa Barbara Tasting Room, 12pm-6pm

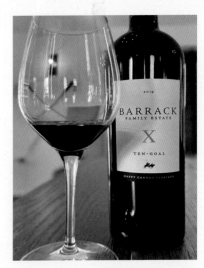

Collection of Wines

Barrack Family Ten-Goal (Cabernet Sauvignon,
Merlot, Cabernet Franc, Petit Verdot, Malbec)
Barrack Family Brand (Merlot, Cabernet Sauvignon,
Cabernet Franc, Petit Verdot, Malbec)
Piocho Reserve (Cabernet Franc, Cabernet Sauvignon,
Merlot, Petit Verdot, Malbec)
Piocho Patrón (Cabernet Sauvignon,
Merlot, Cabernet Franc, Petit Verdot, Malbec)
Piocho Red Blend (Cabernet Sauvignon,
Merlot, Cabernet Franc, Petit Verdot, Malbec)

Piocho Rosé (Sauvignon Blanc)
Barrack Family Blanc (Sémillon, Sauvignon Blanc)
Piocho Sauvignon Blanc (Sauvignon Blanc, Sémillon)

J ust like the French, they are exclusively blending Bordeaux varietals.

BORDEAUX BLENDS

Being a Bordeaux wine lover, and knowing their style is to always blend the Bordeaux varietals off their property, this was a great discovery to find the same here. All their wines are Bordeaux blends, and all the varietals are grown in their vineyards on the property here in the Happy Canyon AVA.

In the Bordeaux style, they make the very traditional styles of Left Bank and Right Bank Bordeaux wines. Left Bank wines are Cabernet Sauvignon centric wines. See our *Exploring Wine Regions – Bordeaux France* book for more information.

Their **Barrack Family Ten-Goal** wine is their Left Bank wine using all five Bordeaux varietals. As a classic Left Bank wine, it leads with 84% Cabernet Sauvignon. This was one of my favorite wines. I tasted there (photo right).

Their **Barrack Family Brand** wine is their Right Bank wine, also using all five Bordeaux varietals. As a Right Bank wine, it leads with 80% Merlot.

I recommend you go visit their estate, **Piocho Ranch**. It is a stunningly beautiful horse property with vineyards on the hillsides (see photo left page). They have two regulation sized polo fields, many powerful polo ponies and the Piocho Polo Club.

The **Estate Vineyard Experience** puts you on the property for wine tasting in their ranch home and a tour of the vineyards. Allow yourself two weeks advance notice for reservations. They will prepare for you and it will be a private experience.

Do you like Sauvignon Blanc? It is one of my more favorite white wines. Happy Canyon Vineyard has a great little twist to make this wine extra delicious. They add 9% Sémillon to make a blend that you will never forget. They call it **Piocho Sauvignon Blanc** (photo right).

$$$-$$$$

5400 Kentucky Road
Santa Ynez, CA 93460

+1 805 691 9065
info@GrimmsBluff.com

GrimmsBluff.com

Open: Every Day
Private Ranch Tours - By Appointment Only
Los Olivos Tasting Room, 11am-5pm (Fri/Sat 6pm)

Los Olivos Village Tasting Room
2445 Alamo Pintado Avenue, Los Olivos

L akeside wine tasting on a beautiful picturesque bluff in the Happy Canyon Appellation.

CABERNET SAUVIGNON

Grimm's Bluff is really Rick Grimm's Bluff. It is 246 acres on top of a bluff in the most eastern portion of the Santa Ynez Valley, on the southern tip of Happy Canyon AVA, overlooking the Santa Ynez River. This is a very beautiful property that makes for a great afternoon to taste wine.

True to being a characteristic bluff, it has a tall face on one side bordering a river. Here, the southern side of the bluff has steep hillsides dropping 300 feet overlooking the Santa Ynez River. And farther south is an expansive view of the Santa Ynez Mountains. Bring your camera.

Rick and Aurora Grimm moved from Monaco to Santa Barbara and purchased this beautiful property in 2010 in order to build their dream retirement home. Well, they sure found a spectacular site for their home.

The land was vacant. Never any agriculture. Virgin. This led to the best opportunity to plant vineyards with organic and biodynamic farming from the very beginning. Hiring a leading biodynamic consultant with extensive vineyard experience, they quickly became certified as no chemicals have ever been used on this property.

They planted sixteen acres of Bordeaux varietals on the bluffs, primarily Cabernet Sauvignon and Sauvignon Blanc. They also planted five acres of three different Tuscan varieties of olive trees. Their olive oil is super delicious.

They primarily make two wines. Their white wine is a Sauvignon Blanc, and the red wine is Cabernet Sauvignon. They have experimented by cultivating both trellised and head-trained Cabernet Sauvignon vines. They bottle them separately so you can taste how different the wines taste, and they also have a blend to combine the qualities.

Make a reservation (required) and come see this beautiful property. You will get a tour of the property in their ATV, exploring the vineyards and the edges of the bluff. The views are outstanding.

They have a beautiful lake (photo left page) where you can taste waterside. Or you can taste inside their barn (photo above), sometimes necessary with weather.

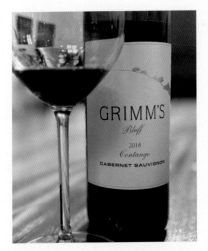

Collection of Wines

Contango Cabernet Sauvignon (Head-Trained)
Cliff Hanger Cabernet Sauvignon (Trellised)
Estate Cabernet Sauvignon (Head-Trained and Trellised)
Balance (Cabernet Sauvignon, Petit Verdot)

River Stone (Rosé of Cabernet Sauvignon)

Reserve Sauvignon Blanc (Oak Aged)
Estate Sauvignon Blanc (Stainless)

$$$-$$$$-$$$$$

2121 Alisos Road
Santa Ynez, CA 93460

+1 805 697 1451
Reservations@StarLaneVineyard.com

StarLaneVineyard.com

Open: Tuesday-Saturday, 10am-4pm
By Appointment Only

Tour one of the most impressive cave systems you will see at any winery.

EXTRAORDINARY CABERNET

The Dierberg family started their interest in the Santa Barbara Winery Region here in the Happy Canyon AVA. Well, actually, it wasn't the Happy Canyon AVA yet when they arrived in 1997. They had a vision for what was possible in this far eastern part of the Santa Ynez Valley.

Jim Dierberg acquired this beautiful canyon (photo left page) in the foothills of the San Rafael Mountain Range after ten years searching the world for the perfect property to grow Cabernet Sauvignon, including Bordeaux. His objective: to produce the finest Cabernet Sauvignon on the planet. He felt this was the perfect terroir for this varietal. And he was right.

The property is 1,500 acres in this canyon, planted primarily on the hillsides. The Star Lane vineyards are now the largest own-rooted Cabernet Sauvignon grown in America, and are Certified California Sustainable.

When their winemaker, Tyler Thomas, was interviewing for the position, he asked if they had a ten-year plan. He wanted to know there was a vision here. He was told: there is no ten-year plan. They had a 250-year plan! It is a long-term vision

that transcends oneself. Tyler wanted to be a part of something that went way beyond him.

Tyler comes from Napa Valley and UC Davis, where he majored in viticulture and oenology. Tyler is also a plant physiologist with degrees in botany and plant molecular biology. Tyler was the perfect winemaker to dig into this canyon, deeply understand its components and bring out the very best of this terroir. And to make great Cabernet!

Inside the winery castle (photo above), everything is a gravity flow through the winemaking process to the depths of a massive cave system. The cave is not just for aging the wines, it holds the 250-year plan: 250 cubbyholes to keep each vintage in private cave tunnels (photo page 304).

The cave is astonishing (photo next page). Nine tunnels in 26,000 square feet, totaling the length of four football fields. It took nine years to build. Tours of the cave come with tasting. Reservations only.

And for the wine. They make three Cabernets. Their basic Estate Cabernet Sauvignon is a Bordelais blend, awarded 94 points. It is deep, rich and yet silky elegant. It embellishes the delicious fruit we love about Cabernet Sauvignon. And an exceptional deal. The other two Cabernets only raise the bar very much higher.

Collection of Wines

Star Cabernet Sauvignon (Single Block of Cabernet Sauvignon)
Astral Cabernet Sauvignon (Cabernet Sauvignon, Petite Verdot, Malbec)
Estate Cabernet Sauvignon (Cabernet Sauvignon, Petite Verdot, Cabernet Franc, Malbec)
Cabernet Franc
Merlot

Rosé of Malbec

Sauvignon Blanc
Chenin Blanc

The massive cave system underground at Star Lane Vineyard

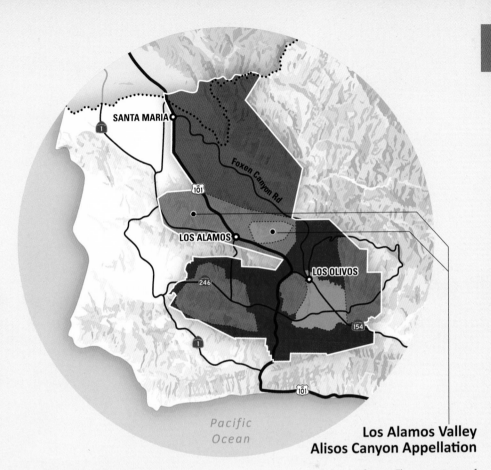

Los Alamos Valley
Alisos Canyon Appellation

Left page: The remote areas of
Alisos Canyon AVA at Dovecote Estate Winery.

A SPECIAL MICROCOSM

The **Los Alamos Valley** is located north and west of the Santa Ynez Valley AVA, and adjacent south of the Santa Maria AVA. When you are driving on Highway 101 through the Los Alamos Valley, you will notice an extensive amount of vineyards. No tasting rooms though as most of the grapes here are exported outside the county to wineries who know the quality of this terroir.

Inside the Los Alamos Valley is a very special appellation called **Alisos Canyon AVA**. It just became the newest appellation in Santa Barbara in 2020. Over the years, it became very well known for its high-quality fruit, so it made sense to define this little area into its own appellation.

Although this appellation is next to the Santa Maria AVA, it is in its own little microcosm not affected much by the marine influence into Santa Maria. Instead, it is much warmer here and conducive for Rhône style wines. I found Grenache, Viognier and Mourvèdre doing very well.

There is only one winery here with a tasting room. Their property is beautiful, tasting is lakeside, wines are excellent, and they can provide gourmet food with reservations.

The historic town of **Los Alamos** is here, a seven-block-long Old West town that time forgot. Expect a saloon and hitching post for your horse. That is the attraction, and amazing restaurants have inhabited the old building, including a Michelin-star restaurant and a host of wine tasting rooms.

Here is the one winery to visit.

• Dovecote Estate Winery, page 389

PHOTOS FROM LEFT TO RIGHT: **Dovecote Rosés**, enjoy a refreshing comparison of the three Dovecote's rosé wines overlooking the beautiful lake; perfectly paired with a **Uni/Caviar**, a locally caught Santa Barbara Uni with Regiis Ova hybrid caviar and mille crêpes; **Steak Frites**, a delicious 8 oz flatiron steak served with maître d'hôtel butter.

$$-$$$

9229 Alisos Canyon Road
Los Alamos, CA 93440

+1 805 344 3440
Info@Dovecote.com

DovecoteWine.com

Open: Every Day, 11:30am-5pm

T his is the location of Thompson Vineyard, a prized source of grapes for 25+ winemakers.

SYRAH EXCELLENCE

In 1989, David Thompson was able to get his hands on the coveted Estrella River Syrah cuttings that were snuck by suitcase into California from the famous Chapoutier Vineyard in Hermitage France. Without root stock, no grafting, Thompson stuck the vines into the bare sandy soil. The vines thrived! And today, this might be the only vineyard of own-rooted Syrah in Santa Barbara County.

These thirty-plus-year-old vines are producing some of the most amazing Syrah you will ever taste. Over 95% of the grapes are sold to well-known winemakers touting this vineyard. And Devocote Estate Winery is producing Thompson Vineyard Noumenon. A Syrah as it is in itself.

This wine is a natural expression of the terroir here, with spontaneous fermentation, sometimes whole cluster bunches, using only 100% native yeast from the vineyard, creating the ultimate expression of this vineyard and land. *Wine Enthusiast* gave this wine 96 points in 2019. If you love Syrah, you cannot miss tasting this wine.

Devecote is located north of the Santa Ynez AVA in the Los Alamos Valley, an AVA to the north and east of the darling little town of Los Alamos along Hwy 101. In 2020, the government granted them a sub-appellation: Alisos Canyon AVA, to reflect their area's unique terroir of climate, soil and geography.

The new owner, Noah Rowles (who made the 96-point Noumenon), has kept the original family (three generations) living on the property to care for the vineyards they know so well. In fact, nobody touches the vines, grapes, harvest, winemaking, except the people who live on this property. This is a very special handmade love of the residence of this remarkable ranch.

The property is expansive and beautiful. You can stay on the ranch. They have homes you can rent (see next page). The wine tasting is extra special. Tasting is at their historic shack alongside a pond surrounded by a grass park and large oak trees (photo left page).

Ask them (ahead of time) for gourmet food and you will taste some amazing cuisine paired with their outstanding wines (inset photos left page).

Collection of Wines

Thompson Vineyard Noumenon (Syrah)
Estate Syrah
Estate Grenache
Estate Petite Sirah

Redtail (Grenache, Syrah, Mourvèdre, Petite Sirah)
Mantle (Co-Fermented Grenache, Syrah)
Redtail and Mantle Are Predominantly Grenache

Rosé (Syrah)
Rosé (Grenache)
Rosé (Grenache, Mourvèdre)

Estate Grenache Blanc
Estate Chardonnay
Estate Viognier

THE CASITA & THE HACIENDA

Stay the night on the Dovecote Estate Winery's ranch. It is very private, with a separate entrance to the ranch, behind the vineyards, with views of the hills and dozens of horses running free (see photo page 386).

The Casita (photos below right) is nestled under oak trees and lavish landscaping. This is a one-bedroom house that was once the home of the ranch's horsemaster. It has been nicely remodeled and decorated. Full kitchen and dining. Two fireplaces. King bed (queen pullout sofa). A private outdoor garden under the trees with fountain and seating.

The Hacienda (photos below left and left page) stands prominent on the side of a hill overlooking a beautiful valley of oak tree, rolling hills and roaming horses. It is a 5,400 sq' custom home that sleeps twelve to fourteen people. Chef's kitchen, formal dining room, a huge living room with a large stone fireplace. This is a great place to entertain or have an event or a wedding. Lots of outdoor space to entertain 50+ people.

$$$ and $$$$$

9229 Alisos Canyon Road
Los Alamos, CA 93440

+1 805 570 0443
Kristen@Dovecote.com

DovecoteRetreats.com

Reservations: On Website

LOS ALAMOS OLD WEST TOWN

Los Alamos is a small Old West town (in the Los Alamos Valley) right off of Highway 101, south of Santa Maria Valley and north of Santa Ynez Valley. Specifically, it is fifteen miles north of Buellton and nineteen miles south of Santa Maria.

Los Alamos has one main road through town, Bell Street, which was once the stagecoach stop. It still looks like an Old West town, a place that time forgot. Except it did not hide from chefs. Los Alamos has become a mecca of exceptionally great restaurants. Michelin has honored the very best restaurant here. Not in the glitzy Santa Barbara city, the only Michelin star in Santa Barbara County is in Los Alamos (**Bell's**, page 397). Another sensational restaurant that Michelin needs to find is **Pico** (page 395). The town has several wine-tasting rooms too (see **Lumen Wines** right page).

Daily Rental Homes (Airbnb)
Pico Cottage • tinyurl.com/ytza8vs3
Greenhouse Cottage • tinyurl.com/4hwm55md

AirBnB.com

Pico Los Alamos has two homes for daily rentals. **Pico Cottage** - (1bed/1bath) is behind the restaurant surrounded by beautiful and edible gardens. Full kitchen and separate bedroom and living room. **Greenhouse Cottage** - (1bed/1bath) is on a quiet road one block off the main street. Kitchenette with open space of bedroom and living room (photos below).

Bob's Well Bread Bakery (Cafe)
+1 805 344 3000 • 550 Bell Street
Open: All Year, Thursday-Monday, 11am-4pm

BobsWellBread.com

Bob is prideful of his artisan breads, handmade in small batches using high hydration combined with long natural fermentation. No preservatives! He bakes in a stone-deck oven which creates irregular open cell structures. He says it's Old-World European tradition. Breakfast and lunch too. And the most delicious caffè latte I get every time I am nearby.

Plenty On Bell (Restaurant)
+1 805 344 3020 • 508 Bell Street
Open: All Year, Tuesday-Sunday, 8am-3pm (Fri 8:30pm)

PlentyOnBell.com

Plenty on Bell is very much a locals' restaurant. Wholesome cooking. American food. Indoor and outdoor seating. Open for breakfast and lunch, and dinner on Fridays. Of course, they're located on Bell Street. Homemade chili (photo below) with beans, ground beef, red onions, cheeses, spices, and topped with sour cream and chives. Exceptionally good.

$$-$$$

458 Bell Street
Los Alamos, CA 93440

+1 805 350 4054
Info@LumenWines.com

LumenWines.com

Tasting Room at Pico Los Alamos Restaurant
Open: Wednesday-Sunday, Noon-7pm

Wine and food pairing at its best... at the Pico Los Alamos restaurant.

COOL CLIMATE WINES

Lumen Wines is the creation of two wine professionals crossing paths and needing each other. Will Henry (descendant of the Henry Wine Group, leading distributors of fine wines in California) wanted to make wine; however, he knew nothing about winemaking, his knowledge and expertise was in wine sales and distribution. Lane Tanner (famous for being the first woman to start her own wine label in Santa Barbara) had lots of excellent wine and did not want to be in the wine business. She just wanted to focus on making excellent wine.

They ran into each other one day in a vineyard. Lane describes the encounter very well: "Will had a label and a concept but needed wine, while I had wine and no label." They needed each other!

The concept, which they share, is to produce wines from the best cool-climate vineyards in Santa Barbara. This primarily means Pinot Noir and Chardonnay. However, they also have a couple of Grenache wines that are extraordinarily delicious (photo right). Pinot Gris too.

They are particular the vineyards they choose. Fruit must be certified sustainable and biodynamic. Everything is small batch, hand made, high quality.

Their philosophy is to pick the fruit on the early side so that the wines are livelier on the pallet, deeper in complexity and lower an alcohol. These are the kind of wines that will age well in your cellar and be particularly good pairing with foods.

Now that you know the quality and partnership of Lumen Wines, let's get to the best part, tasting them. The tasting room is in the **Los Alamos General Store**, now a restaurant, bar, tasting room and wine shop.

While they have a separate tasting room for the Lumen Wines, I suggest you take a seat in the restaurant (open space) and enjoy their wines with great food. The restaurant is **Pico Los Alamos** (next page), also owned by Will Henry. The Pico cuisine is very creative, gourmet and ever so flavorful.

By the way, they donate 1% of all wine sales to environmental causes.

Collection of Wines

Pinot Noir (Presqu'le Vineyard)
Pinot Noir (Julia's Vineyard)
Pinot Noir (Sierra Madre Vineyard)
Pinot Noir (Santa Maria Valley)

Grenache (Martian Ranch)
Grenache (Portico Hills)

Chardonnay (Santa Maria Valley)
Pinot Gris (Sierra Madre Vineyard)

WINE TASTING, RESTAURANT, WINE SHOP, BAR

The *Pico Los Alamos* restaurant is located on the main street in the small Old Western-town of Los Alamos. It is located in the original general store built in 1880 in this historic town. The restaurant's namesake comes from Solomon Pico. He was an 1850's rancher here who lost his wife to gringo invasion. So, he became a bandit in revenge, a train robber, stealing gold from miners on trains. So skilled with horses, he would ride all night to Los Angeles (receiving fresh horses from his fellow ranchers) so it would look like he was never there, or done the crimes. He was never caught; however, he was banned from Los Alamos, allowing the town to be officially founded in 1879. The next year, the **Los Alamos General Store** was built.

In the general store is now **Lumen wine tasting**, their **wine shop**, a **full bar**, and the **Pico restaurant**. This is an ideal location to enjoy it all. The restaurant has both indoor dining (photo right) and a beautiful outdoor terrace and garden for dining as well. Service is extraordinary. They have a wine steward if you want to pair your foods. You can do a full food and wine pairing if you like. Their chef, Cameron, has brought a high level of creativity and quality to this restaurant. He believes in using only local purveyors, and in knowing the farmers and ranchers personally. And so, he gets their best!

The food is both creative and flavorful. And unique. Two first timers for me: a **pig snout** cooked with olive oil, chives, parsley and lemon juice, and a **crispy pig ear**, cooked in a water bath with duck fat for forty-two hours. It was like a beef jerky. Flavorful.

Here are a few examples of the yumminess here...

Port & Beans (photo left page): celebrating this American classic with special pork from Winfield Farms and shelling beans from Bautista Farms. Bruce of Winfield Farms (locally in Buellton) raises perfect mangalista pigs where he figured out a way to force better intermuscular fat growth in the pigs making the flavor insanely good. This dish is unbelievably delicious!

Potato Tortaloni (photo below left): a play on a soup from the chef's mom, boiling olive oil into potato broth giving out the illusion of creaminess, and then adding parmigiana and basil. A simple four-ingredient dish.

Mussels Escabeche (photo below right): fresh mussels hand-harvested twenty minutes from the restaurant, served with pickled fennel and special habanero peppers created by Michael Mazourek at Cornell University (not liking hot spices, he bred a pepper with all the flavors of habanero and none of the heat).

SANTA BARBARA **LOS ALAMOS** ■
Restaurant, Wine Tastings
PICO LOS ALAMOS

$$$-$$$$-$$$$$

458 Bell Street
Los Alamos, CA 93440

+1 805 344 1122
Pico@LosAlamosGeneralStore.com

LosAlamosGeneralStore.com

Open: Wednesday-Sunday
Dinners: 3pm-9pm
Plus Weekend Brunch: 10am-2pm

BELLS. VERY FRANCH.

Yes, Very Franch, as Greg and Daisy Ryan call their restaurant. A French bistro of five inspiring plates in a well-orchestrated prix fixe menu. Executive Chef Daisy is Culinary Institute of America trained, with illustrious experience at the Michelin three-star Per Se, Thomas Keller's acclaimed New York interpretation of The French Laundry. General Manager Greg manages the high-level customer experience at the Bell's. He is also trained with front-of-the-house expertise at Per Se.

So, you might easily say that this could be one of the best restaurants you'll experience in all of Santa Barbara County. And they have already received their first star from Michelin. The only Michelin-star restaurant in Santa Barbara County. The restaurant is located on Bell Street (hmm, the name) in the tiny Old West town of Los Alamos.

And now for a sample of the delectable cuisine...

Santa Barbara Sea Urchin on Mille Crêpe (photo left page): fresh Santa Barbara sea urchin caught by marine biologist Stephanie Mutz of Sea Stephanie Fish, served over mille crêpe with creme fraiche and chives (mille means a thousand exaggerated layers). This has become the iconic dish of Bell's and most commonly stays on the evolving menu.

Crudo of Kanpachi (photo below): raw yellowtail fish, slightly seared, in a rich a tomato consommé made with Finley Farms organic tomatoes. Clementines sourced from Eye of the Day, plus green-onion rings and Peruviana beans.

Mediterranean Sea Bass (photo right): sea bass with grilled Finley Farms sweet peppers. The fruits de mer beurre blanc sauce is freshly caught sea urchin and halibut stock. Topped with sweet Marcona almonds and Kandarian Farms coriander.

SANTA BARBARA **LOS ALAMOS** ■
Restaurant
BELL'S RESTAURANT

$$$$-$$$$$

458 Bell Street
Los Alamos, CA 93440

No Phone Number
Info@BellsRestaurant.com

BellsRestaurant.com
Website For Reservations

Open: Thursday-Monday
Lunch: 11am-3pm • Dinner: 5pm-8:30pm

Michelin Star Awarded

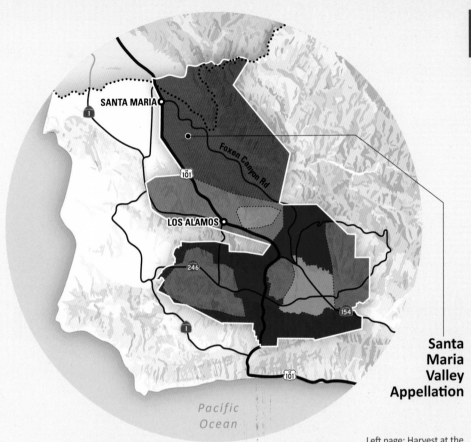

**Santa
Maria
Valley
Appellation**

FIRST APPELLATION

The **Santa Maria Valley AVA** is the northernmost appellation in Santa Barbara County and is the region's first officially approved American Viticultural Area (AVA) in 1981. Plus, it is California's second-oldest appellation.

Santa Maria Valley is the second coldest appellation in California. Just fifteen miles from the ocean, this valley gets cool winds and fog flowing extensively from the Pacific Ocean making it perfect terroir for Pinot Noir and Chardonnay, its two primary wines.

This cooling effect is significant. It is consequential to influence the growing season in this region, lengthening it (the growing season is among the longest in the world), and contributing positively to the sugar/acid balance of the grapes.

In 1973, the Miller family planted 300 acres of Pinot Noir and Chardonnay on the northwestern portion of the Santa Maria Valley AVA. The Millers did not just give birth to these excellent vineyards, a brand emerged as the iconic *Bien Nacido Vineyard* name becoming the most designated vineyard on wine labels anywhere in the world (over 15,000 different wine labels).

There are many wineries up and down this valley. I present to you three wineries from very different locations, different styles of wines and completely different tasting experiences.

Here are these three wineries.
- Bien Nacido Estate, page 401
- Foxen Vineyard & Winery, page 403
- Presqui'le Vineyard, page 405

$$$-$$$$

4705 Santa Maria Mesa Road
Santa Maria, CA 93454

+1 805 318 6600
TastingRoom@BienNacidoEstate.com

BienNacidoEstate.com

Open: Every Day, 10am-4pm

B ien Nadido is the most designated vineyard on wine labels anywhere in the world.

LEGENDARY VINEYARD

I'm sure you've seen the Bien Nacido Vineyard named on a wine label. Probably many times. This vineyard has become an icon as winemakers from all over want these grapes, and they make wines touting the Bien Nacido Vineyard name on the bottle. What a special place.

Bien Nacido (meaning "well born" in Spanish) was originally planted in 1973 by the Miller family, starting with 300 acres of Pinot Noir and Chardonnay in this special location of the Santa Maria Valley AVA. The Millers did not just give birth to these excellent vineyards, the family has continuously grown and managed this amazing property with five generations giving their hands and hearts to the care of this land and vines.

Imagine the depth of honor from winemakers over their fifty-year history as over 15,000 different wine labels have designated Bien Nacido as the single vineyard in their bottles. It is hard to realize all that success, yet it helps us understand the impact to this California acclaim!

I will say it again, terroir is everything! The Bien Nacido Estate is located very close to the ocean where the cold fog smothers their land. The way the mountains surround them, it creates a pocket whereby the fog does not generally disperse until the afternoon. This creates a mesoclimate of milder weather and less diurnal range, perfect for slowly ripening Pinot Noir. The results are amazing!

The Millers are farmers and sold all their grapes until 2005 when they decided to make a little wine for themselves and friends. In 2007, the wine went commercial. They established a tasting room in the Los Olivos Village and began distribution across the country. In 2023, they opened a beautiful tasting facility on the estate. This is an excellent opportunity to see the Bien Nacido location, where these iconic grapes grow.

Both tasting rooms offer **tasting flights** of their Bien Nacido Estate and Solomon Hills Estate wines. You can also have a **pairing flight** with charcuterie and cheese.

Collection of Wines

Black Label Collection
The Captain Pinot Noir
Bien Nacido Old Vines Pinot Noir
The XO Syrah

Bien Nacido Estate Collection
Bien Nacido Pinot Noir
Bien Nacido Syrah
The Bench Red Wine (Pinot Noir, Syrah)
Bien Nacido Estate Chardonnay
Bien Nacido Viognier

Solomon Hills Estate Collection
Solomon Hills Pinot Noir
Solomon Hills Vin Gris (Rosé of Pinot Noir)
Solomon Hills Chardonnay
Belle of the Ball Chardonnay

$$$-$$$$

7600 Foxen Canyon Road
Santa Maria, CA 93454

+1 805 937 4251
TastingRoom@FoxenVineyard.com

FoxenVineyard.com

Open: Every Day, 11am-4pm

Original Tasting Barn
7600 Foxen Canyon Road
Thursday-Sunday from 11am-4pm

Collection of Burgundian Wines

Pinot Noir (Bien Nacido Vineyard - Block 43)
Pinot Noir (Bien Nacido Vineyard - Block 8)
Pinot Noir (Julia's Vineyard)
Pinot Noir (Riverbench Vineyard)
Pinot Noir (John Sebastiano Vineyard)
Pinot Noir (Santa Maria Valley)
Rosé of Pinot Noir

Chardonnay (Bien Nacido Vineyard - Block UU)
Heritage Chardonnay (Tinaquaic Vineyard)
Chardonnay (Tinaquaic Vineyard)

F rom a blacksmith shop to an advanced fully solar-powered winery; 35 years of great wines.

LEGENDARY JULIA'S VINEYARD

It was Thanksgiving a few years ago that I opened a fifteen-year-old Pinot Noir magnum from Foxen Vineyard & Winery. I can't even tell you how many times people have told me that Pinot Noir does not last that long. You cannot age it. You need to drink it young, right away. I imagine you have heard the same, or even thought so yourself.

This bottle was extra special to me. Not just because it was a 2001 vintage, it was their *Julia's Vineyard Pinot Noir*. This is by far my favorite Pinot Noir wine they make. Even more special though is that Dick Doré and Bill Wathen autographed the bottle for me. Dick and Billy are the founders of this winery from way back in 1985.

The wine was perfect. It held its beautiful Pinot fruit in an ever-so-smooth manner. It was delicate. Sophisticated in its range of flavors throughout the mouth experience. I cannot wait to do this again. You should too! Quality Pinot ages! So, after spending the morning with Dick (photo above at the historic Shack), I had to leave with his autograph on another magnum of Julia's Vineyard.

This is the fun story about this wine's origin. Legendary Jess Jackson, Kendall Jackson Wines, walked into the Foxen tasting room one day and was impressed with their wines. He found Dick and asked how he could help. Dick responded: sell us some of your best grapes. And that is how they got a hold of the extraordinary Julia's Vineyard grapes. They have kept this great relationship ever since. You must taste it!

Foxen winery is located in the far east and south side of the Santa Maria Valley AVA. They are easily accessible from the Santa Ynez Valley AVA as Foxen Canyon Road (where numerous wineries reside) goes over the hill arriving in Santa Maria Valley and Foxen winery. Guess where the road got its name? Captain Foxen was Dick's great-great-grandfather, who purchased Rancho Tinaquaic 200 years ago.

Do you remember the first tasting room at Foxen? It was a shack. It was once a blacksmith shop. They still keep **The Shack** open for fun weekends only, Saturdays and Sundays from 11am to 4pm for their Bordeaux and Italian wines.

$$$-$$$$

5391 Presqu'ile Drive
Santa Maria, CA 93455

+1 805 937 8110
Info@PresquileWine.com

PresquileWine.com

Open: Every Day, Noon-5pm (Sat/Sun 11am)

Beautiful architectural winery with views across the valley to the mountains and ocean.

STATE-OF-THE-ART WINERY

Presqu'ile is located in the southwestern corner of the Santa Maria Valley AVA, easily accessible from Highway 101. This property is beautiful rolling hills of vineyards with the winery and tasting area perched at the top of the hill for spectacular views across their landscape. This is cool, Santa Maria climate where they focus on Pinot Noir, Chardonnay and cool climate Syrah.

Just ten years old, this winery has stunning modern architectural design (see photo above). There is a lot of outdoor tasting spaces, both under the expansive eaves and through a step-down landscape that gives everybody the impressive views.

There is a lot of diversity in the vineyards here. Many different elevations, sun exposures and types of soils that they mix with different varietals and varying clones within the varietals. This gives their winemaker a huge palette of distinctions for blending excellent complex wines.

While Presqu'ile has **standard tasting flights** and an incredible **food and wine experiences** (see next page), the ultimate experience here is their

Presqu'ile Wine & Food Tour. This is a guided walking tour throughout the winery, inside and out.

As you move through this architecturally striking building, the back wall leads into their caves. You get to walk through 240 feet of caves where their wines are aging (photo left page). Your guide will explain how the winery works as you traverse backwards through the winery process.

You will enter the winery from the cave and go through the different floor levels that the wine moves and ultimately outside to the platform where the grapes are received. There is much to see in the winery as this is one of the most well-designed wineries I have witnessed, extreme state-of-the-art, with unique winemaker attributes.

Behind and above the winery is their hilltop pond where you will have views in every direction of their vineyards, the San Rafael Mountains, Soloman Hills and you can actually see the Pacific Ocean.

Ultimately you settle into a private lookout terrace to enjoy a food and wine prepared with estate sparkling wine and single-vineyard wines.

This is an unforgettable experience!

Collection of Wines

Presqu'ile Vineyard Pinot Noir
Bien Nacido Vineyard Pinot Noir
Santa Maria Valley Pinot Noir
Carbonic Gamay
Gamay Nouveau
Estate Syrah

Rosé (Pinot Noir)
Presqu'ile Vineyard Chardonnay
Santa Maria Valley Chardonnay
Sauvignon Blanc

Sparkling Rosé (Pinot Noir)
Blanc de Blancs Sparkling
Brut Cuvée Sparkling
Non Vintage Brut Cuvée Sparkling

EXTRAORDINARY FOOD AND WINE PAIRINGS

Presqu'ile has created an incredible food and wine tasting experience. Each day they create a group of foods that pair well with their wines. This is not a restaurant; however, they are delivering creative gourmet foods that are specifically intended to pair with their wines for the day.

The **Mezze Picnic Wine & Food Experience** is the ultimate picnic. Not just because it is paired with a delicious tasting flight of Presqu'ile's new and current estate wines, it is because the food is creatively gourmet. Presqu'ile has an estate chef who creates five to six family-style small plates featuring a seasonal bounty from their one-acre estate garden and other ingredients from local purveyors (see four photos below).

Check out the environment. Indoors is a grand, open, spacious tasting. A romantic fireplace if you choose. Living room style. And a step-up bar (photo left page). Outside is beautifully designed with multiple levels of umbrella covered tables. The view is extraordinary. You can see across the valley and even see the ocean from this hilltop vantage.

They also put on a half dozen professional concerts here during the summer months. Check their website for artists and concert times.

$$$-$$$$

5391 Presqu'ile Drive
Santa Maria, CA 93455

+1 805 937 8110
Info@PresquileWine.com

PresquileWine.com

Open: Every Day, Noon-5pm (Sat/Sun 11am)

Classic Chickpea Hummus
(left page, left): garlic, tahini and lemon juice, garnished with a piquillo pepper and currant relish.

Housemade Farmers Cheese
(left page, right): burrata, goat cheese and sheep's milk, blended with olive oil and salt, then hand strained. Accompanied by heirloom tomato jam (cardamom, cinnamon, ginger) and garnished with pumpkin seeds.

Pork Cheek Adobo
(below left): braised in tamari, duck stock, sherry vinegar, star anise, and black pepper, garnished with quick pickled Armenian cucumber salad and toasted sesame seeds. Served with Calrose white rice.

Grilled Shishito and Heirloom Tomato Salad
(below right): dressed with tamari, sesame oil, roasted garlic, ginger, basil, and cilantro.

Remembering the beautiful autumn colors as the vines begin to rest for the winter, at Roake Ranch in Sta. Rita Hills.

Harvest occurring in the vineyards of Valle de Guadalupe

Wine may be your attraction to travel here; however, the culinary scene in Valle de Guadalupe is beyond-your-imagination extraordinary. Gastronomy is setting the stage for the future here.

VALLE DE GUADALUPE

Have you seen, as I have been reading, that the wines from Valle de Guadalupe, México are getting high scores from major critics? The wineries have been hiring excellent winemakers from California, UC Davis, France and Spain to come elevate the qualities of their wines. And it is working!

The wines are winning competitions against California and French wines. Most characteristic to their success is that **The French Laundry** (a three-star Michelin restaurant consistently on "The World's 50 Best Restaurants") has Valle de Guadalupe wines on its wine list. Great wine is really beginning to happen here. You must go check it out.

In this small fourteen-mile long agricultural valley, with a population of less than 7,000 people, you will find an abundance of extraordinary restaurants. I do not mean quality Méxican foods. The cuisine here is creative international gourmet dishes that you would experience in the world's largest cities by talented educated executive chefs.

It was a special occasion to start my journey by meeting Fernando Perez Castro, the owner of two wineries in Valle de Guadalupe. I was tasting with him at his La Lomita winery. I love his wines, he loves my books. And he loves the project of my new book about Valle de Guadalupe and Ensenada. We hit-it-off and became instant friends.

Fernando introduced me to some amazing restaurants. Little did I realize in that moment, that he was showing me the jewels of the area: extraordinary foods. Many of these restaurants are now in this book for you to enjoy. Thank you very much, Fernando.

This is an agricultural region, so produce is in abundance. The Pacific Ocean is right there, so fresh fish is prolific. Just like needing quality grapes to make great wine, you need excellent ingredients to make outstanding cuisine. This is the source here!

On my last day of this first trip, Fernando and I met for dinner at his Lunario restaurant (photos above and left) to debrief my two-week journey. The astonishment for me was the quality of food, so creative, gourmet and artistically presented. For Fernando, the extraordinary cuisine has become the inspiration motivating winemakers to produce wines of the same exceptional caliber.

The cuisine in Valle de Guadalupe is surprisingly amazing, more than your expectations, truly extraordinary. These two gastronomic creations came from Executive Chef Sheyla Alvarado at Restaurante Lunario located in Valle de Guadalupe.

Olive Wood Smoked Carrot Soup
(photo left page): a unique soup made from carrots smoked with olive wood, served with a rainbow of organic carrots (purple, yellow, orange, and white), topped with raw cream and a nasturtium leaf. Served with a 24-hour fermented buckwheat sourdough bread.

Corn Mousse Camembert Ice Cream
(photo above): sweet corn mousse, candied pecans and cacao nibs, topped with ice cream made from their homemade camembert cheese.

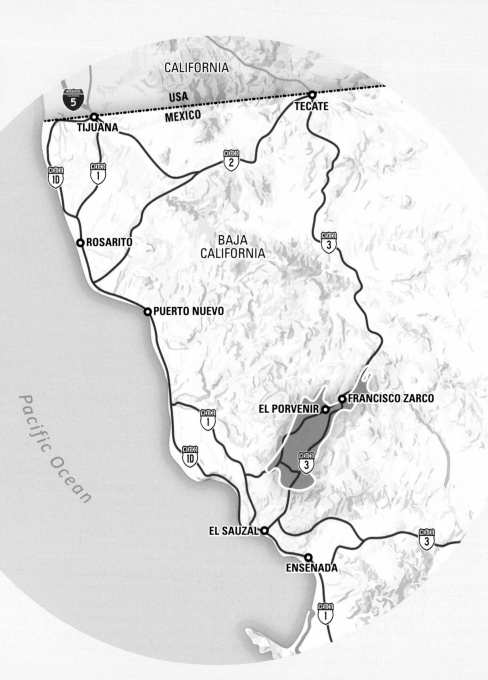

VALLE DE GUADALUPE

THE NEXT BOOK
Exploring Wine Regions – México

I n the past twenty years, this valley has grown from only a few wineries to hundreds of wineries today. Most accept visitors, many have food.

VALLE DE GUADELUPE

Valle de Guadalupe is a valley benefiting from the cold Pacific Ocean influence, just as the other California coastal wine regions. They get warm days from the inland heat, followed by cool evenings from the cold ocean influx. They get these large diurnal temperature swings important for viticulture. You may think this is just hot México; however, this is a real wine region with the right kind of terroir to make excellent wines.

There are no official appellations in México, yet. In Valle de Guadalupe, you can consider the valley an appellation in the sense of defining the viticulture area. There are three sub-areas within the valley called **Cañada de Trigo, Cañada de Guadalupe** and **Valle de Calafia**, which are considered unique growing areas within the valley. You could consider them sub-appellations in that general meaning. Even though there is no official appellation, it is clearly about unique terroir in these distinctive areas.

Valle de Guadalupe is fourteen miles long (west/east) and five miles wide, with most of the wineries on the north side of the valley facing the sun.

Nobody could give me a confident number of wineries here. The range varied from 100 to 350 wineries. Why? Because the growth is so rapid to keep track and there are many winemakers inside other wineries. Especially the small guys are hard to keep track. Anyway, the abundance here is for our enjoyment. I share with you wineries I know you can count on to be good.

As it is in any wine region, it is very much about the right varietals being planted in their best terroir. Here, I found the terroir worked optimum for **Nebbiolo, Mourvèdre, Grenache, Tempranillo, and Syrah**. These wines you will definitely like.

And don't forget the food. The culinary scene here is extraordinary. I promise you. Michelin is going to find this place soon, as they have their quality. The cuisine might end up being the primary reason you will travel here.

MÉXICO WINE REGIONS

There are several other wine regions in México to explore. One of my Argentina winemaker friends has move to Guanajuato Mexico. Apparently, there are several Argentina winemakers establishing themselves here. My winemaker friend is an excellent winemaker. I know her wines from Mendoza Argentina, so I trust there must be something good going on there.

Nearby is San Miguel de Allende. Not only is this a beautiful historical colonial-era city with baroque Spanish architecture and cobblestone streets, it also has a vibrant arts scene, cultural festivals and wineries. Yes, this high elevation area (6,234') is growing grapes and making wine. It is time to go explore and include this place in our México book for you explore as well.

And there may be more regions to explore, so look out for the next book. With half the book already completed, I expect it published in 2024.

MY CENTRAL COAST DISCOVERIES?

This has been an incredible journey. I thought I knew California's Central Coast until I had to dig in and create this book. It is so true that the teacher learns more than a student. Looking back now, it's hard to imagine that I spent twenty-nine weeks in the wine regions of these three counties. Fortunately, there were excellent people, true professionals, that helped introduced me to quality wineries, excellent restaurants and interesting attractions. They created great itineraries for me. I am so appreciative, as this made all the difference.

This was two solid years of traveling up and down the central coast of California. Mostly in the summer and fall, one week in the wine region and one week home. I always looked forward to an extra week or two home to get caught up on photo editing, designing and writing the book. I also made a few trips in the winter and spring to capture these seasons.

Most special about my trips was meeting remarkable winemakers and talented chefs. For me, it is all about unexpected amazement in wine and food experiences. I love learning what makes each of them individual and special. The central coast definitely has outstanding chefs and winemakers.

Prior to this journey, I enrolled in the California Wine Appellation Specialist course at the San Francisco Wine School. This made a huge difference in learning about each individual appellation in the Central Coast. There happen to be thirty-two appellations in these three counties. As you know, I believe it's all about terroir, and appellations distinguishing the terroir.

While I have been making a big deal about terroir, and the importance of your learning the appellations and which grapes excel in each appellation, what surprised me most in this journey to create the book was discovering terroir and appellations that were everything to finding great wines I had not yet discovered. How funny is that? I actually began to like wines that previously were uninteresting to me. For example, Syrah. It's a nice big bold red wine; however, there are others I would prefer. Now that I have tasted Syrah in extraordinary terroir, I uncovered unbelievably great Syrah wines that I can't wait to drink again and again. And Chardonnay. I simply don't drink that stuff. Yet, now I have found places in the Central Coast where the terroir so exceptional for Chardonnay that I now think of foods to pair with it. This has been a surprising discovery in enjoying new wines.

Now it is your turn. Go! I promise you will be pleasantly surprised that the wines in the Central Coast are phenomenal, the restaurants amazing, and the tourism is excellent. And mostly, the people are amazing, warm and inviting, and desirous to share with you everything special.

Happy Tasting,

Michael C. Higgins, PhD

Michael C. Higgins, PhD
Author, Photojournalist & Publisher

What is next...

Originally, I was going to include Valle de Guadalupe, in Baja California México in this book. This region is still California, just a different country. When I focused my book more closely on the Central Coast of California, I decided to make the Valle de Guadalupe section its own book. I had already visited twice for four weeks, and fell in love this wine region. The food is extraordinary. And I focus you in on finding the great wines in this valley.

As you certainly noticed, my last three books have been quite substantial in size. They are between 350 and 500 pages, each! These books have taken three years of research, plus an additional year for completion, printing and publishing. They are grand projects. I want to do some small book now, and go to some smaller wine regions. I can deliver books to you faster, and I want the simplicity.

While I had a couple of small wine regions in mind, Greece contacted me. They want me to do my next book on Greece. And they will organize everything to make it easy to explore their regions. So I am very excited. Greece is small, and the islands are spectacularly beautiful. I can't wait to get there and share everything with you.

2024 - Exploring Wine Regions – México
2026 - Exploring Wine Regions – Greece

THE INDEX
Finding Your Way Around Easily

WINERIES	PAGES
■ Monterey County (MRY)	**24**
Albatross Ridge (MRY, Carmel Valley Village)	82
Albatross Ridge (MRY, Carmel-By-The-Sea Village)	88
Bernardus Winery (MRY, Carmel Valley Village)	85
Blair Estate (MRY, Carmel Valley Village)	90
Boekenoogen Wines (MRY, Carmel Valley Village)	85
Caraccioli Cellars (MRY, Carmel-By-The-Sea Village)	90
Chalone Vineyard (MRY, Chalone)	69
De Tierra Vineyards (MRY, Carmel-By-The-Sea Village)	90
Folktale Winery & Vineyards (MRY, Carmel Valley)	81
Hahn Estate (MRY, Monterey, Santa Lucia Highlands)	59
Holman Ranch (MRY, Carmel Valley)	75
Holman Ranch (MRY, Carmel Valley Village)	82
I. Brand Winery (MRY, Carmel Valley Village)	83
Joyce Estate Winery (MRY, Arroyo Seco)	63
Joyce Estate Winery (MRY, Carmel Valley Village)	82
KORi Wines (MRY, Carmel-By-The-Sea Village)	91
Lepe Cellars (MRY, Carmel-By-The-Sea Village)	91
Odonata Wines (MRY, Monterey, Santa Lucia Highlands)	47
Pessago Winery (MRY, Monterey, Santa Lucia Highlands)	51
Puma Winery (MRY, Monterey, Santa Lucia Highlands)	55
Rustique Wines (MRY, Monterey, Santa Lucia Highlands)	49
Scheid Vineyards (MRY, Arroyo Seco)	65
Scratch Wines (MRY, Carmel Valley Village)	83
Silvestri Vineyards (MRY, Carmel-By-The-Sea Village)	91
Windy Oaks Estate (MRY, Carmel Valley Village)	83
Wrath Wines (MRY, Monterey, Santa Lucia Highlands)	57
■ San Luis Obispo - York Mountain	**98**
Epoch Estate Wines (SLO, York Mountain)	101
■ San Luis Obispo - Paso Robles (Paso)	**102**
Adelaida Vineyards & Winery (SLO, Paso, Adelaida)	153
Allegretto Vineyard Resort (SLO, Paso, Estrella)	117
Alta Colina (SLO, Paso, Adelaida)	171
Ancient Peaks Winery (SLO, Paso, Santa Margarita)	219
Barton Family Wines (SLO, Paso, Willow Creek)	191
Booker Vineyard (SLO, Paso, Willow Creek)	185
Bovino Vineyards (SLO, Paso, El Pomar)	149

WINERIES	PAGES
Cass Winery (SLO, Paso, Geneseo)	139
Castoro Cellars (SLO, Paso, Templeton Gap)	201
Daou Vineyards (SLO, Paso, Adelaida)	163
Denner Vineyards (SLO, Paso, Willow Creek)	183
Eberle Winery (SLO, Paso, Geneseo)	127
Hope Family Wines (SLO, Paso, Templeton Gap)	203
Hunt Cellars (SLO, Paso, Willow Creek)	195
J. Lohr Vineyards & Wines (SLO, Paso, Estrella)	113
JUSTIN Vineyards & Winery (SLO, Paso, Adelaida)	155
La Cuvier Winery (SLO, Paso, Adelaida)	165
LAW Wine Estates (SLO, Paso, Adelaida)	175
McPrice Myers Winery (SLO, Paso, Adelaida)	167
Niner Wine Estates (SLO, Paso, Willow Creek)	187
Opolo Vineyard (SLO, Paso, Willow Creek)	179
Paris Valley Road Winery (SLO, Paso, Geneseo)	135
Peachy Canyon (SLO, Paso, Templeton Gap)	209
Pomar Junction Vineyard (SLO, Paso, El Pomar)	147
Robert Hall Winery (SLO, Paso, Geneseo)	133
Summerwood Winery (SLO, Paso, Templeton Gap)	205
Six Mile Bridge (SLO, Paso, Adelaida)	173
Villa San-Juliette (SLO, Paso, Estrella)	115
Tablas Creek Vineyard (SLO, Paso, Adelaida)	161
Turley Wine Cellars (SLO, Paso, Willow Creek)	197
■ San Luis Obispo County (SLO)	**230**
Absolution Cellars (SLO, SLO Coast, North)	247
Alapay Cellars (SLO, SLO Coast, South)	250
Center of Effort (SLO, SLO Coast, Edna Valley)	275
Chamisal Vineyards (SLO, SLO Coast, Edna Valley)	269
Claiborne & Churchill (SLO, SLO Coast, Edna Valley)	271
Dunites Wine Company (SLO, San Luis Obispo Downtown)	295
El Lugar Wines (SLO, Downtown Industrial Park)	294
Harmony Cellars (SLO, SLO Coast, North)	245
Hearst Ranch Winery (SLO, SLO Coast, North)	239
Kynsi Winery (SCO, SLO Coast, Edna Valley)	273
La Lomita Ranch (SCO, SLO Coast, Edna Valley)	261
Laetitia Vineyard (SLO, SLO Coast, Arroyo Grande)	281
Lindquist Wines (SLO, SLO Coast, South)	282

WINERIES	PAGES
Peloton Vineyards (SLO, SLO Coast, South)	250
Ragtag Wine Company (SLO, San Luis Obispo Downtown)	295
Saucelito Canyon (SLO, SLO Coast, Edna Valley)	277
Sinor-LaVallee (SLO, SLO Coast, South)	251
Stephen Ross Wine (SLO, Downtown Industrial Park)	294
Stolo Vineyards (SLO, SLO Coast, North)	243
Talley Vineyards (SLO, SLO Coast, Arroyo Grande)	279
Timbre Winery (SLO, SLO Coast, South)	283
Tolosa Winery (SLO, SLO Coast, Edna Valley)	265
Verdad Wines (SLO, SLO Coast, South)	282
Wolff Vineyards (SLO, SLO Coast, Edna Valley)	267
■ Santa Barbara County (SBA)	**298**
Alma Rosa Winery (SBA, Santa Ynez, Sta. Rita Hills)	347
Beckmen Vineyard (SBA, Santa Ynez, Ballard Canyon)	359
Bien Nacido Estate (SBA, Santa Maria Valley)	401
Brave & Maiden Estate (SBA, Santa Ynez, Los Olivos)	363
Crown Point Vineyards (SBA, Santa Ynez, Happy Canyon)	377
Dierberg Estate (SBA, Santa Ynez, Sta. Rita Hills)	343
Dovecote Estate Winery (SBA, Alisos Canyon)	389
Fess Parker Winery (SBA, Santa Ynez)	323
Folded Hills Ranch Winery (SBA, Santa Ynez)	311
Foxen Vineyard & Winery (SBA, Santa Maria Valley)	403
Gainey Vineyard (SBA, Santa Ynez, Los Olivos)	367
Grimm's Bluff (SBA, Santa Ynez, Happy Canyon)	381
Happy Canyon Vineyard (SBA, Santa Ynez, Happy Canyon)	379
Lumen Wines (SBA, Los Alamos Downtown)	393
Margerum Wine Company (SBA, Santa Ynez, Buellton)	327
Peake Ranch (SBA, Santa Ynez, Sta. Rita Hills)	349
Presqu'ile Vineyard (SBA, Santa Maria Valley)	405
Roblar Winery (SBA, Santa Ynez, Los Olivos)	365
Rusack Vineyards (SBA, Santa Ynez, Ballard Canyon)	355
Stolpman Vineyards (SBA, Santa Ynez, Ballard Canyon)	357
Sunstone Winery (SBA, Santa Ynez, Los Olivos)	369
Star Lane Vineyard (SBA, Santa Ynez, Happy Canyon)	383
The Hilt Estate (SBA, Santa Ynez, Sta. Rita Hills)	345
Zaca Mesa Winery (SBA, Santa Ynez)	325

THE INDEX
Finding Your Way Around Easily

RESTAURANTS	PAGES
■ *Monterey County (MRY)*	**24**
Anton & Michel (MRY, Carmel-By-The-Sea Village)	88
Coastal Kitchen (MRY, Monterey Downtown)	34
Cultura, Comida Y Bebida (MRY, Carmel-By-The-Sea Village)	88
Folktale Winery & Vineyards (MRY, Carmel Valley)	81
Lucia Restaurant & Bar (MRY, Carmel Valley)	84
Luigi's Italian Restaurant (MRY, Gonzales Downtown)	52
Montrio Bistro (MRY, Monterey Downtown)	32
Tarpy's Roadhouse (MRY, Carmel-By-The-Sea)	89
Taste of The Pinnacles Wine Bar (MRY, Soledad Downtown)	52
■ *San Luis Obispo - Paso Robles (Paso)*	**102**
Allegretto Vineyard Resort (SLO, Paso, Estrella)	117
Ancient Peaks Winery (SLO, Paso, Santa Margarita)	217
Barton Family Wines (SLO, Paso, Willow Creek)	193
Bovino Vineyards (SLO, Paso, El Pomar)	149
Buona Tavola (SLO, Paso Downtown)	224
Cass Winery (SLO, Paso, Geneseo)	141
ETTO Pasta Bar (SLO, Paso, Tin City)	211
In Bloom Restaurant (SLO, Paso Downtown)	228
Jeffry's Wine County BBQ (SLO, Paso Downtown)	224
JUSTIN Vineyards & Winery (SLO, Paso, Adelaida)	157
La Cuvier Winery (SLO, Paso, Adelaida)	165
Les Petites Canailles (SLO, Paso Downtown)	223
Niner Wine Estates (SLO, Paso, Willow Creek)	189
Opolo Vineyard (SLO, Paso, Willow Creek)	179
Paris Valley Road Winery (SLO, Paso, Geneseo)	137
Robert Hall Winery (SLO, Paso, Geneseo)	133
Six Test Kitchen (SLO, Paso, Tin City)	213
The Hatch (SLO, Paso Downtown)	224
Thomas Hill Organics (SLO, Paso Downtown)	225
Villa San-Juliette (SLO, Paso, Estrella)	115
■ *San Luis Obispo County (SLO)*	**230**
Blue Moon Over Avila (SLO, Avila Beach Village)	250
Buona Tavola (SLO, San Luis Obispo Downtown)	286
Galley Seafood Grill (SLO, Morro Bay Village)	246
Gina's Italian Cuisine (SLO, Arroyo Grande Village)	282
Giovanni's Fish Market (SLO, Morro Bay Village)	246
Giusepp's Cucina Rustica (SLO, San Luis Obispo Downtown)	286
Lido Restaurant (SLO, SLO Coast, South, Pismo Beach)	254
Mason Bar & Kitchen (SLO, Arroyo Grande Village)	283
Mistura (SLO, San Luis Obispo Downtown)	286
Novo Restaurant & Lounge (SLO, San Luis Obispo Downtown)	292
Ox + Anchor (SLO, San Luis Obispo Downtown)	291
Park 1039 (SLO, San Luis Obispo Downtown)	287
Robin's Restaurant (SLO, Cambria)	240

RESTAURANTS	PAGES
Sea Chest Oyster Bar (SLO, Cambria)	240
■ *Santa Barbara County (SBA)*	**298**
Alisal Ranch (SBA, Santa Ynez)	319
Bell's Restaurant (SBA, Los Alamos Downtown)	397
Bob's Well Bread Bakery (SBA, Los Alamos Downtown)	392
Coast Range (SBA, Santa Ynez, Solvang Downtown)	339
Copenhagen Sausage Garden (SBA, Solvang Downtown)	331
First & Oak (SBA, Santa Ynez, Solvang Downtown)	337
Hitching Post II (SBA, Buellton)	326
Industrial Eats (SBA, Buellton)	326
Leonardo's Cucina Italiana (SBA, Solvang)	330
Mad & Vin (SBA, Santa Ynez, Solvang Downtown)	335
Paula's Pancake House (SBA, Solvang Downtown)	330
Peasant FEAST (SBA, Solvang Downtown)	338
Pico Los Alamos (SBA, Los Alamos Downtown)	395
Plenty On Bell (SBA, Los Alamos Downtown)	392
Presqu'ile Vineyard (SBA, Santa Maria Valley)	407
Roblar Winery (SBA, Santa Ynez, Los Olivos)	365
S. Y. Kitchen, Cucina Rustica (SBA, Santa Ynez Downtown)	330

LODGING	PAGES
■ *Monterey County (MRY)*	**24**
Holman Ranch (MRY, Carmel Valley)	77
Pessago Winery (MRY, Monterey, Santa Lucia Highlands)	53
Puma Winery (MRY, Monterey, Santa Lucia Highlands)	53
Monterey Plaza Hotel (MRY, Monterey Downtown)	35
■ *San Luis Obispo - Paso Robles (Paso)*	**102**
Allegretto Vineyard Resort (SLO, Paso, Estrella)	117
Cass Winery (SLO, Paso, Geneseo)	143
JUSTIN Vineyards & Winery (SLO, Paso, Adelaida)	159
McPrice Myers Winery (SLO, Paso, Adelaida)	169
Opolo Vineyard (SLO, Paso, Willow Creek)	181
Summerwood Winery (SLO, Paso, Templeton Gap)	207
The Lofts, at The Market (SLO, Paso, Downtown)	229
■ *San Luis Obispo County (SLO)*	**230**
Hotel San Luis Obispo (SLO, San Luis Obispo Downtown)	289
La Lomita Ranch (SLO Coast, Edna Valley)	263
Cambria Pines Lodge (SLO, SLO Coast, North, Cambria)	241
Dolphin Bay Resort (SLO, SLO Coast, North, Cambria)	255
■ *Santa Barbara County (SBA)*	**298**
Alisal Ranch (SBA, Santa Ynez)	321
Dovecote Estate Winery (SBA, Alisos Canyon)	391
Pico Cottages (SBA, Los Alamos Downtown)	392
Sunstone Winery (SBA, Santa Ynez, Los Olivos)	371
The Landsby (SBA, Santa Ynez, Solvang Downtown)	333

THE APPELLATIONS	PAGES
MONTEREY COUNTY (MRY) (Central Coast North)	24
■ Monterey	36
◆ Santa Lucia highlands	44
◆ Arroyo Seco	60
■ Chalone	66
■ Carmel Valley	72
◆ Carmel Valley Village	82
◆ Carmel-By-The-Sea	86
SAN LUIS OBISPO COUNTY (SLO) (Central Coast Central)	92
■ York Mountain	98
■ Paso Robles (Paso)	102
◆ Estrella	108
◆ Geneseo	122
◆ El Pomar	144
◆ Adelaida	150
◆ Willow Creek	176
◆ Templeton Gap	198
◆ Tin City	210
◆ Santa Margarita Ranch	214
■ SLO Coast	230
◆ Edna Valley	258
◆ Arroyo Grande	277
SANTA BARBARA COUNTY (SBA) (Central Coast South)	298
■ Santa Ynez Valley	306
◆ Sta. Rita Hills	340
◆ Ballard Canyon	352
◆ Los Olivos District	360
◆ Happy Canyon	374
■ Alisos Canyon	386
■ Santa Maria Valley	398
MÉXICO, BAJA CALIFORNIA (Next Book)	410

Left page: Wooden fermentation tanks at Crown Point Vineyards in Happy Canyon

Above: Concrete fermentation tanks at Crown Point Vineyards in Happy Canyon

DEFINITIONS
Glossary of Wine Terminology

Origins of the Grapes in this Book

BORDEAUX GRAPES
Red – Cabernet Sauvignon, Cabernet Franc, Merlot, Malbec, Carménère, Petit Verdot
White – Muscadelle, Sauvignon Blanc, Sauvignon Gris, Sémillon

BURGUNDIAN GRAPES
Red – César, Gamay Noir, Pinot Gris, Pinot Noir
White – Aligoté, Chardonnay, Melon de Bourgogne, Pinot Blanc, Sacy

RHÔNE GRAPES
Red – Counoise, Cinsault, Folle Blanche, Grenache, Mataro, Mourvèdre, Muscardin, Petite Sirah, Syrah, Terret Noir, Vaccarèse
White – Bourboulenc, Clairette Blanche, Grenache Blanc, Marsanne, Picardan, Picpoul Blanc, Rousanne, Viognier

CROATIA GRAPES
Red – Dobričić, Plavac Mali, Refosco, Terrano, Zinfandel
White – Grk Bijeli, Malvasia, Pošip, Welschriesling

ITALIAN GRAPES
Red – Aglianico, Barbera, Corvina, Dolcetto, Falanghina, Grignolino, Lagrein, Lambrusco, Montepulciano, Nebbiolo, Nero d'Avola, Rondinella, Sangiovese, Teroldego
White – Arneis, Catarratto, Fiano, Friulano, Greco, Moscato (Muscat), Pigato, Ribolla Gialla, Teroldego, Trebbiano, Verdicchio, Vermentino

SPANISH GRAPES
Red – Alicante Bouschet, Bobal, Carignan, Garnacha, Graciano, Mencia, Mission (Misión), Monastrell, Tempranillo
White – Airén, Albariño, Garnacha Blanca, Getariako Txakolina, Godello, Palomino, Rías Baixas, Txakoli, Verdejo, Vijariego, Viura, Xarel·lo

GREEK GRAPES
Red – Agiorgitiko, Moschofilero and Xinomavro
White – Assyrtiko, Malagousia, Moschorlero, Savatiano

WORDS

Acidity – A tartness that makes wine refreshing and your tongue salivate to want another sip. Harvesting early increases acidity. Acidic wines tend to go extra well pairing with foods.

Appellation – A legally defined and protected geographical area used to identify where wine-grapes are grown. Also known as an AVA.

AVA – **A**merican **V**iticultural **A**rea is a specific type of appellation of origin used on wine labels. An AVA is a delimited grape-growing region that affects how grapes are grown with specific geographic and climatic features that distinguish it from surrounding regions.

There are currently 267 established AVAs in the United States, California has the most with 147.

    California Central Coast AVA - 1
    Monterey AVAs - 9
    San Luis Obispo AVAs - 5
     - Paso Robles AVAs - 11
    Santa Barbara AVAs - 7

Clone – A twig, a separate vine genetically identical to its mother vine, certified like a pedigree.

Tannins – Naturally occurring molecules extracted from the grape skins, seeds, stems, and oak barrels. They impart flavor to red wines, contain antioxidants, yet have no smell or flavor itself. They constitute a basic building block of red wines, contributing much to texture, balance and aging potential. Tannins have a dry chalkiness in your mouth.

Terroir – Soil, climate and people

Toast – Burnt wood inside the wine barrel

Varietal – Type of grape used in making wine

Vat – Tank (stainless steel, concrete and wood)

Vinification – Fermenting the grape juice

Vintage – Year of harvest

Vintner – The winery owner

Alcoholic Fermentation – Biochemical process in which sugar is converted into alcohol.

Malolactic Fermentation – The process in winemaking in which tart-tasting malic acid, naturally present in "grape must," is converted to softer tasting lactic acid.

Meniscus – Edge of the wine in the glass, the color determines the vintage, age of the wine.

CONCEPTS

Pruning – Pruning changes the form and growth of a plant. Pruning can also be considered preventive maintenance for both insect and disease damage. Grapes vines should be pruned during their dormancy, usually in late winter. Mature vines should be pruned yearly to remove all growth except new one-year-old fruiting canes and renewal spurs which is where the new fruit will grow.

Tipping – Removing new growth at the top of the vines so the energy can flow to the grape clusters.

Leaf Removal – Removing leaves so more air flows into the vines and more sun shines on the grapes.

Green Harvest – Removing some of the green clusters of grapes so the other clusters get more nutrition and energy from the plant.

Veraison – Onset of the grapes ripening, as grapes turn from green to red, as grapes change from growing to ripening.

Stages of winemaking – Harvest, sort, crush, ferment, press, clarify, age, and bottle.

ACTIVITIES IN THE VINEYARD

January – Pruning
February – Till soil and remove vine shoots
March – Staking and tying (to training wires)
April – Bud break and till soil (at vine base)
May – Bud pruning
June – Flowering and tipping (removing tops)
July – Fruit sets and leaf thinning
August – Veraison, green harvest and leaf thinning
September – Monitor ripeness and harvest
October – Harvest and fermentation
November – Plowing vineyards
December – Pruning

TRAVEL EASIER
WITH OUR
E-BOOK TRAVEL EDITIONS
On Apple Books and Amazon Kindle

THE BENEFITS

I get it. The books are too nice and you do not want to get them damaged while traveling. Plus, they are big, take up space, and weigh down your bag. I understand, as I carry the books with me when I travel. So we have created a great solution... **eBOOK TRAVEL EDITIONS**. They go on your smart phone and tablet. It has all the exact same content and is more convenient than the printed book for traveling. And more...

In these digital Travel Editions, we have made the websites, phone numbers, emails, and physical addresses *live links* so you can easily click and go directly to the page of the winery, restaurant, resort, attraction, etc.

• Time to navigate? Click on the *address link.*
• Want to call them? Click on the *phone number link.*
• Need more information? Just click on their *website link.*
• Want to email with questions or book a visit? Click on the *email link.*

For me, the **eBook Travel Editions** are indispensable. Easy. Handy. Everything is at my fingertips. And no added weight.

Available on
Amazon Kindle
and **Apple Books**

OUR OTHER BOOKS
The Exploring Wine Regions Book Series

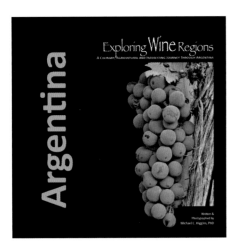
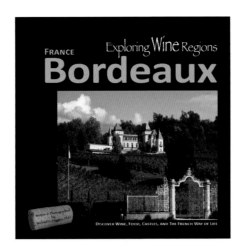
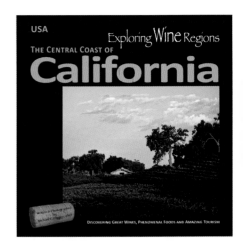

EXPLORING WINE REGIONS – ARGENTINA
A Culinary, Agricultural and Interesting Journey Through Argentina

Exploring Wine Regions – Argentina is our debut book that has won "Best Travel & Wine Book 2016" and "Best Travel Book 2017". This first book of the series sprung from my personal quest. Will I ever meet a Malbec I don't like? What is Argentina's secret to producing the best Malbec?

Argentina offers so much more than just Malbec. Our journey unveiled Bonarda, Tempranillo and Torrontés wines just to name a few. Torrontés is indigenous to Argentina. And Asado, delicious steaks cooked slowly over live wood embers. Tango! A most beautiful dance to go with the beauty of their people and landscape. There is so much to see and do here. Jump into all the adventures Argentina has to offer.

Follow us to this magnificent country's top three wine regions: Mendoza, Salta and Patagonia. Mendoza produces extraordinarily great Malbec that put Argentina on the map as the fifth largest wine country in the world, Salta boasts the world's highest elevation vineyards, and Patagonia makes delicious Pinot Noirs thanks to its cool climate.

A must-have book for those wanting to explore one of the world's top wine regions. And learn the answer to my question.

EXPLORING WINE REGIONS – BORDEAUX
Discover Wine, Food, Castles, and The French Way of Life

Exploring Wine Regions – Bordeaux France is the second book in the series and has won ten awards. It takes you on a journey of the long and fascinating history of wine, gastronomy, castles, and *joie de vivre*, the French way of living life.

Bordeaux is complicated, so I have worked meticulously to make Bordeaux comprehendible for you. The wines are presented by each region separately to better appreciate their nuances. Exploring the Left Bank of the Médoc, Graves and Sauternes, as well as the Right Bank of Saint Émilion, Pomerol and Fronsac, leads us to a greater understanding and distinction of the regions here. Plus, a side trip to Cognac and the Entre-Deux-Mers wine regions.

We help you navigate your own way through this historic wine region with detailed maps and insider tips. We highlight the châteaux worth visiting, including the ones where you can stay in their castles, as well as excellent restaurants and unique tourism experiences.

Everyone can learn how to develop a palate to appreciate the finest wine and food the French have to offer. A must-have book for expanding your knowledge of Bordeaux and wines itself.

EXPLORING WINE REGIONS CALIFORNIA CENTRAL COAST
Discovering Great Wines, Phenomenal Foods and Amazing Tourism

Exploring Wine Regions – California Central Coast is the third book in the series exploring a lesser-known area of the wine regions in California. Most everyone knows of Napa Valley and Sonoma County; however, the Central Coast Wine Regions are producing top-level, high-quality wines, and the tourism is extraordinary.

Twenty million years ago, the Pacific Plate arose from the ocean hitting the North American Plate (Canada, United States and Mexico) leaving a sliver of land above the water along California's coast south of San Francisco. This sliver of land has its own very special terroir highly conducive to making high-quality wines. This book takes you on a journey to discover these amazing wines.

Also, the tourism along the central coast of California is unmatched. The beaches, mountains and valleys are ever so enchanting. The wineries are engaging, have lots of tourism activities available, and are especially inviting and friendly, unlike other wine regions. It's not uncommon to find the vintner or winemaker at the tasting room wanting to share their stories and their love of wine with you.

OUR OTHER BOOKS
The Exploring Wine Regions Book Series

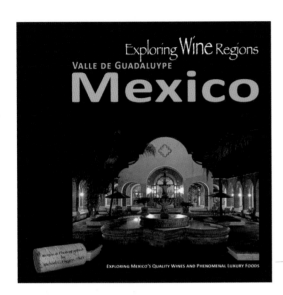

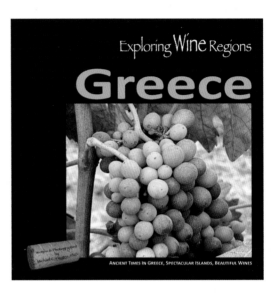

COMING SOON
EXPLORING WINE REGIONS – BAJA CALIFORNIA
Exploring México's Quality Wines and Phenomenal Luxury Cuisine

Are you familiar with Valle de Guadalupe in Baja California? It is a wine region valley inland from Ensenada México, an hour and a half south of the San Diego international border. This is set to be the fourth book in the series, and expected to be published in 2024.

Valle de Guadalupe enjoys the same marine influence on the wine regions as are occurring along the entire coast of California. The Pacific plate running along the edge of California also includes Baja California México, Having the same very special terror of the California Central Coast wine regions.

Okay, so you might be suspect of the wines in México. I felt the same way. Until I started reading the great reviews from prominent wine critics that made me realize something is going on there. And then to find out that wines from Valle de Guadalupe are now on the famous French Laundry wine list, I had to go explore and discover. Now that I have visited many wineries there, and tasted a significant number of their wines, I have figured out which varietals do really well there and which wineries have the great wines. This is what this book does very well in guiding you in the right direction.

Also, the quality food in this valley is beyond your imagination. You can find cuisine here at the same top-level quality you find in Los Angeles, New York, Chicago, and San Francisco. At a significantly better price. As one winemaker said to me, the chefs in this valley are setting the high standards, which is motivating winemakers to higher levels of quality wines.

COMING SOON
EXPLORING WINE REGIONS – GREECE
Ancient Times in Greece, Spectacular Islands, Beautiful Wines

I must admit, I have never tasted any wines from Greece. You? I did not know if they were good or not good. And I wondered why they had been off my radar all this time. All I knew is the country was beautiful, the islands stunning.

We received an email from Greece asking if we would consider doing our next book on Greece. We started with them shipping a couple of good bottles of wines to try. I went to the owner of a local authentic Greek restaurant and asked him to make foods to pair with the wines. From here we had a four-hour Zoom food and wine pairing experience together. I was hooked, and ready to complete the current books so I could begin this journey to Greece.

Have you seen the names of their grapes? For example, Xinomavro, Assyrtiko and Moschofilero. The first thing I realized is I needed to learn how to pronounce their wines, especially how to properly spell the grape names.

Apparently, the Crete Island is one of the best destinations for us wine lovers, with about thirty-five wineries on the island primarily producing the indigenous varieties of Vidiano, Vilana, Malvasia, and Kotsifali. They have 4,000 years of Cretan winemaking tradition that will be interesting to discover.

What I do know for sure is that the food is incredible delicious, the islands stunningly beautiful, the Greek people are warm and friendly, and an ancient history of winemaking and mysticism that will be so fascinating to uncover.

We are expecting a two-year journey to complete this book, estimating a 2026 publishing date.

SPECTACULAR WINE CELLARS
We take you into the most
amazing wine cellars.

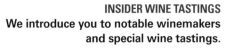

INSIDER WINE TASTINGS
We introduce you to notable winemakers
and special wine tastings.

TRAVEL WITH US

ACTIVITIES

COME JOIN US...
on extraordinary trips
exploring wine regions all over the world!

We put together over-the-top trips that are unforgettable! Our groups are small and intimate, carefully selected, to ensure the best possible experience for everyone. Our events are exclusive and unlike anything available to the general public.

We go in the back-door, so-to-speak, as our friends are the "who's who" in wine and travel. They create the most amazing experiences for us.

Our trips are unique. We have been organizing special trips since 2005, ranging from spectacular to luxurious.

If you would like to be on our special private invite list, please email us at:
JoinUs@ExploringWineRegions.com

TESTIMONIALS

"The best part about Michael organizing our tour: all the hard work was already accomplished, the best locations were chosen. There was nothing left to do but enjoy. Being on a tour with other wine lovers was extra enjoyable because we already had something in common with everyone else and could share stories of other trips and wine experiences."

– Lee and Carolyn Jones

"Dr. Higgins does everything 1st class or not at all!"

– Mike Goering

More testimonials on our website:
ExploringWineRegions.com/testimonials

OUR WEBSITE
ExploringWineRegions.com

Exploring Wine Regions

ABOUT   BLOGS   BOOKS   TRAVEL   SHOP   JOIN US   FREE E-BOOK

Visit The Most Spectacular Wineries
We reveal the most interesting and amazing wineries

KNOW MORE

FOLLOW US ON SOCIAL MEDIA

FACEBOOK: Exploring Wine Regions

INSTAGRAM: @ExploringWineRegions

exploringwineregions   Edit Profile

869 posts   26.3k followers   846 following

Exploring Wine Regions
🍷 INSIDER TRAVEL GUIDES 🍷 to exploring the world's wine
regions... sharing the lifestyle of extraordinary food and wine
experiences. #ewr
ExploringWineRegions.com/books

GIVE AUTOGRAPHED BOOKS

Personally autographed by the author, including customized messages if you desire.

Perfect for gifts!

ExploringWineRegions.com/Books

Bring Wine Home Safely with Wine Luggage

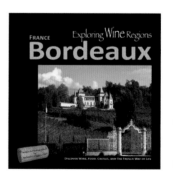

FRANCE
Exploring Wine Regions
Bordeaux

DISCOVER WINE, FOOD, CASTLES, AND THE FRENCH WAY OF LIFE

**To Get Autographed
Copies of the Books**
$10.00 off, use code: 10$OFF

GET EXTRA CHAPTERS – FREE
There is more and more to share with you!

As of the printing of this book, I have already written more chapters to share with you. There are so many more things to tell you about. I have discovered additional interesting places to stay in the vineyards that I did not get to review in time for the book. I have organized my favorite hot spots and romantic places. I share some of my valuable travel tips. And so much more! I will send them to you digitally at no extra charge. Just ask, as I am happy to share. Here are a few of the chapters...

Receive Extra Chapters (for free)

Send us your full name, email, zip code, and where you purchased this book to:

Extra@ExploringWineRegions.com

SHIP WINE HOME... FOR FREE

This is not a list of wineries that will ship for free when you buy their wines. Some wineries will do that though, if you buy enough of their wine. I am referring to how to ship multiple bottles from many different wineries, all for free.

International shipping can be very expensive, especially for wine because it weighs a lot. Discover my little secret in how to ship dozens of bottles for free. I will also give you important packing tips to protect your precious wines.

HOW TO PACK A CARRY-ON LUGGAGE FOR LONG TRIPS

YES! It really is possible to travel for a month or more with only carry-on luggage. I do it. All the time! It works so well that this is now the only way I travel.

A carry-on is so much easier at the airport. Fewer lines. Less cumbersome. Shorter advanced arrival time. You move through with ease and grace.

I know you do not believe me, as I was initially doubtful I could do it. And ladies, I promise you can do it too. I have seen it firsthand.

This includes casual clothes, business clothes and nice evening wear, as well. At first, I did it for three weeks. Then for five weeks, a couple of times. Last year, I did it for two months. Twice! That's right, just one carry-on luggage piece.

There are numerous techniques to make this all possible. I detail everything in this extra chapter.

TOP TEN ROMANTIC PLACES

Would you like to know the most magical places to share a kiss? How about the most romantic places to dine? Inside, outside, or underground in caves? How about the best places to cuddle up with your sweetheart?

This chapter is for the lovers of the heart, those with passion and desire. I am insatiable and never miss discovering those magical romantic settings.

I was there. Took pictures. Indulged. And now I am sharing them with you.

ROMANTIC HOT SPOTS

SECRET BEDROOMS

ACCOMMODATIONS IN THE VINEYARDS

HOW TO GET INTO A PREMIER GRAND CRU

SPECIAL SUB-APPELLATIONS

ACKNOWLEDGEMENTS

The Exploring Wine Regions Team

Michael C. Higgins, PhD
Author, Photojournalist & Publisher

Danielle Ballantyne
Copy Editor

John Irvin
Proofing

Gregory Franco
Map Design & Production

Juliana Alexandra Alvarez
Social Media & Marketing

Arlind Rexhmataj
Web Development & Administration

Baker & Taylor Publisher Services
Worldwide Distribution

Dany Rolland, Richard Sanford, Ian Brand, and David Glancy
The Foreword

Reach us through our website at:
ExploringWineRegions.com/Contact
Or call us at: +1 (626) 618-4000

International Exploration Society
Box 93613 • Pasadena, CA 91109 USA

It Takes a Team...

This book is the culmination of many individual's efforts. Extensive or tiny, each person has had a meaningful mark on the quality of this book. I am endlessly appreciative and thank you all. There are three people who have been on this journey with me all the way and I would like to give them some extra acknowledgment.

I have known **Chris Taranto** for at least fifteen years. We worked together on editorials for my Flying Adventures magazine. Chris is the communication director of the Paso Robles Wine Country Alliance. Creating this book made it exciting to be able to work with Chris again. Chris is a true professional and in love with Paso Robles. While I know Paso Robles very well through the years of visiting and writing stories, Chris always knows it better. He continues to introduce me to everything new and exciting going on in Paso Robles. It is because of the thoughtful and thorough itineraries that he created for my visits that Paso Robles takes on the most robust part of the book. I always love sharing wine with Chris, appreciate our friendship and have so much gratitude for what he has done to help make this book excellent. Thank you, Chris.

Dan Fredman is a very special person. It is a true pleasure to know him. It's not just that he extensively knows the wineries in San Luis Obispo County, it is his availability and great attitude about making things happen that was infinitely valuable to me. Dan would never stop thinking about how he could contribute to the book, as I would get phone calls of great ideas on a regular basis from him. Dan even helped me with wineries and restaurants to visit in a different county where he knew I was not getting much help from their association. Dan, I am forever grateful for your love of our publication and your endless contributions to making it great. Dan is a sommelier, wine consultant and public relations professional. He represents the SLO Coast Wine Collective (the wineries in the San Luis Obispo County).

Another important thank you is to **Kim Stemler**. Kim is the executive director of the Monterey County Vintners & Growers Association. I really needed an education on the Monterey wine regions as it is set up completely different from other wine regions in terms of visiting the wineries and tasting rooms. Kim was instrumental in helping me set up the best way to present the wineries, giving us the greatest opportunities in visiting Monterey. Further, Kim knows everyone there, giving me the ability to visit the right wineries. She would make a simple phone call when needed and make things happen, even at the last minute.

My appreciation and gratitude go out to many people who made this book a reality. I thank you very much!

• **David Glancy** - Master Sommelier, Certified Wine Educator, Founder of San Francisco Wine School • **Ian Brand** - Winemaker & Proprietor, I. Brand Winery
• **Chris Taranto** - Communications Director, Paso Robles Wine Country Alliance • **Steve Peck** - Vice President of Winemaking, J. Lohr Vineyards • **Mike Dawson** - Travel Paso Robles
• **Dan Fredman** - Sommelier, Wine Consultant and Public Relations Professional, SLO Coast Wine Collective • **Richard Sanford** - Vintner, Pioneer of the Sta. Rita Hills Appellation
• **Anna Ferguson-Sparks** - Stiletto Marketing • **Barry Prescott** - General Manager, The Landsby • **Phil Carpenter** - Director of Operations, Santa Barbara Vintners
• **Kim Stemler** - Executive Director, Monterey County Vintner & Growers Association • **Emerson Brown** - Monterey Bay Aquarium • **Garrett Bowlus** - Winemaker, Albatross Ridge

NEED A PROFESSIONAL SPEAKER
Fun and Entertaining Education

EXPERIENCES WITH MICHAEL

Michael is a natural storyteller... engaging, charismatic and full of personality! With his immense knowledge of wine and wine regions around the world, Michael is the ideal speaker for your event, no matter its size. Whether it is a corporate function or fun social gatherings for connoisseurs or novices, he is guaranteed to entertain and educate your group! Pick from one of the options below or we can easily come up with something perfectly suited for your group.

An Evening Exploring Wine Regions. Choose Argentina, Bordeaux or California! Michael offers a fun, entertaining and educational evening with an amazing food and wine pairing from the subject country. Learn about what makes the particular wine region special and how to choose their wines. Enjoy authentic cuisine, excellent wines and engage in fascinating conversations.

How to Find Your Wine. Michael will show you how to find wines you like in a fun and approachable way. It's very common for people to not understand their preferences. They are intimidated by the restaurant wine list and end up simply ordering the house wine. They walk into a wine shop and are completely overwhelmed. Michael can help! He will teach you easy ways to sift through the long lists and unfamiliar options to uncover the wines you love! Let Michael help you taste your way to success.

Send us an email at: Booking@ExploringWineRegions.com or call us (626-618-4000) for more ideas or to book your event.

Need editorial? Need content for the development of your story? Need some spectacular photography? Need a good interview? On or off camera, Michael makes for a very interesting interview. With his vast knowledge of travel, wine and wine regions, he is the perfect resource for everything you may need to know.

Gorgeous sunsets over the Merlot vineyards at the Sunstone Villa Castle in the Los Olivos AVA in Santa Barbara County